PRO FOOTBALL
at
WRIGLEY FIELD

Photographs by Ron Nelson
Text by Beth Gorr

The place was different. Going to the North or left field it was like kicking downhill. The other way was uphill. For the season I was paid $500.00 for extra points, $500.00 for Field goals and kickoffs. And that was paid if I was the primary kicker. Really enjoyed playing there. *-Roger LeClerc*

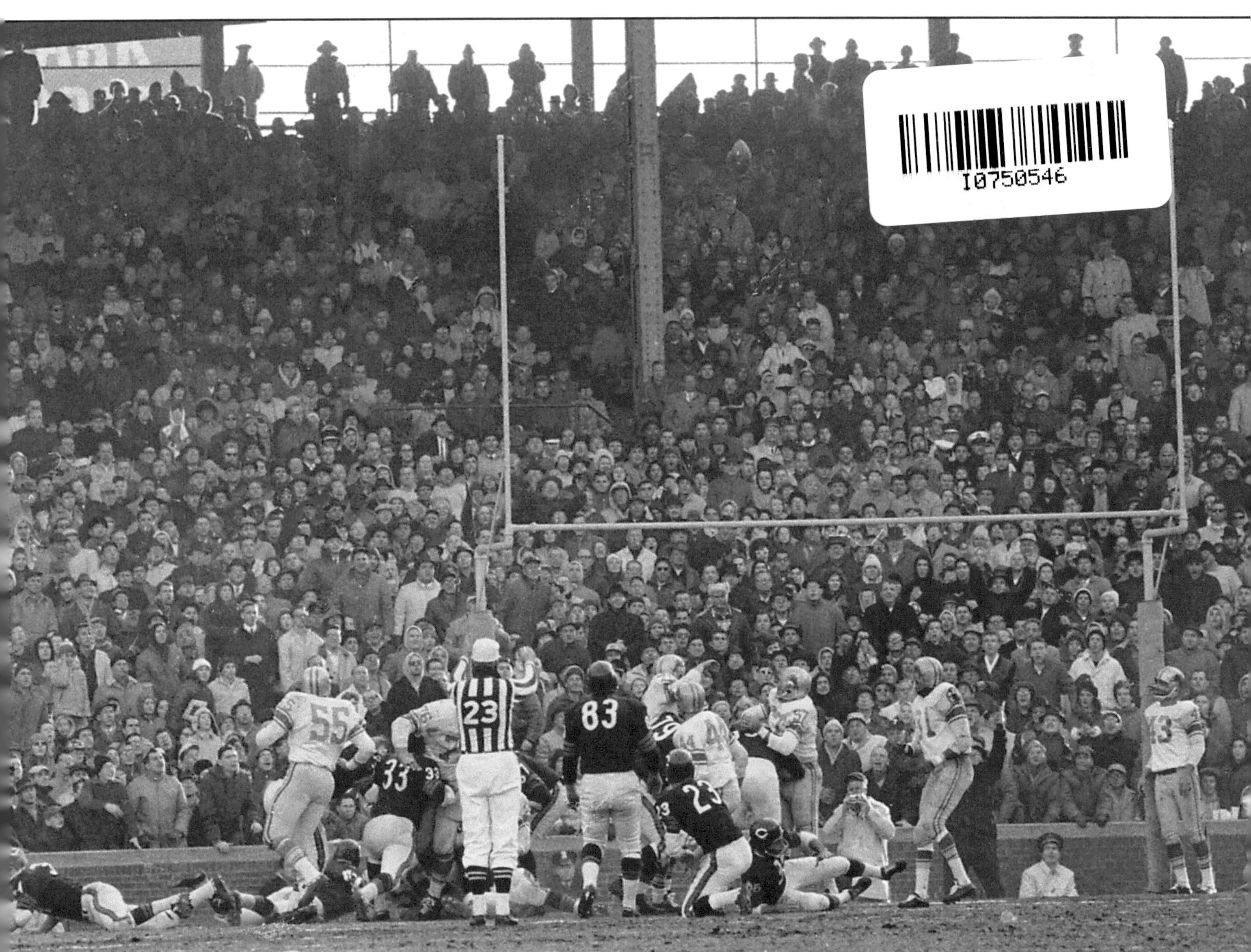

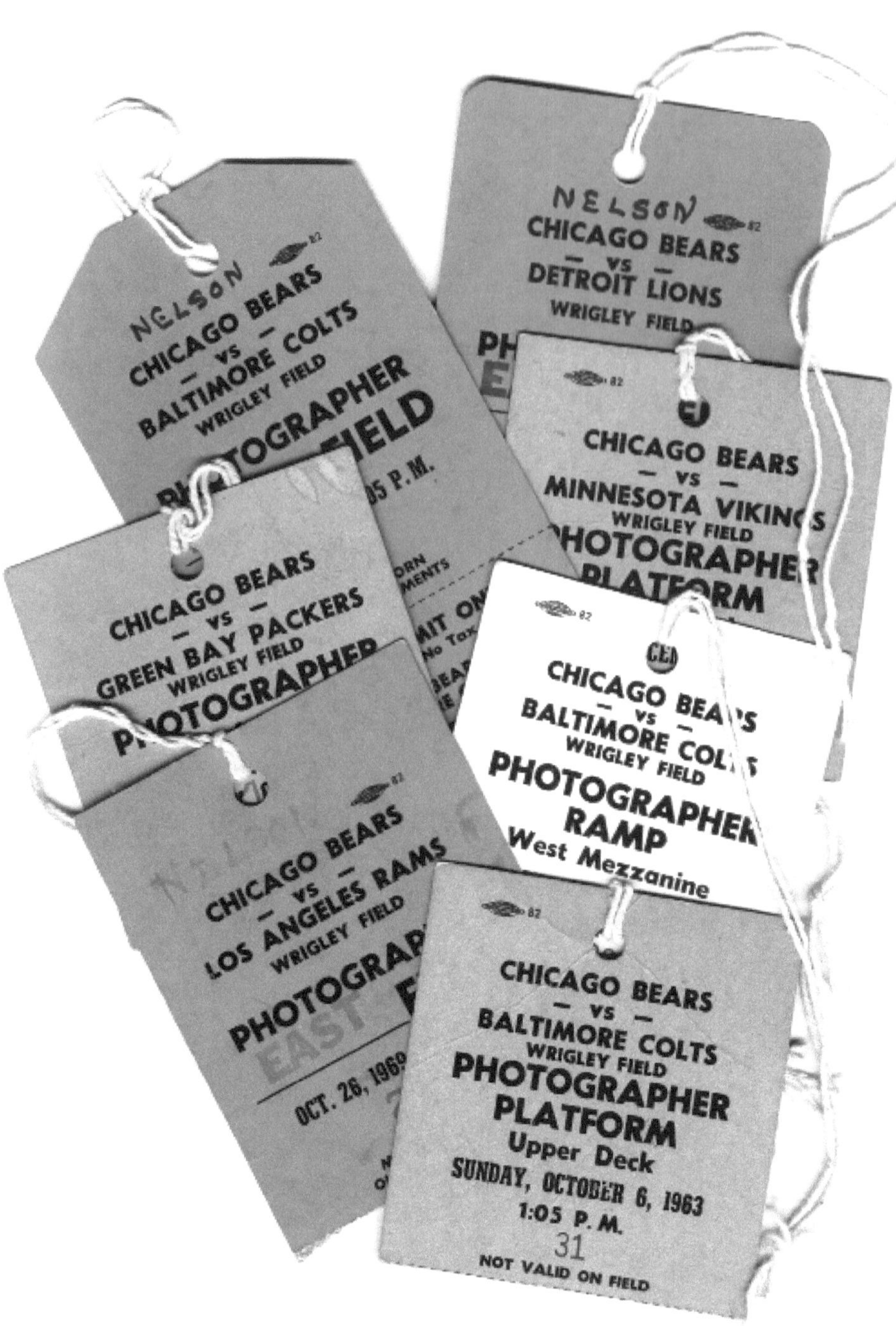

Early on a friend on military leave from Japan showed me his 35mm camera with a telephoto lens. I admired it and he said "Take it, I'll get another one when I get back to Japan". That was the beginning of my life long love of photography.

I became a midwest photographer for Competition Press and started shooting the Indy 500, Watkins Glen, Road America and many racing events in the midwest.

Always a Bear fan, in 1961 I went to Wrigley field and bought a ticket for a left field bleacher seat and took my camera with me. The following week I printed my photographs, went down to the Bear office and met with the Bears business manager, Rudy Custer. He really liked the photographs , reached in his desk drawer, and handed me my first sideline pass. I was on my way.

I didn't have a motor-drive so it was one shot at a time. So, anticipating the action became very important. Over that period of time Rudy and I became good friends. My work is now part of the permanent displays in Soldier Field, Halas Hall and in many private collections. I also have been published in several books on auto racing and football.

I hope you will enjoy looking at these photographs as much as I enjoyed taking them.

Ron Nelson

ISBN: 9780615396118

Written by Beth Gorr
Cover and book design by Tim Didier

visit my websites:
www.prairiestreetart.com
www.classicvintagemortorsports.com

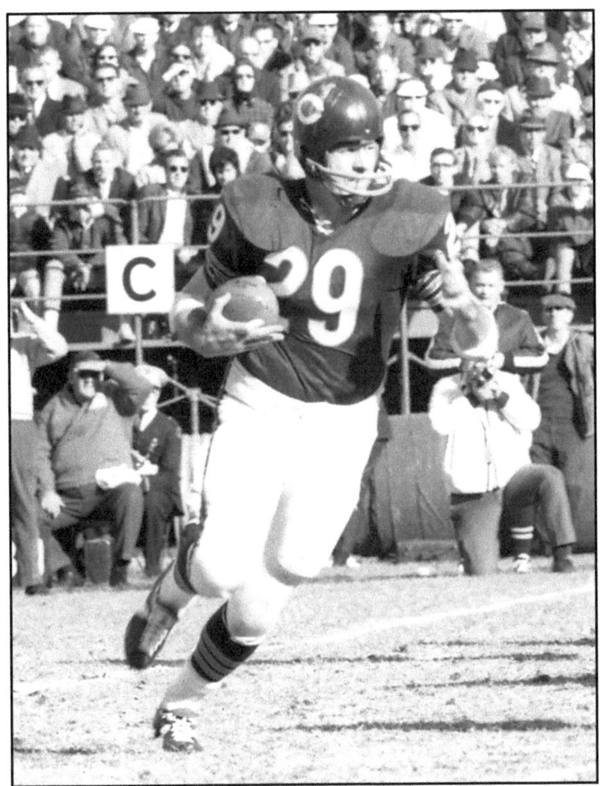

Ronnie Bull remembers Wrigley Field

When the football game between Northwestern and the University of Illinois was announced recently, I must confess to feeling somewhat nostalgic. It's been a long time since football was played at what I always felt was the best stadium in the NFL.

What the players always noticed when we played in Chicago was the proximity of the fans. The positive energy was palpable. Interestingly enough, no fan ever tried to reach down and touch us during a game although they certainly could have done so. There was a mutual respect. We liked to hear them cheer for us and they enjoyed watching us play.

I'm a native of Texas so I was not a person who enjoyed cold weather. And believe me, Wrigley could get very cold with the winds howling off of the lake. But my teammate Bill George told me something that I've since found to be true: "You don't notice the cold so much when you win."

I always found the turf at Wrigley Field to be in remarkable shape. Halas hired an excellent grounds crew. As a running back, however, I noticed one thing-the field was slanted. Remember, baseball was played there during the summer and the grounds were configured for that. If we ran toward the infield, we were running uphill. If we headed for the outfield, we were running downhill. It was strange but we all got used to it eventually.

The locker room was adequate for our needs. I liked the fact that each individual locker was deep enough so a player could lay back inside. That was the perfect place to get our game faces on.. The players on the team who smoked soon learned little hideaways. They could light up but still see Halas or one of the other coaches coming.

Meeting rooms were marginal. The offense met upstairs next to the training room. It was a space about the size of a closet. The defense met downstairs near the locker room. I suspect that Halas was still barely scraping by financially so there weren't many improvements in the structure. We all learned to make due with what was there.

We played some exhibition games in Soldier Field and I never grew fond of the place. The fans were too far away, separated from the players by a racing track. The locker room was horrendous. There was usually no hot water and the showers backed up. Of course the facility they have at Soldier Field today is state of the art.

The NFL mandated that the Bears relocate to Soldier Field toward the end of the 1960s. The rule was that a stadium had to hold at least 55,000. Wrigley held 48,000 if you really crammed them in. And we did exactly that. It sold out every single week. It didn't seem right that a rule like that would force a team to leave a place they had played in for decades. If not for the NFL, I believe the Bears would still be there, running uphill and downhill in Wrigley Field.

Ronnie Bull

DEDICATION

This book is dedicated to
my best friend and
dear wife Adrienne,
and my wonderful family.

ACKNOWLEDGEMENTS

Published by:
Prairie Street Art
www.prairiestreetart.com
www.classicvintagemotorsports.com

Many thanks to Beth Gorr for research and writing. To Tim Didier for Design and Digital production. To former Bear players, and my friend Joe Coletta who gave me encouragement along the way.

CHICAGO BEARS

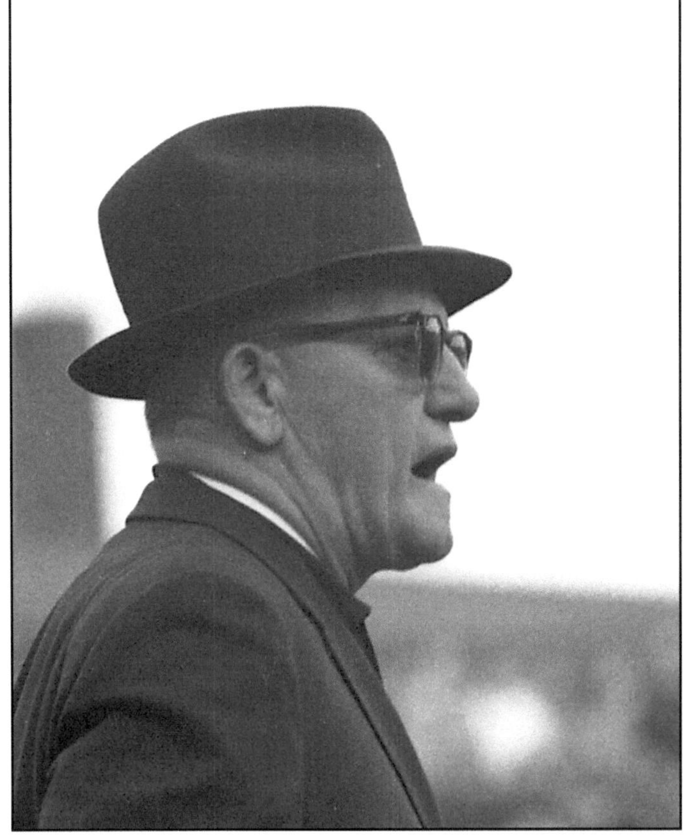

The Bears at Wrigley-the NFL Championship Game December 29,1963 Bears 14 - New York Giants 10

The weather was so cold that frigid December day that fans heading for their seats in Wrigley Field stopped by the stores of local news vendors before entering the arena. The goal in mind wasn't to catch up on the day's events but to use the newsprint to stuff coats, boots and gloves in an effort to provide an extra level of comfort to frozen bodies, fingers and toes.

Wrigley Field could be a difficult venue in which to hold a football game in the dead of winter. The stadium was notorious for capturing the cold and holding it close. And, as the sun set over slightly thawed turf, the field more often than not would turn into an ice rink.

"Footing? What footing" Rosey Taylor said when asked about the conditions at Wrigley in December.

The forecast was so dire that NFL Commissioner Pete Rozelle had asked Bears coach George Halas to move the game to nearby Soldier Field. The rationale was not only to provide extra seating capacity, but to take advantage of a bowl-like stadium that would allow more of the feeble winter sunlight to warm the field, the players and the fans.

Halas refused so Roselle set the game time for 12:05 p.m. The earlier hour had virtually no effect on the temperature within the confines of Wrigley, which hovered between 9-11 degrees.

Chicago quarterback Bill Wade remembered what conditions were like.

"I was so cold I could hardly stop shaking enough to throw the darned ball. And when it reached my receivers, it was as if I had thrown a large block of ice. You can imagine the difficulty of catching anything in those conditions."

All the big name Bears were there on the field for Chicago that day: Mike Ditka, Mike Pyle, Stan Jones, Ed O'Bradovich, Joe Fortunato, Rosey Taylor, Richie Petitbon, Ronnie Bull, Doug Atkins, Willie Gallimore, Johnny Morris to name a few.

The game played out back and forth over what must have seemed like an eternity to most of them. The score was 10-7 in the Giants' favor at the half.

"All I know is that I was more than ready to get off of the field and back into our warm locker room" Doug Atkins would later recall.

Y.A. Title, the Glants outstanding quarterback, had gone down hard in the second quarter after a vicious hit by Larry Morris. The Bears hoped that perhaps Tittle was done for the day. Tittle came back, however, after the half aided in part by a combination of cortisone, Novacaine and taping. What worked to the Bears advantage was the fact that Tittle now had to throw off of his left foot to spare his injured knee.

Ed O'Bradovich took advantage of the situation and grabbed an interception deep in Giants territory that set up a Bears score, bringing the game to 14-10, Bears. With ten seconds left, the Giants closed in on the Bears end zone. Richie Petitbon darted in front of Tittle's receiver in the end zone and saved the day for the Bears. The Championship went to Chicago.

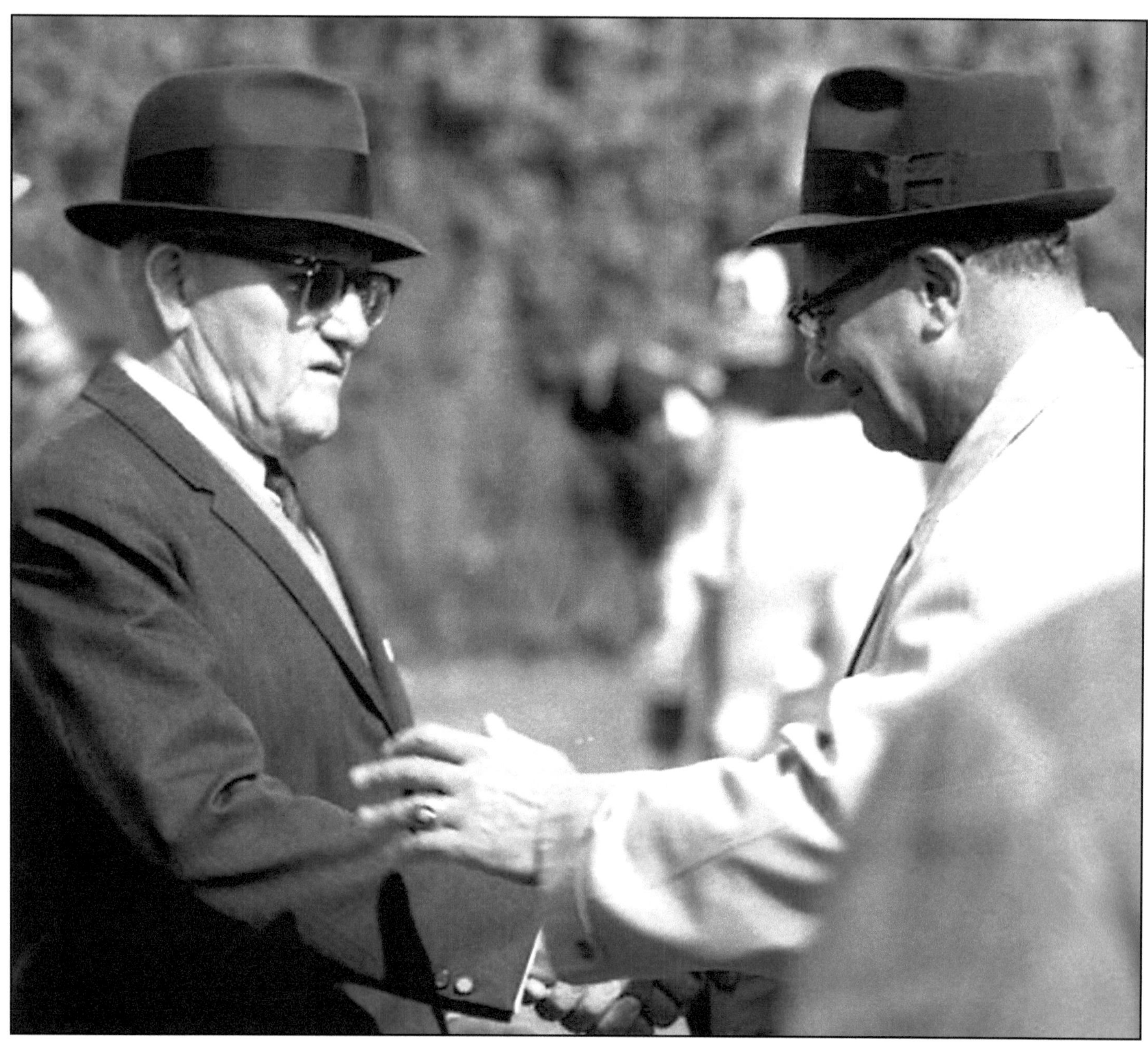

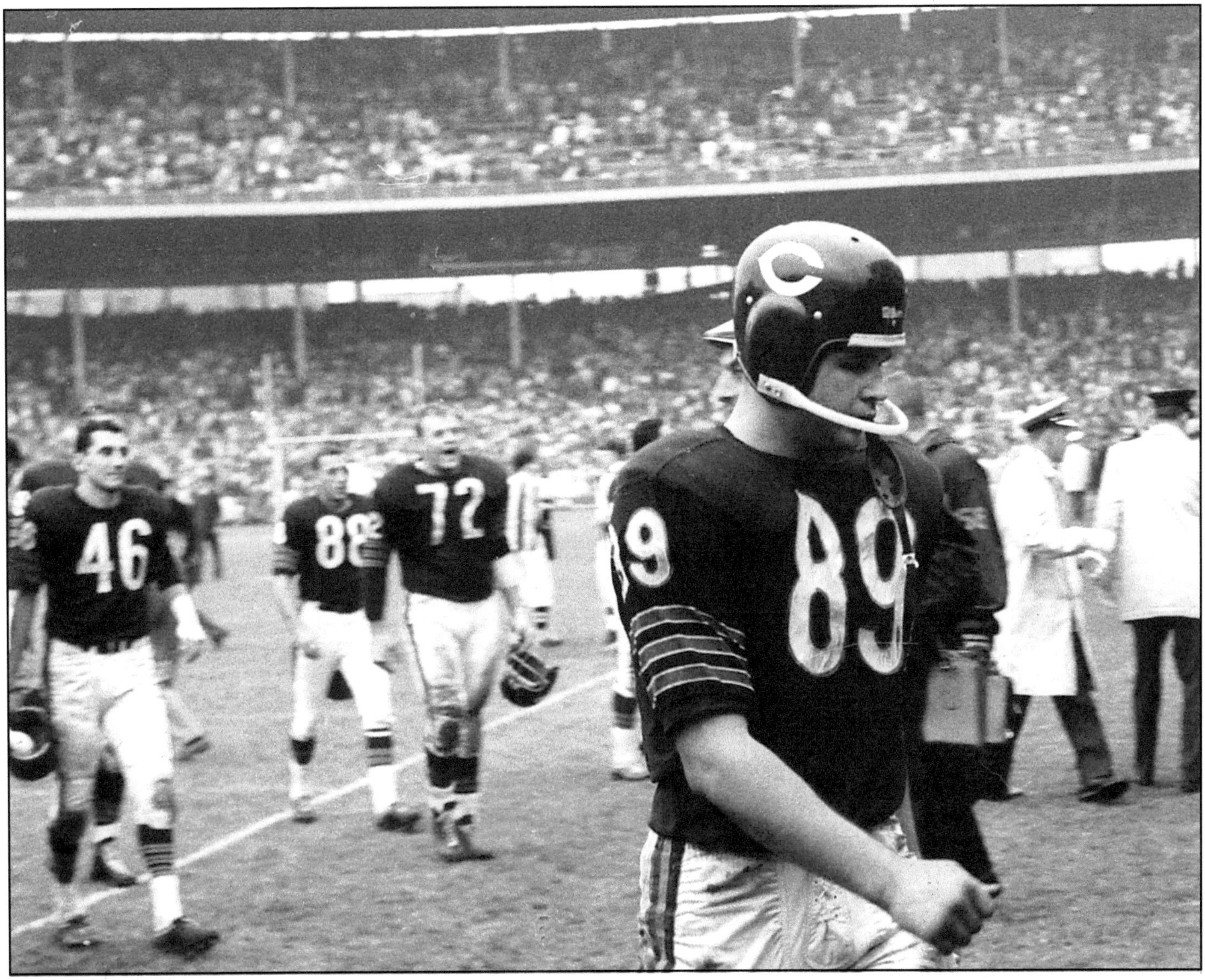

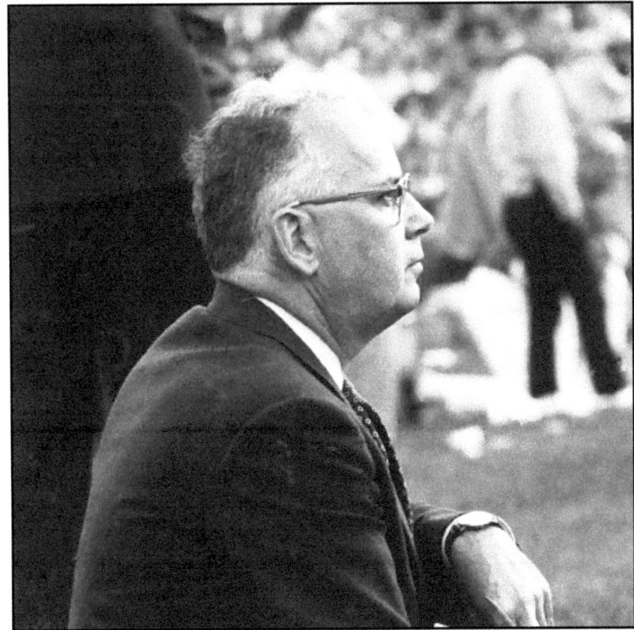

Rudy Custer, the man who opened the door for me.

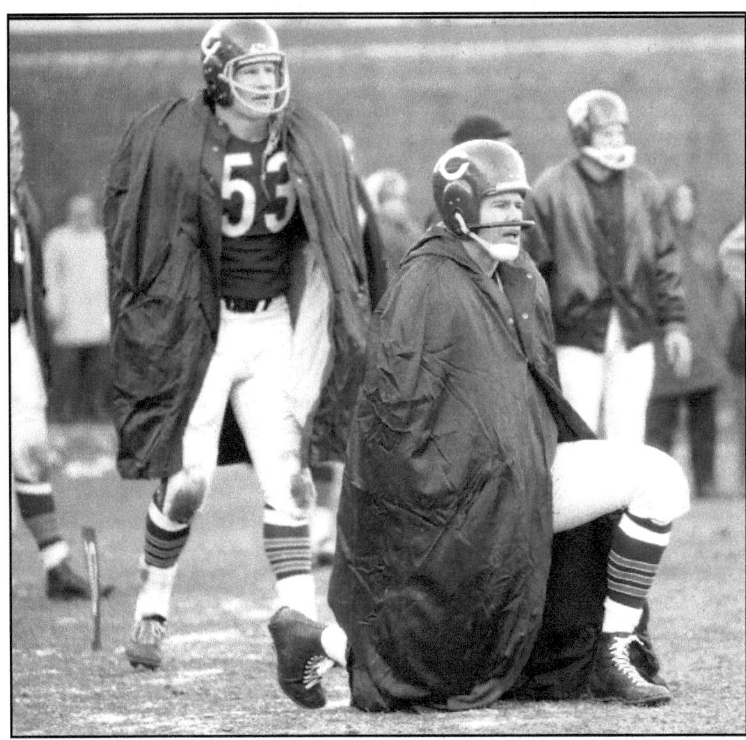

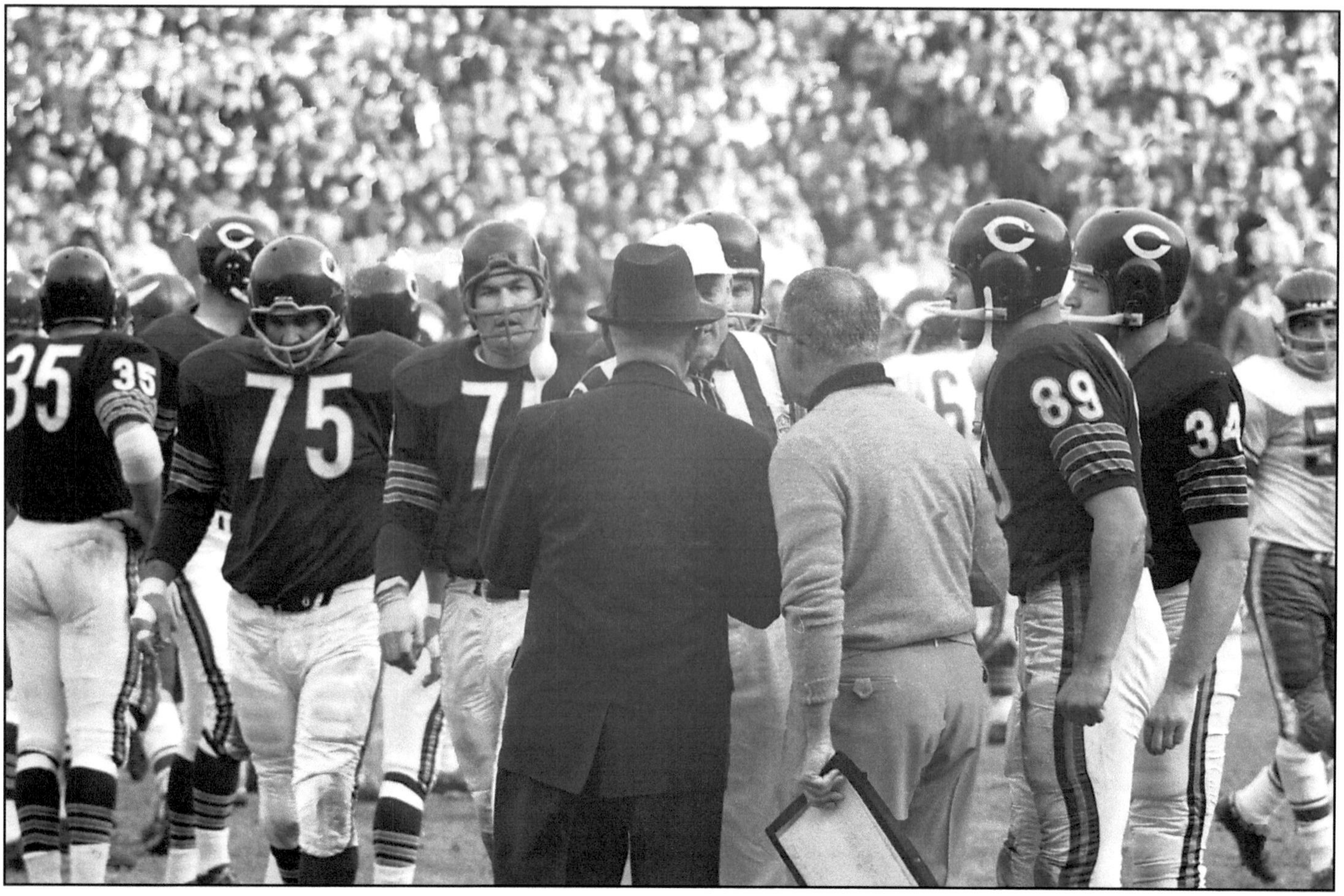

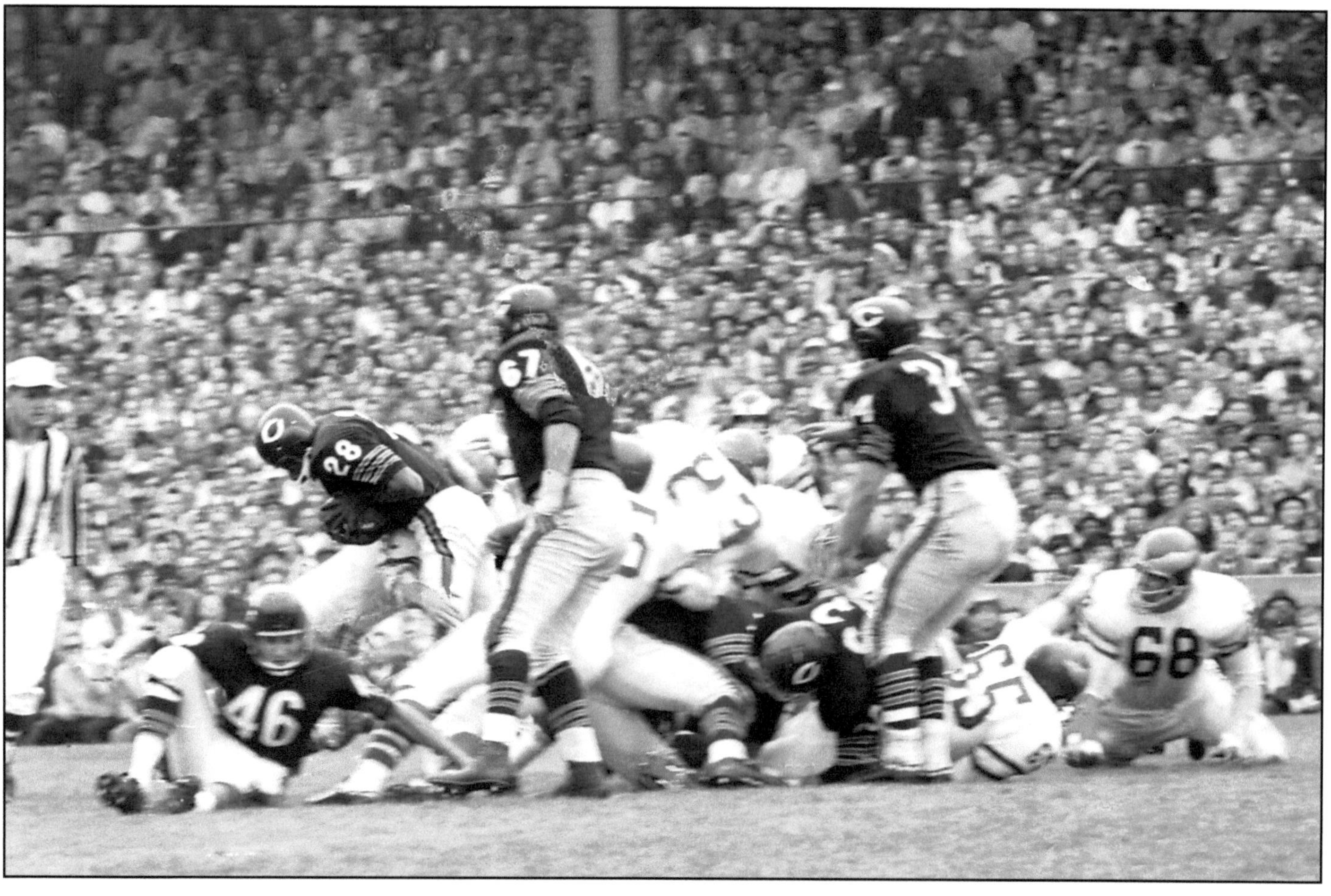

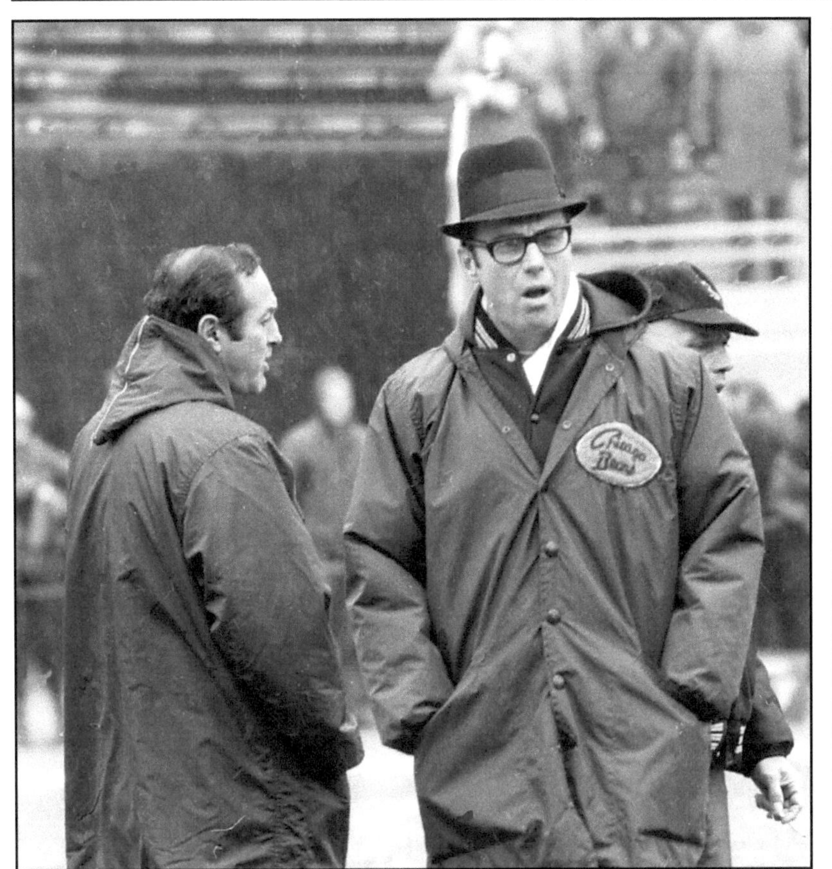
Chicago Bears

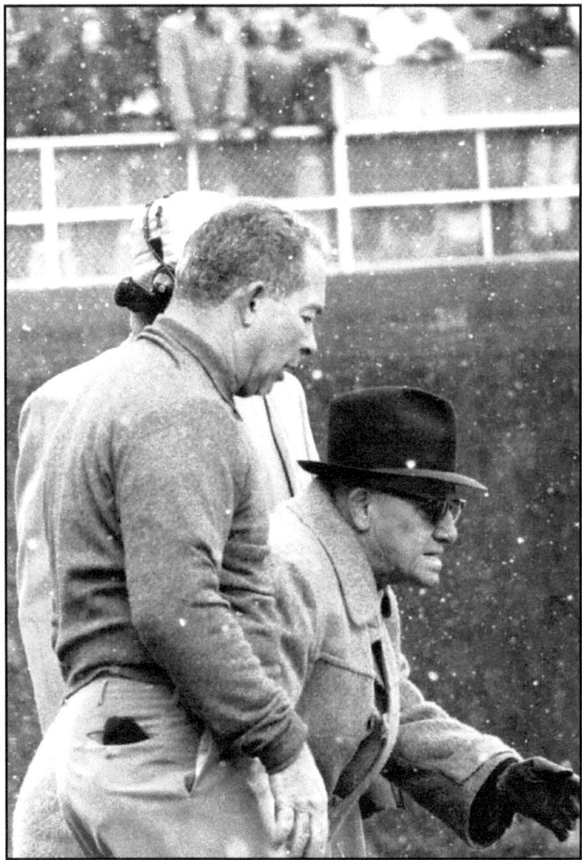

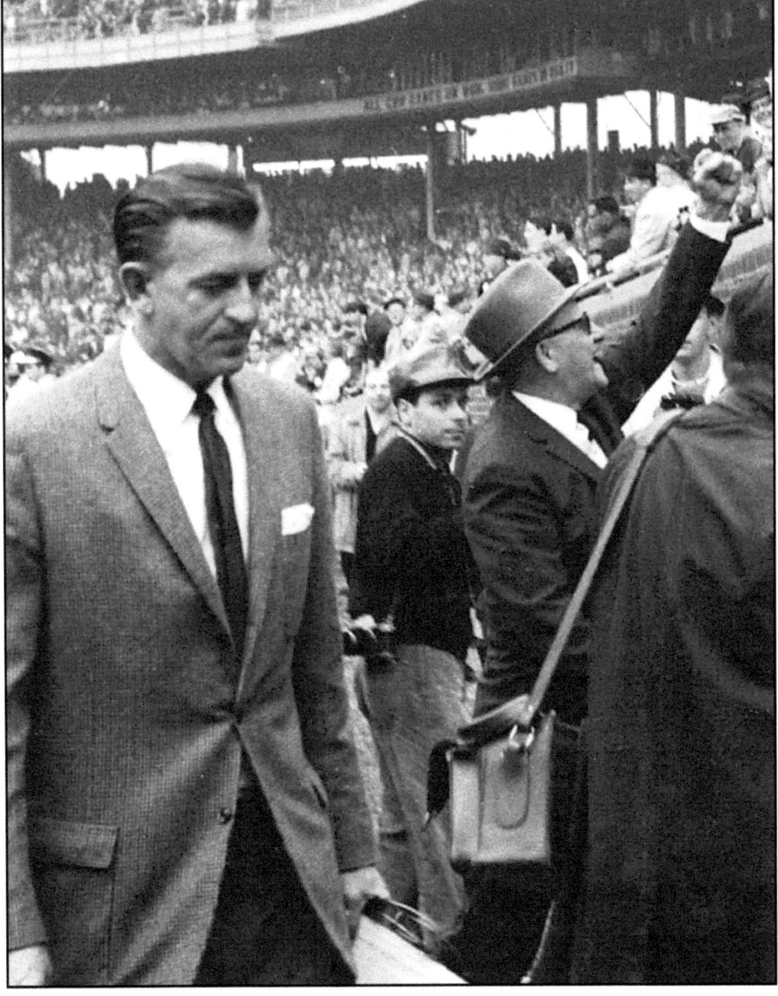

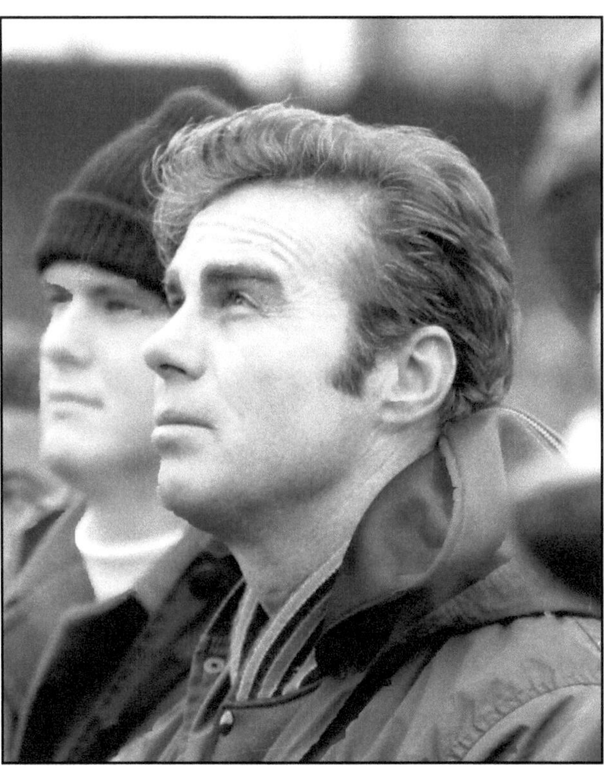

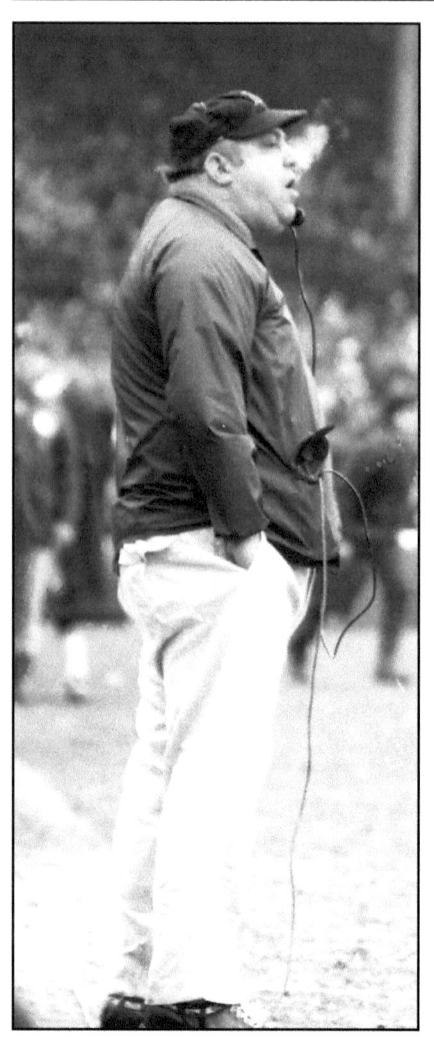

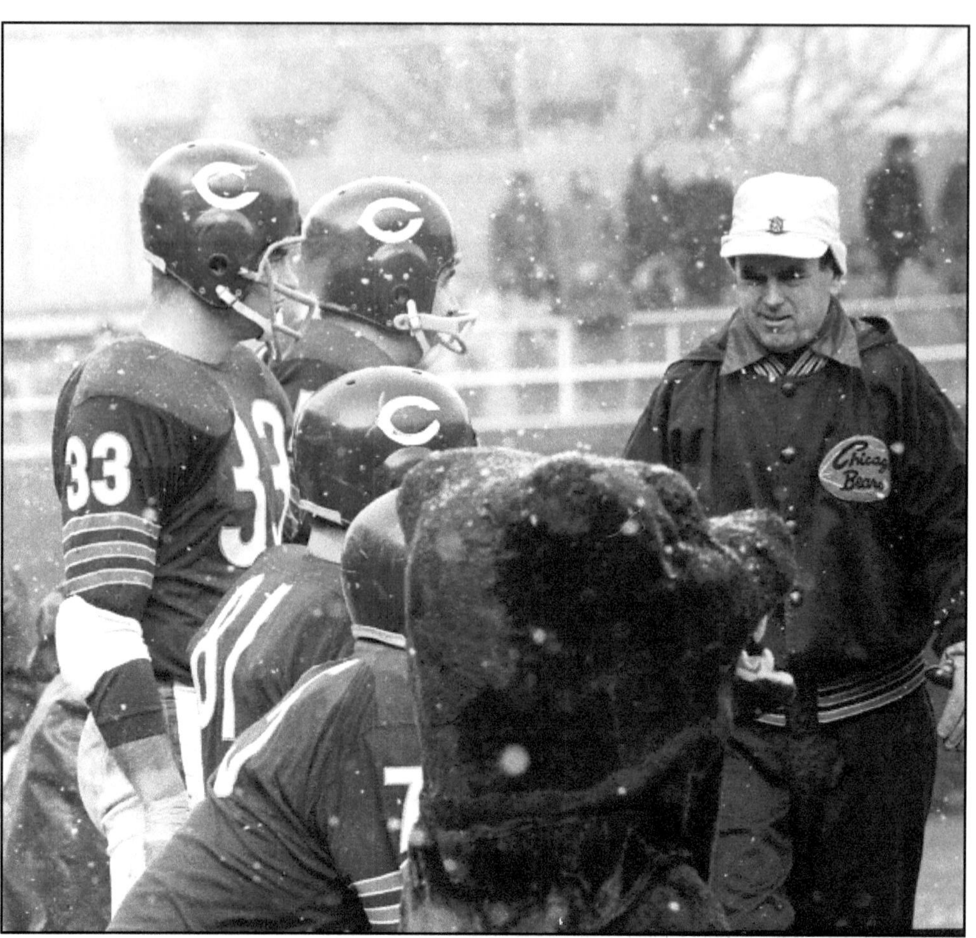

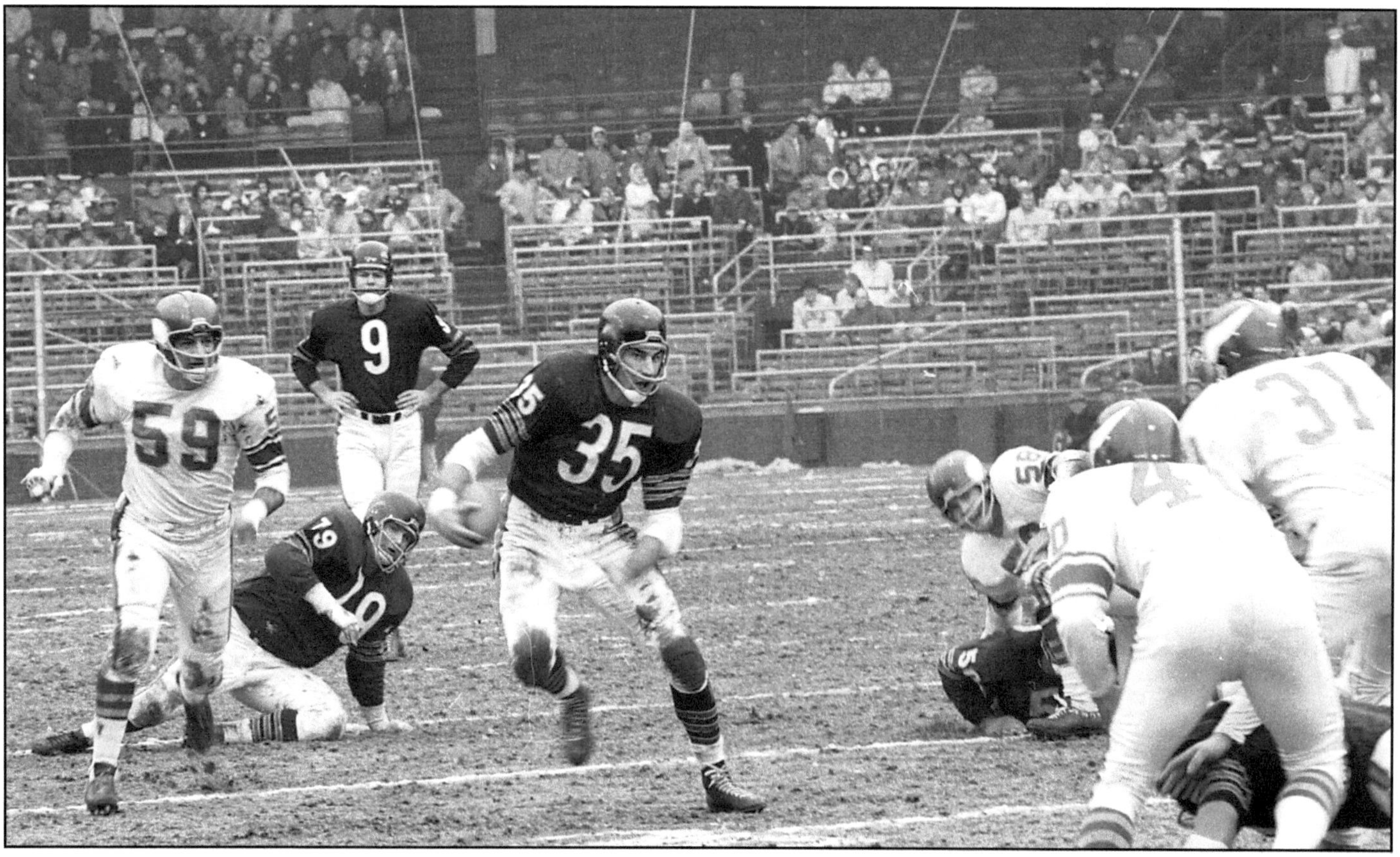

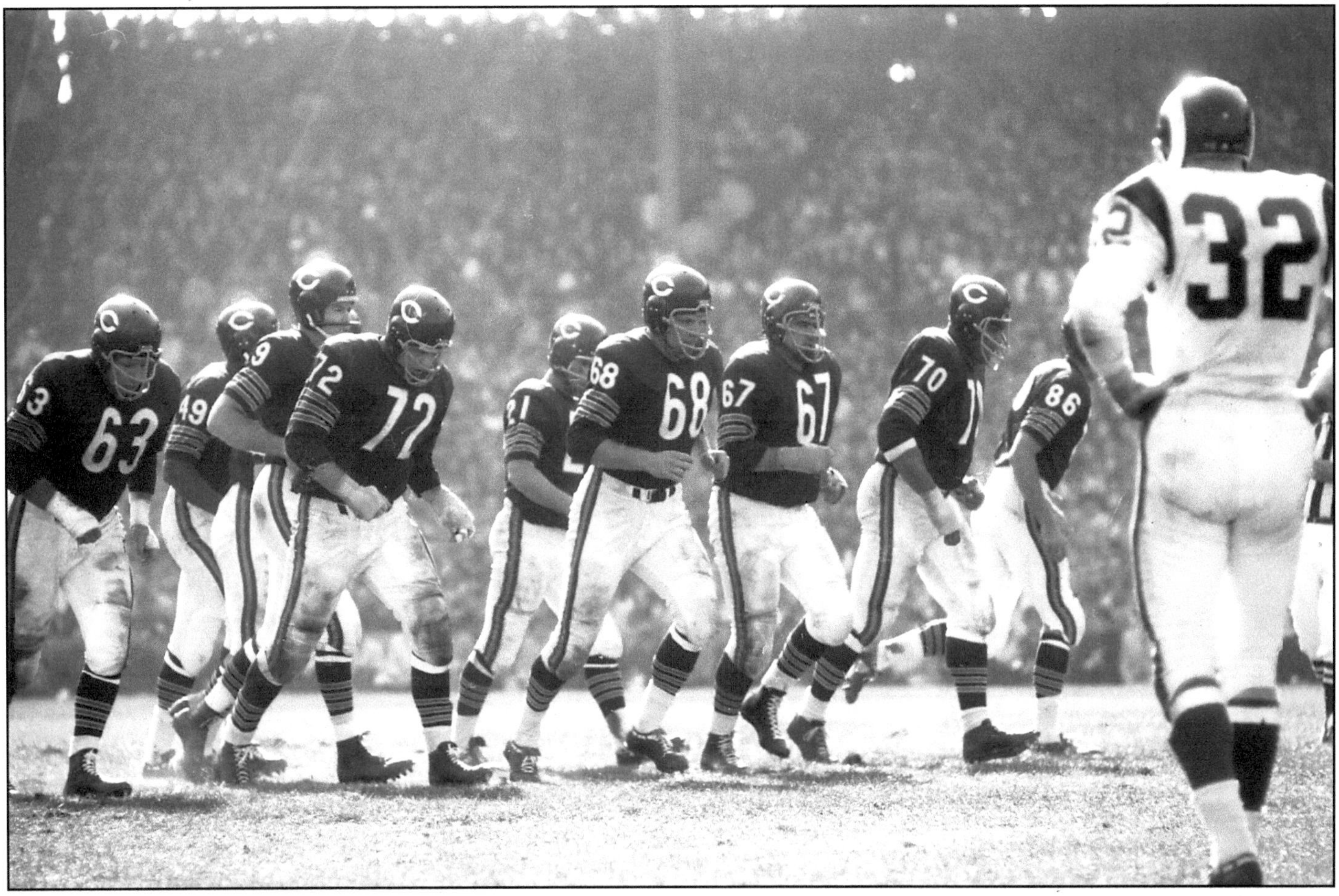

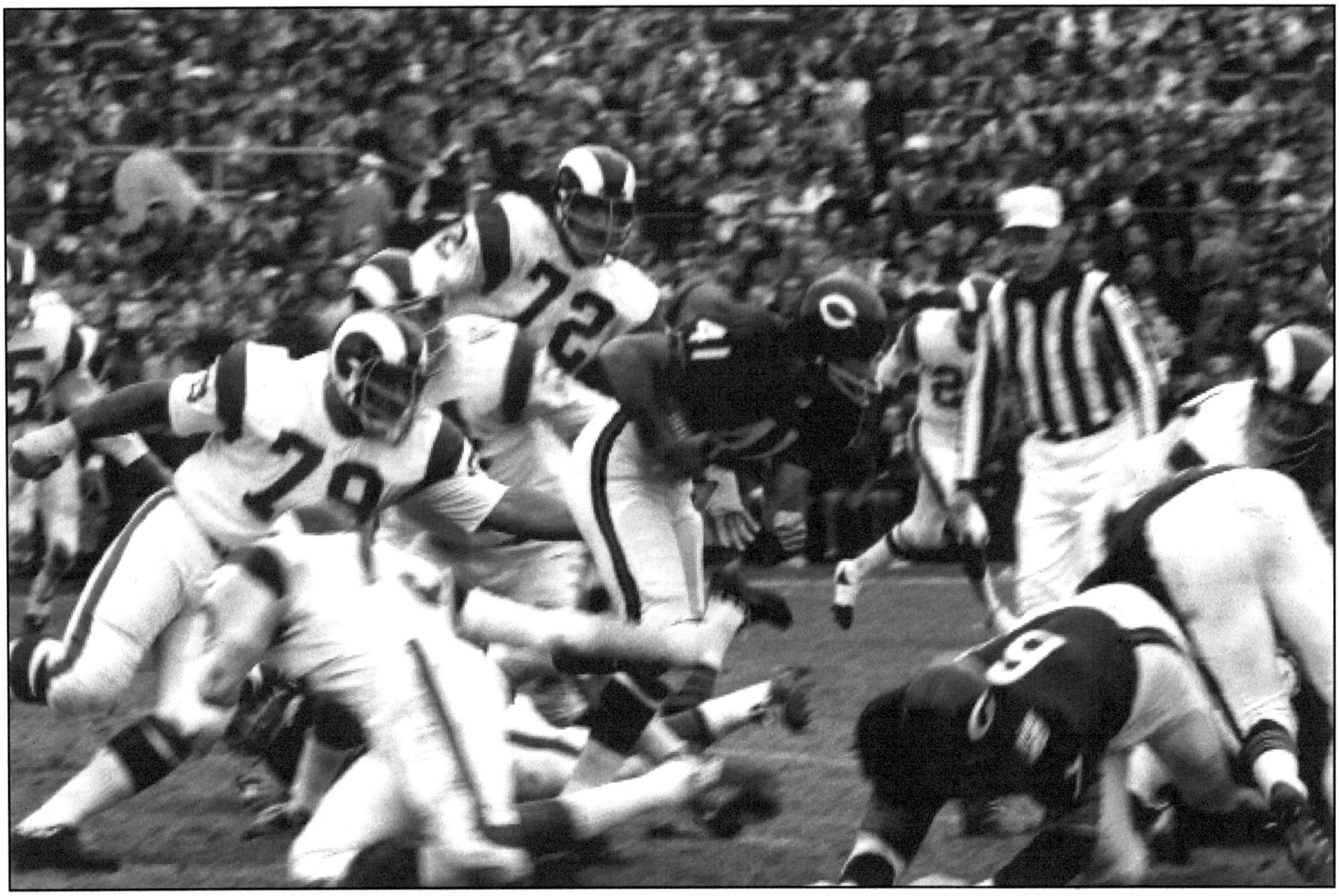

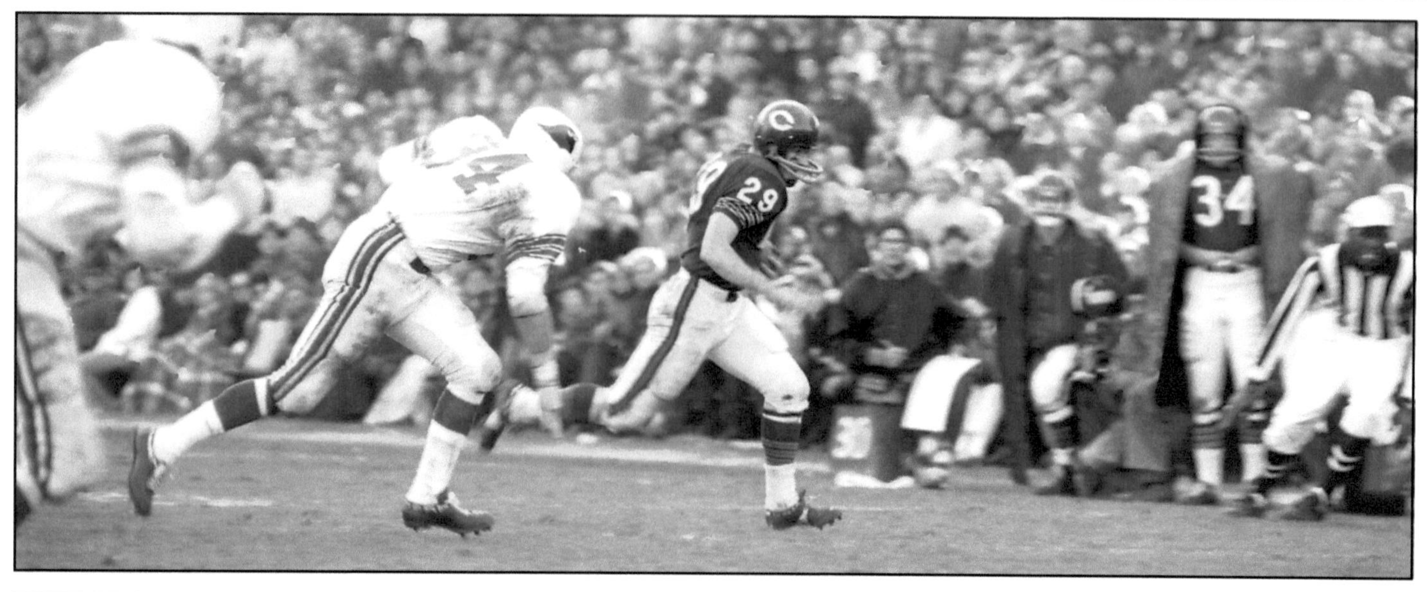

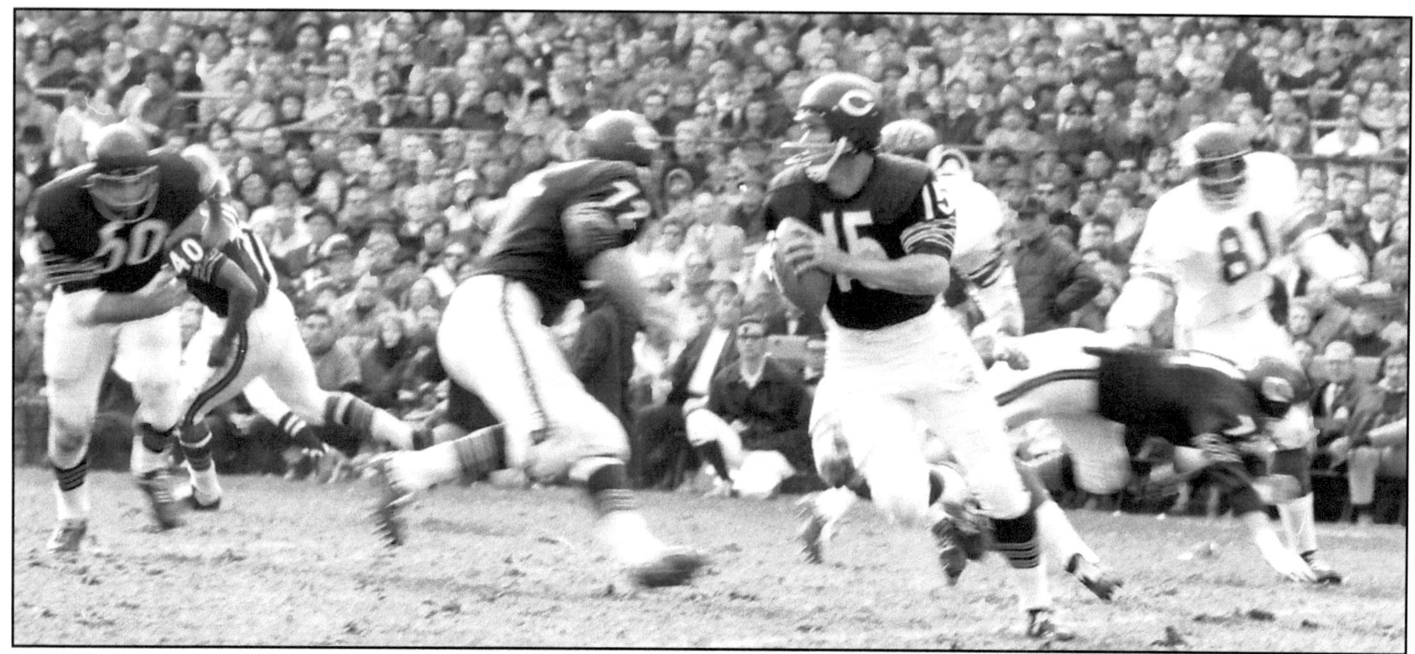

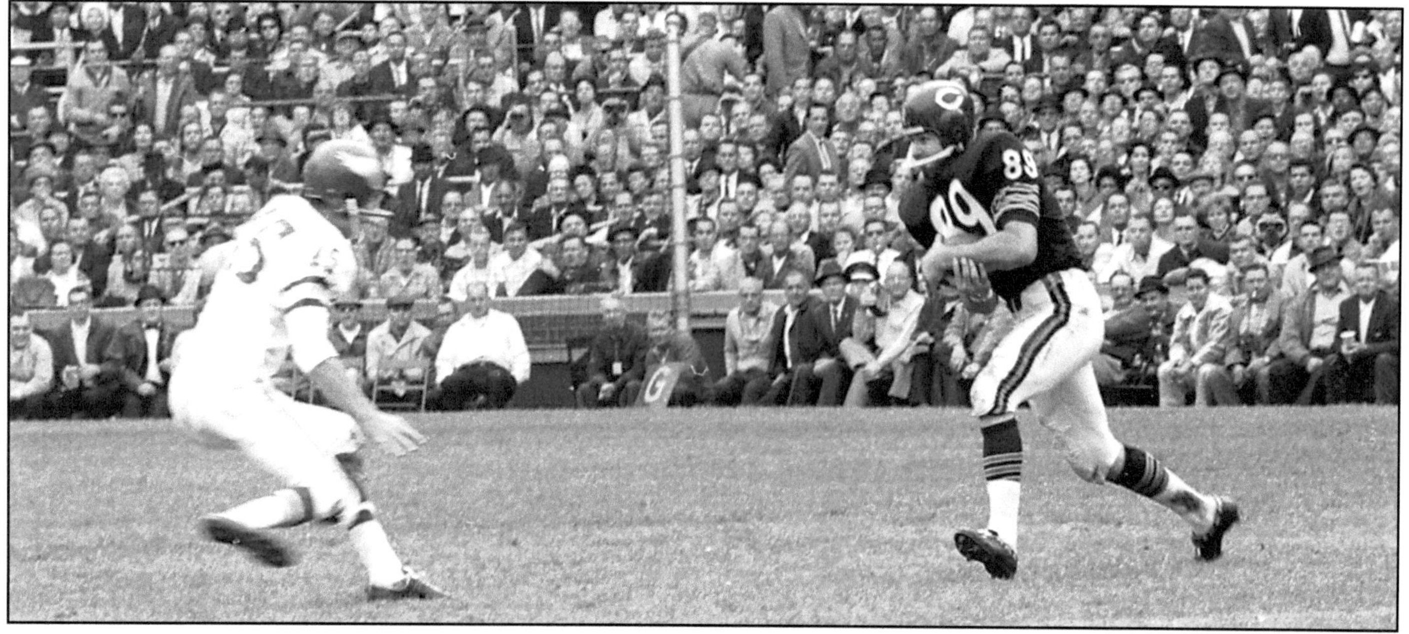

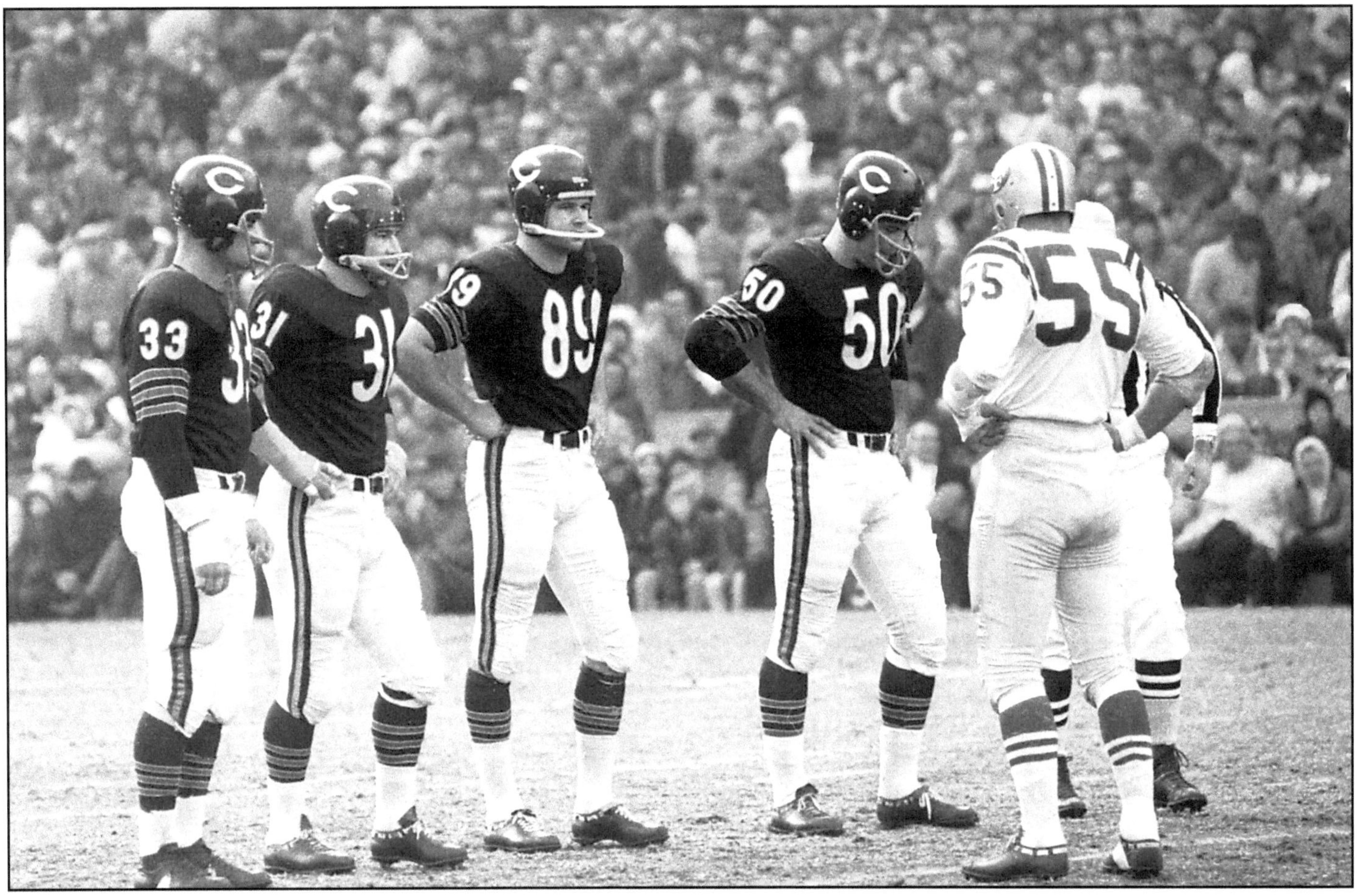

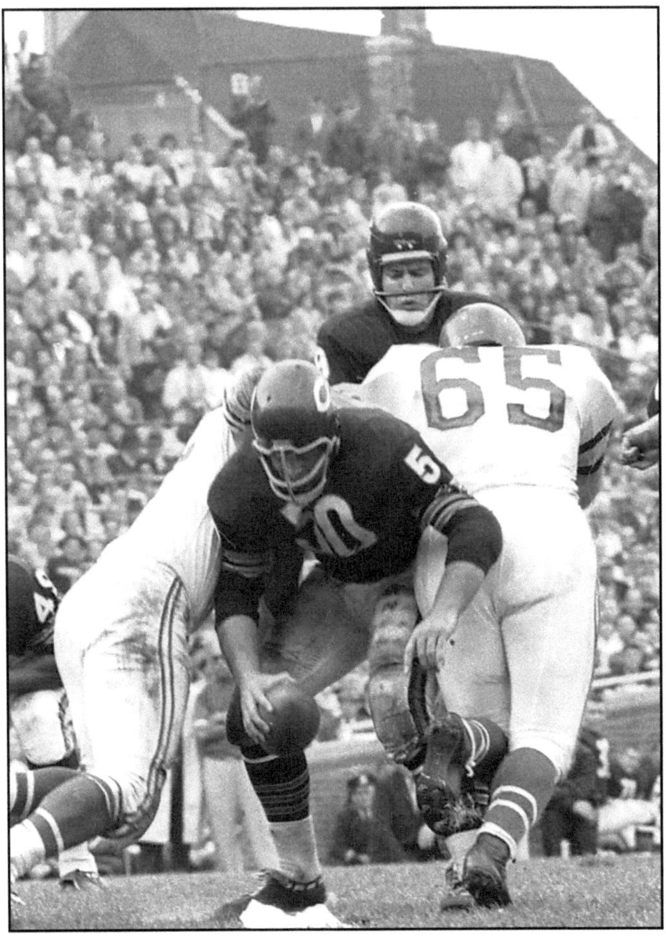

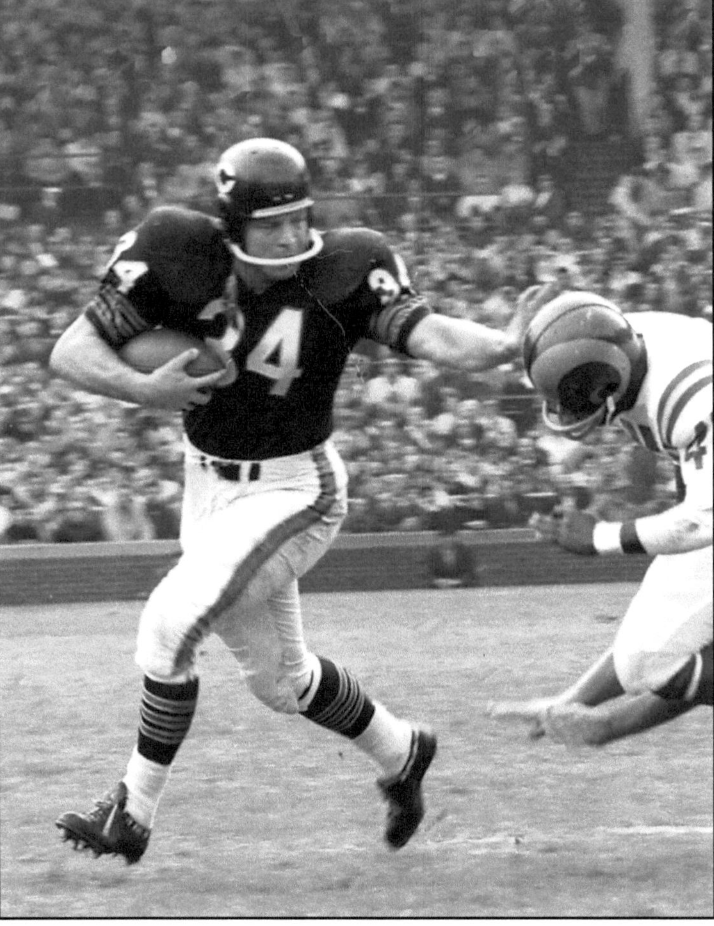

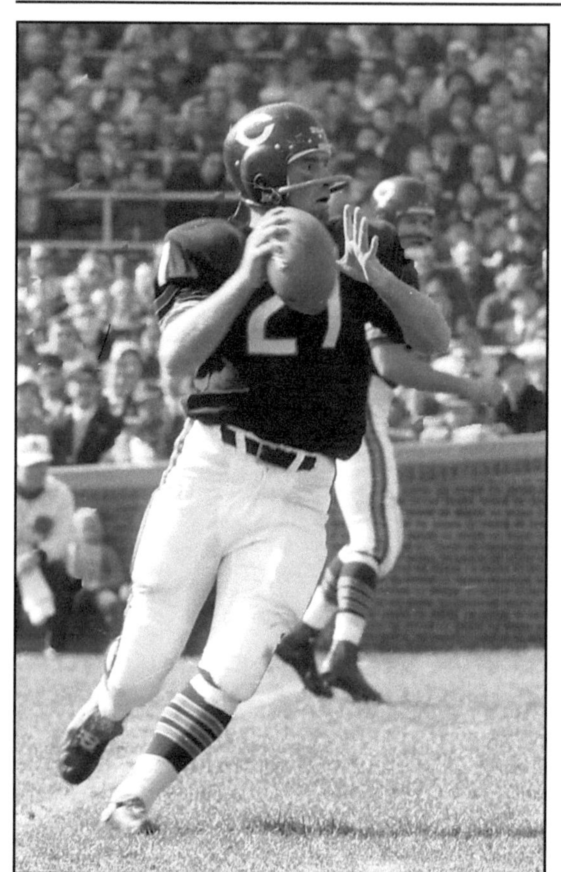

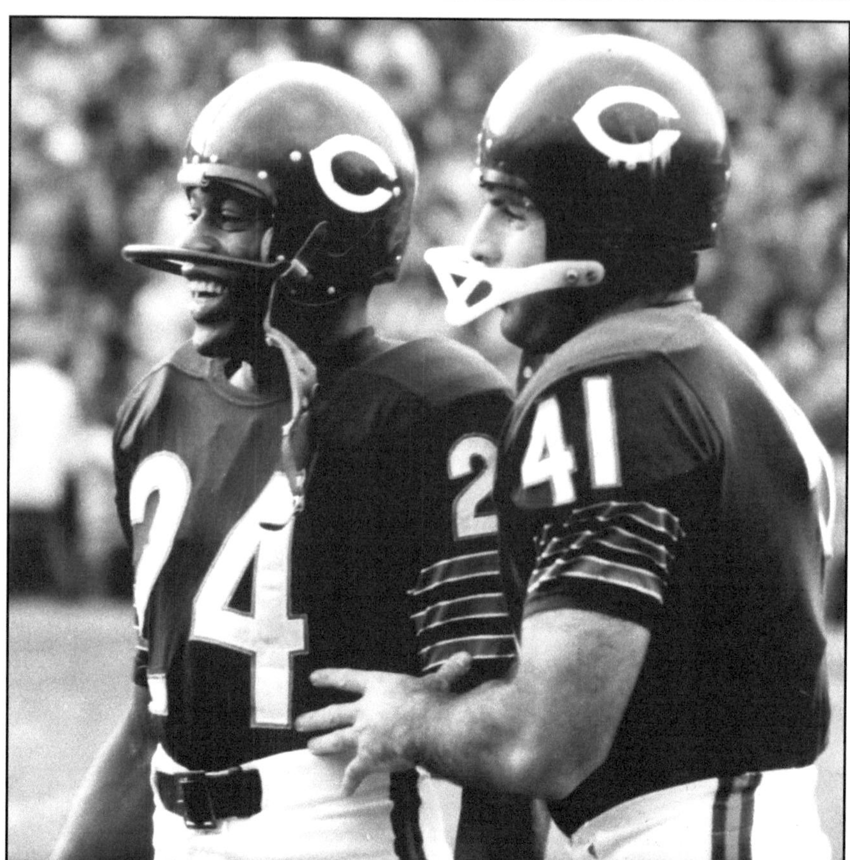
24
41

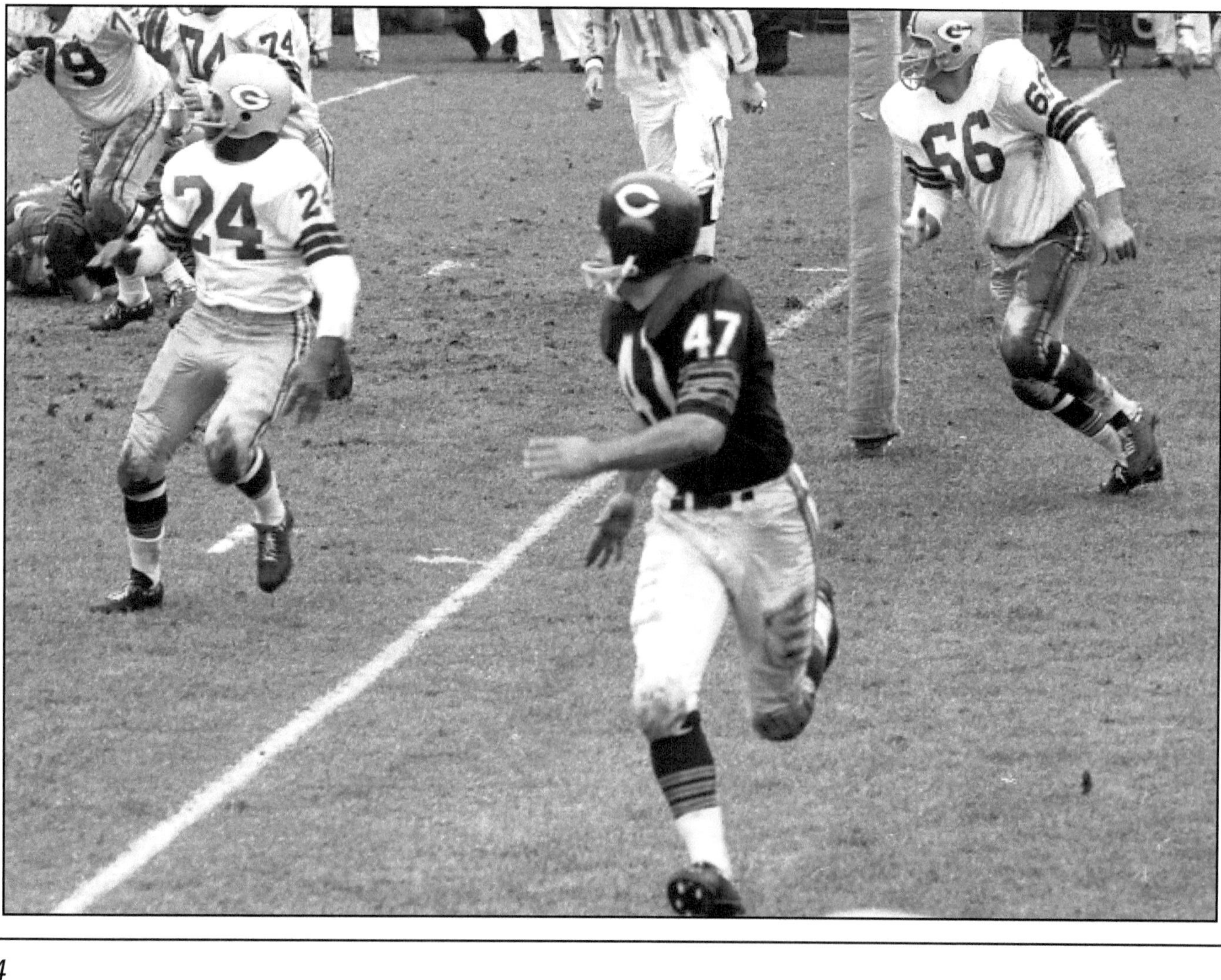

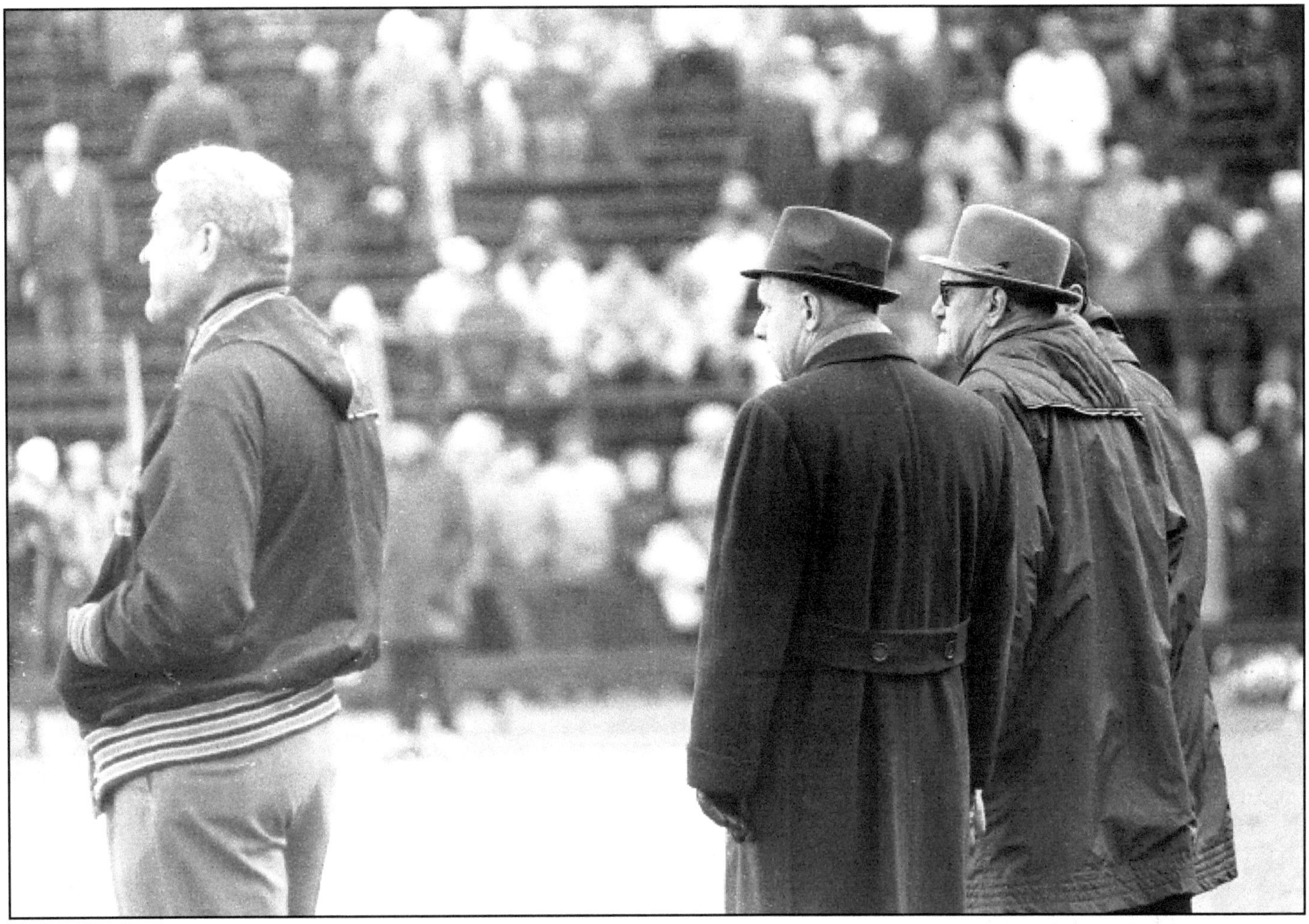

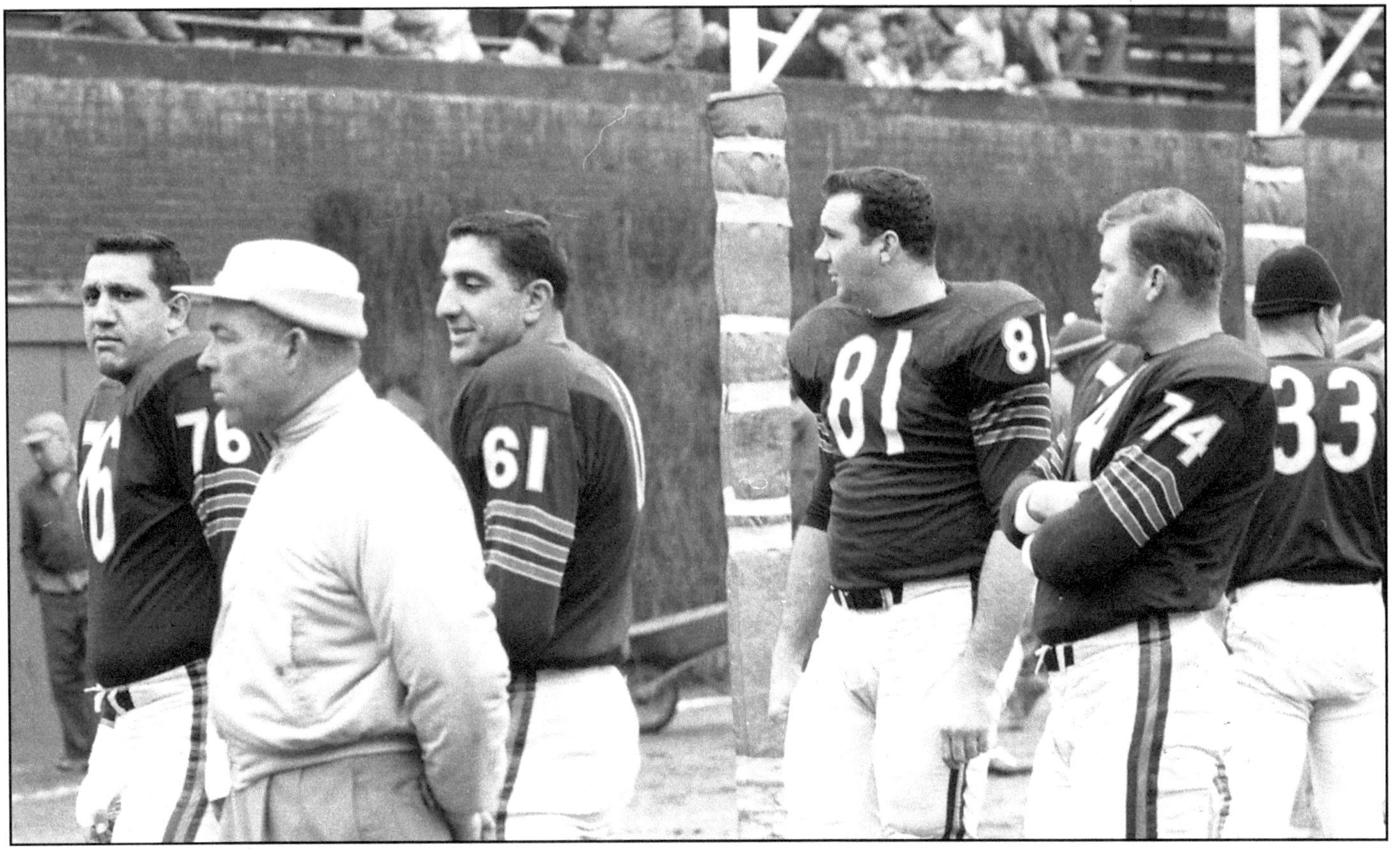

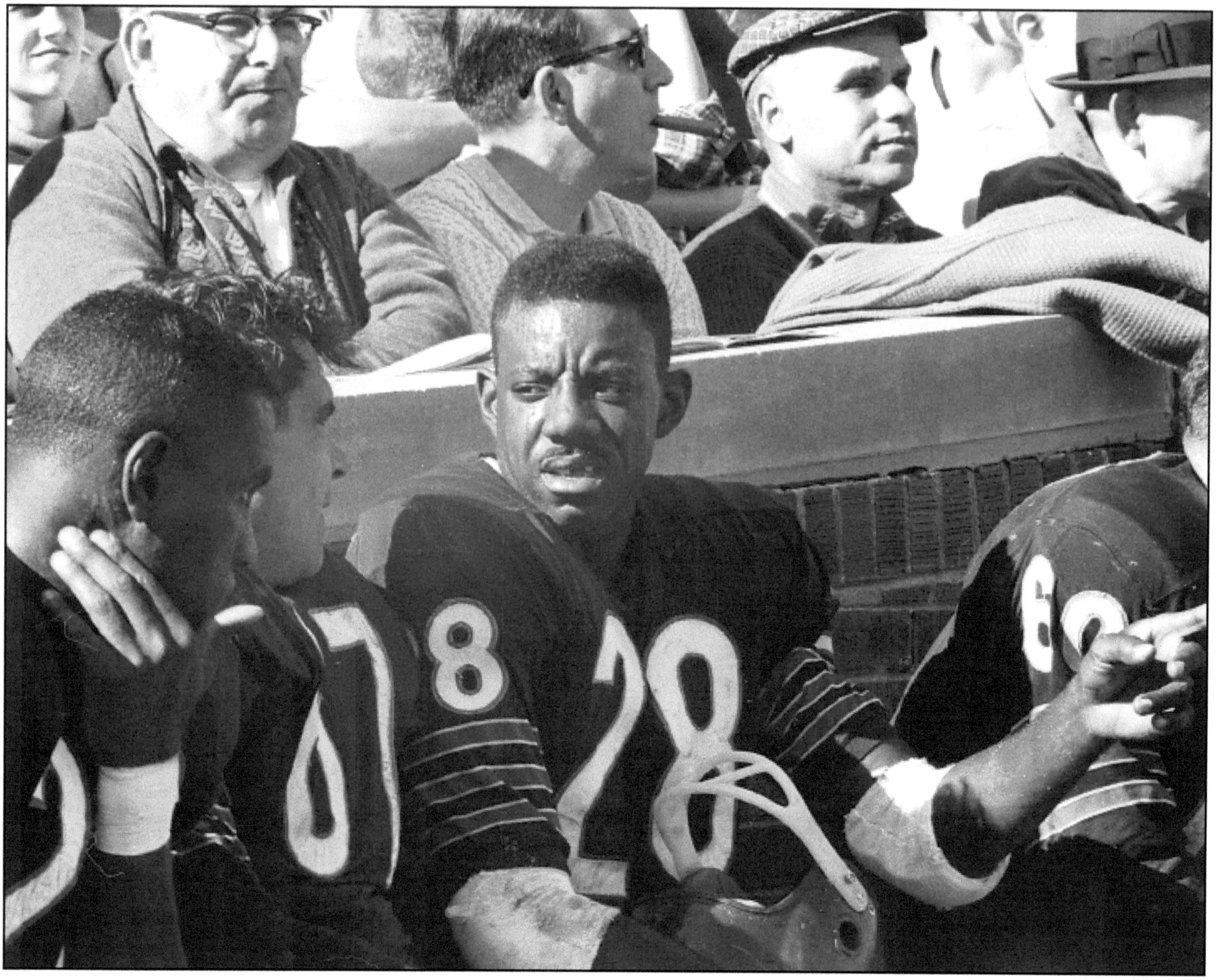

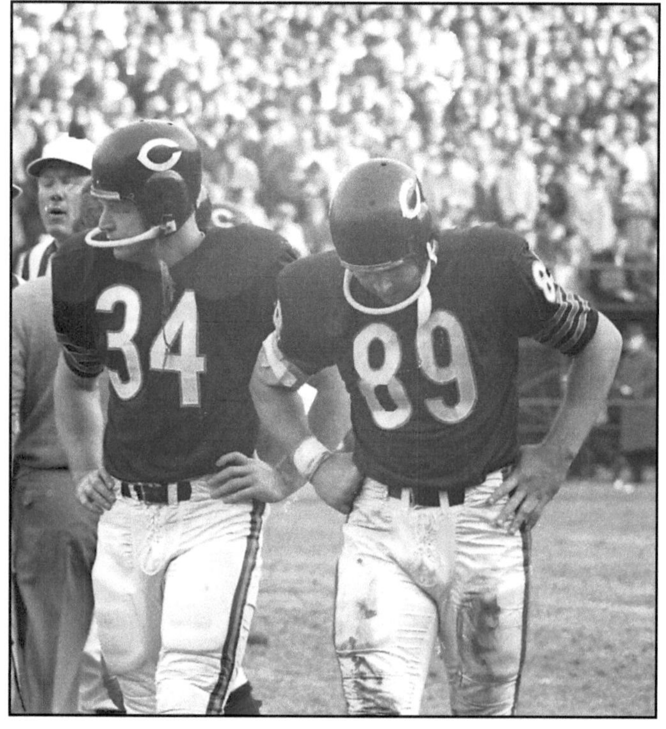
34
89

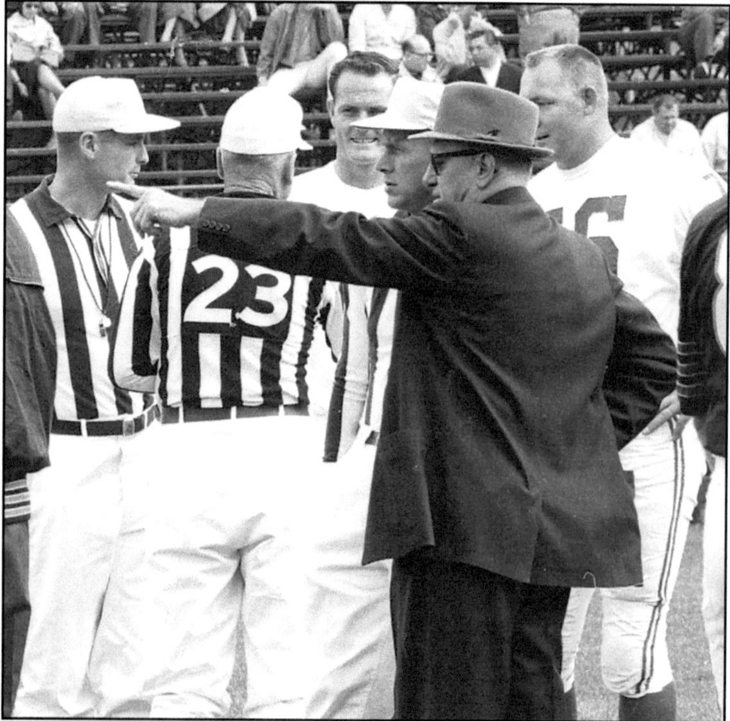
23

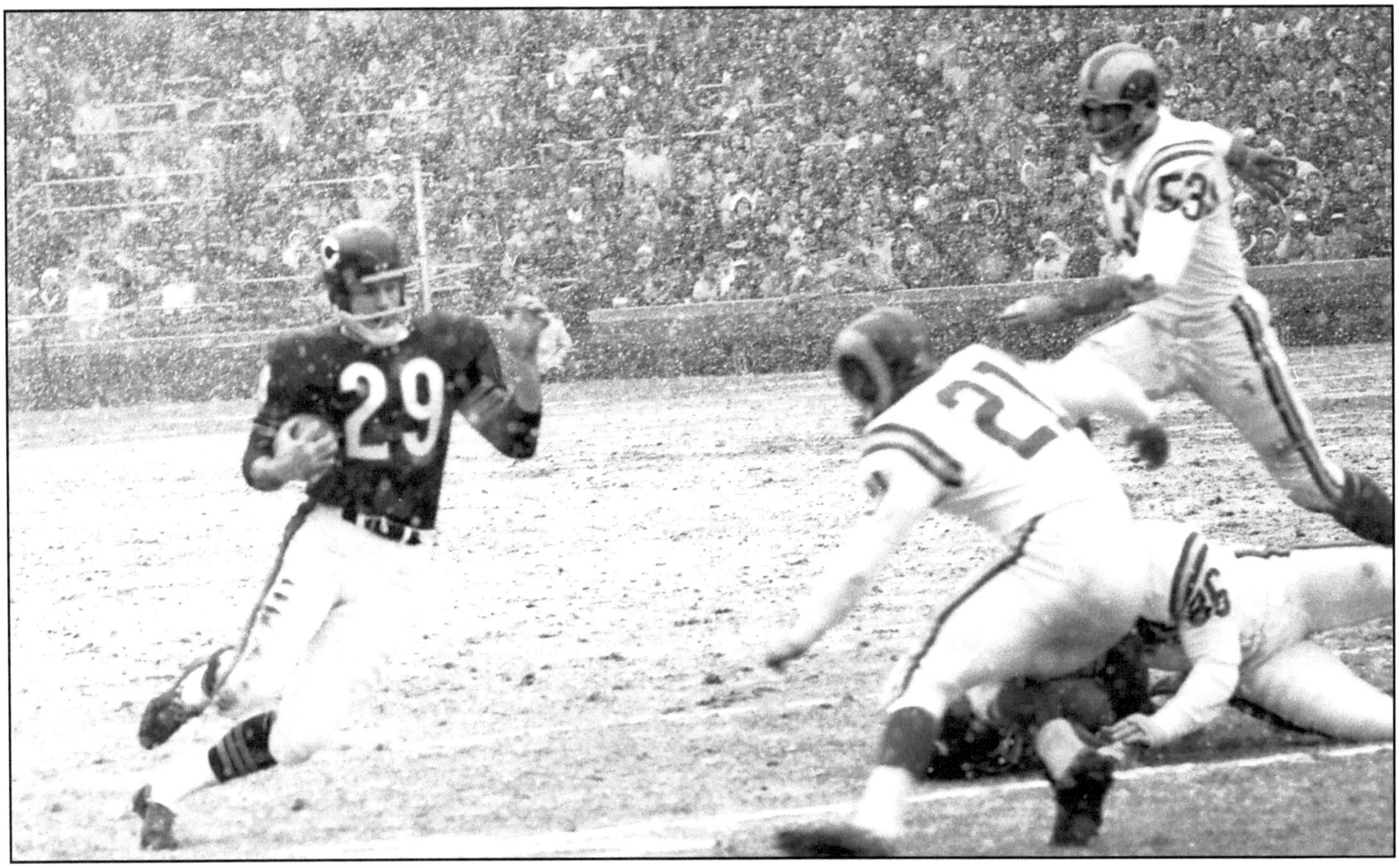

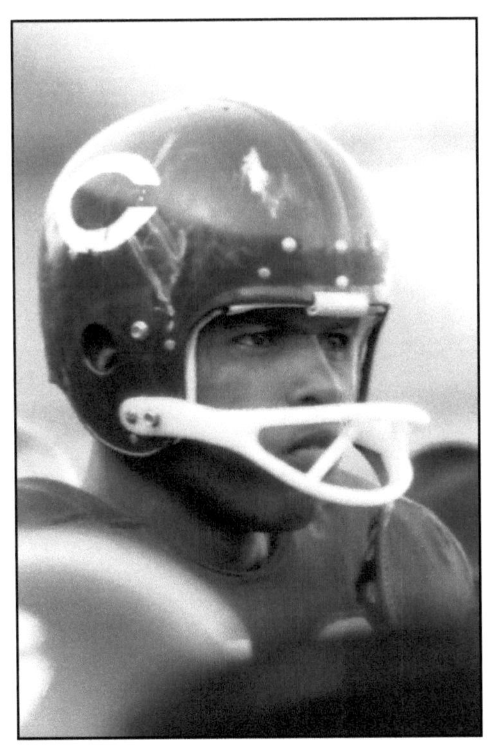

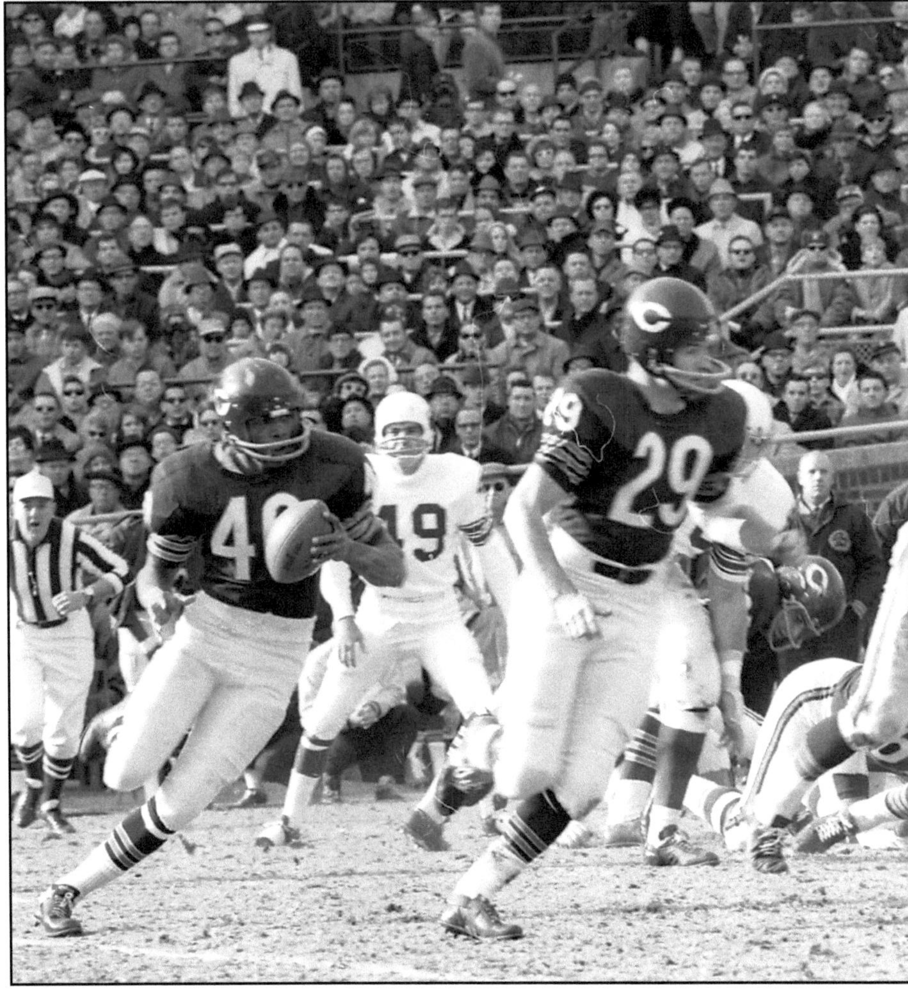

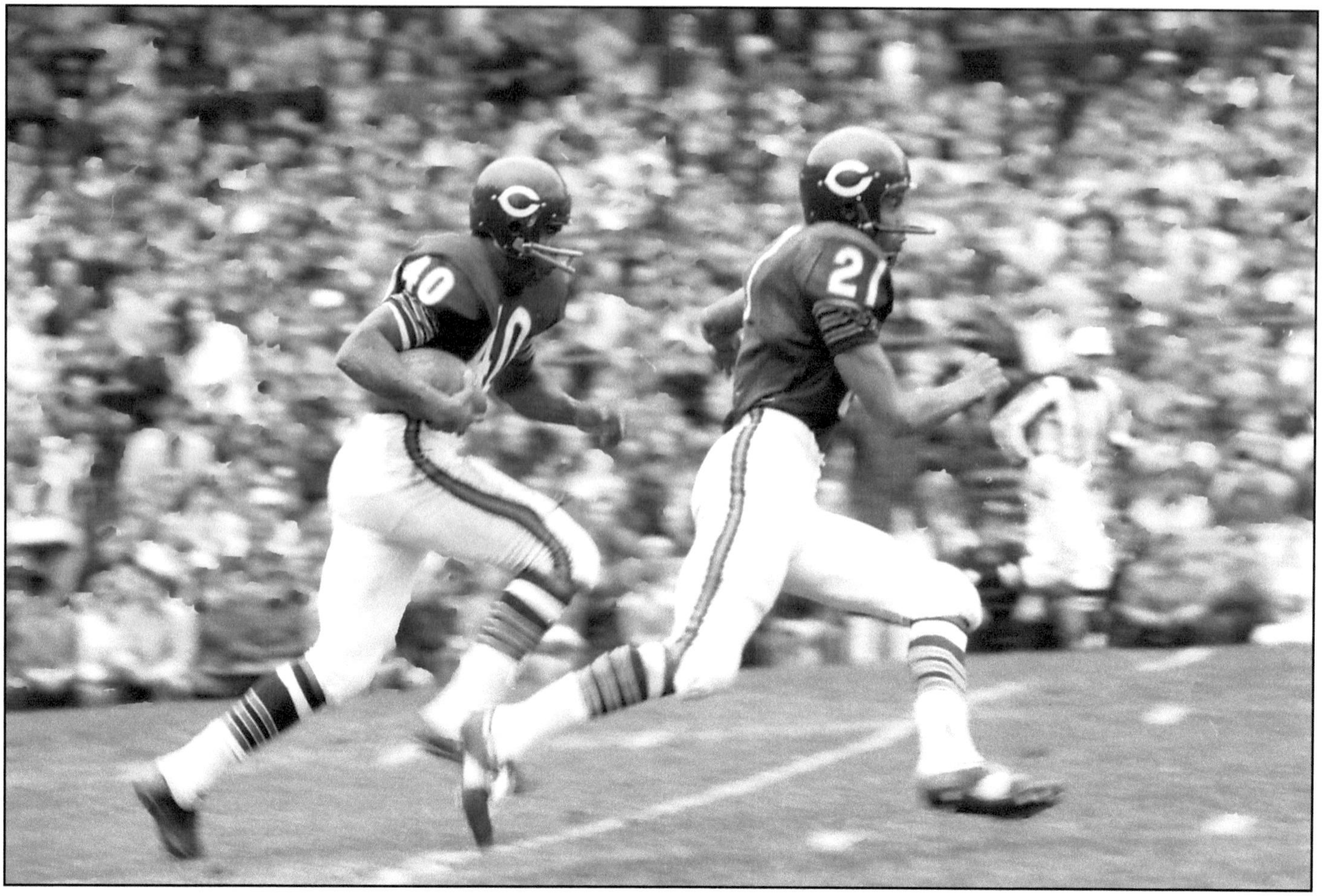

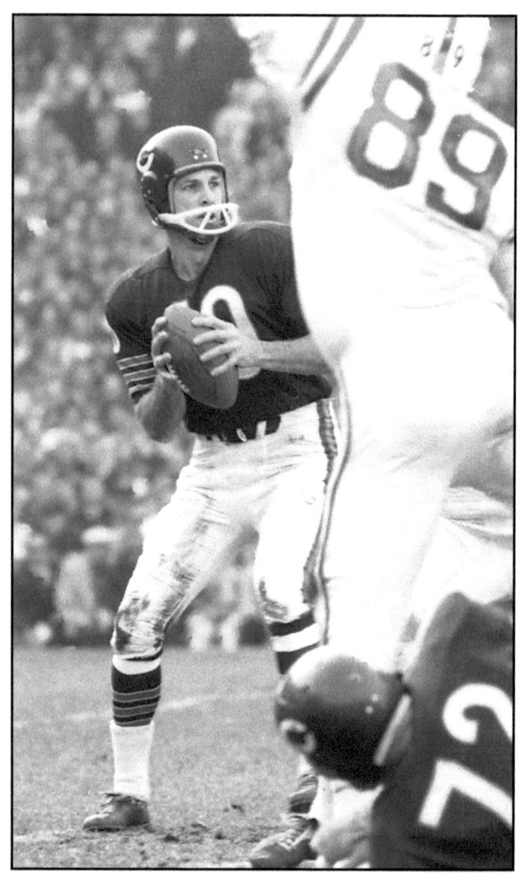

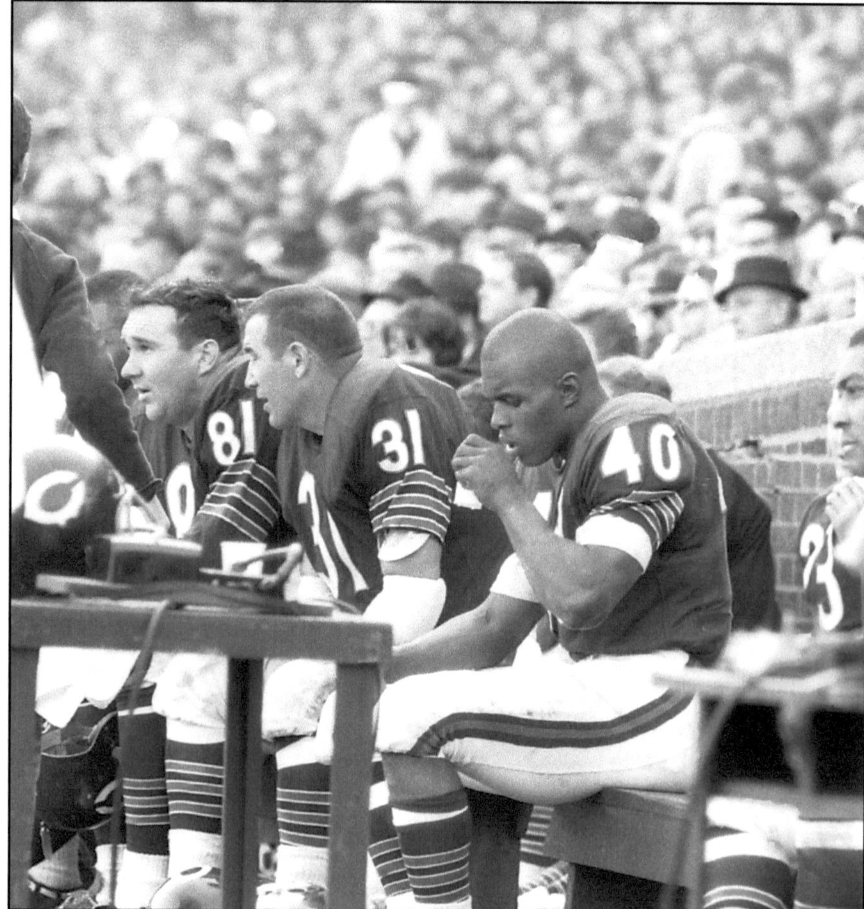

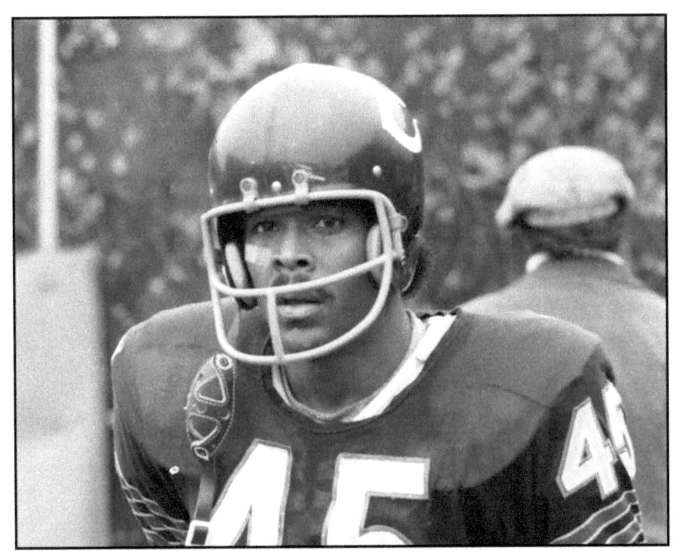
45

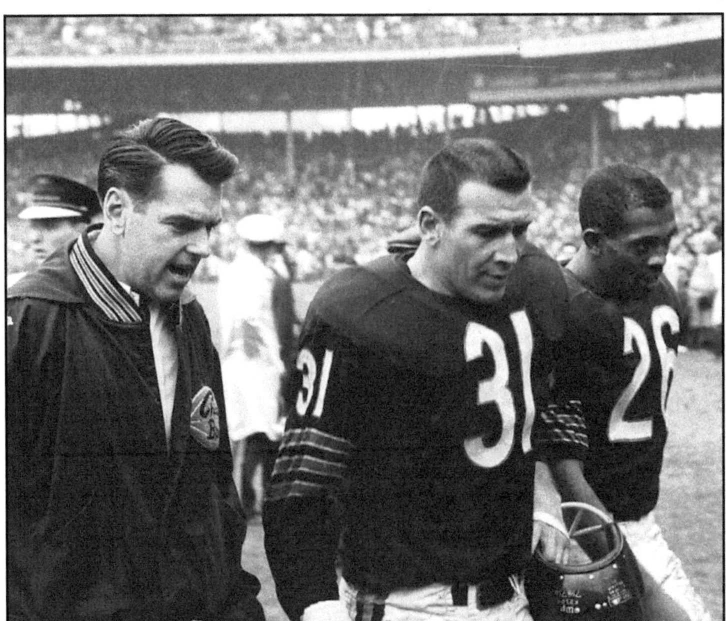
31
31
26

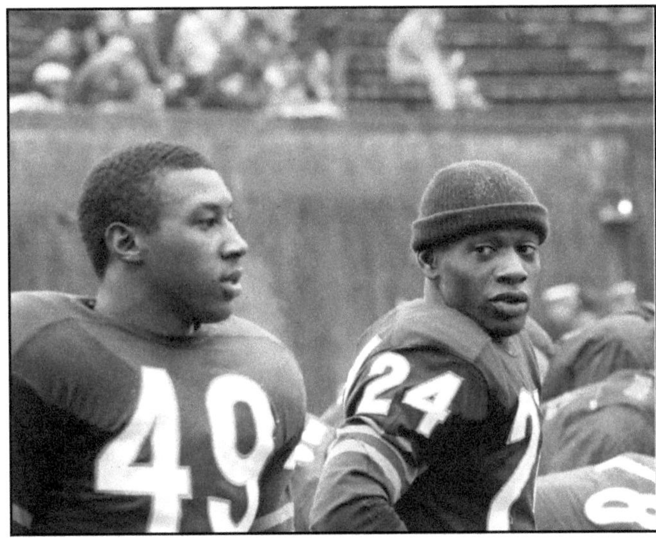
49
24

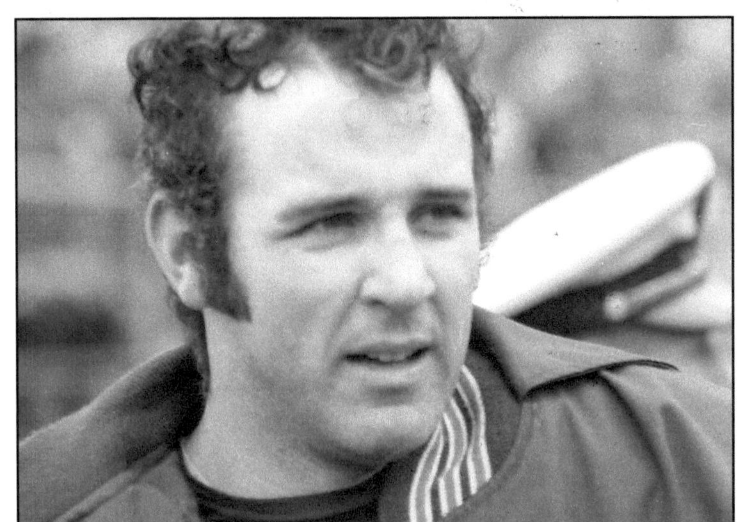

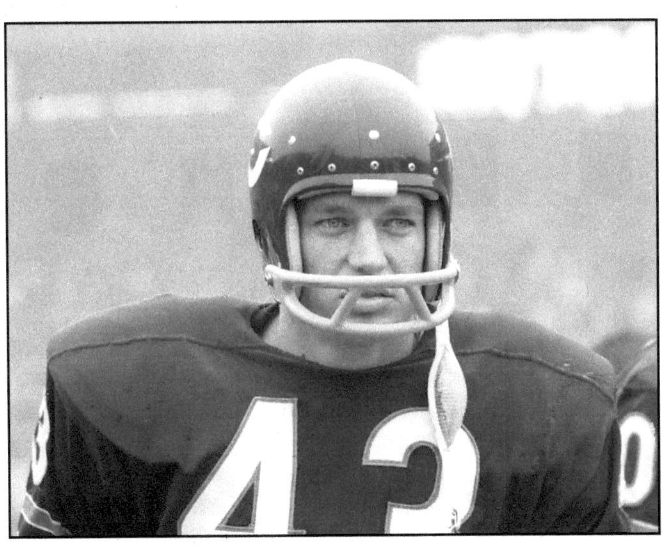

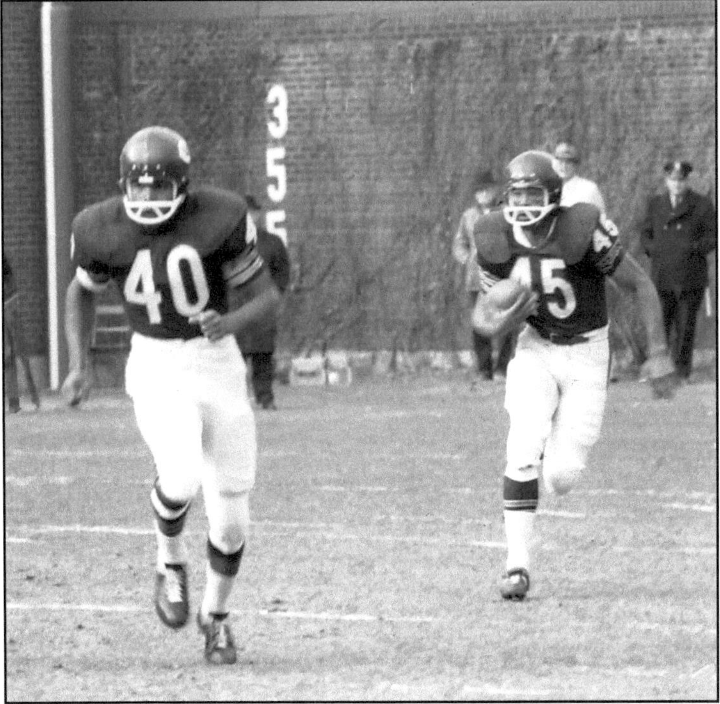
355
40
45

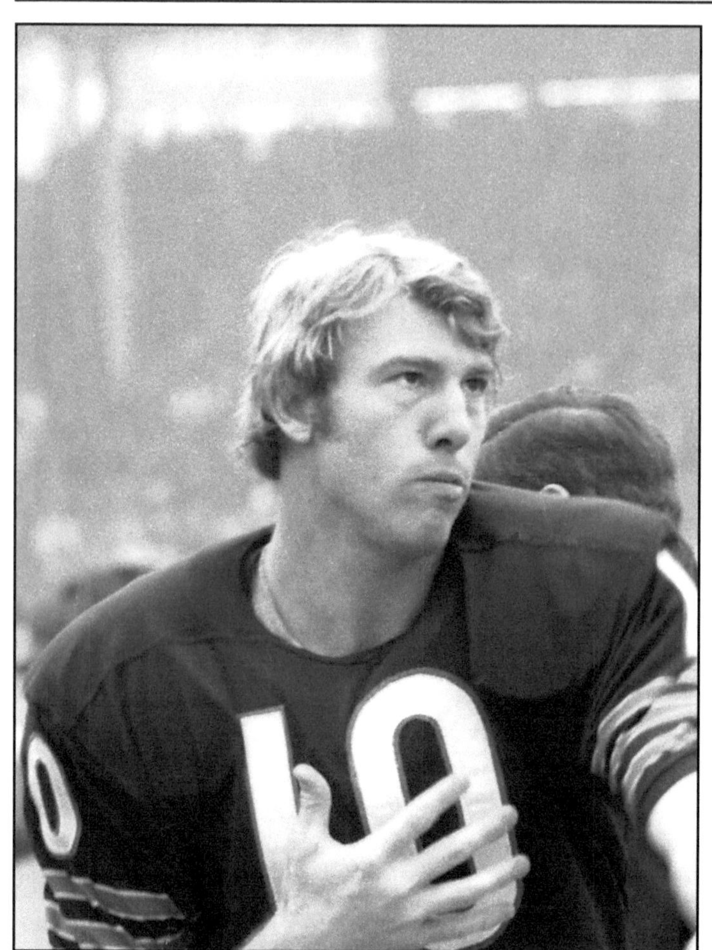
10

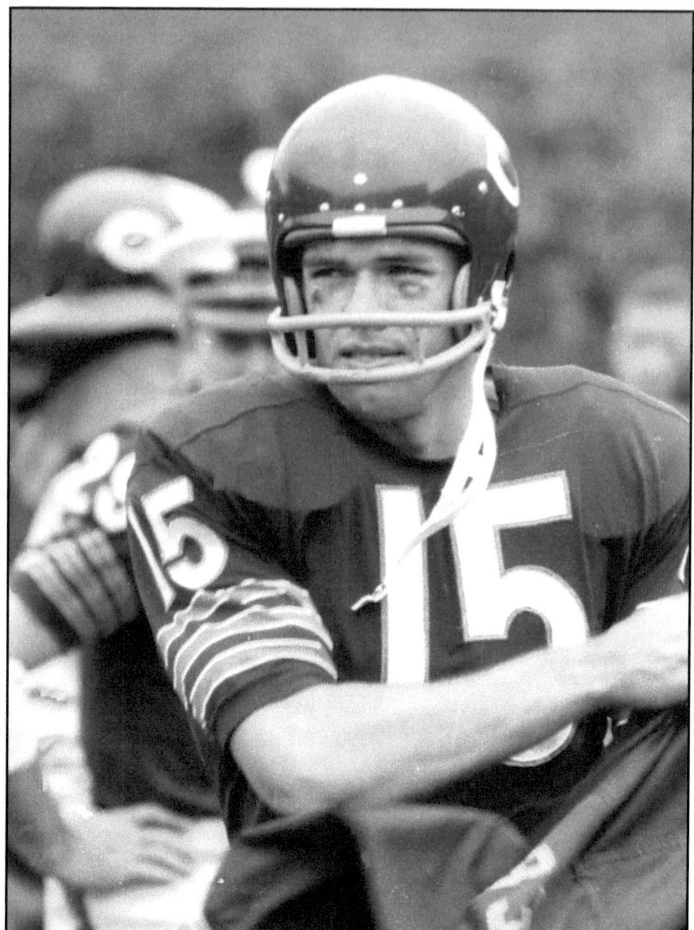
15

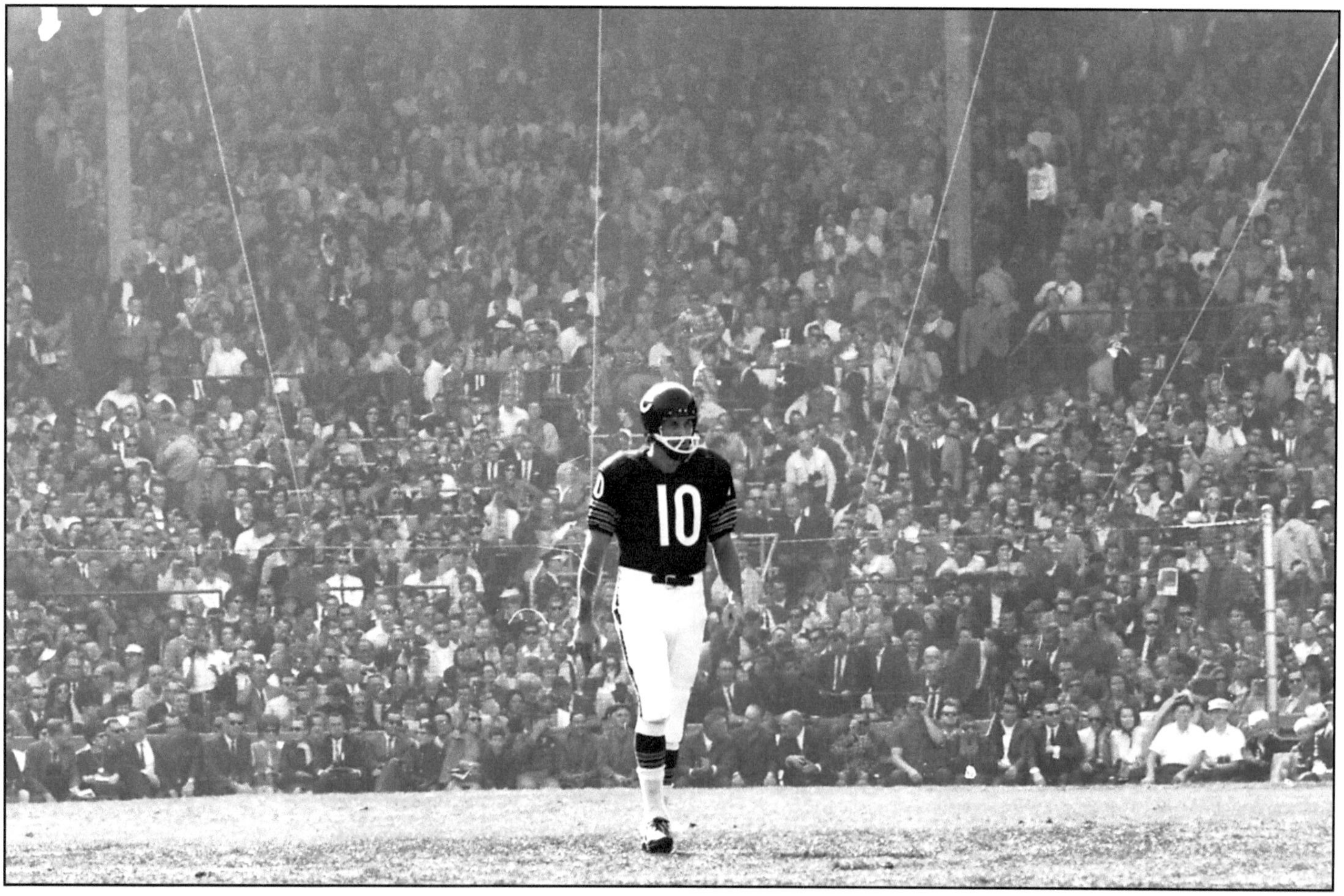

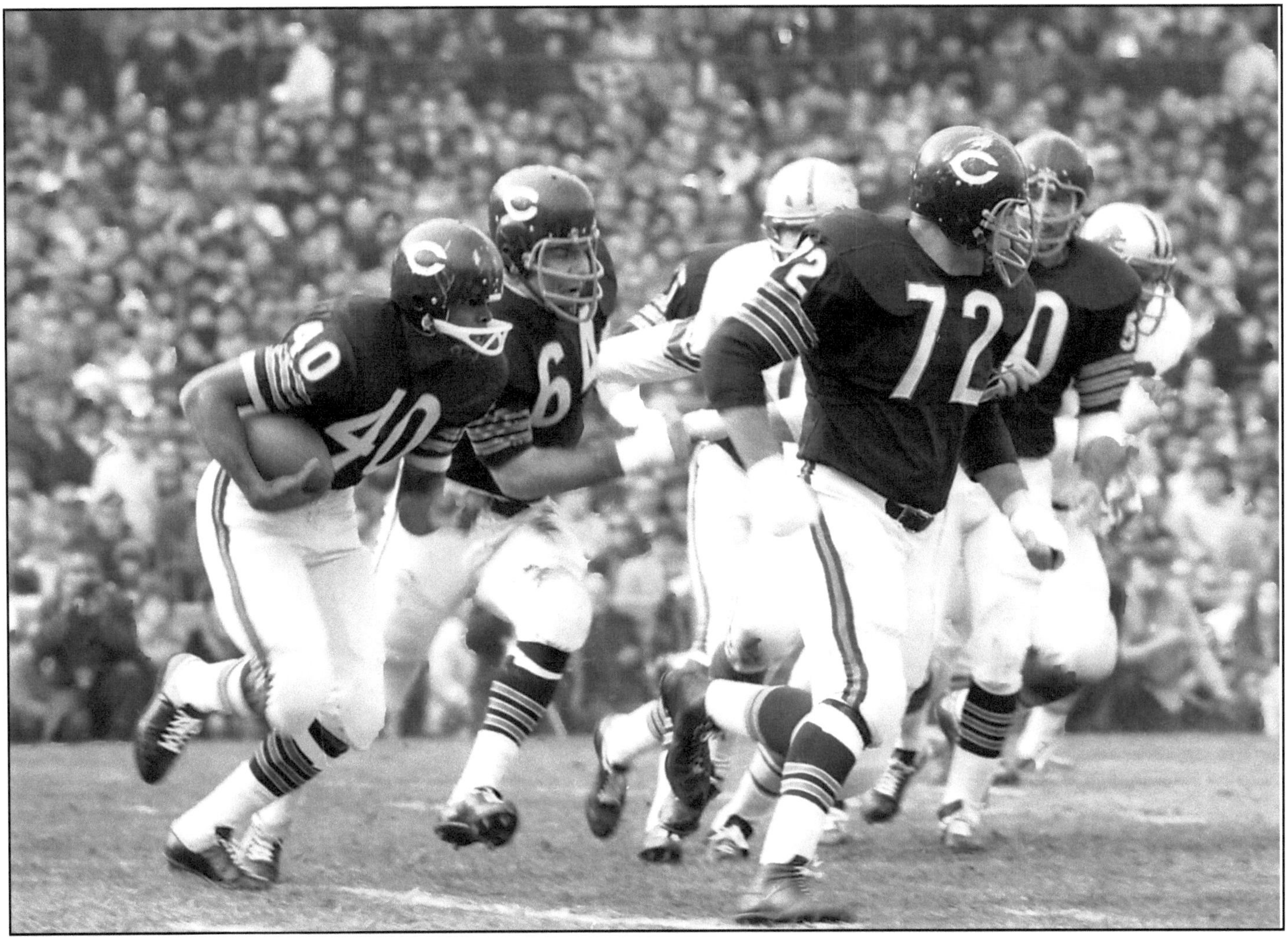

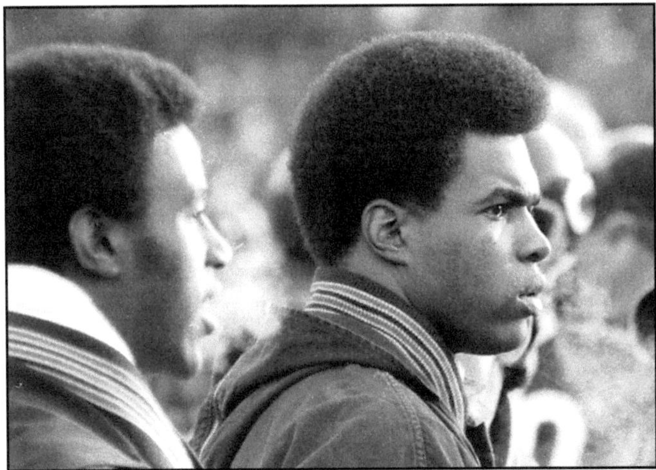

"The closeness of the fans and the right field stands made that place special. Someone asked if I would rather play in a big stadium like Yankee Stadium or the other big parks. I always said the field is 50 yards wide and 100 yards long and I don't care where they put it. The fans at Wrigley always gave us a big advantage. It was a great place to play"

- Gale Sayers

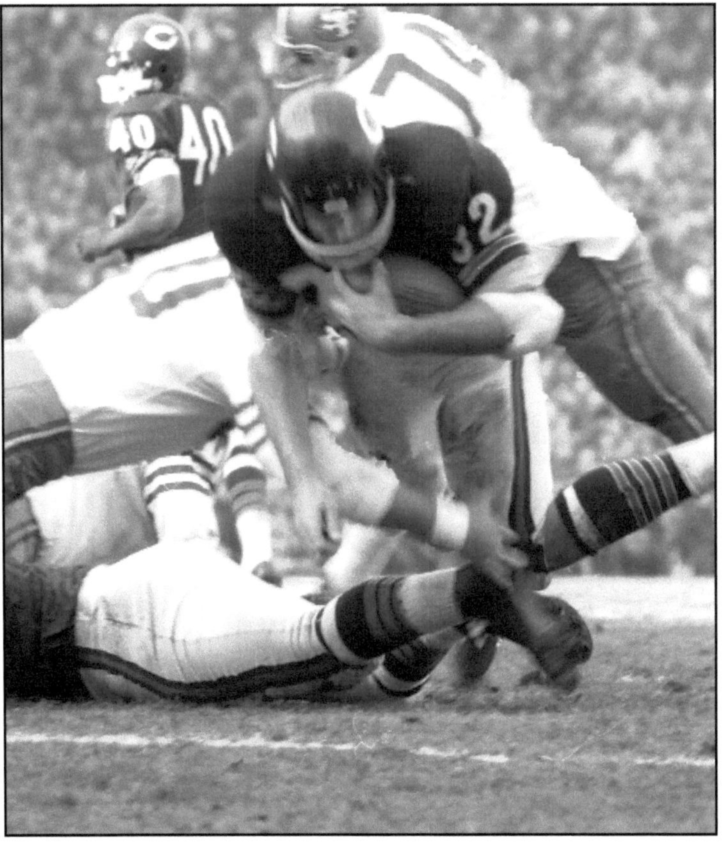

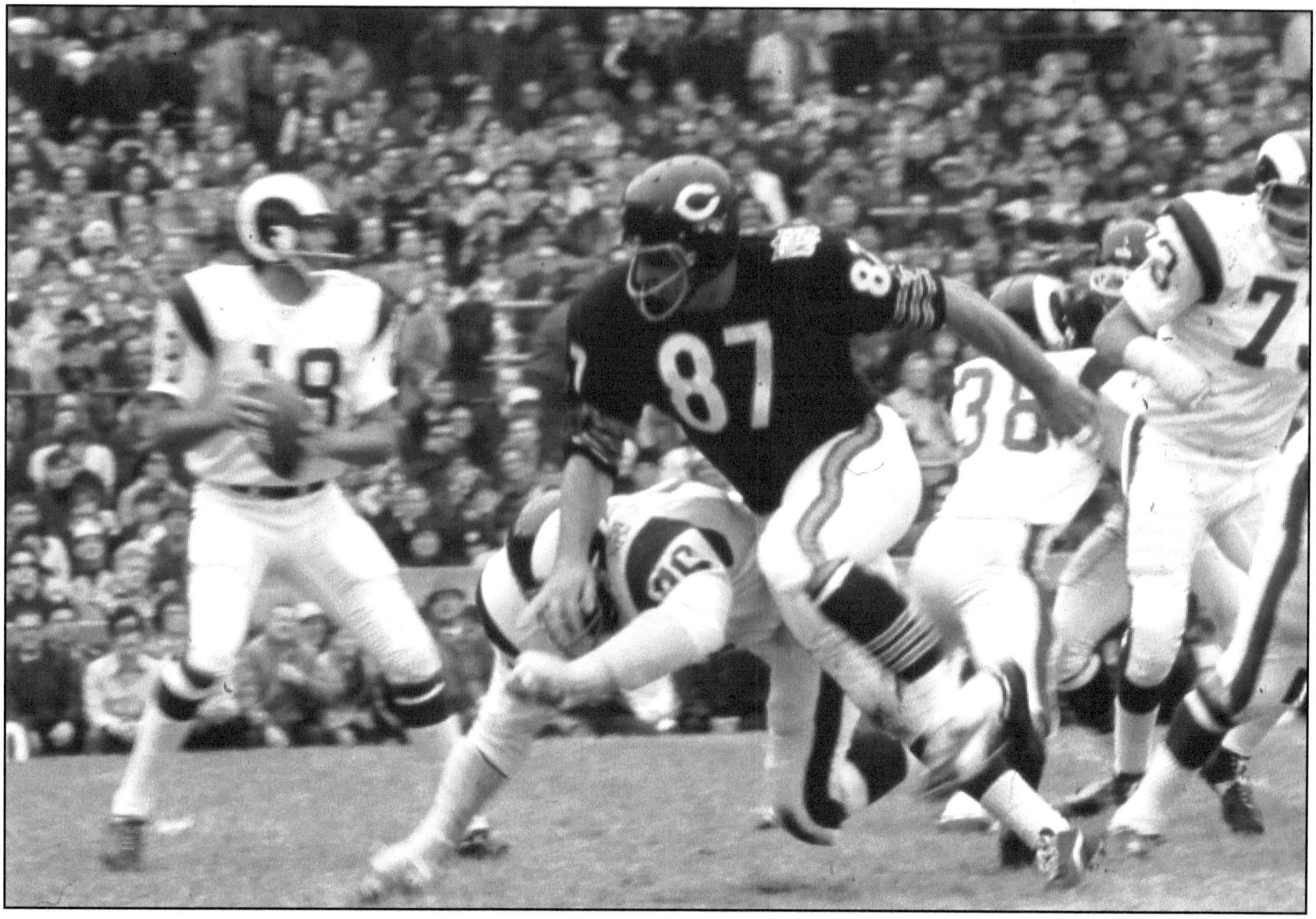

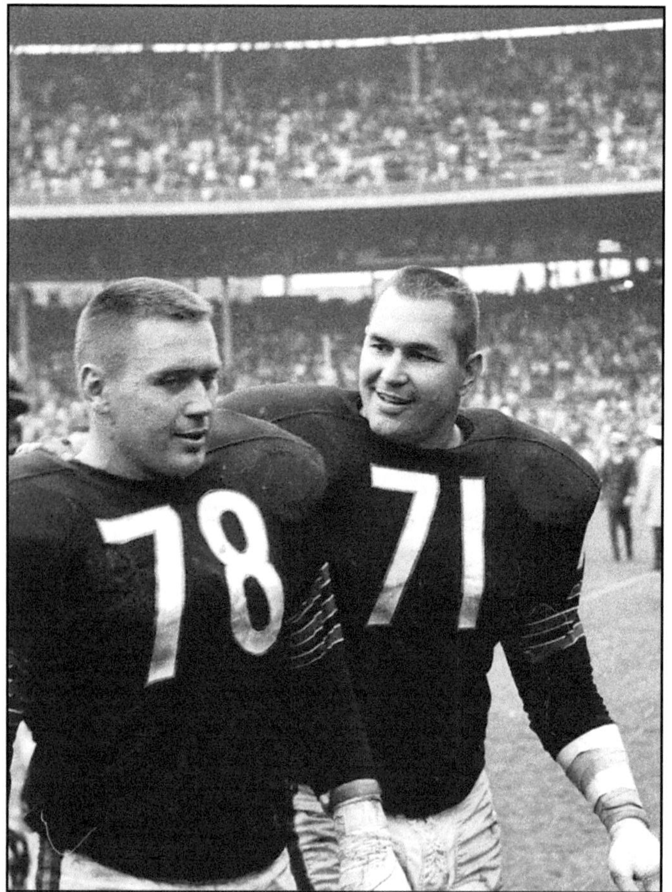

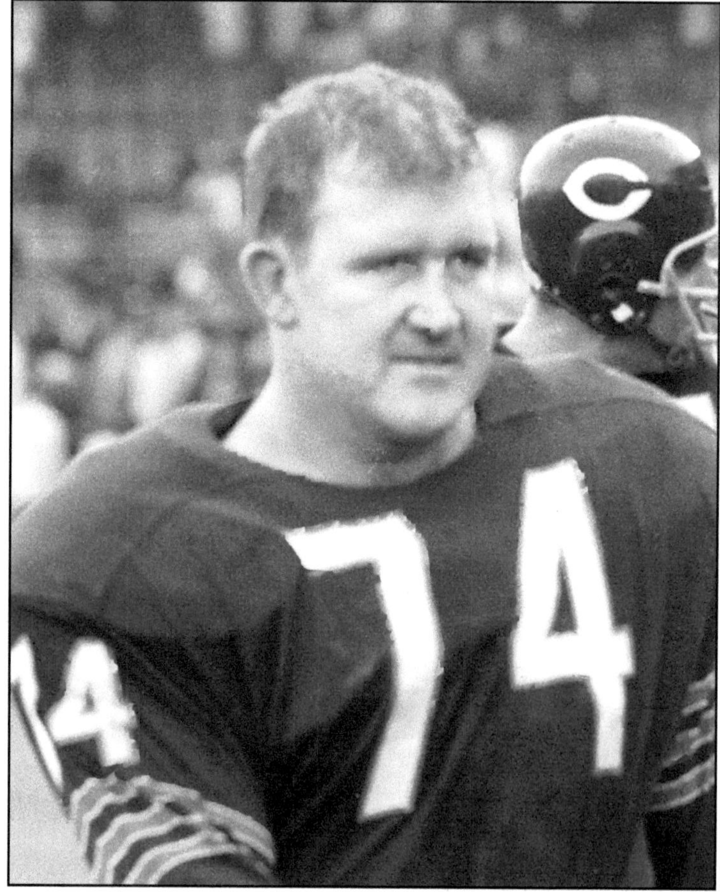

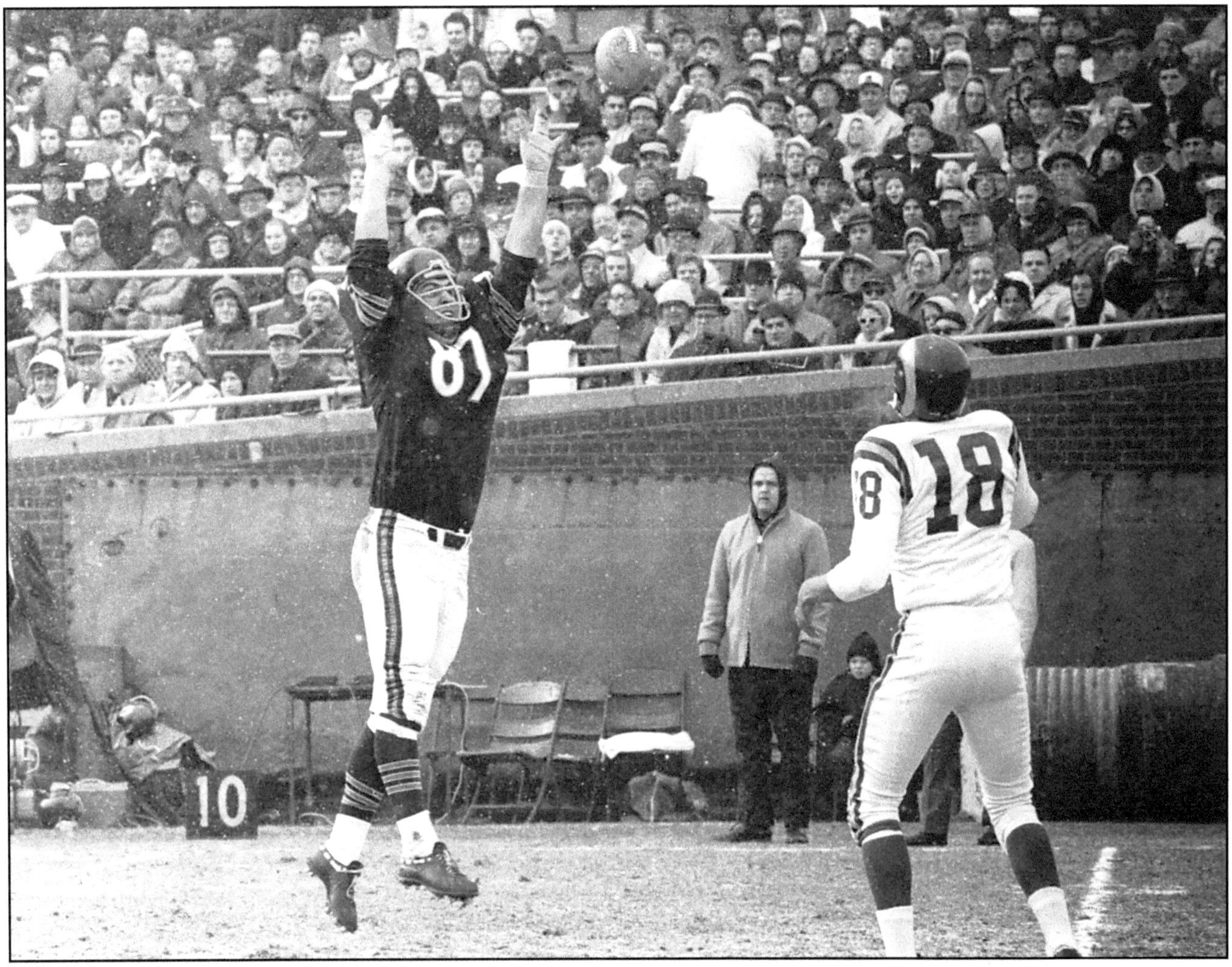

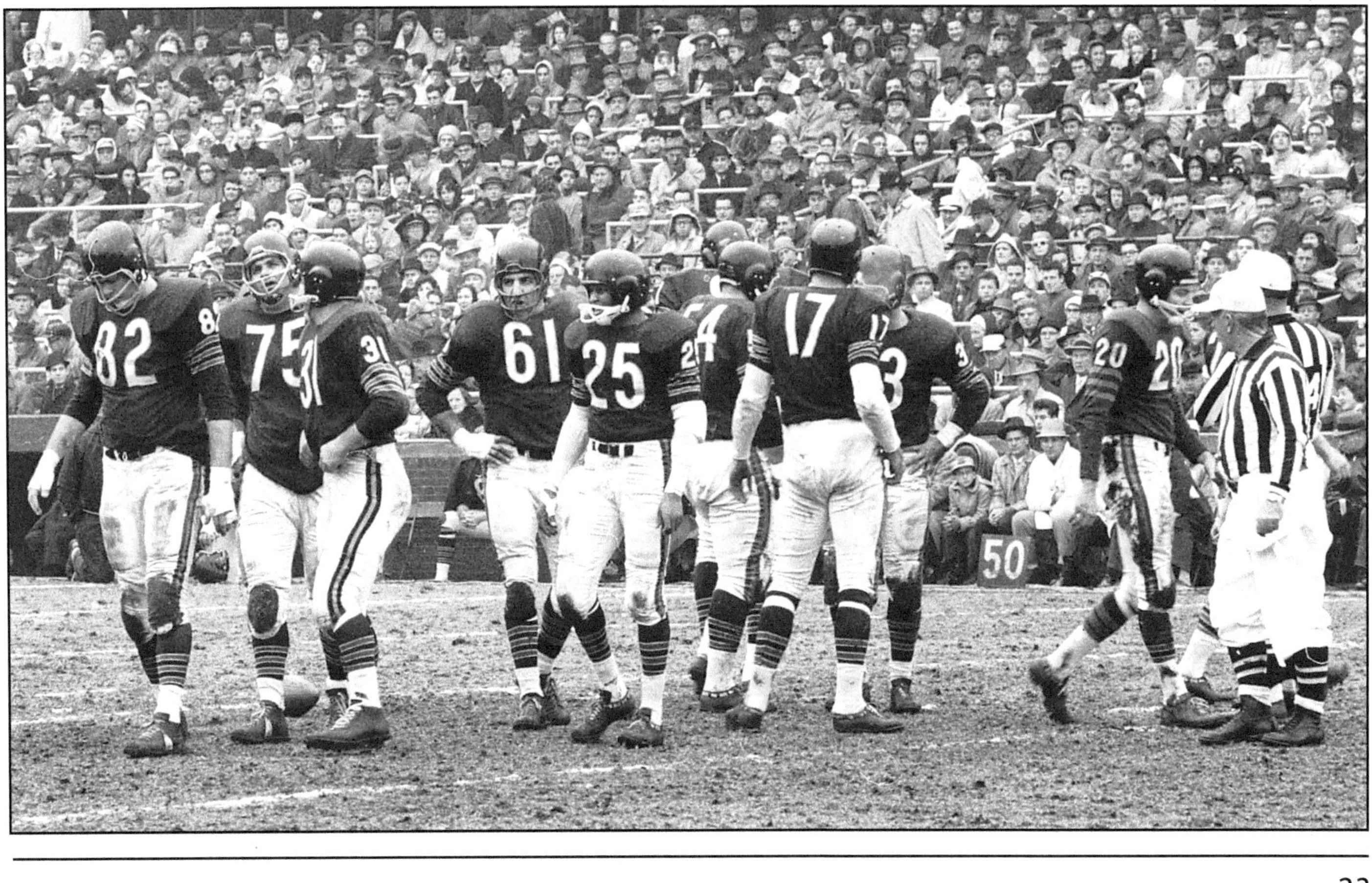

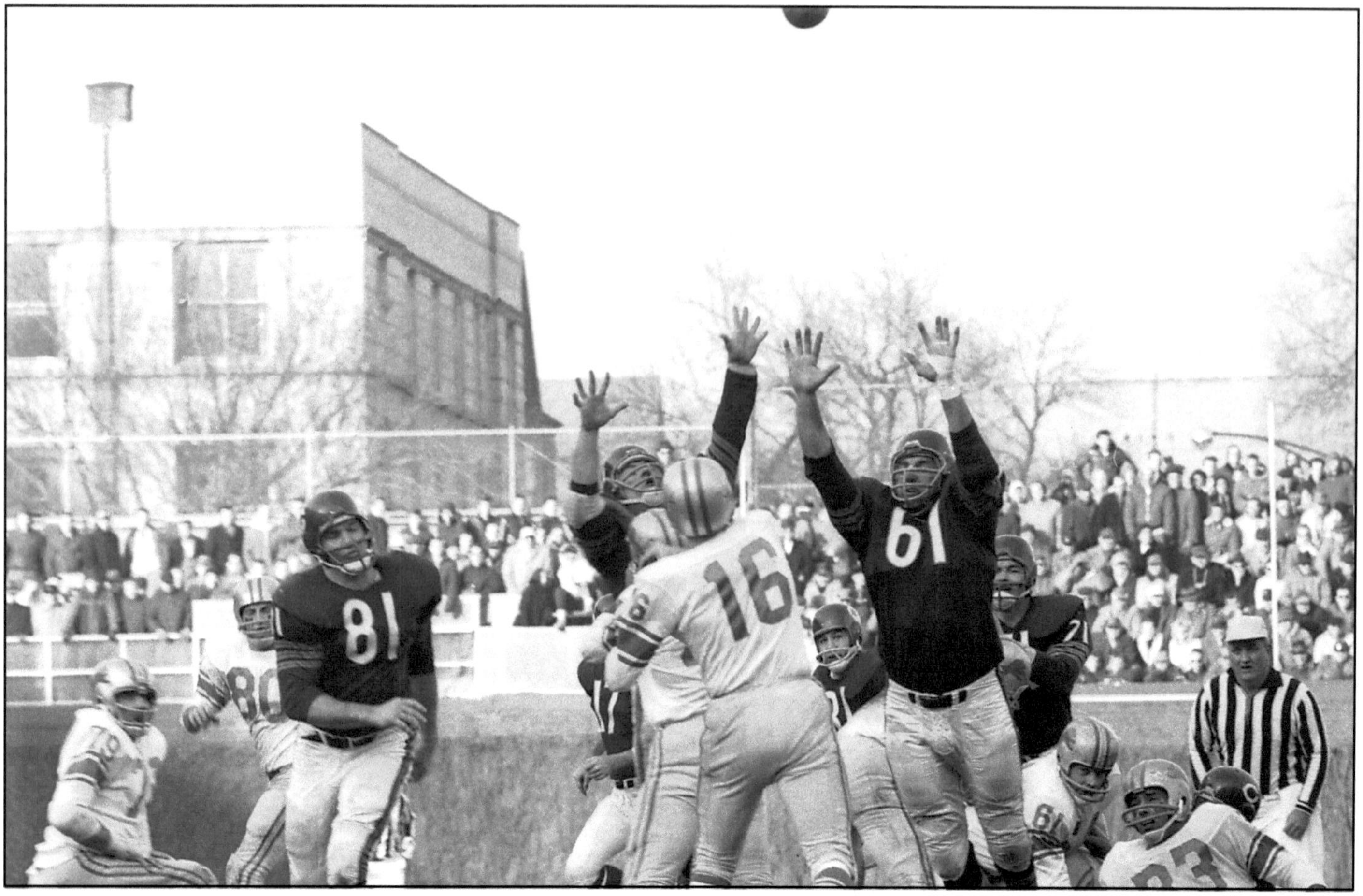

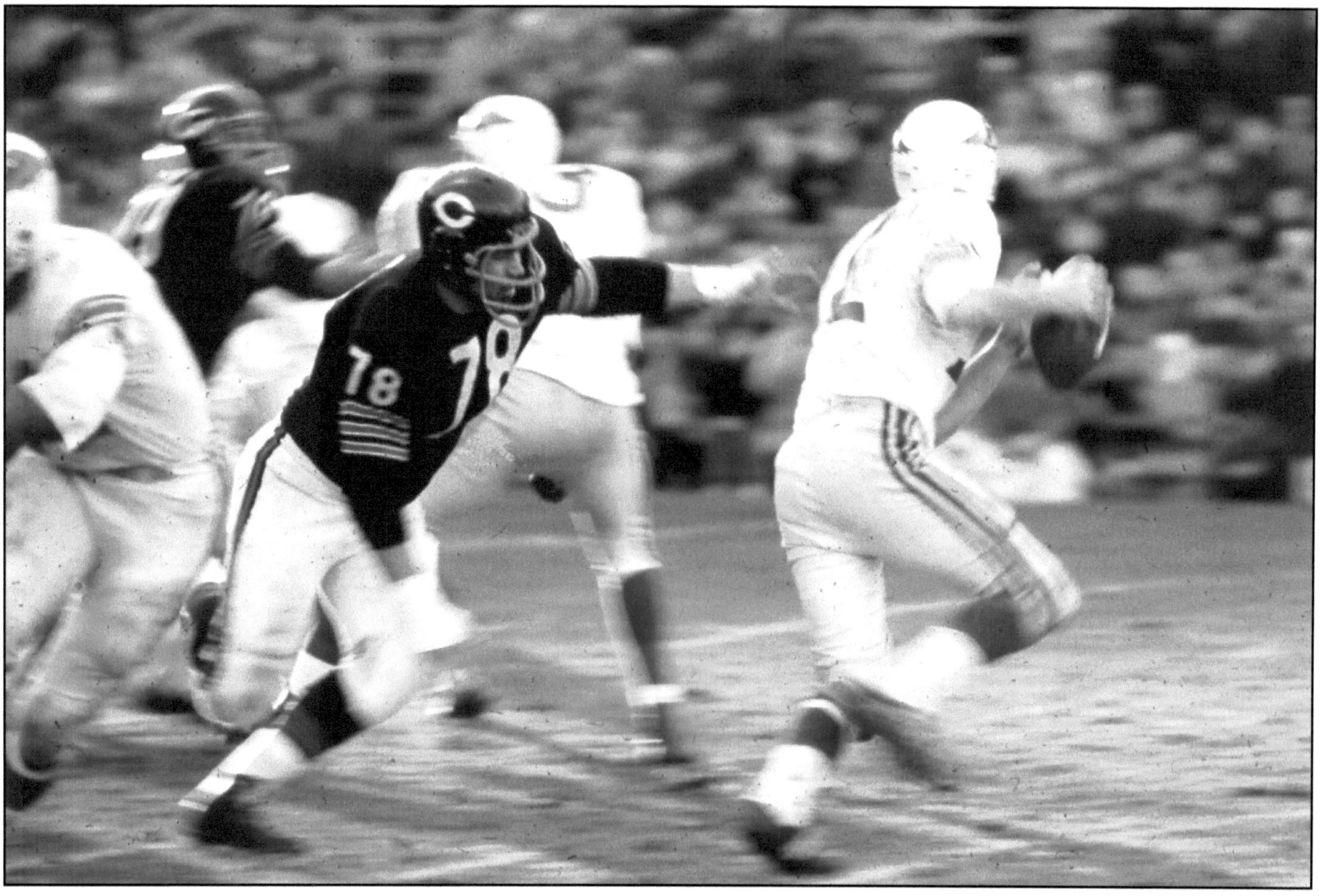

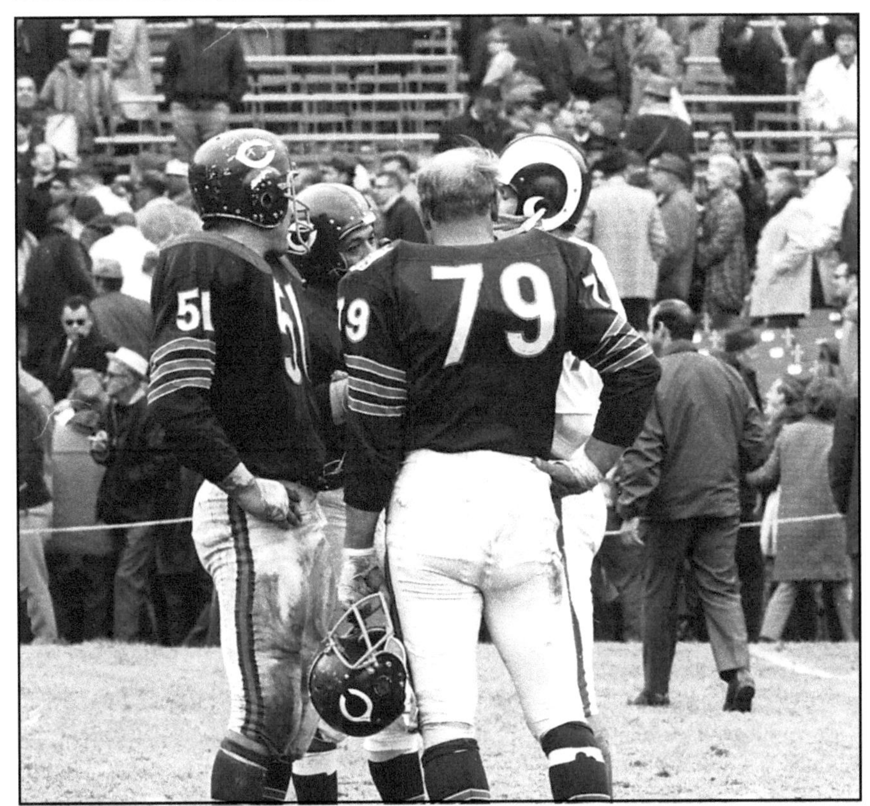
51
79

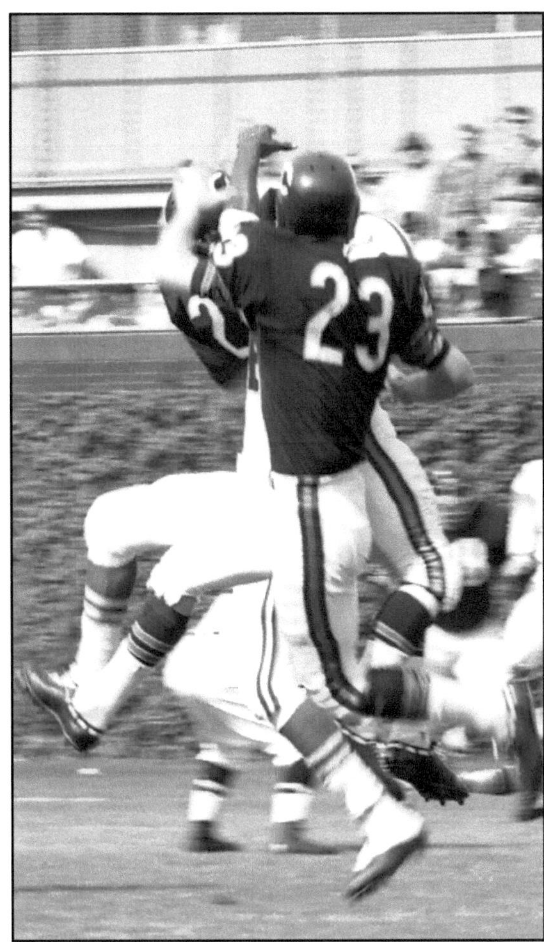
23

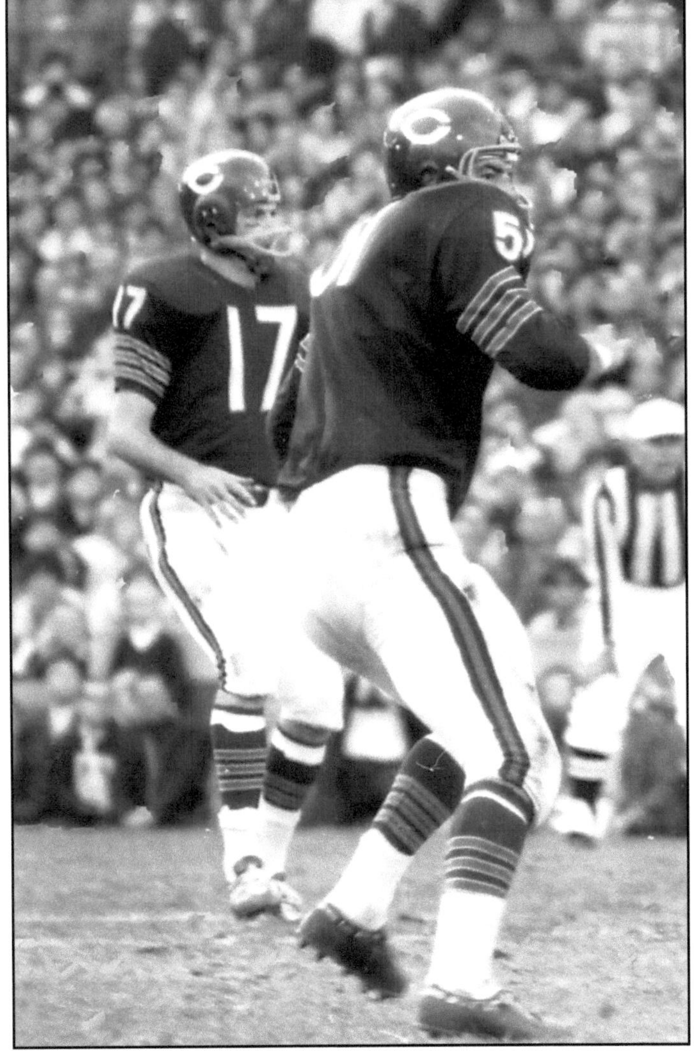
17

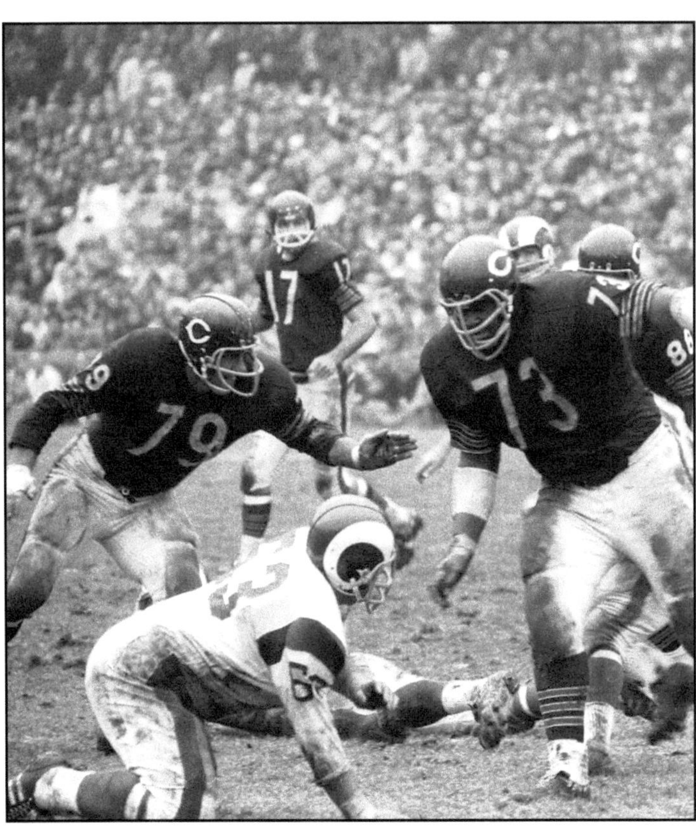
17
79
73

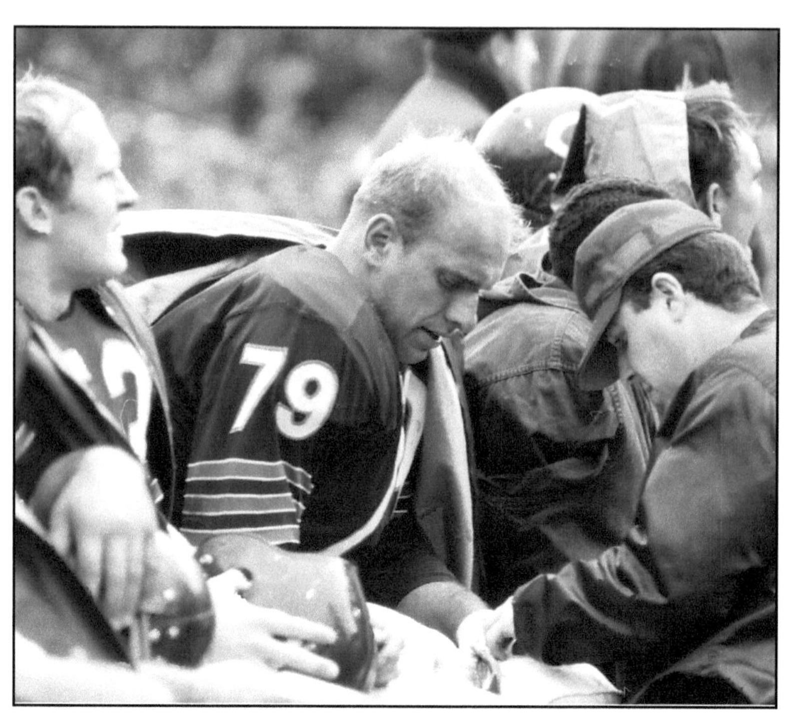
79

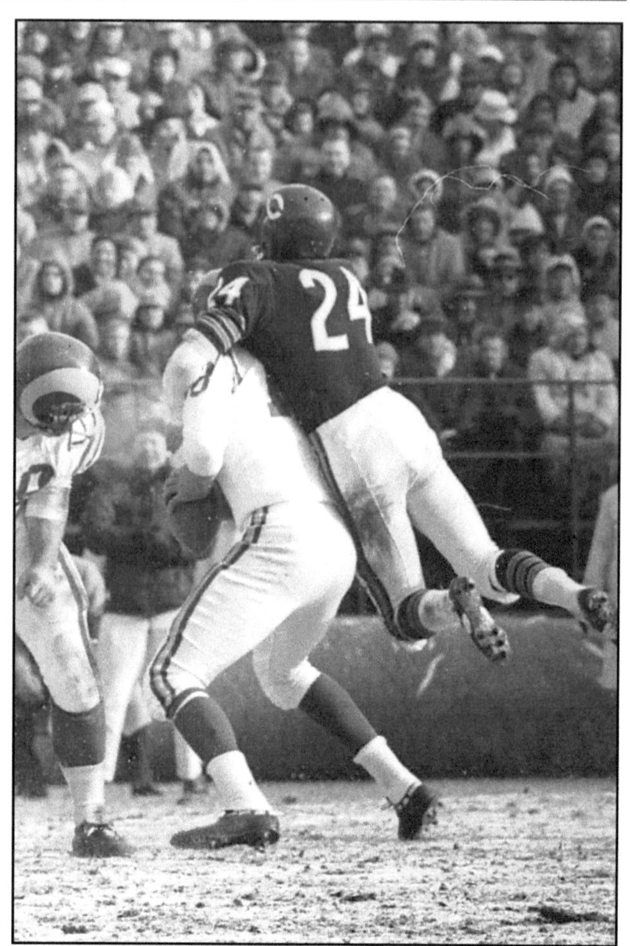
24

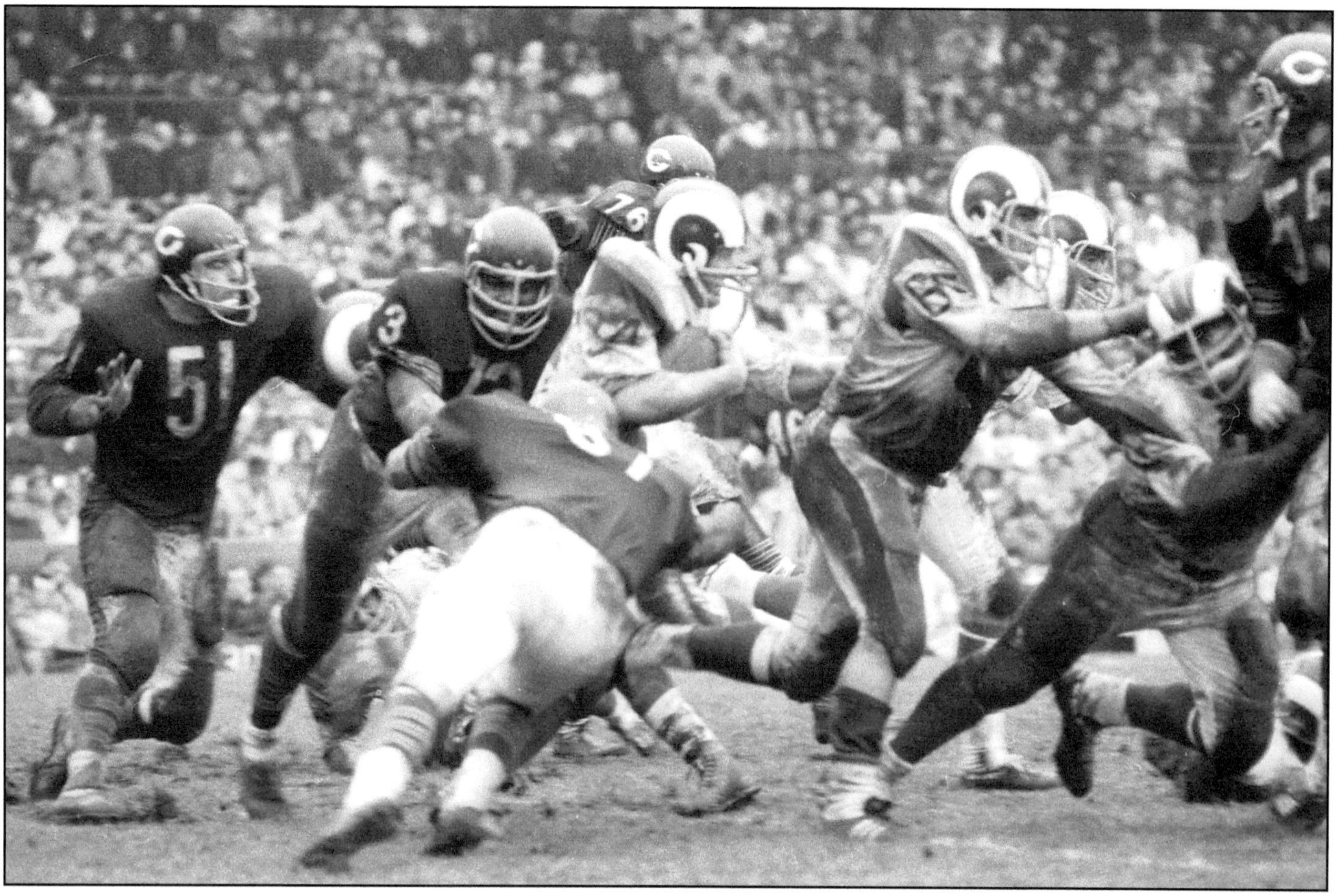

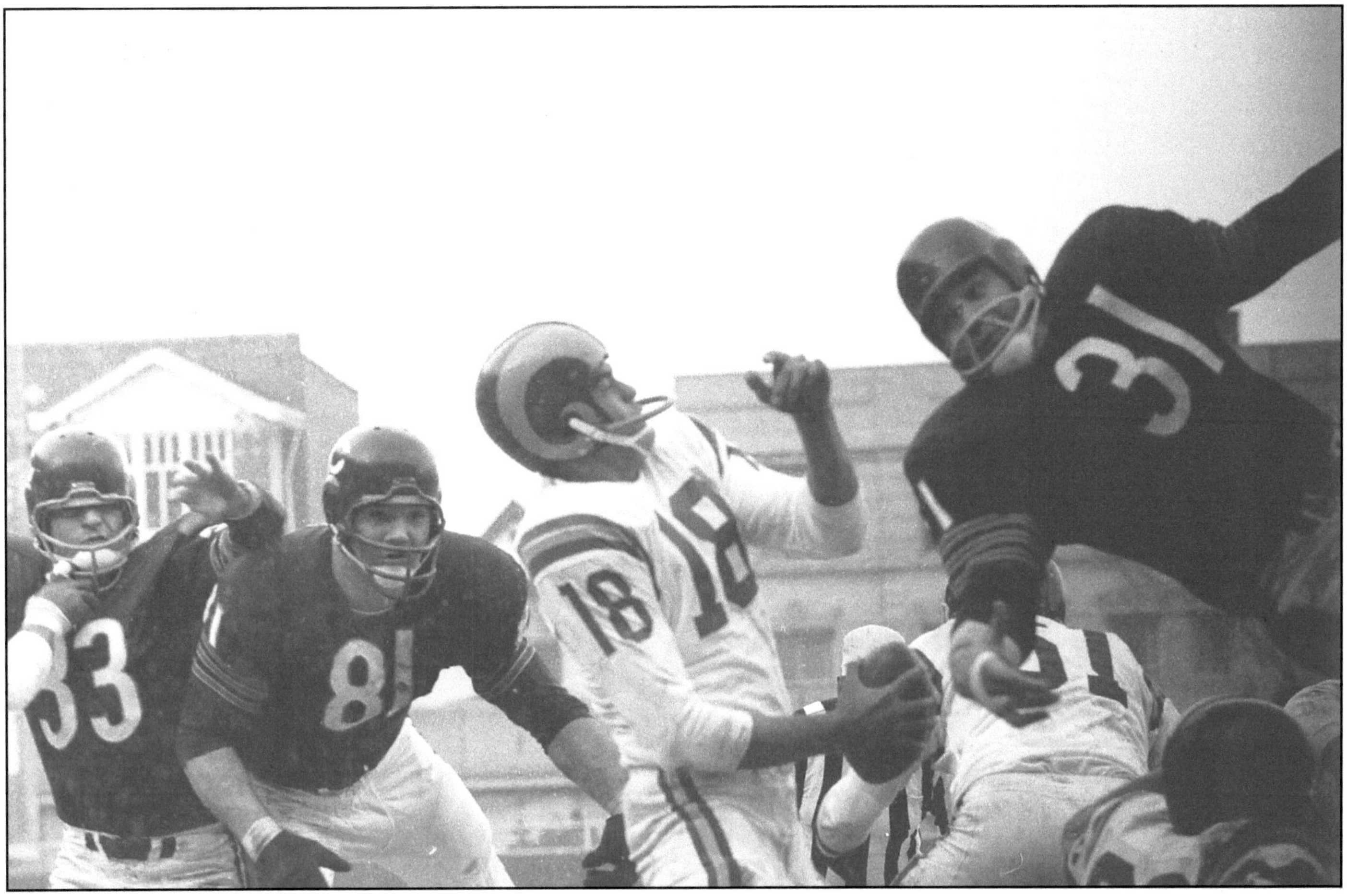

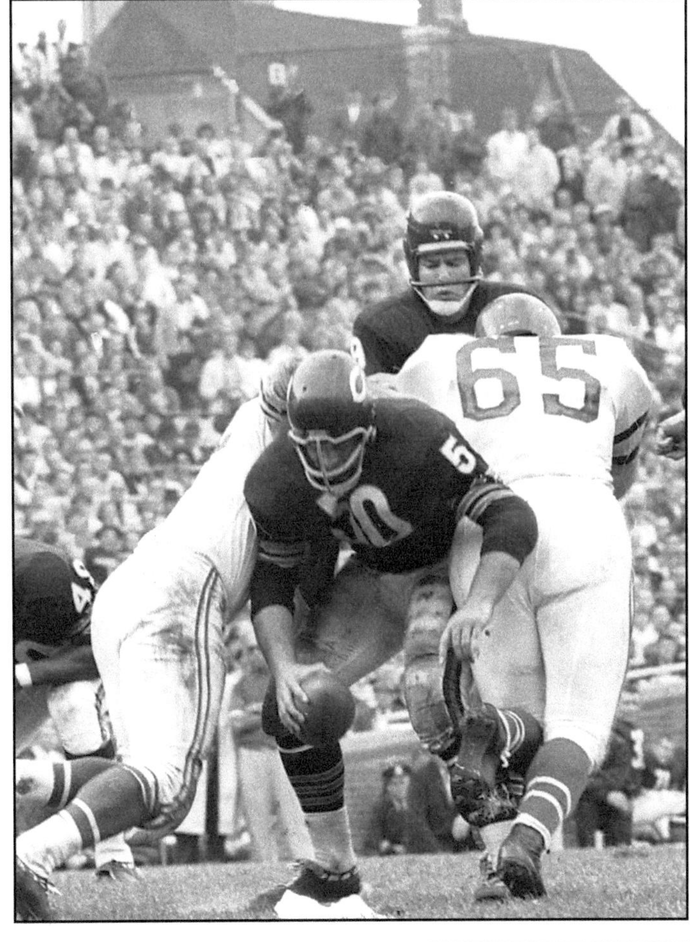

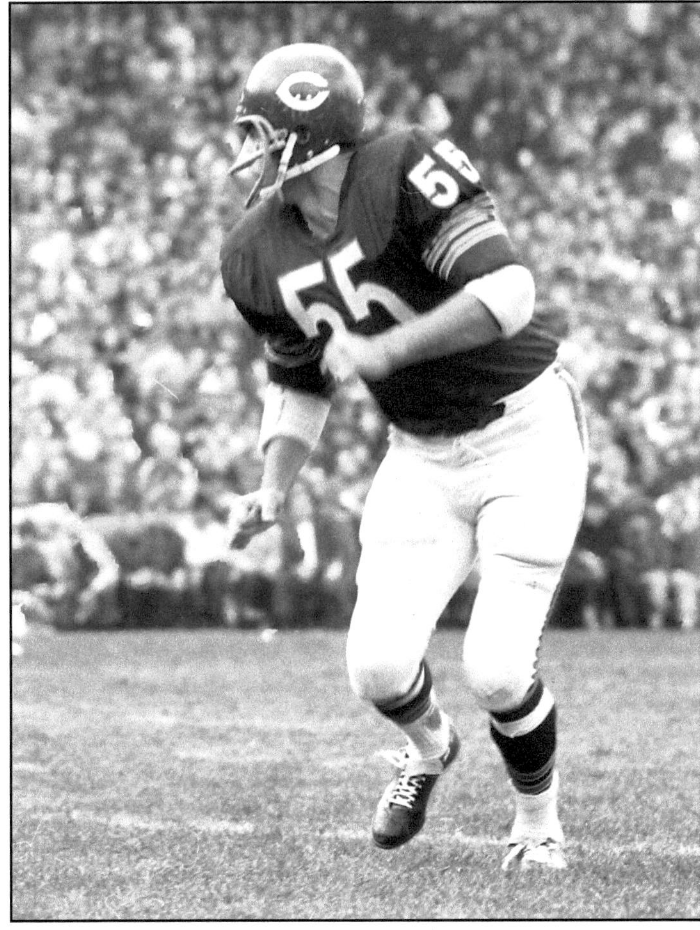

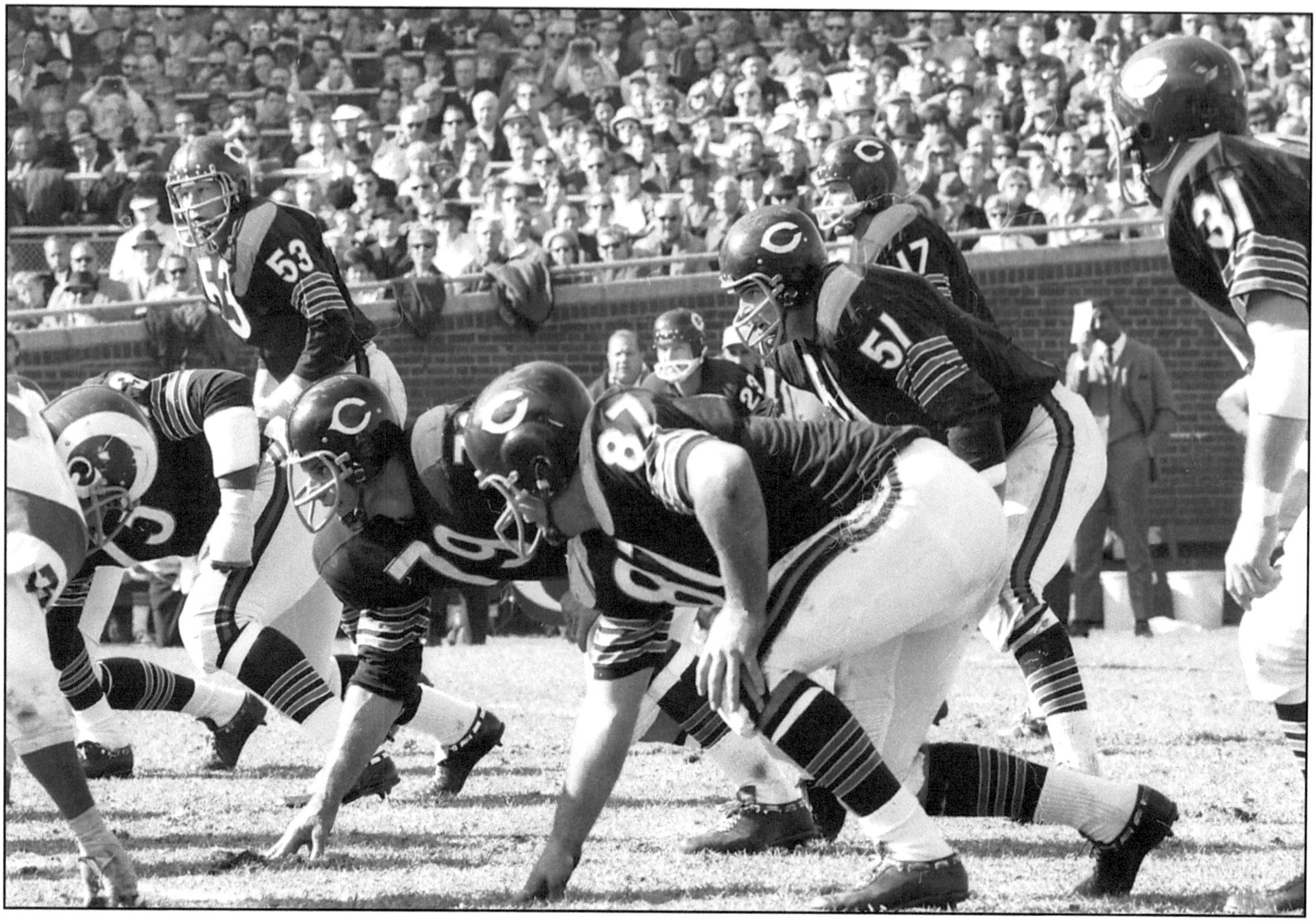

"It was always a thrill to play on a field that held so many memories of past players and coaches that played and coached in this great stadium. My last time there was in a very cold TV box with Bill Connor and Red Grange while they covered the '63 Championship game." -Maury Youmans

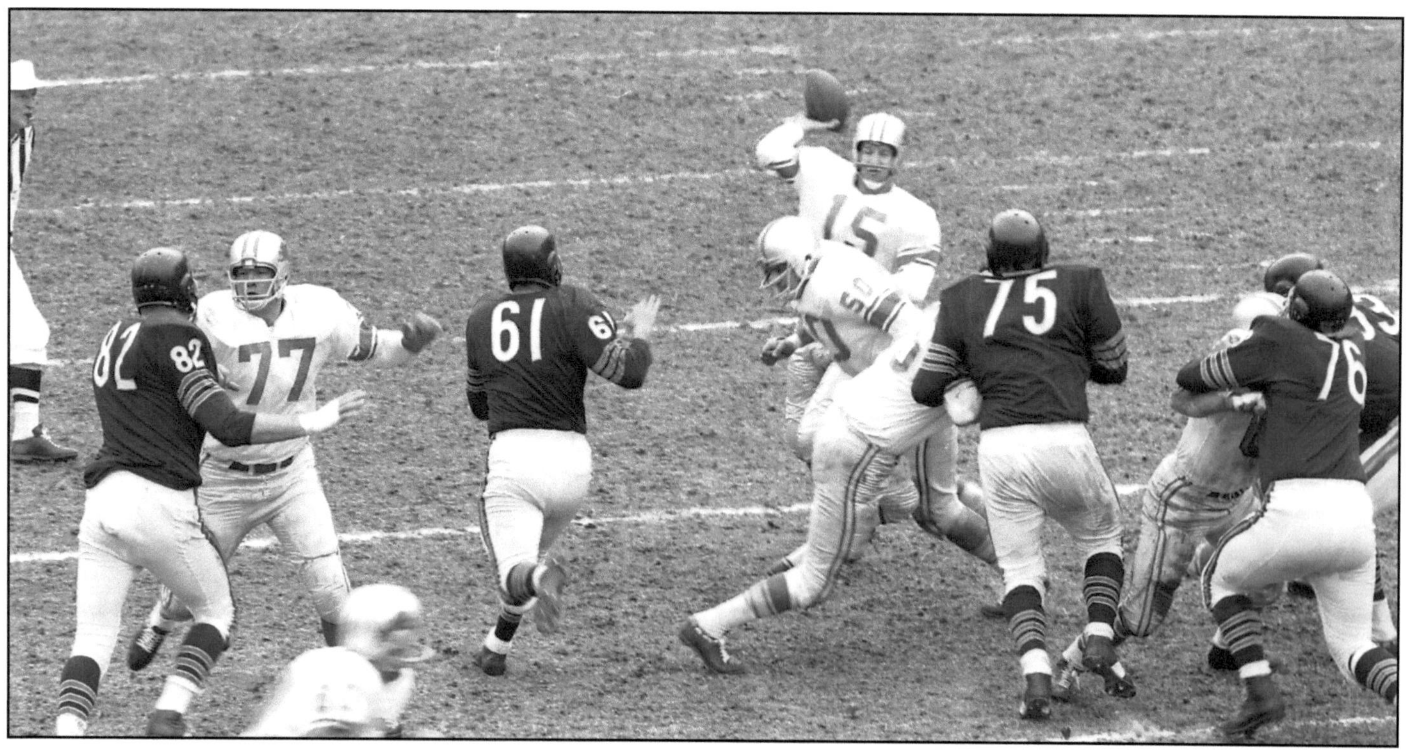

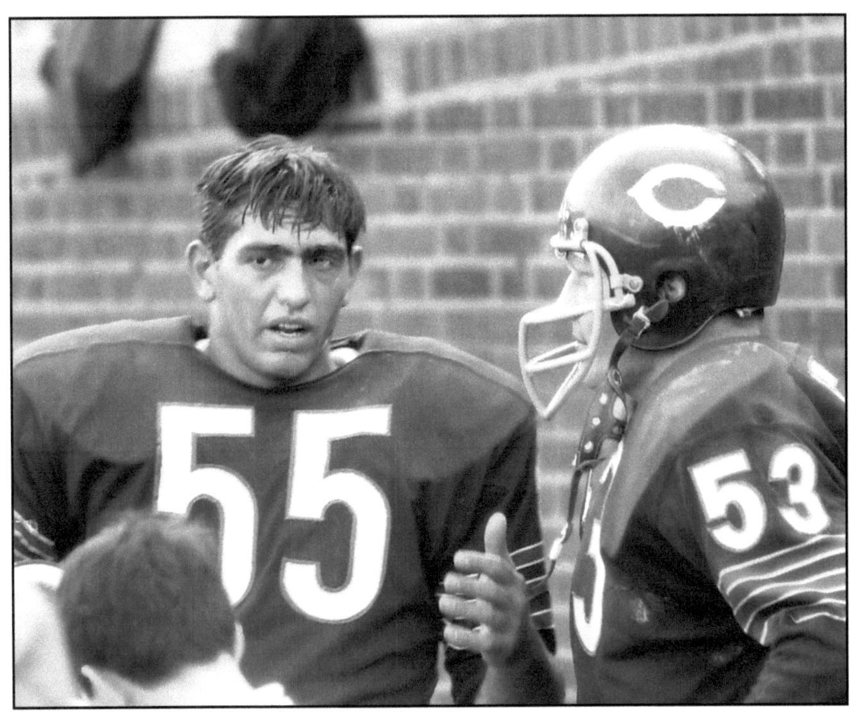

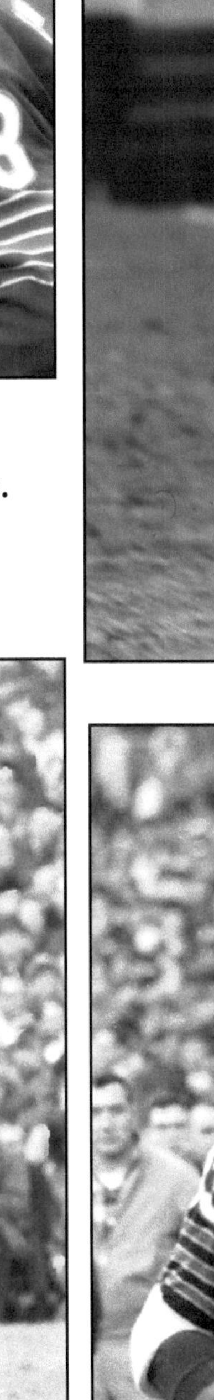

"One time after a loss to Detroit I was angry and complained to Coach Gibron I really hated losing to those guys. He responded, 'Don't feel so bad Doug, we put 9 of the Lions out of the game!' " -Doug Buffone

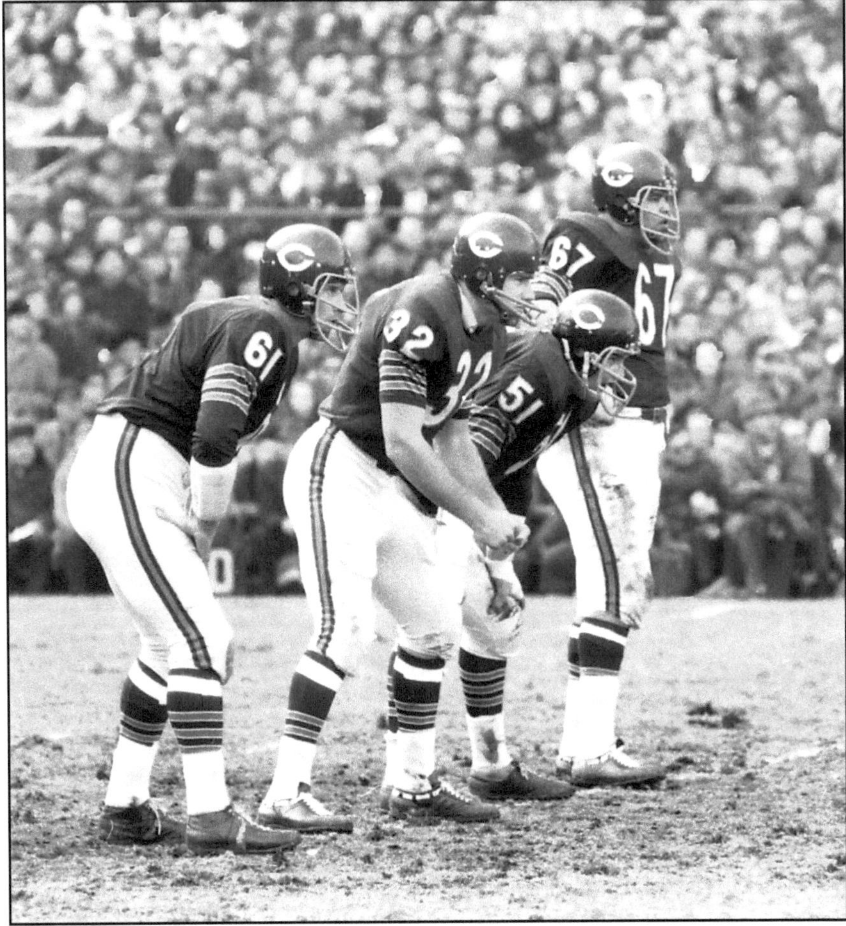

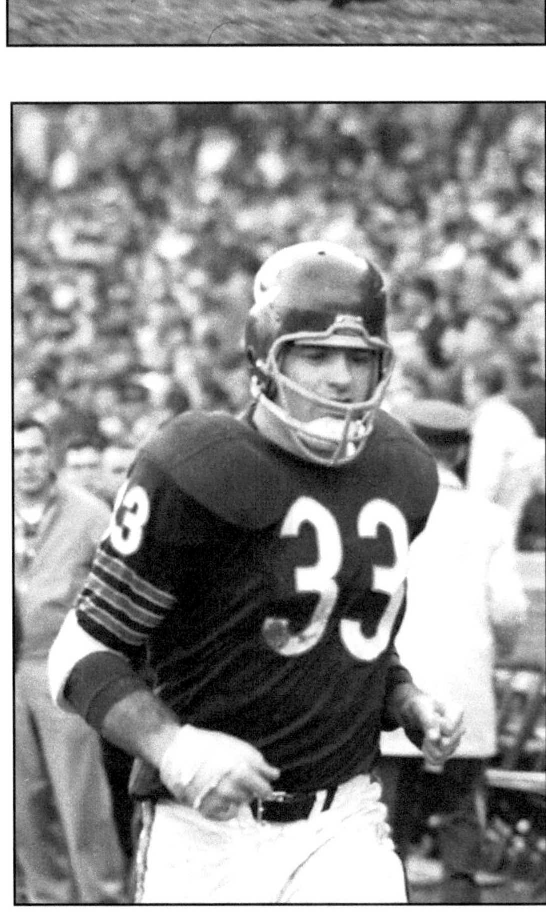

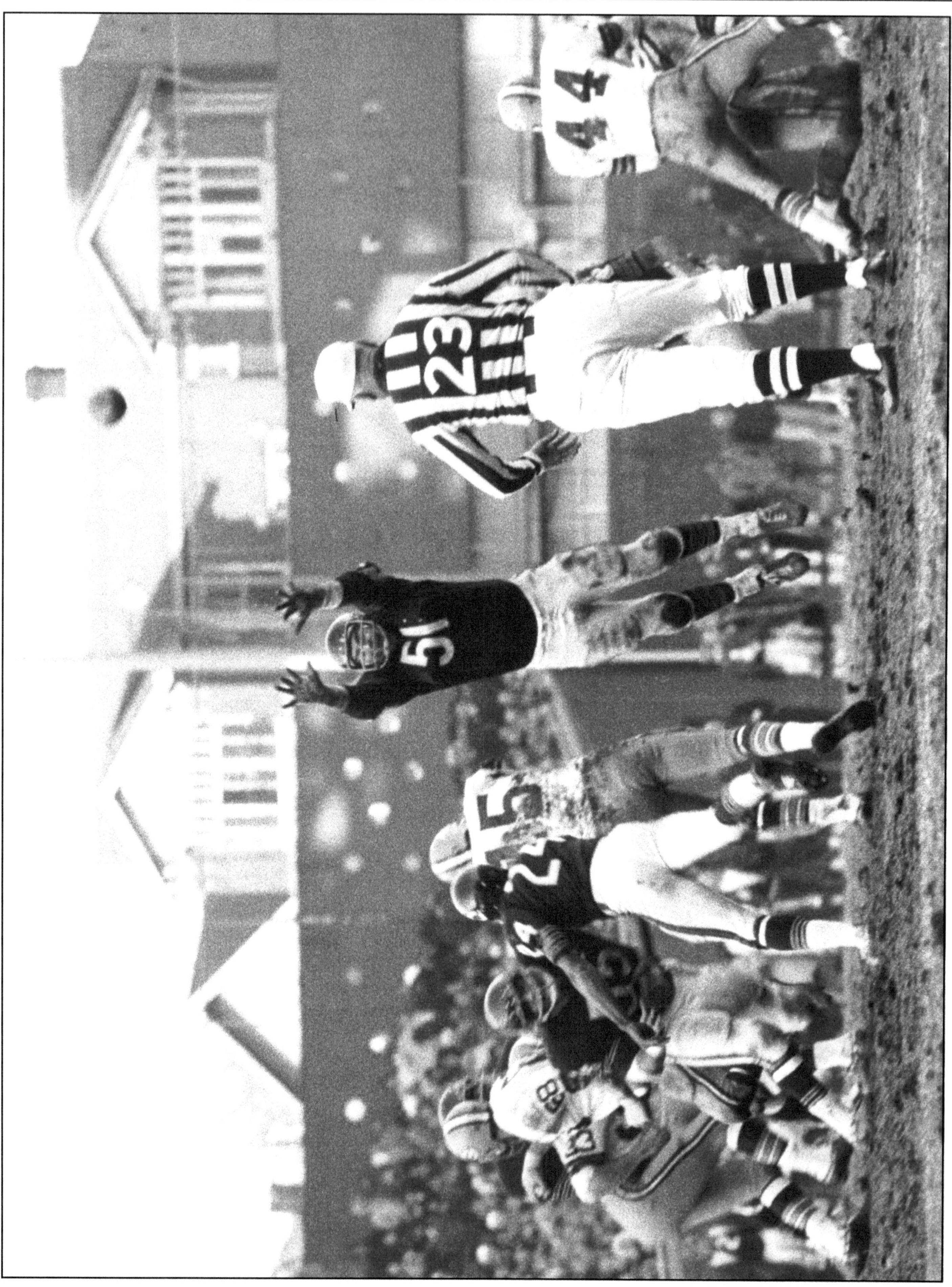

GREEN BAY PACKERS

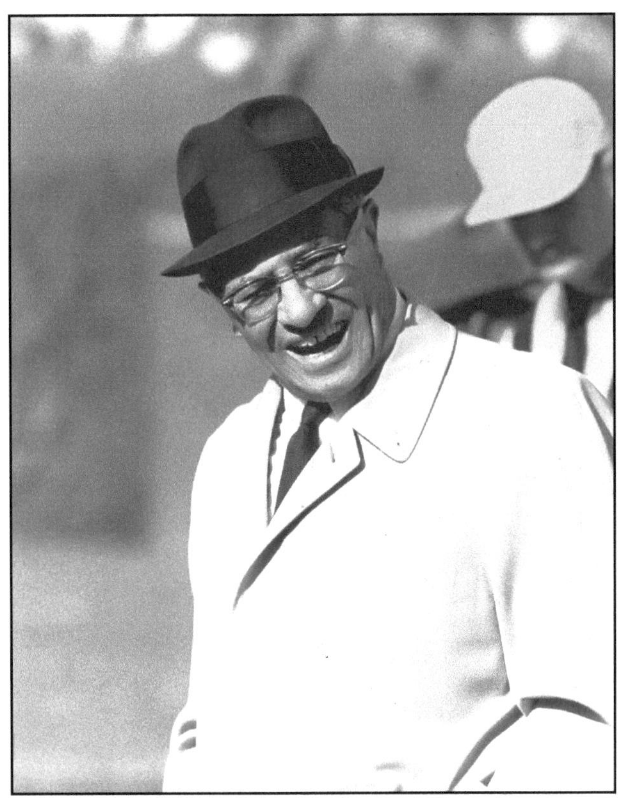

	Bears	Packers
1960	13	41
1961	28	31
1962	7	38
1963	26	7
1964	3	17
1965	31	10
1966	0	17
1967	13	7
1968	27	28
1969	3	21

During the Lombardi era, from 1959 through the completion of the 1967 season, the Packers never finished lower than second in their division. Football was a priority in this town of 100,000 where Packers green and yellow could be seen decorating storefronts and worn on the backs of its citizens 365 days a year.

It was not surprising that the teams of Chicago and Green Bay would become bitter rivals almost from the time that these franchises were formed. It wasn't just geographical proximity that cried out for bragging rights, but also a string of strong willed coaches and enthusiastic fans on both sides of the state line.

In 1960 Packers quarterback Bart Starr faced off against Eagles' Norm Van Brocklin in Philadelphia for the NFL Championship. The Eagles were victorious 17-13. Packers star Paul Hornung ran for 617 yards in the season, caught 28 passes and scored 15 touchdowns for a record setting 176 points.

The Packers continued to roll in 1961 after adding Herb Adderley, Elijah Pitts and Ron Kostelnik to the roster. The team won the Western Division title then went on to win the Championship game over the Giants by a score of 37-0. It was the team's seventh title.

Although Hornung went down with an injury early in 1962, the Packers continued to dominate the league with another NFL championship win over the Giants. Taylor scored a record 19 season touchdowns, Wood led in interceptions and Starr led the league in passing.

1963 was a year that Packer backers would rather forget. Hornung was suspended by the NFL for gambling, Starr broke his hand and the Packers lost two games to the Bears. The Packers finished half a game behind the Bears in the division race and had to settle for a 40-23 victory over Cleveland in the Playoff Bowl.

By 1964 the Packers had to settle for a record of 8-5-1 record. The team lost to St. Louis Playoff Bowl by a score of 24-17. In 1965 the team struggled both with a series of injuries to starters and with the loss of the team's founder Curly Lambeau. The Packer's field was renamed in Lambeau's honor. Bart Starr was injured but the Packers still beat the Brows in Lambeau Field on January 2.

The Packers signed Jim Grabowski in 1966 . The team won the NFL title over Dallas by a score of 34-27. The first Super Bowl was played in Los Angeles Memorial Coliseum where the Packers beat Kansas City 35-10. Starr was the game's MVP.

The Packers went up against Dallas in the NFL Championship in 1967. The weather was a recorded -13 with a wind chill of -37. The Packers were victorious on Starr's one-yard quarterback sneak. The drama was even higher in Green Bay when Vince Lombardi resigned in 1968 and named his assistant as his successor. Green Bay finished at 6-7-1. By 1969, the Packers still struggled with the loss of their coach and repeated injuries to players . The year wound down with a record of 8-6.

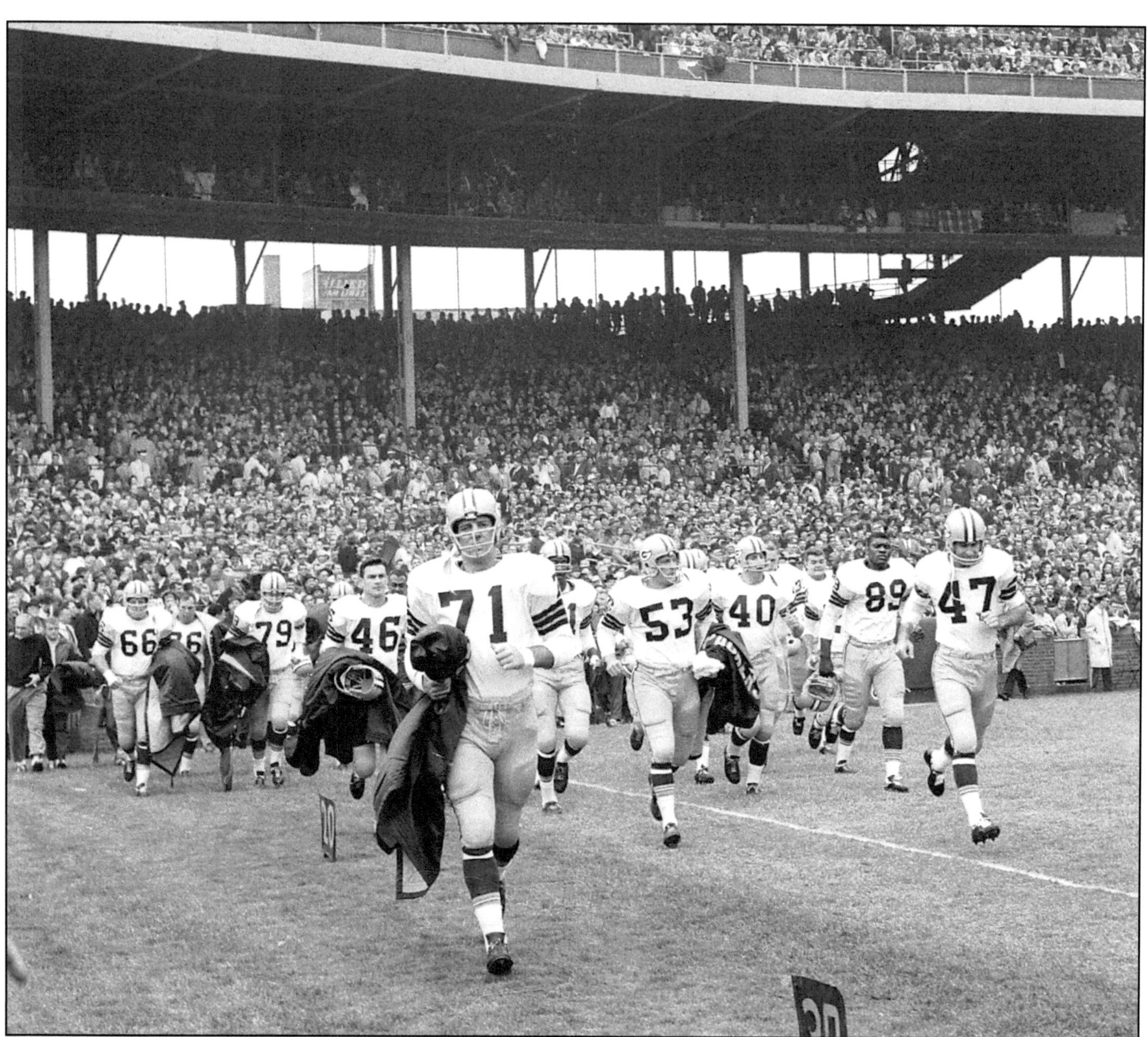

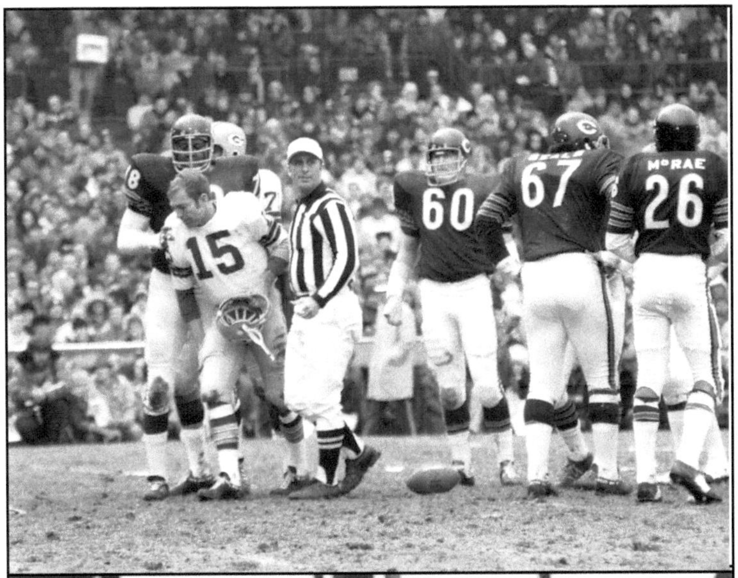

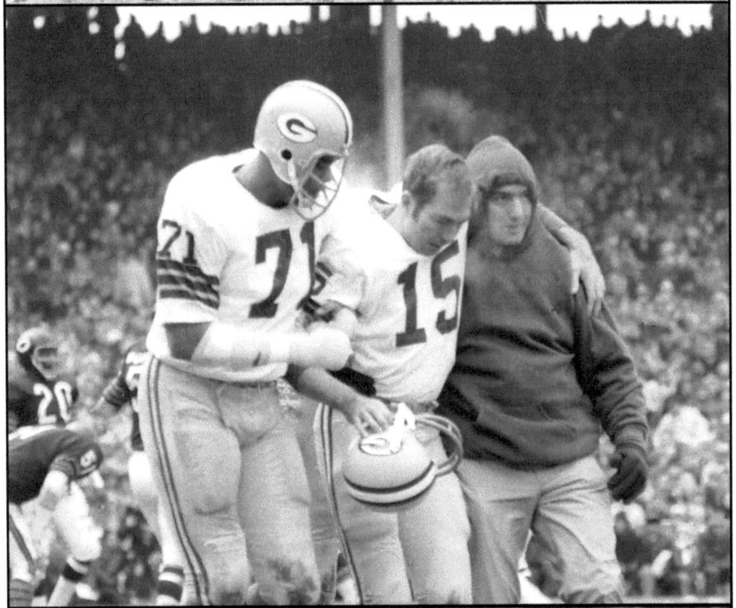

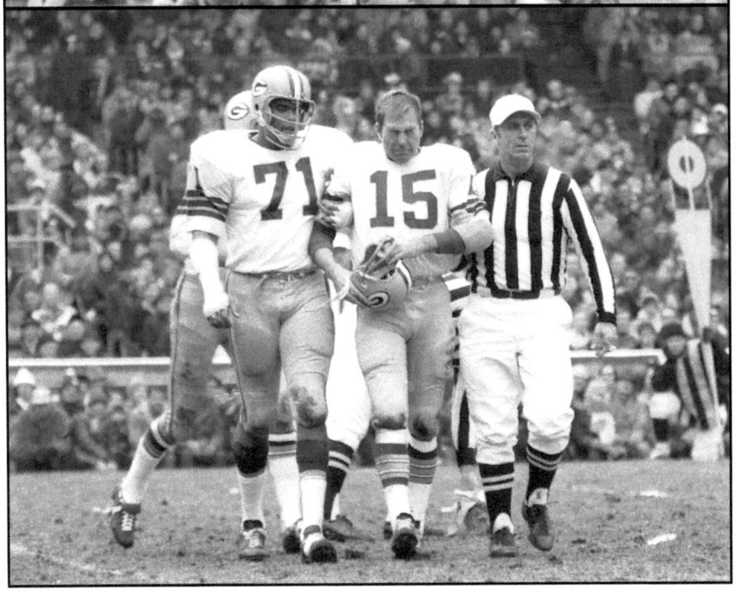

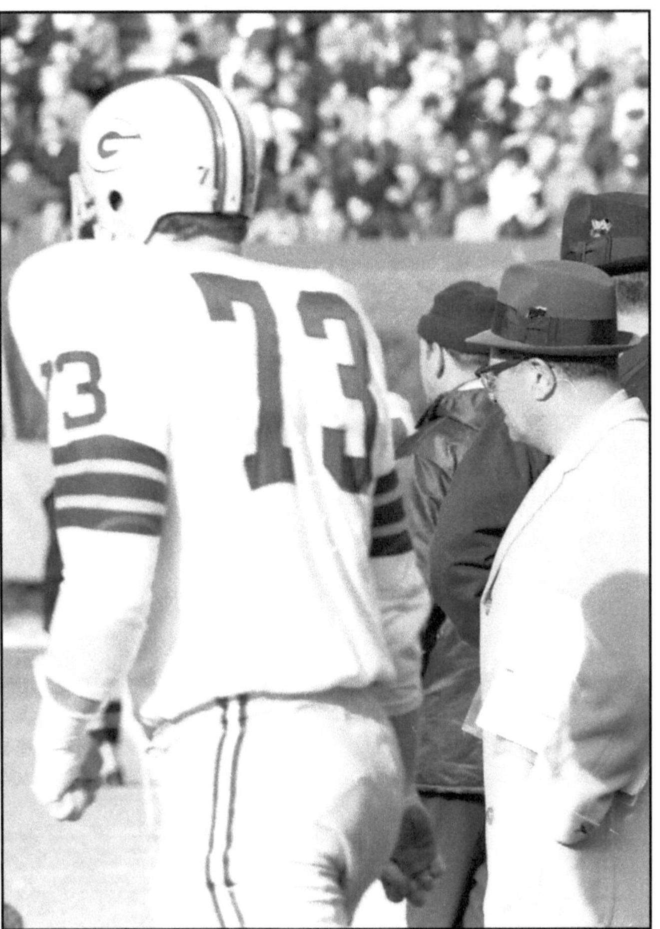

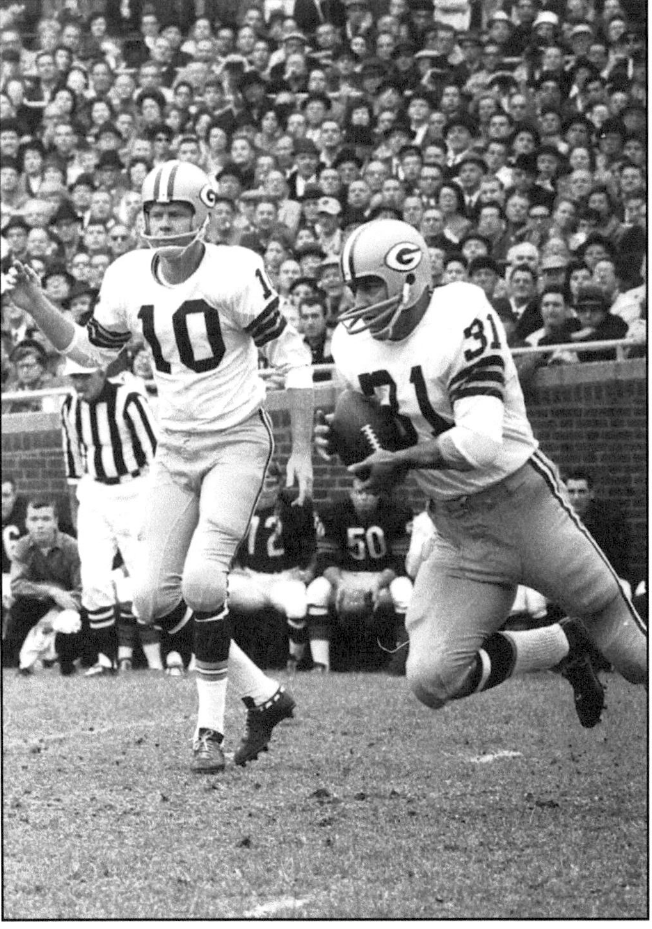

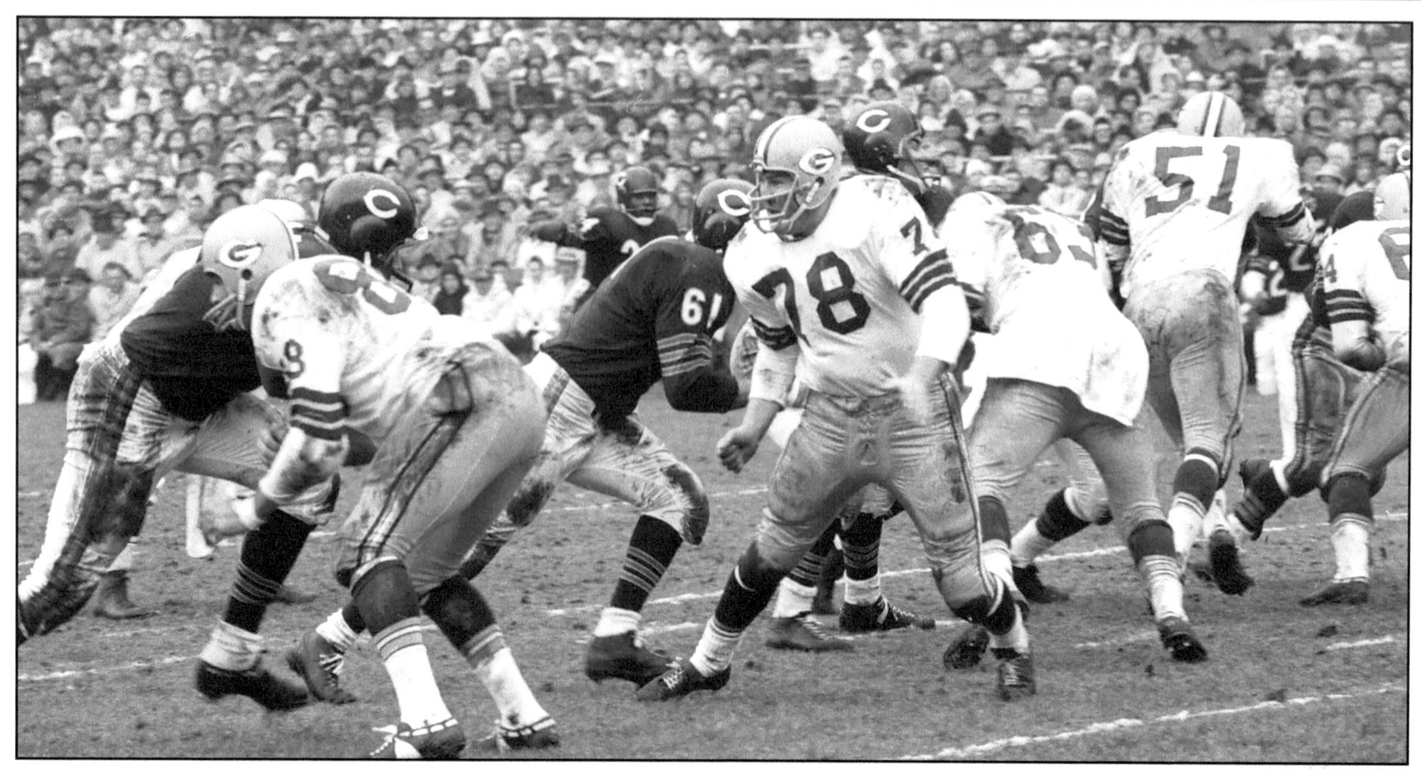
51
78
61

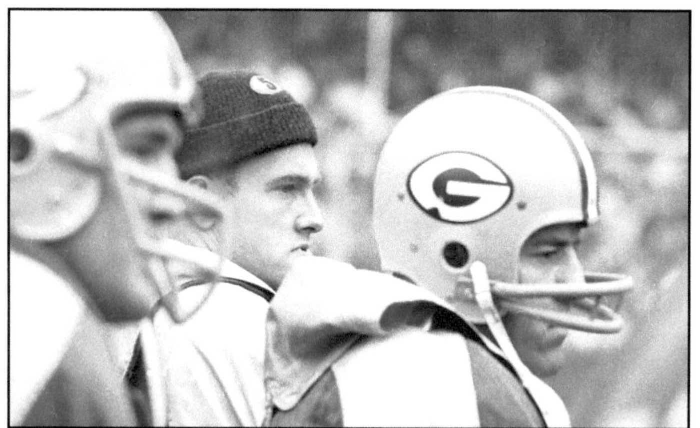

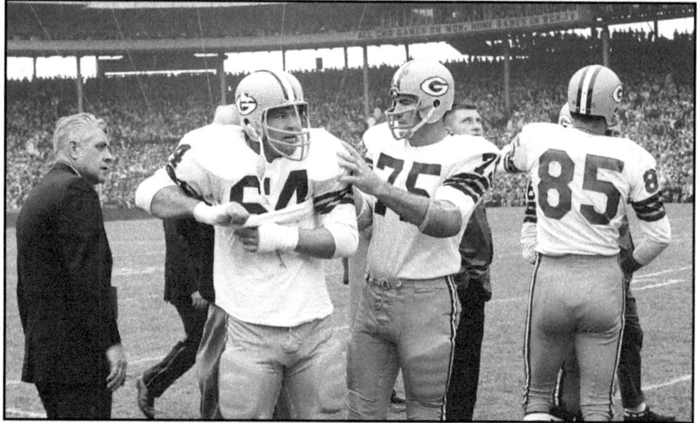
75
85

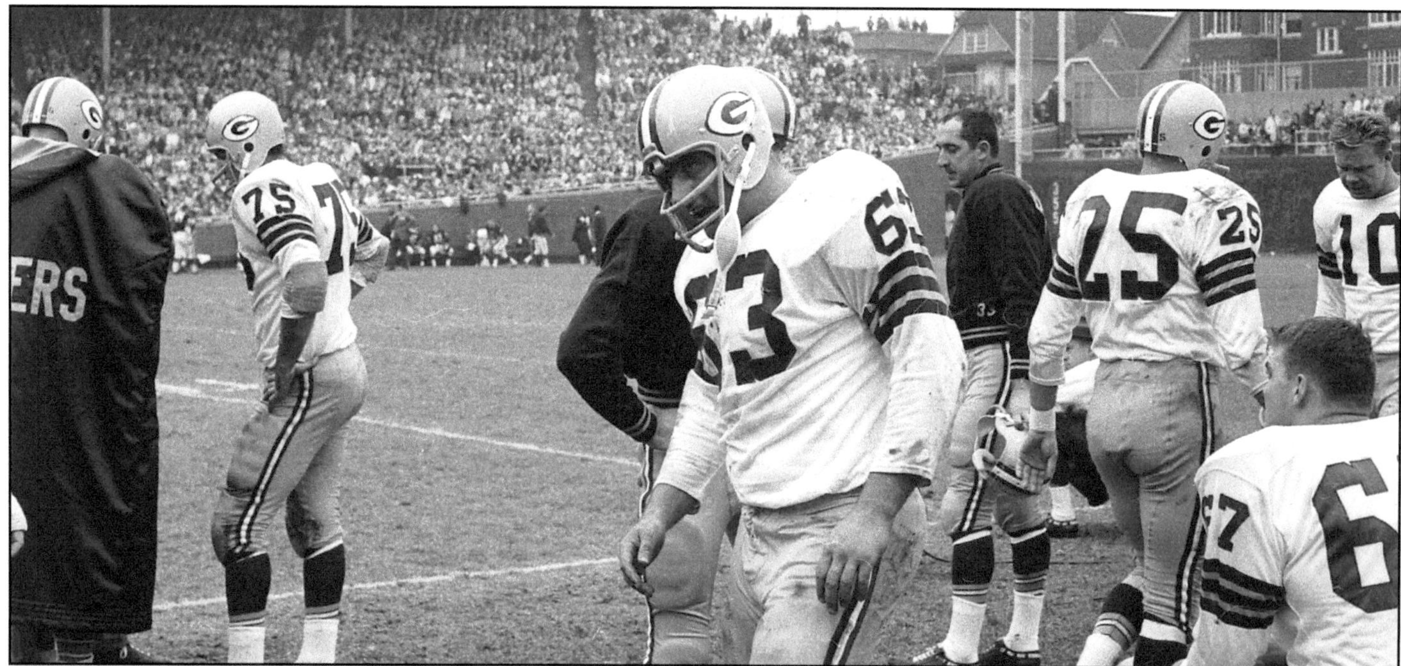
ERS
75
63
25
10

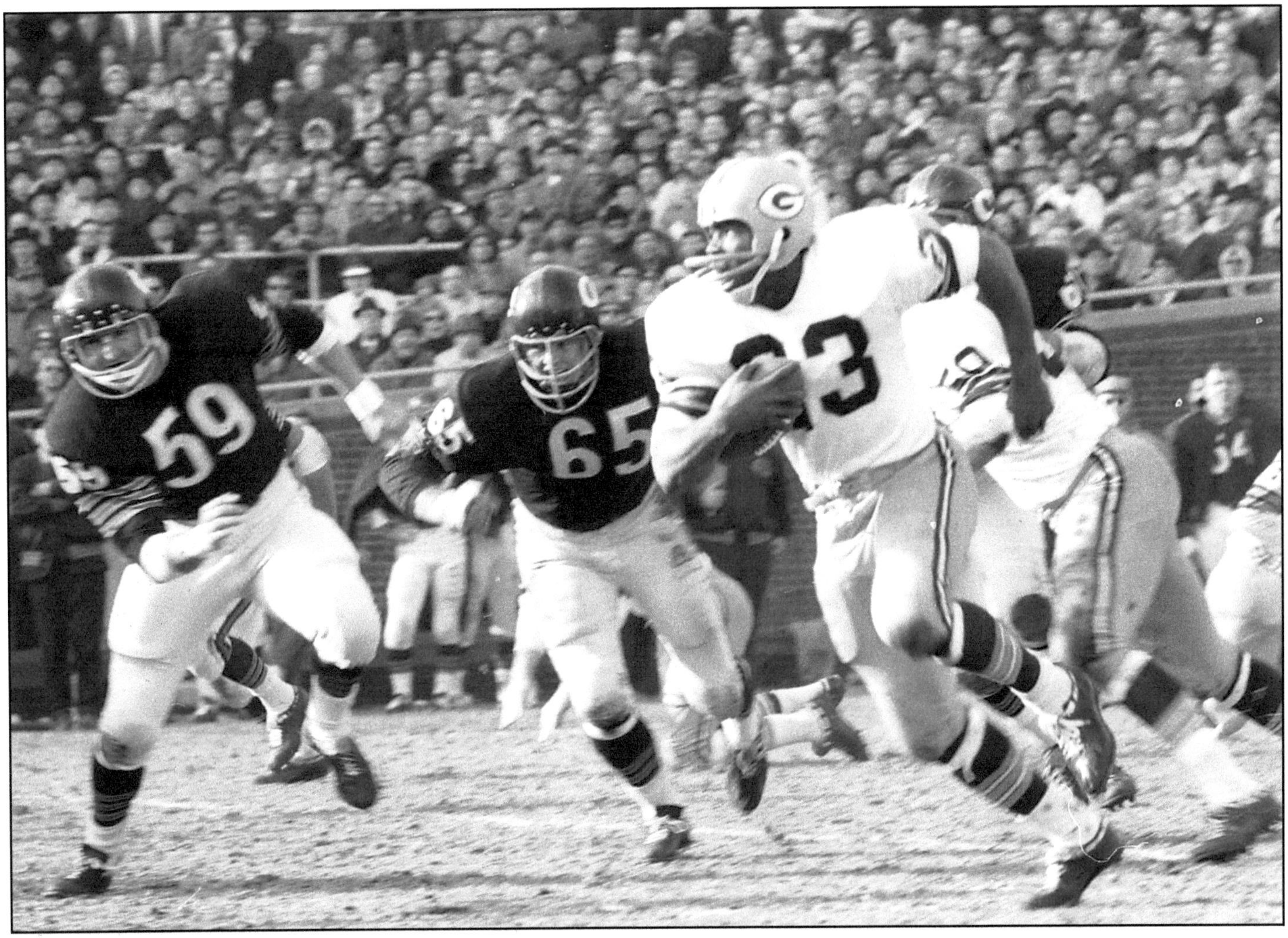

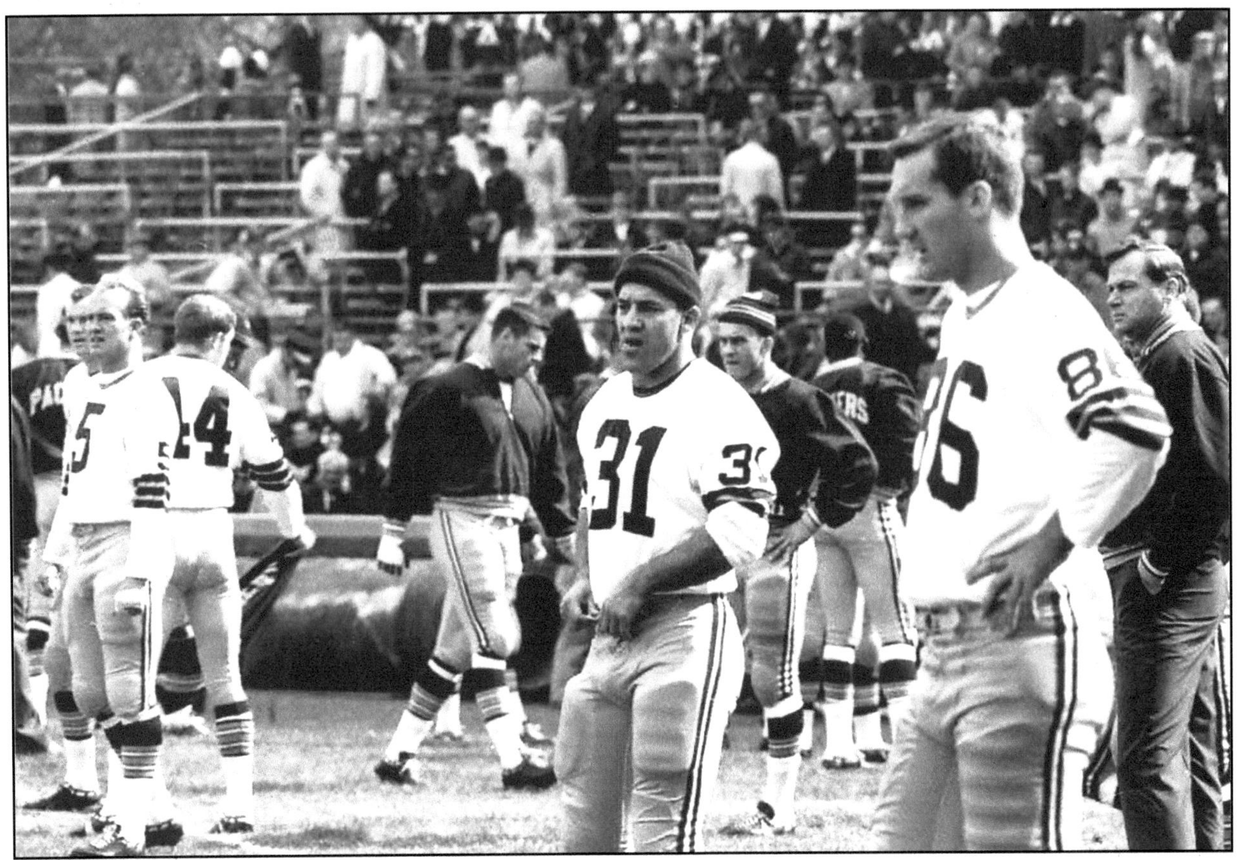

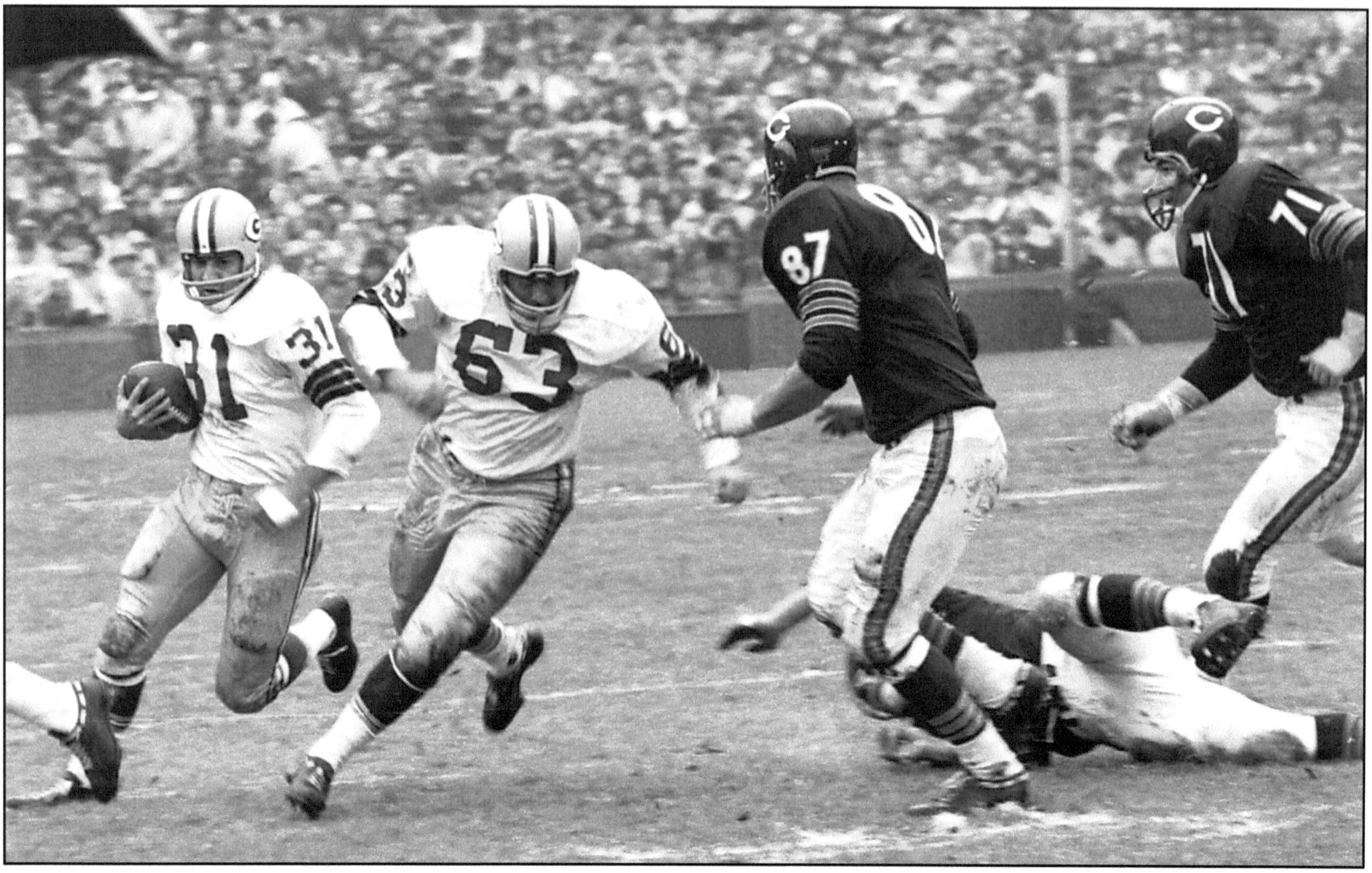

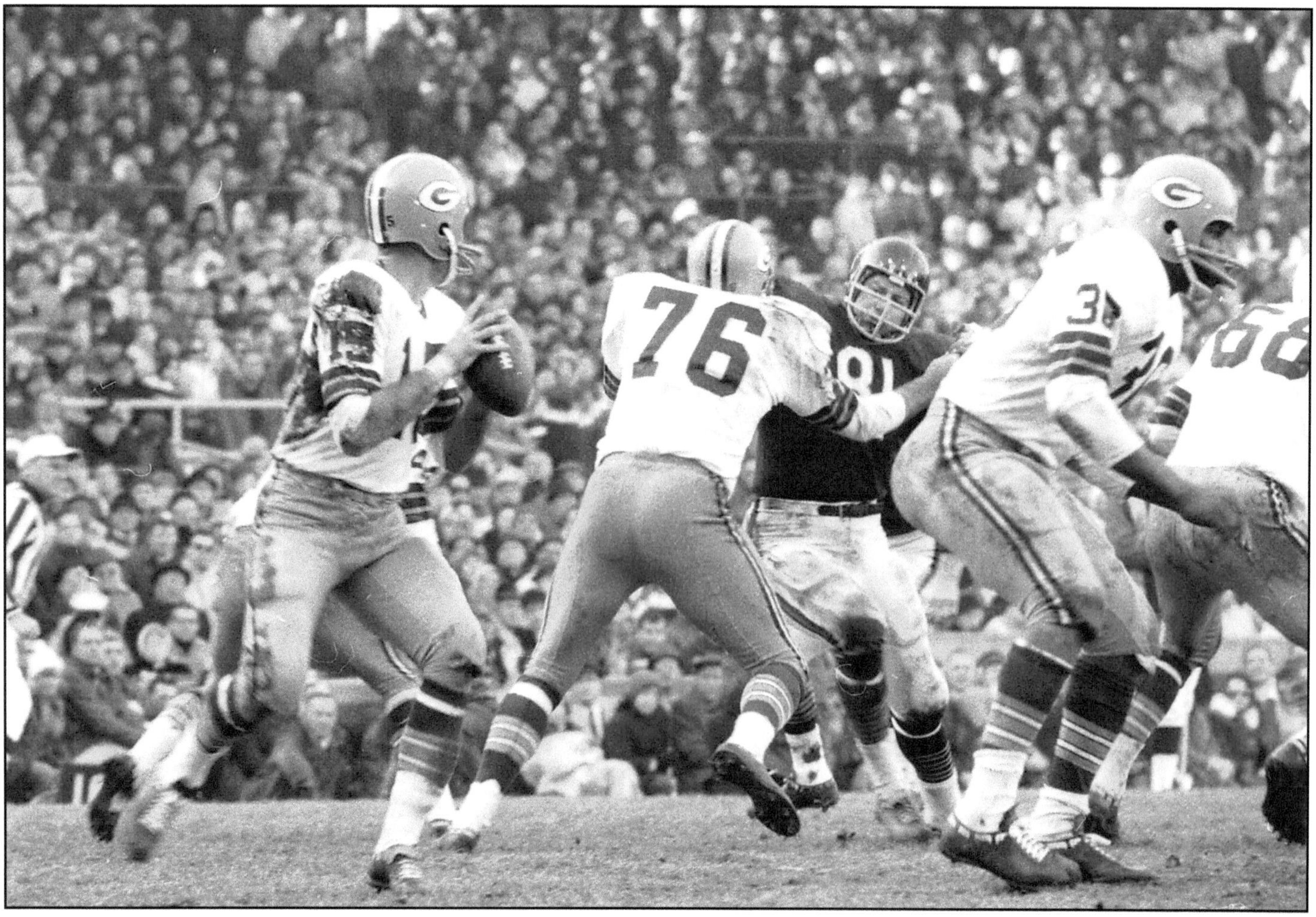

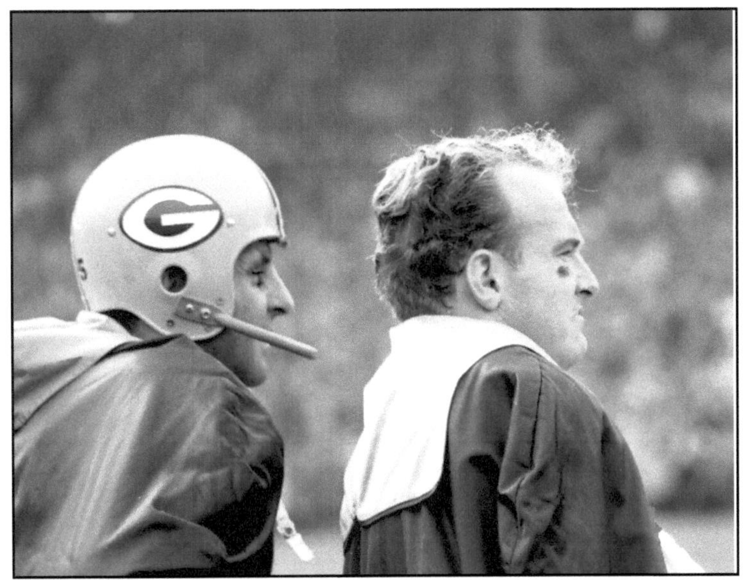

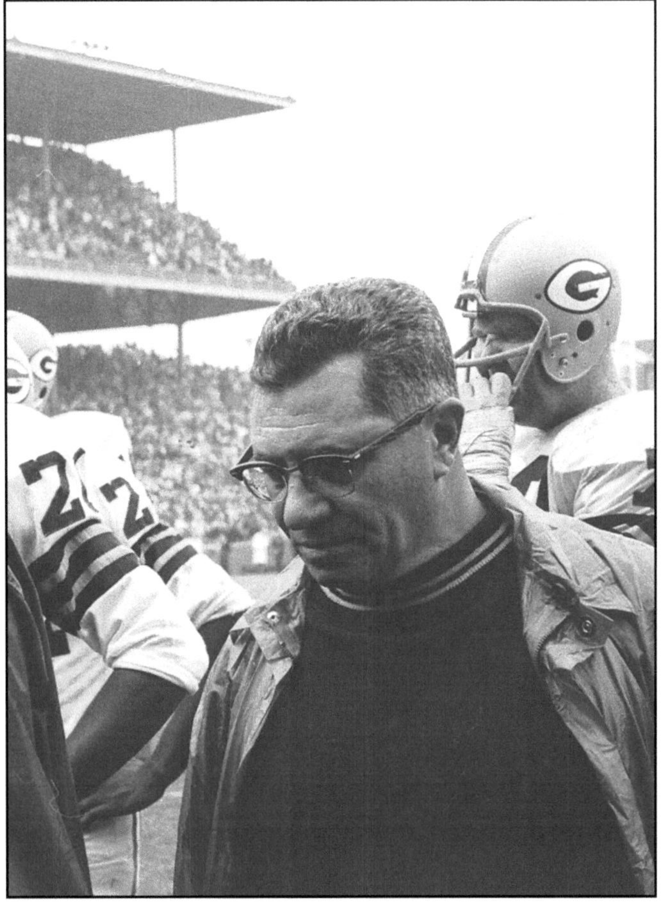

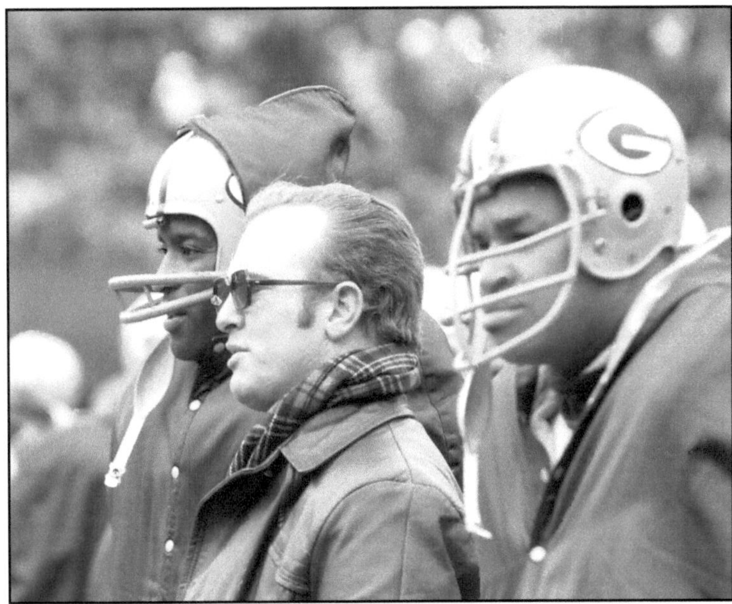

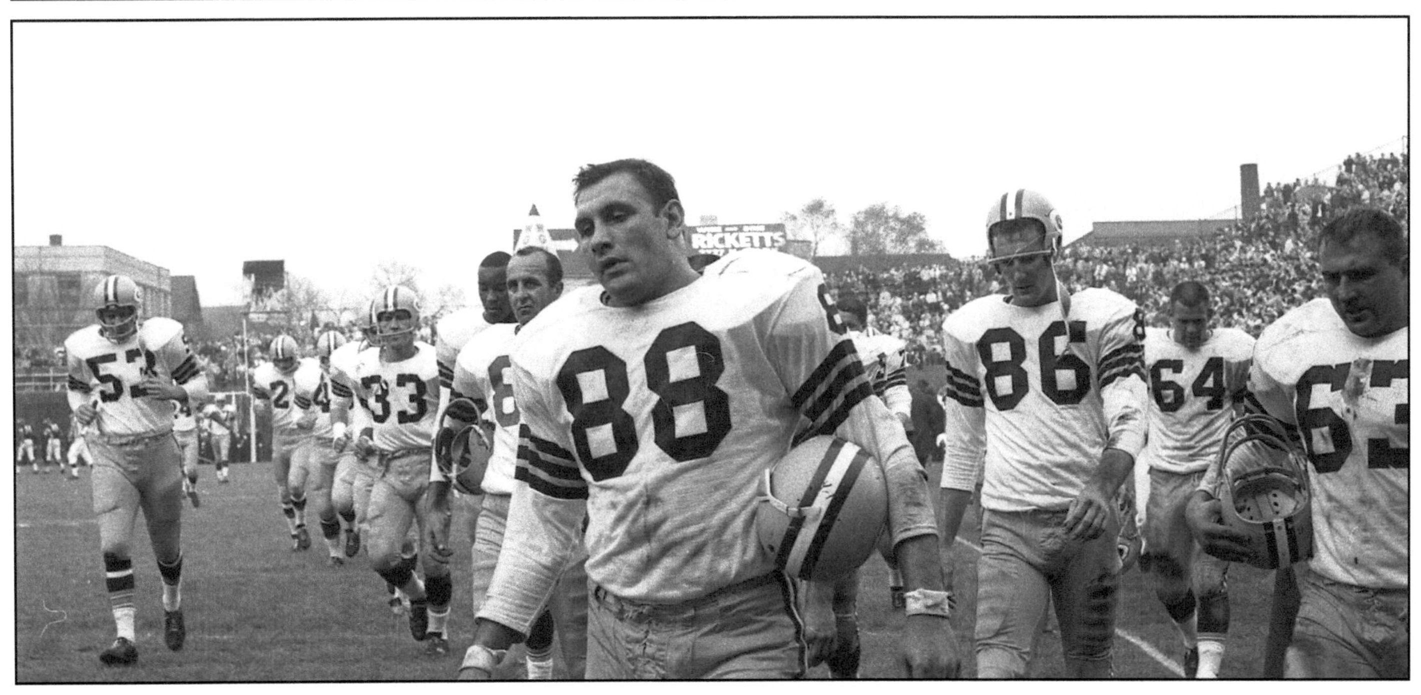
RICKETTS
33
88
86
64

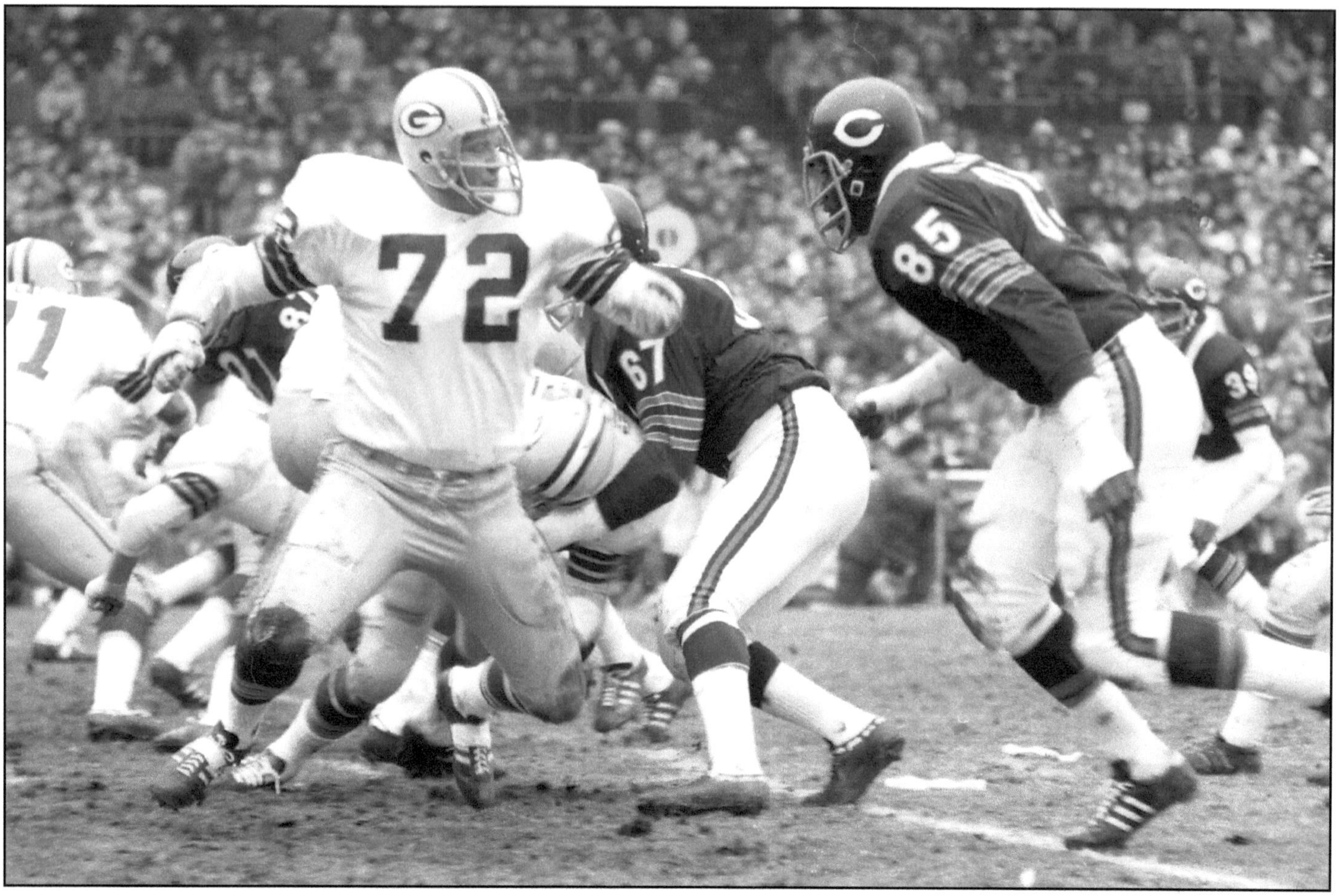

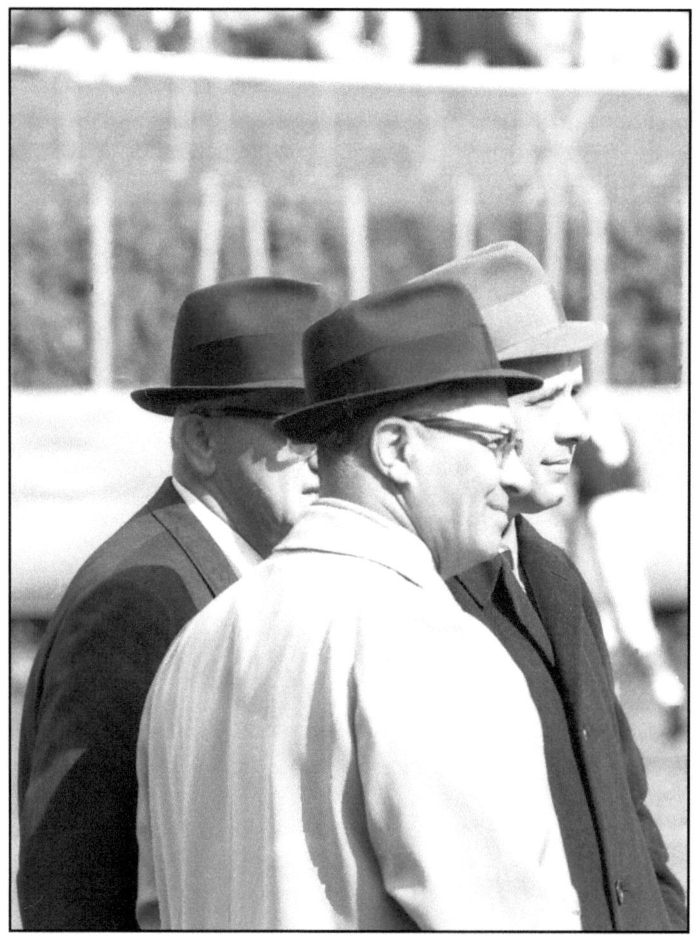

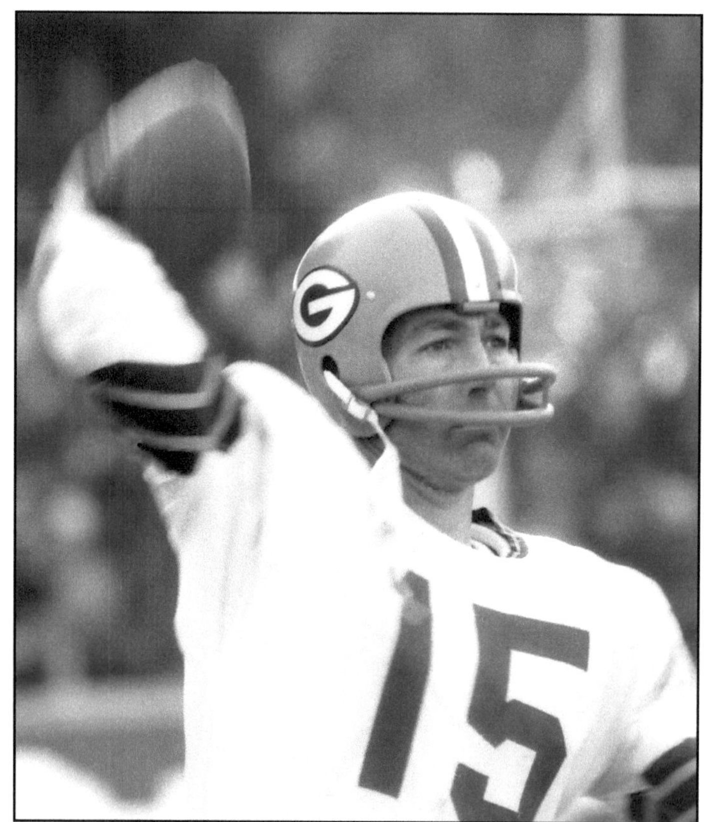

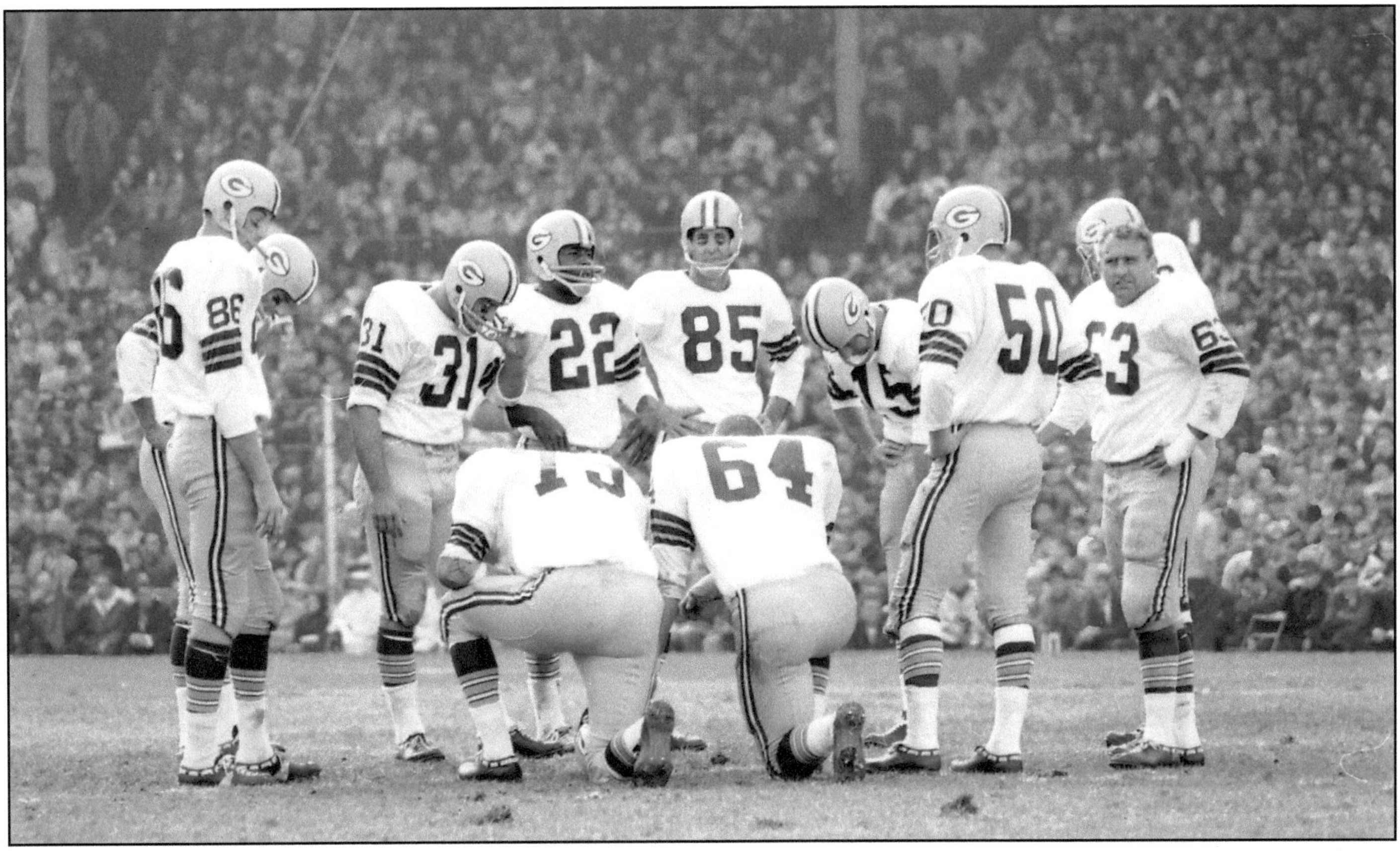

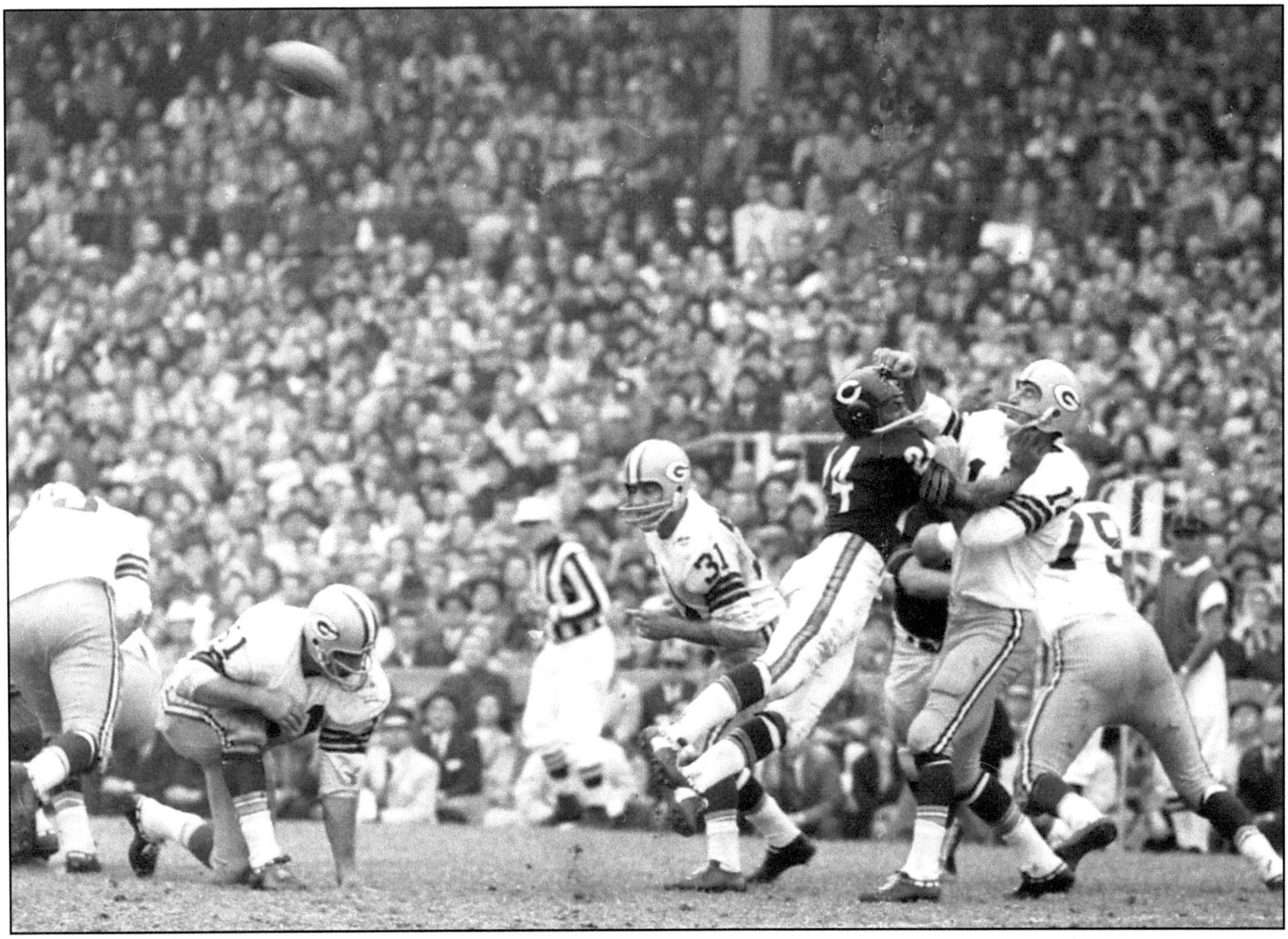

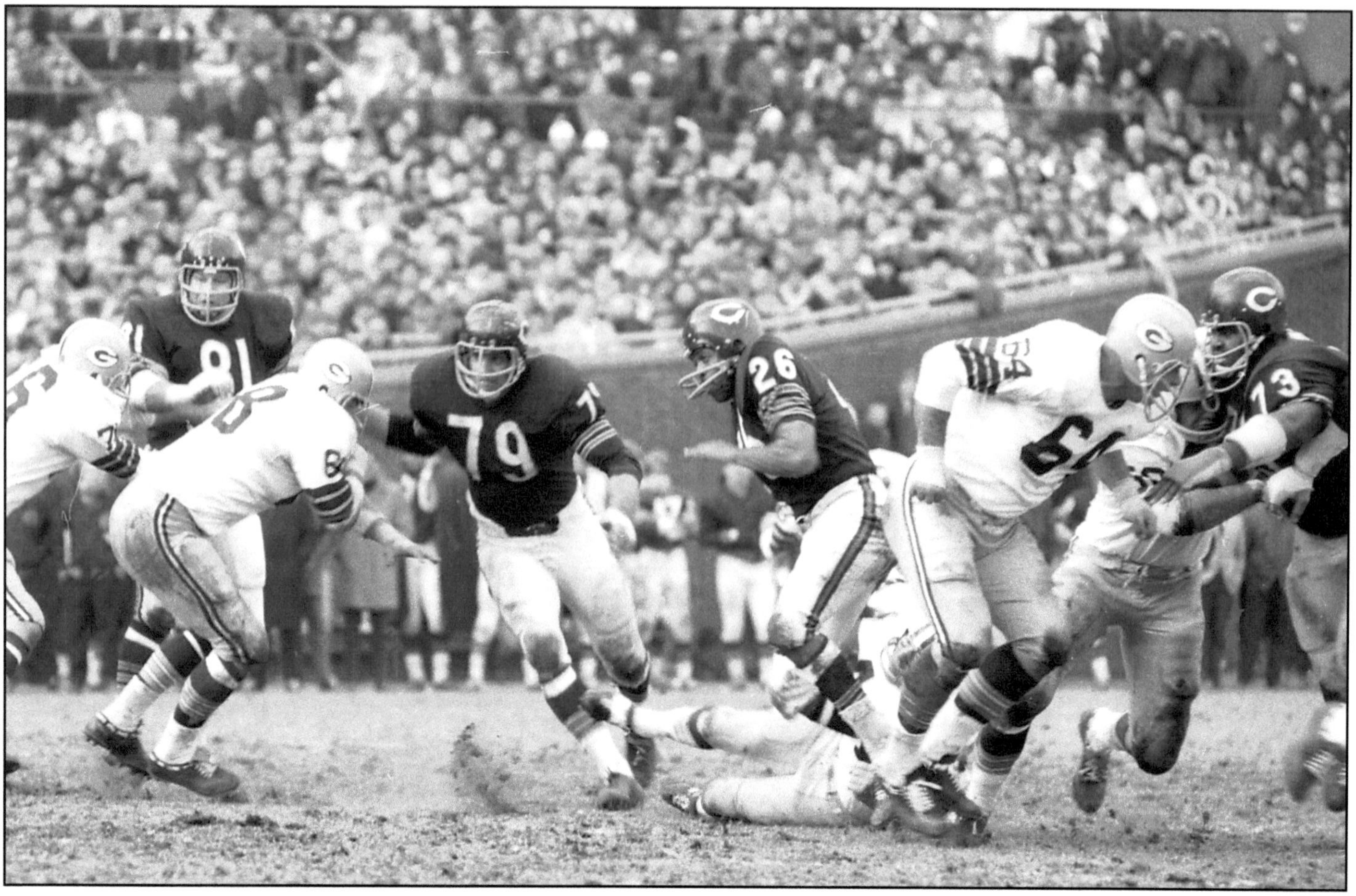

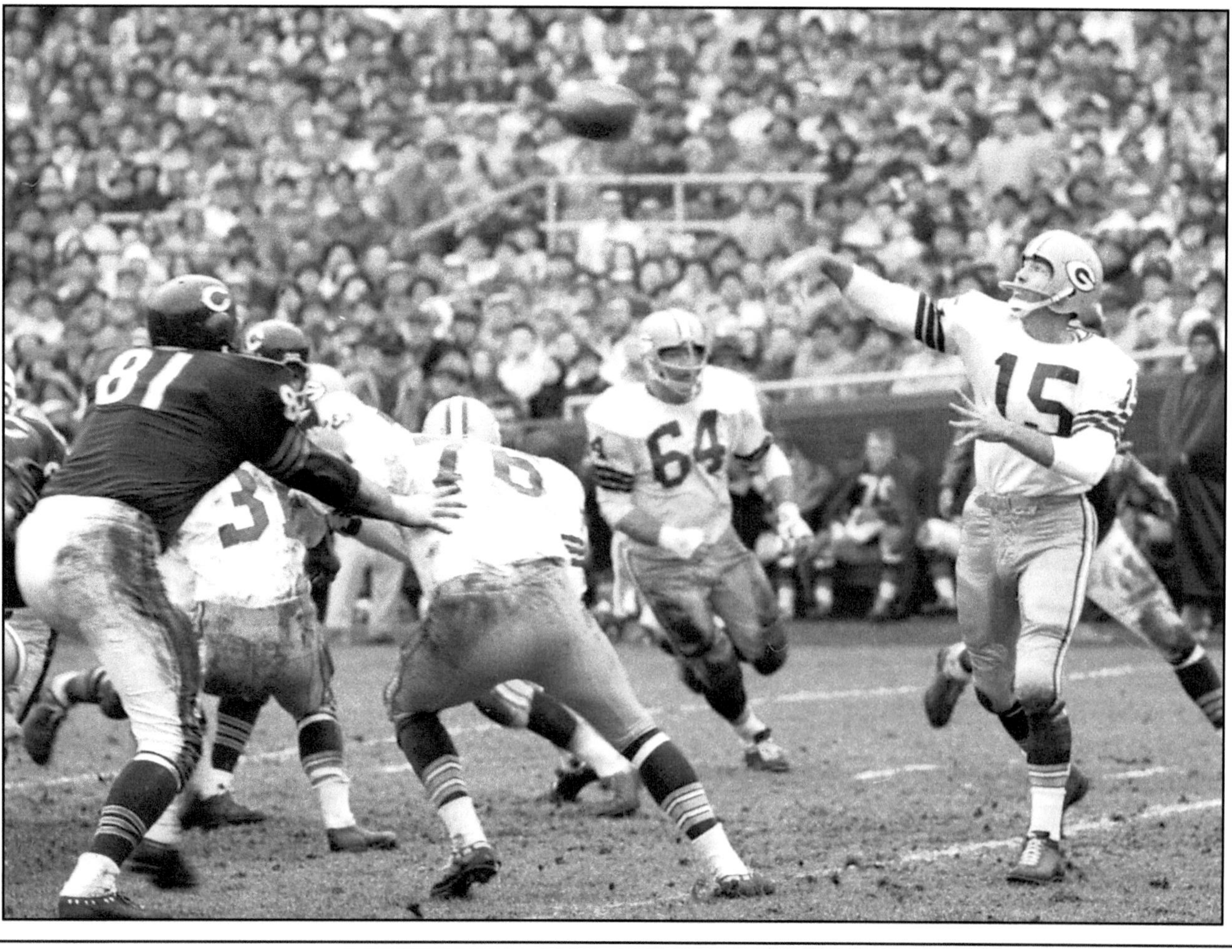

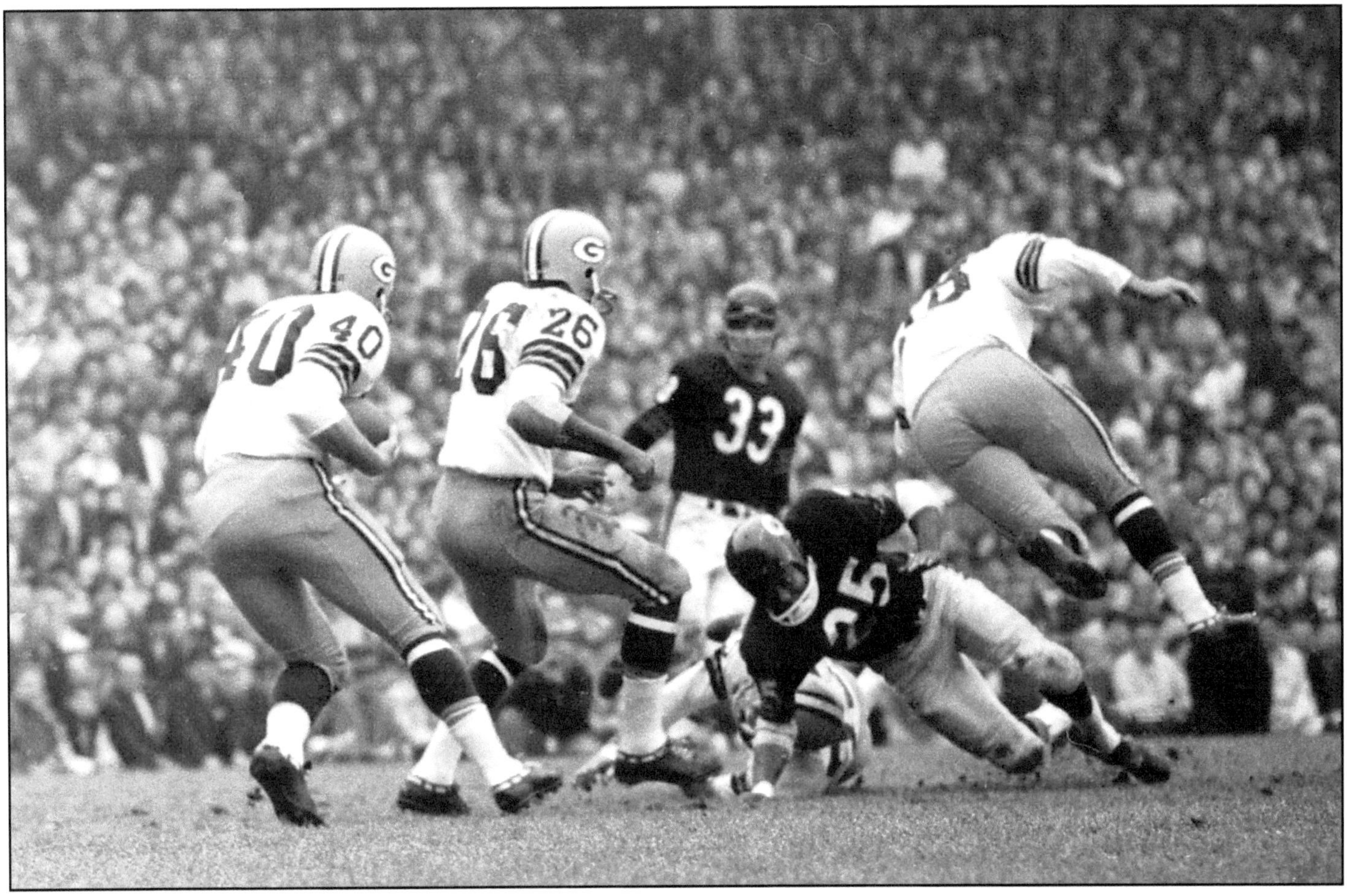

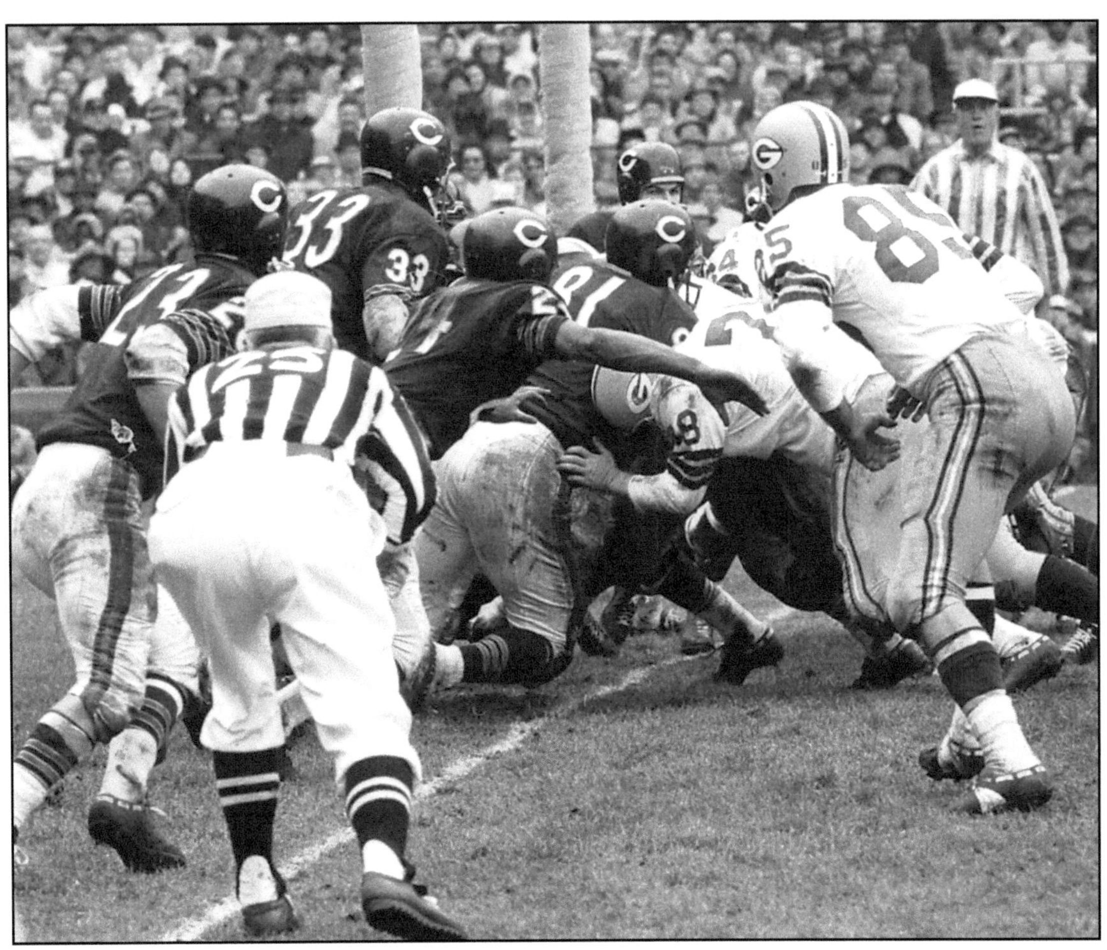

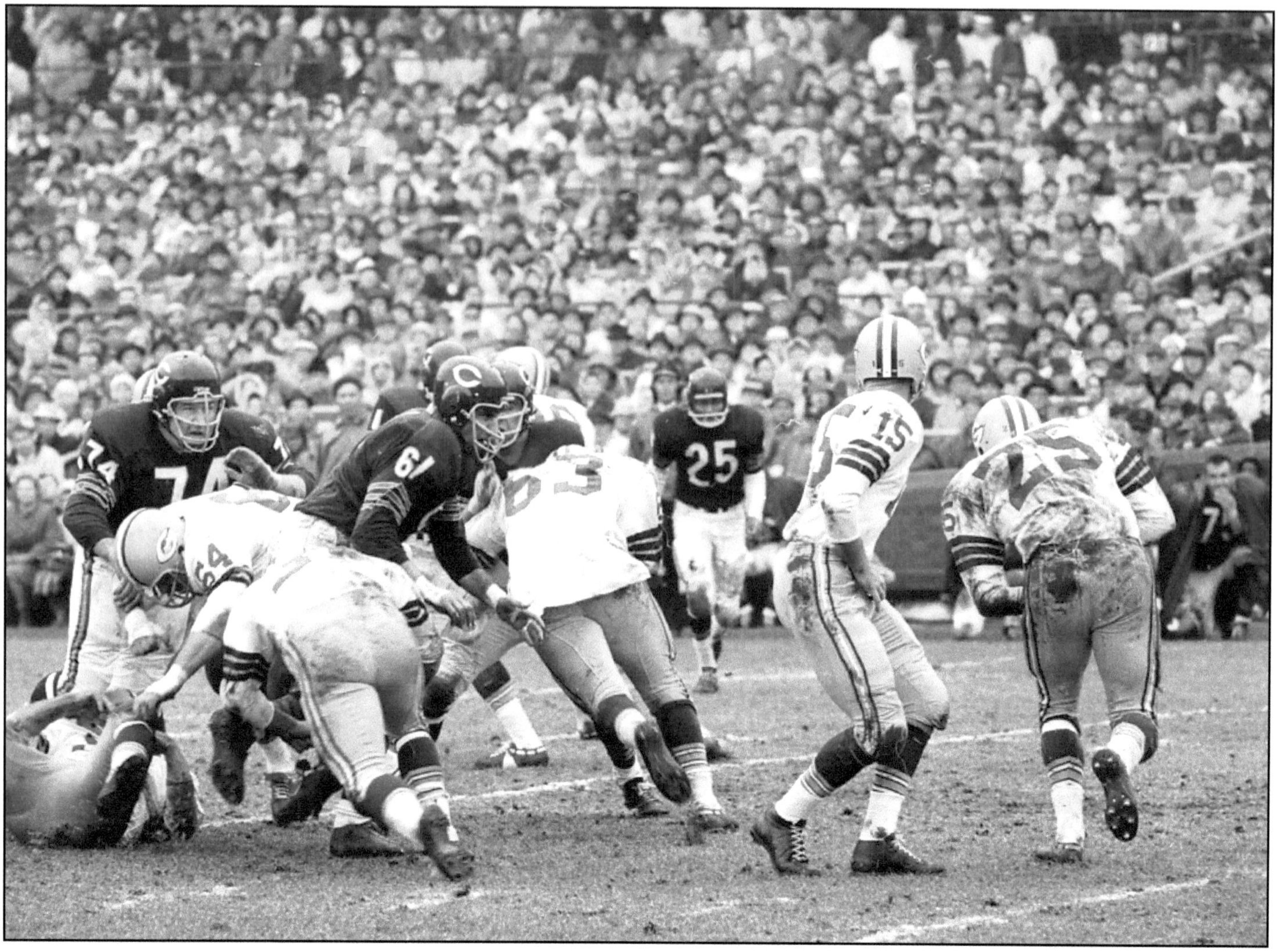

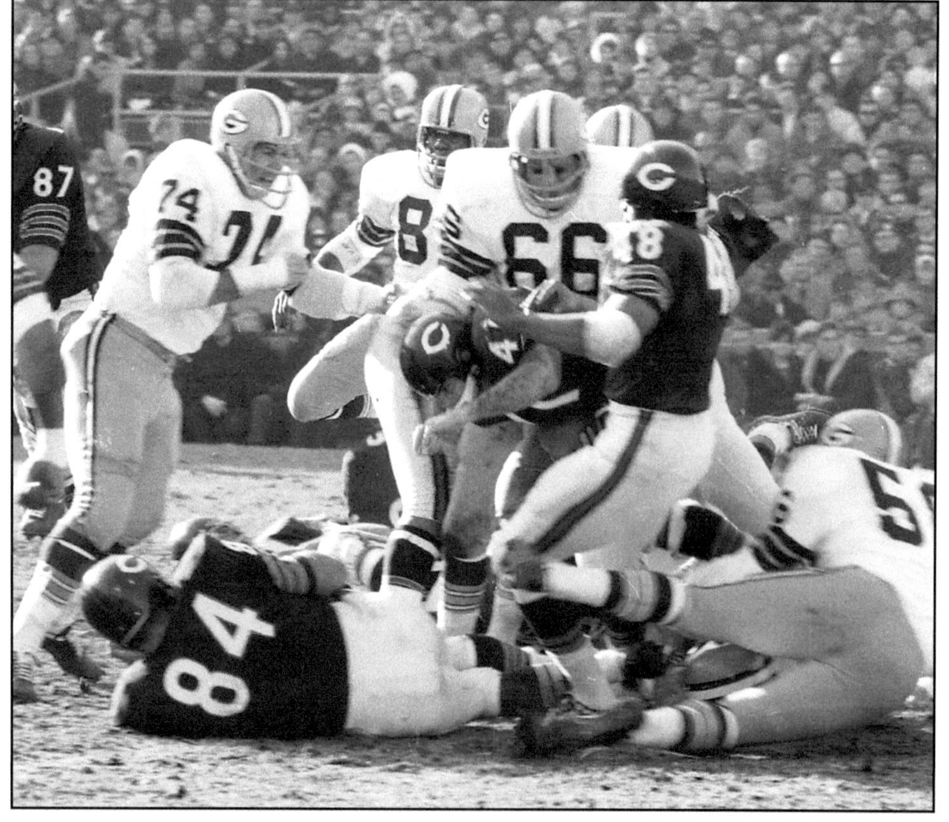

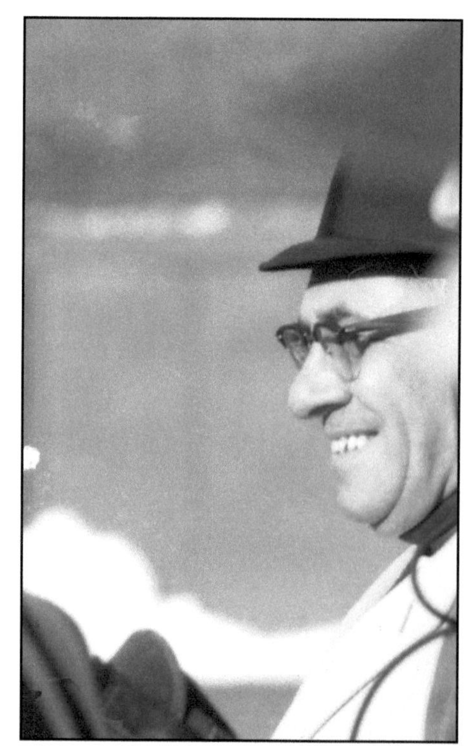

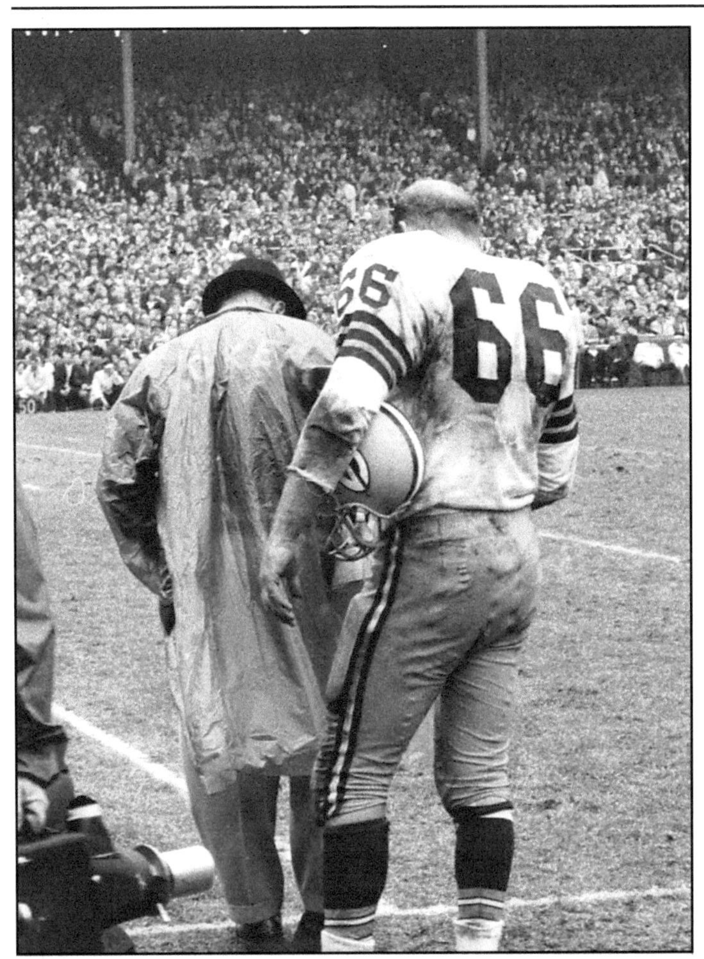

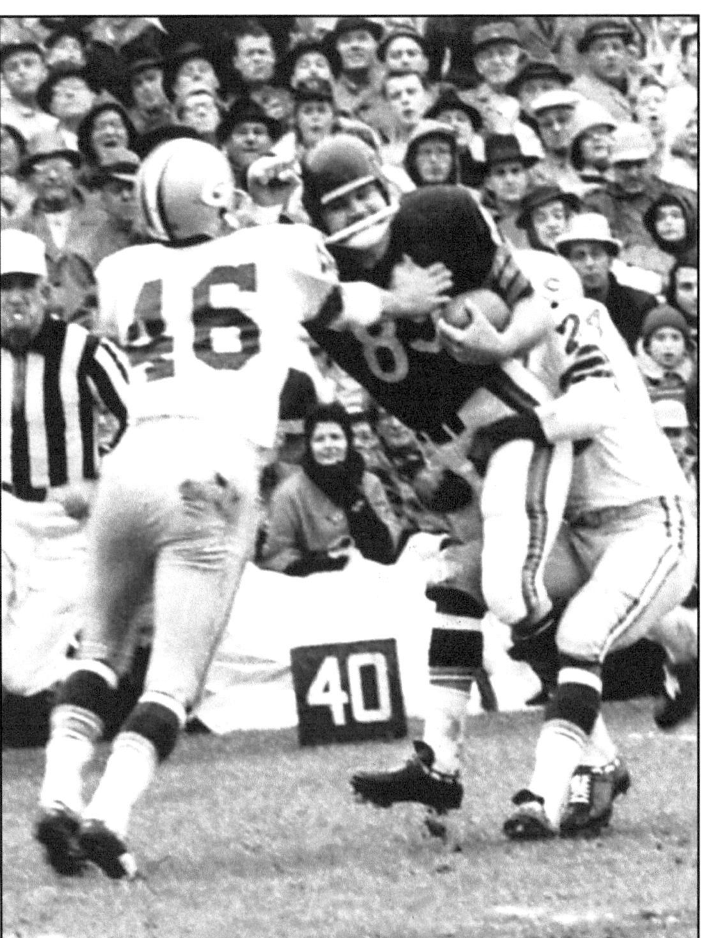

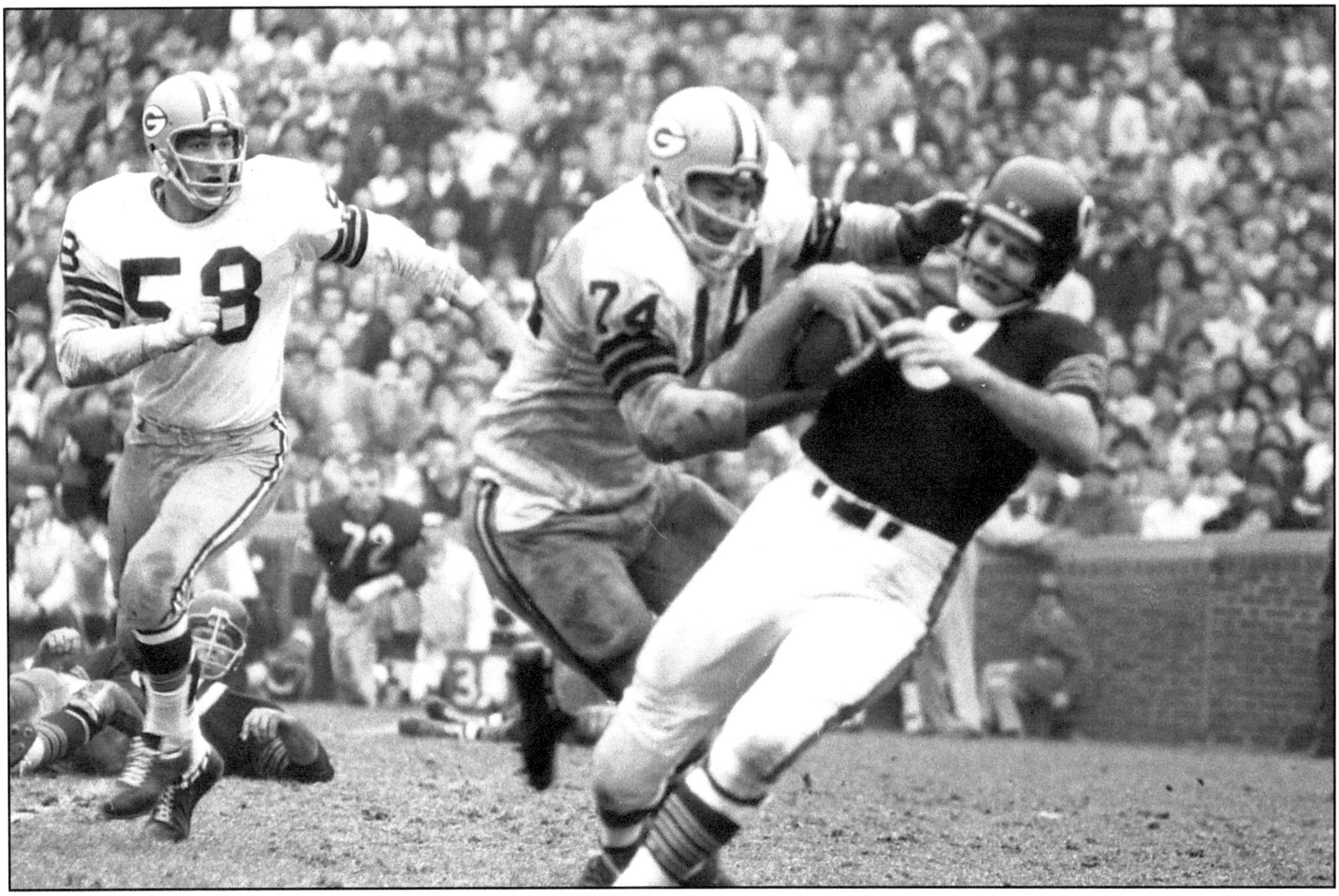

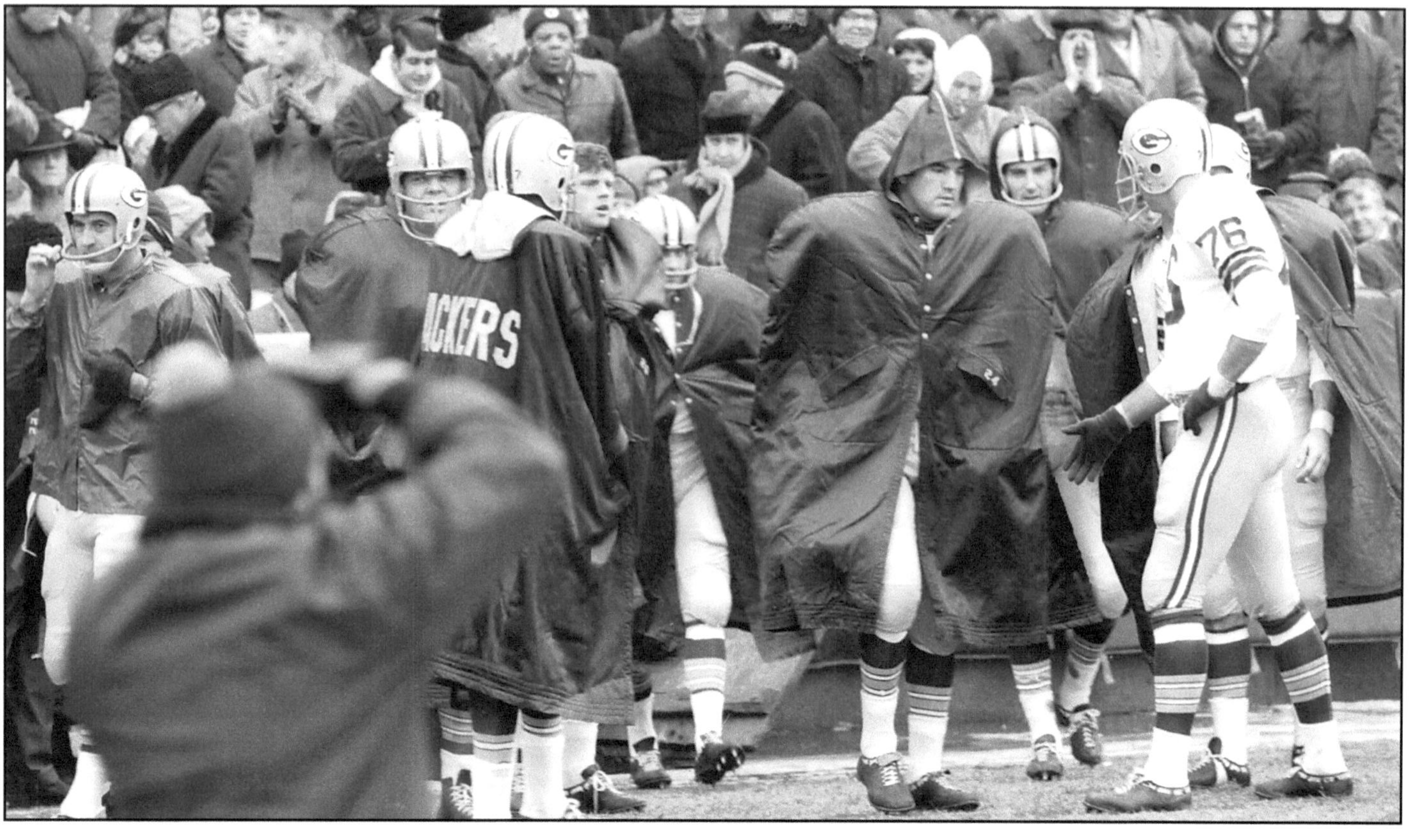

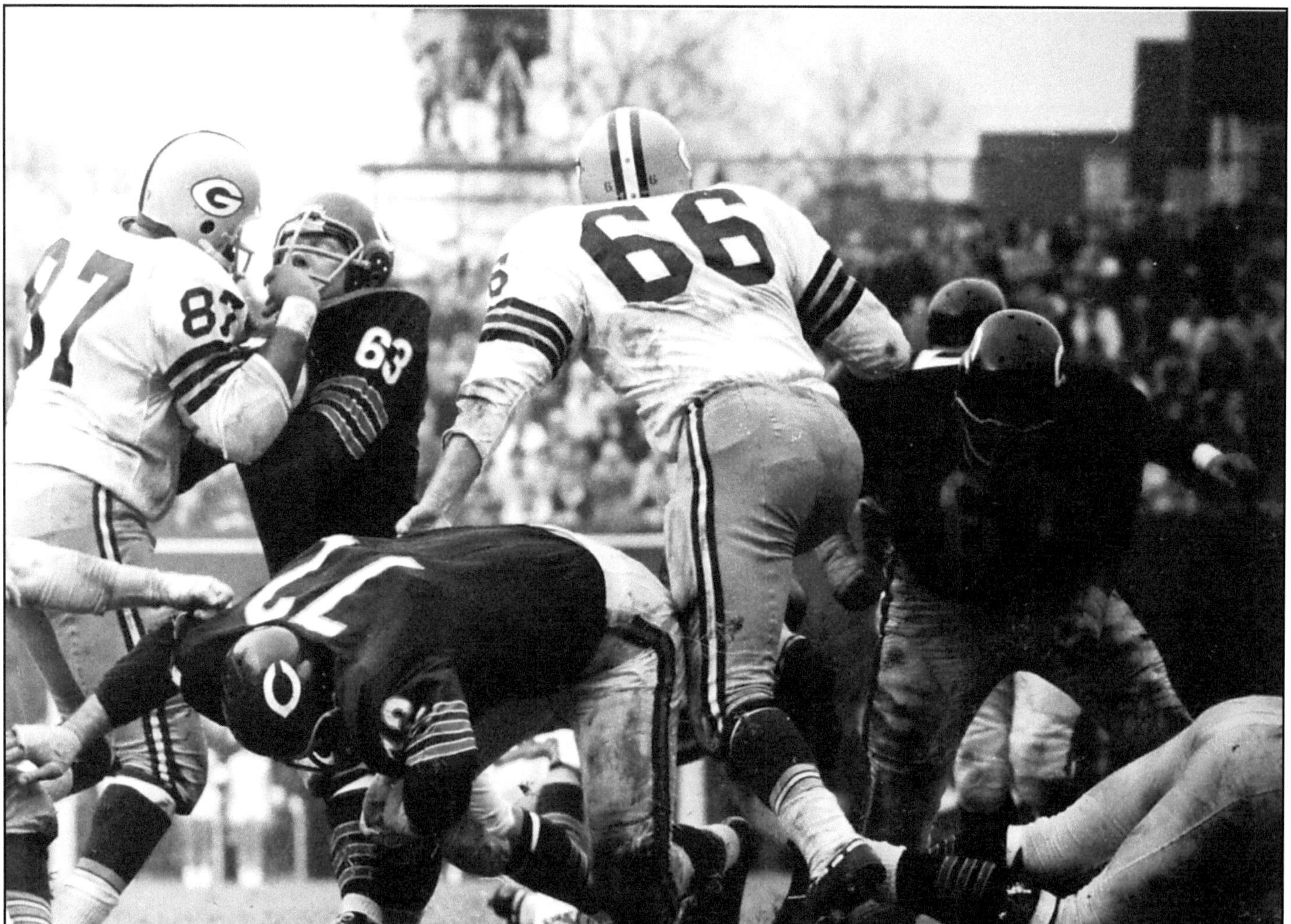

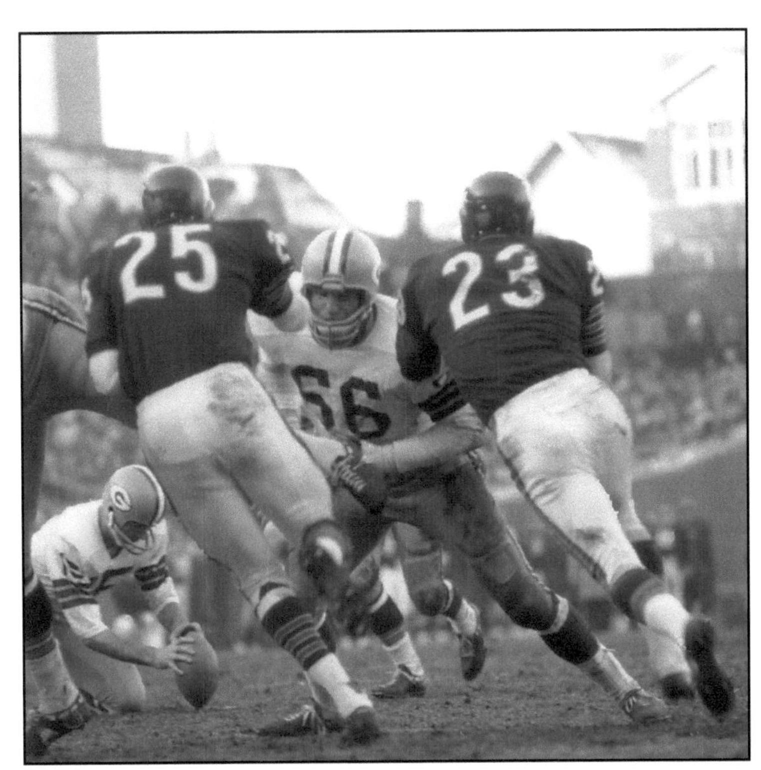
25
66
23

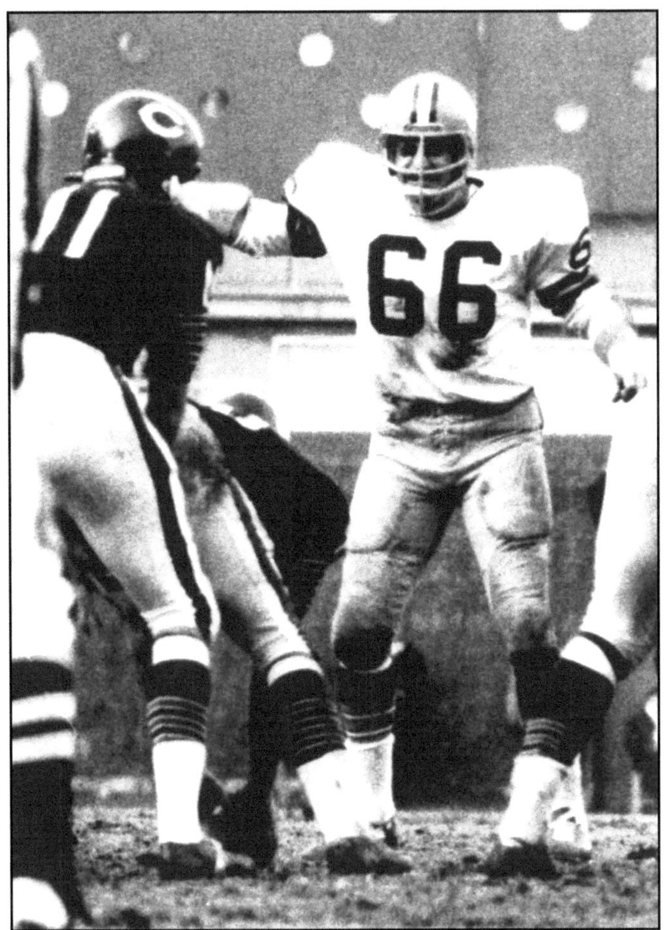
66

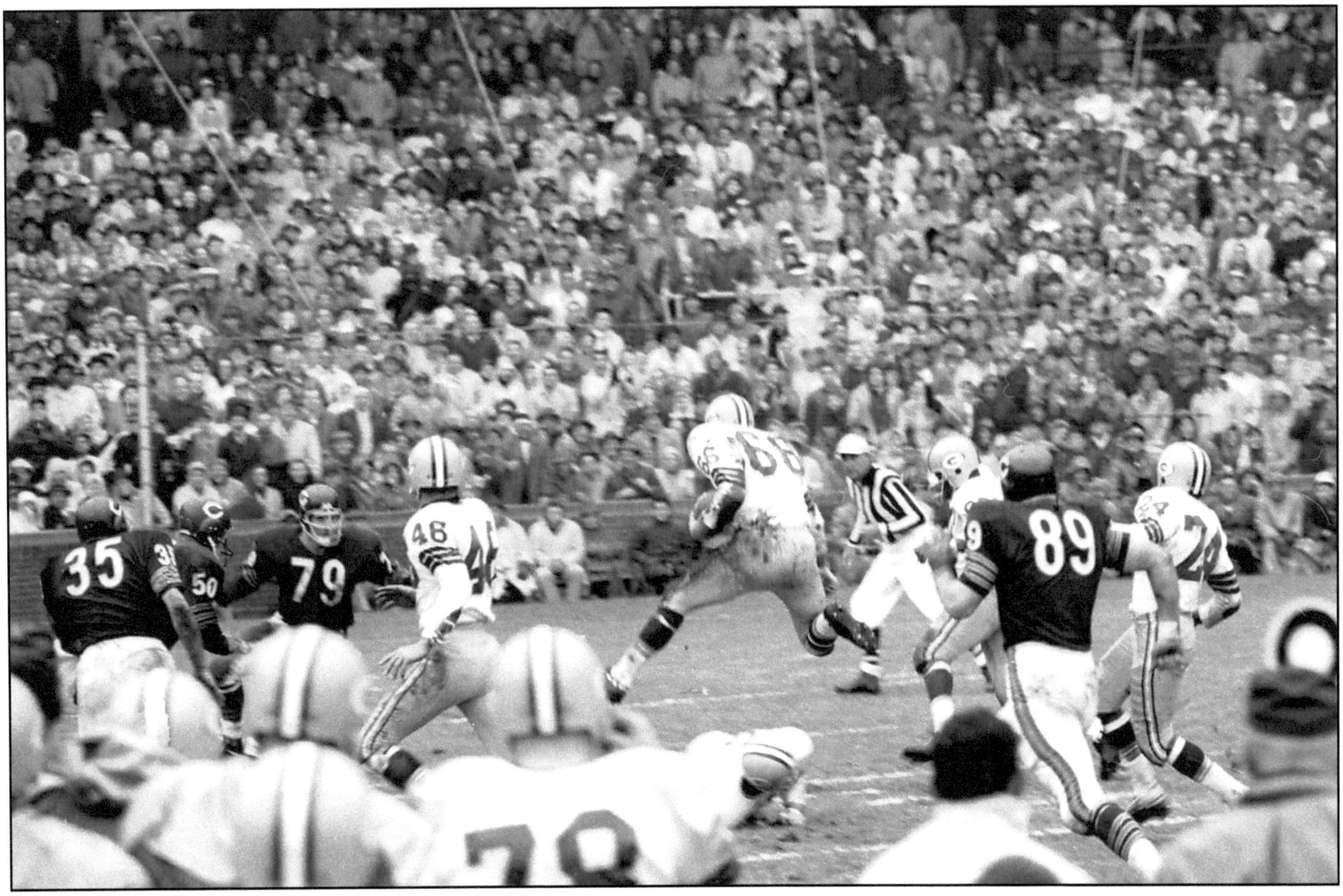

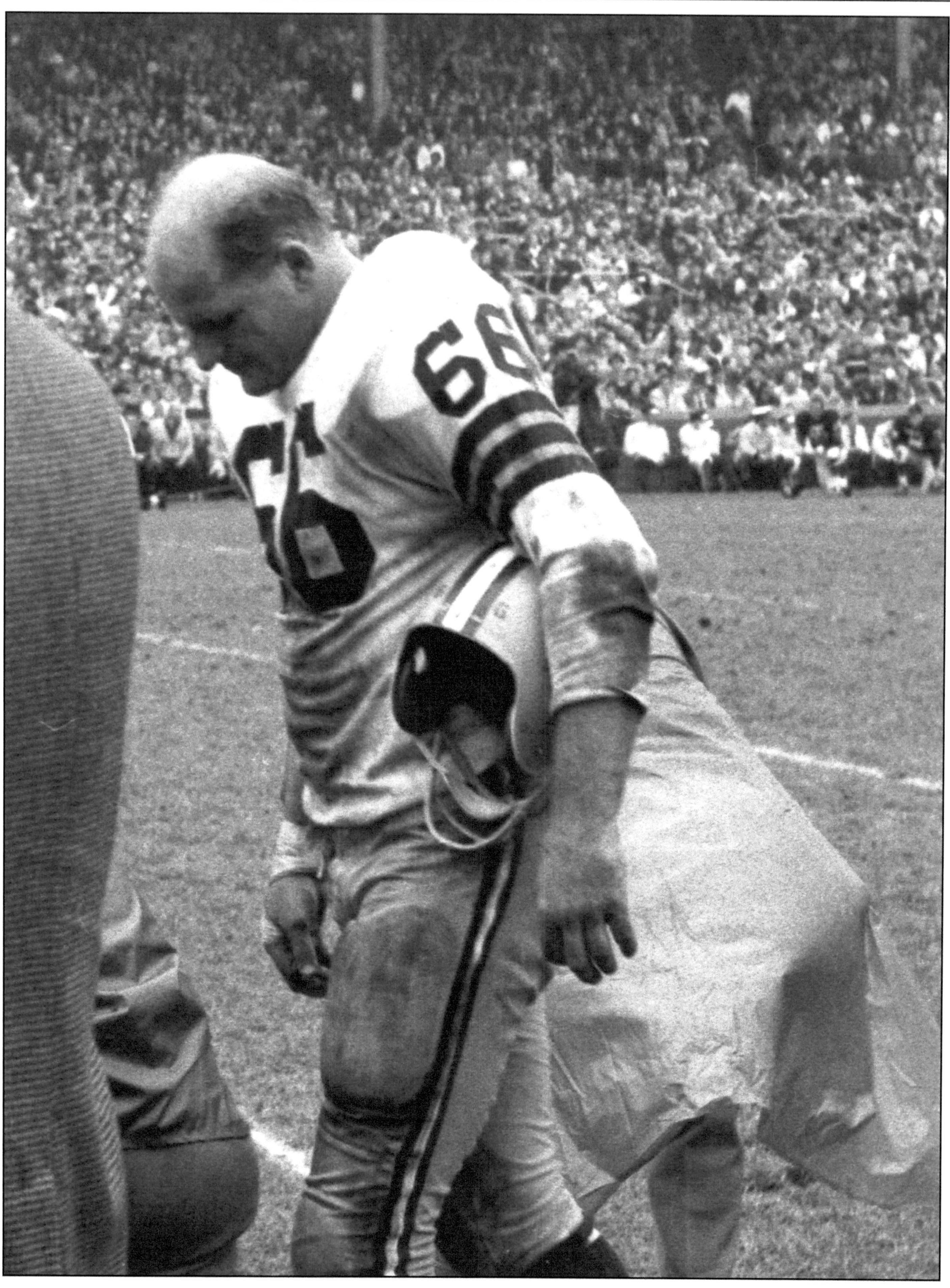
66

DETROIT LIONS

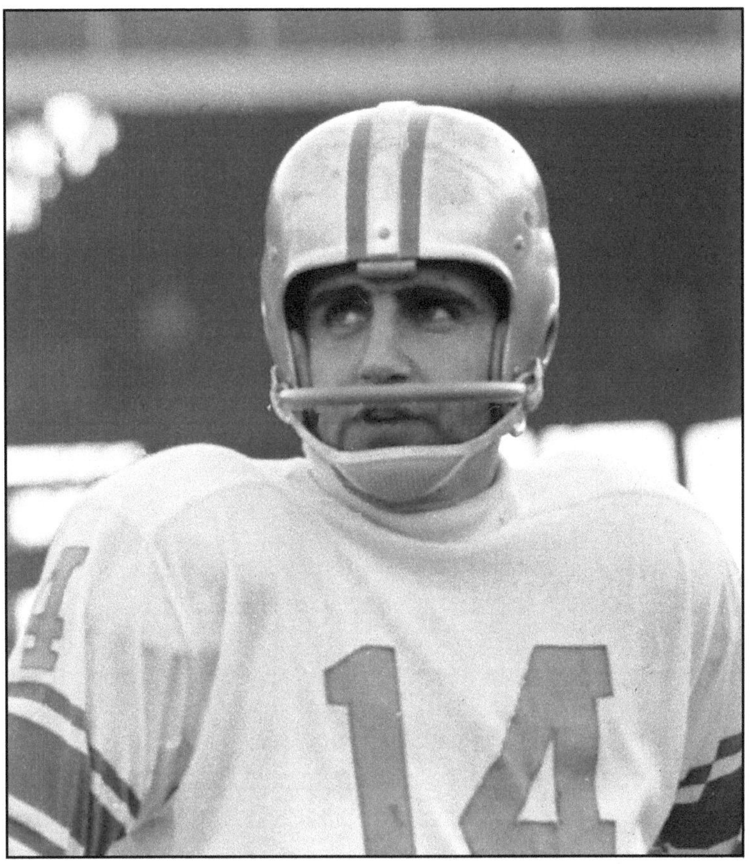

	Bears	Lions
1960	28	7
1961	15	16
1962	3	0
1963	24	14
1964	0	10
1965	38	10
1966	10	10
1967	14	3
1968	10	28
1969	3	20

In 1930, The Portsmouth, Ohio Spartans entered the NFL Purchased for $15,000 by George Richards, a local businessman, the Spartans moved to Detroit and became the Detroit Lions after a radio contest was held to rename the team. From that time the Lions were featured regularly n the Bears' schedule.

In 1960 300 pound defensive tackle Roger Brown and defensive back Night Train Lane became two of the most formidable forces in the NFL. The team won six of their last sever games that year and beat the Browns 17-16 in the Playoff Bowl.

1961 brought an embarrassing 8-5-1 season including a 49-0 loss to the 49ers. In 1962 Matt Plum joined the team at quarterback and Detroit won 11 games, the most in franchise history. The Lions beat the Eagles 38-10 in the Playoff Bowl. After a league instigated investigation for gambling among its players in 1963, the Lions plummeted to a 5-8-1 record. Not all the news was bad for Lions fans however as Terry Barr caught 66 passes for a record setting 1,086 yards and 13 touchdowns.

In 1964 William Clay Ford took over the team and Alex Karras was reinstated after the gambling scandal. A 7-5-2 season led Ford to fire all Lions assistant coaches. The head coach, Wilson, resigned shortly thereafter. Harry Gilmer from the Vikings took over coaching duties in 1965 but the team finished with a 6-7-1 record. By 1966 resentment within the ranks of Lions players grew and the team finished dead last in their division.

Gilmer was fired in 1967 but the struggles remained leading to a dismal 5-7-2 season. In 1968 the team drafted quarterback Greg Landry from Massachusetts but the LIons went 16 consecutive quarters without a touchdown. By 1969 both the Lions offense and defense began a turnaround leading to a record of 9-4-1.

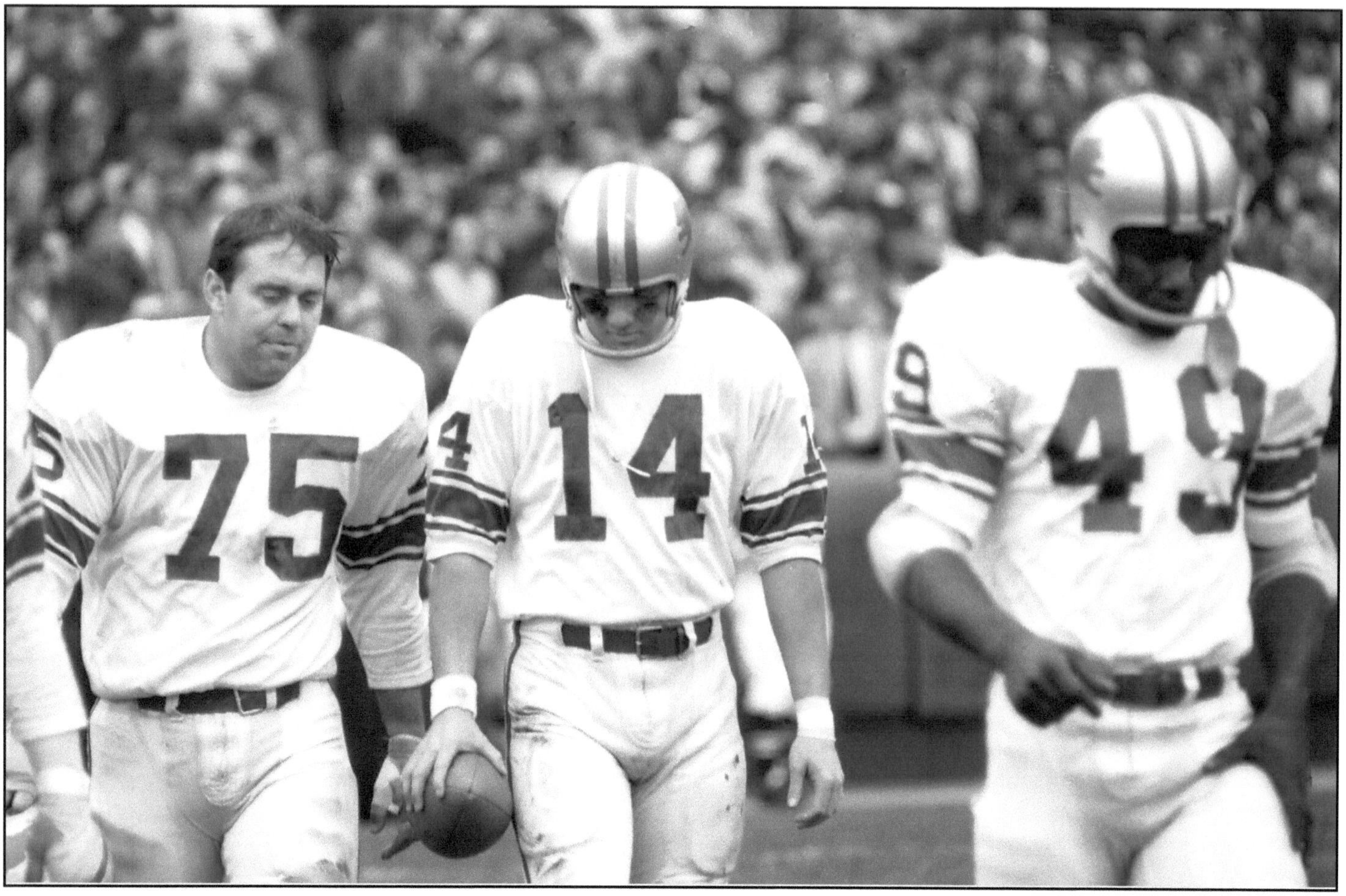

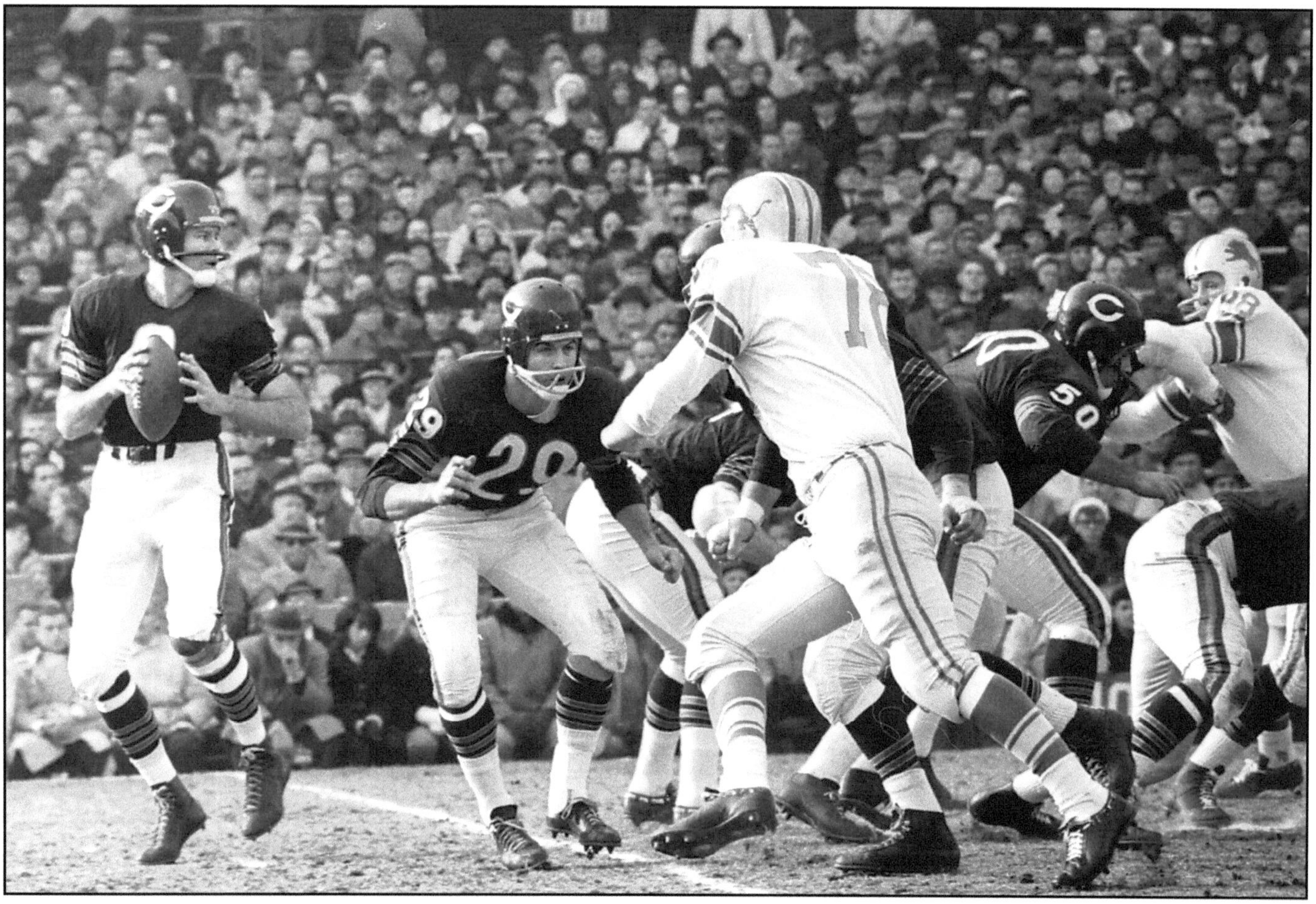

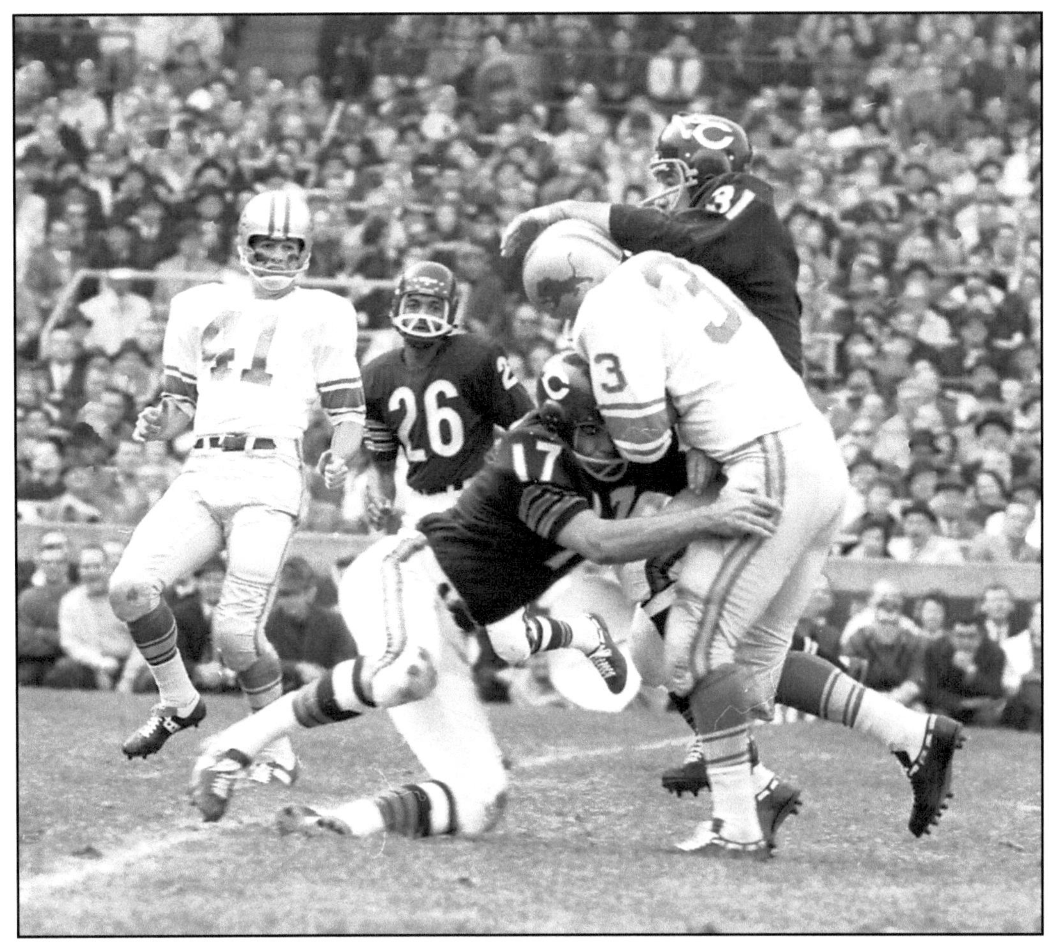

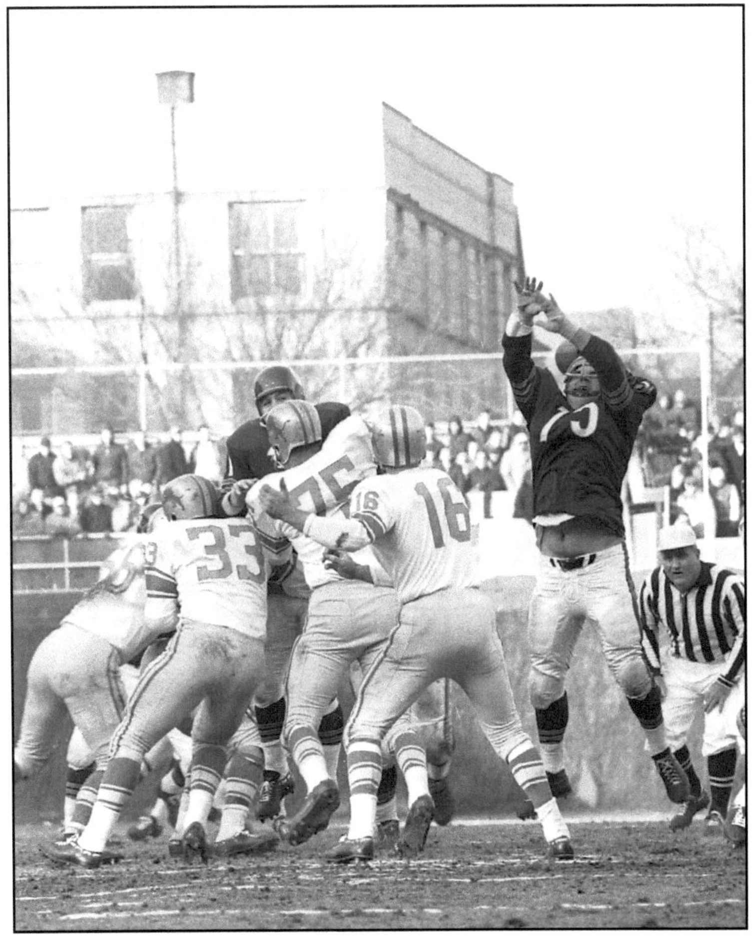

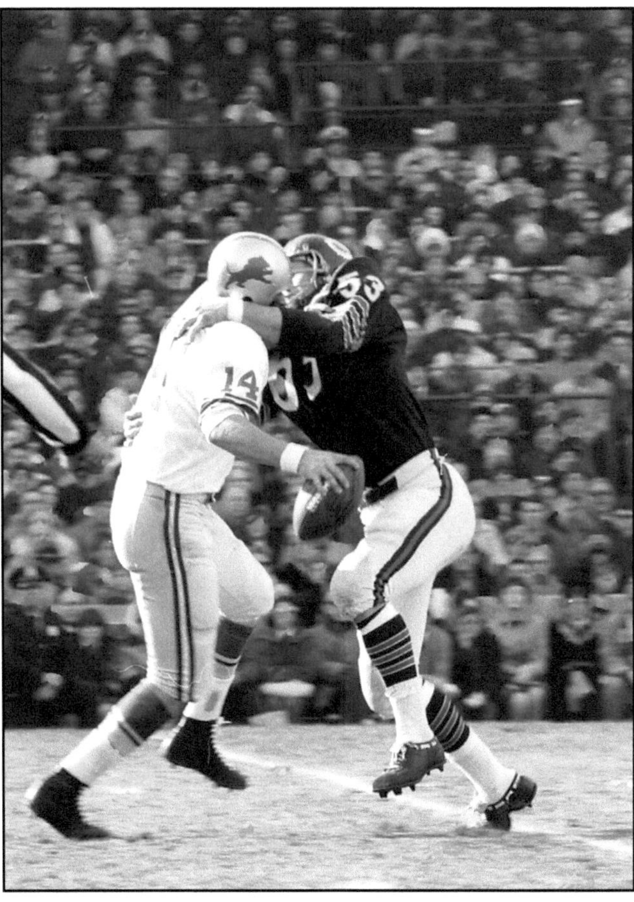

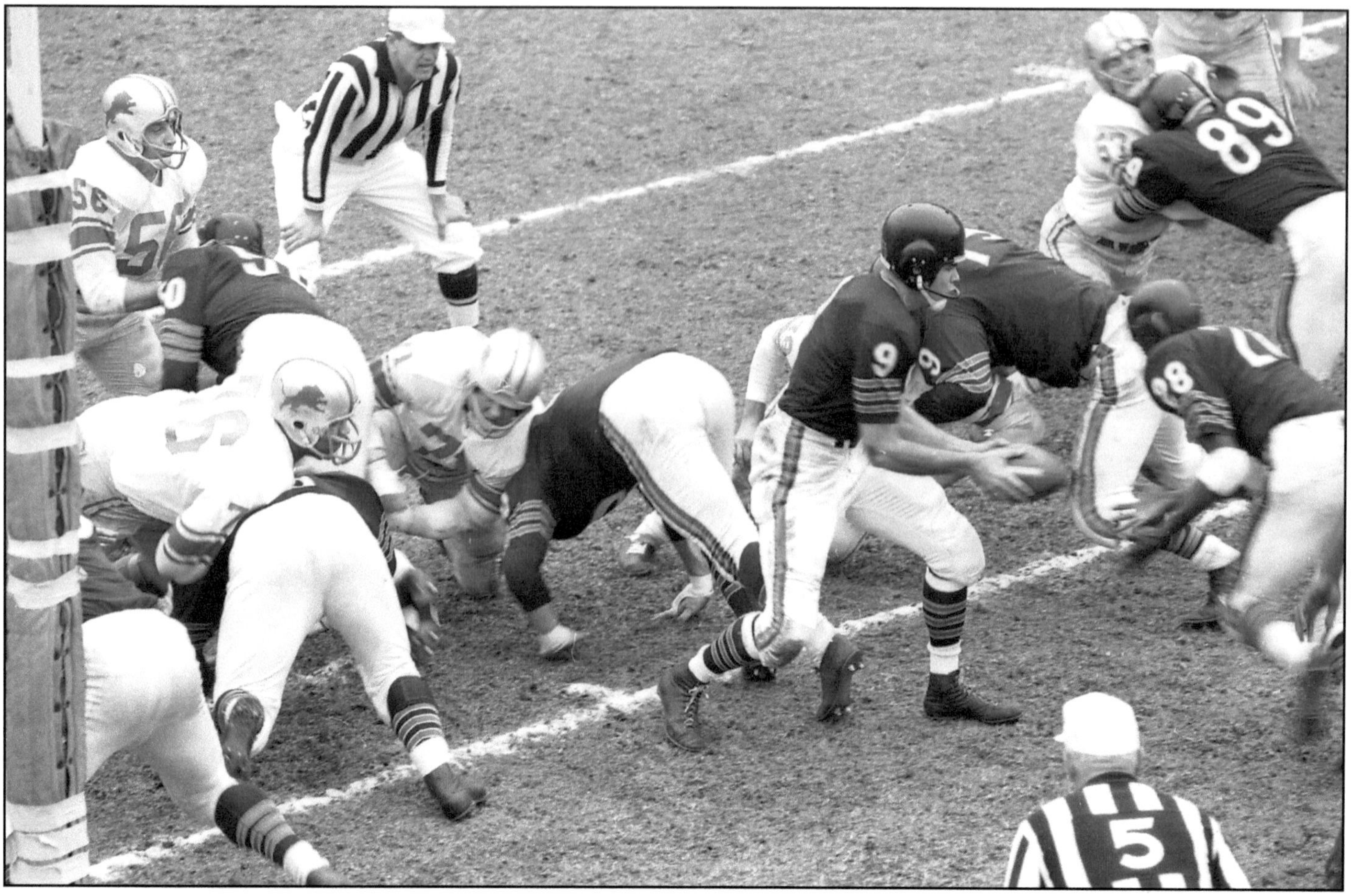

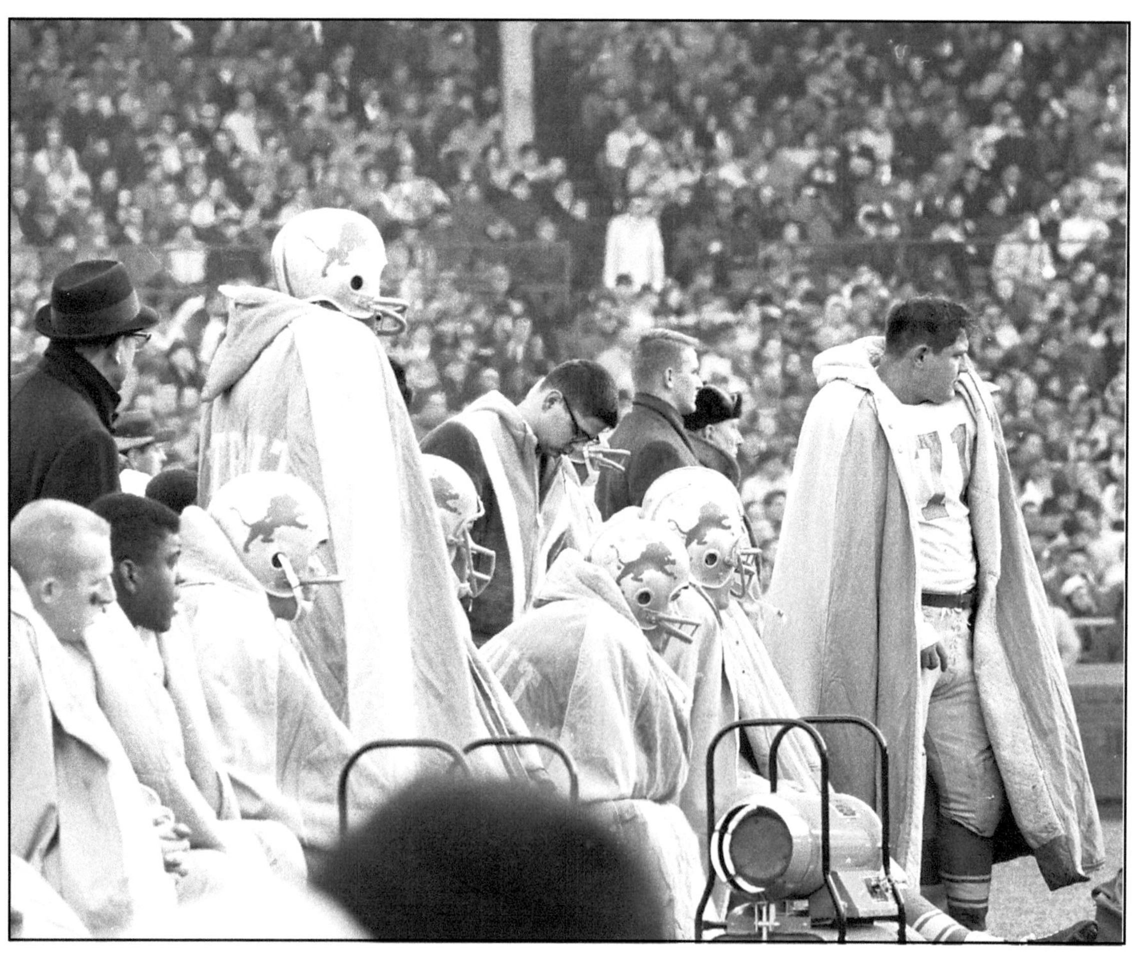

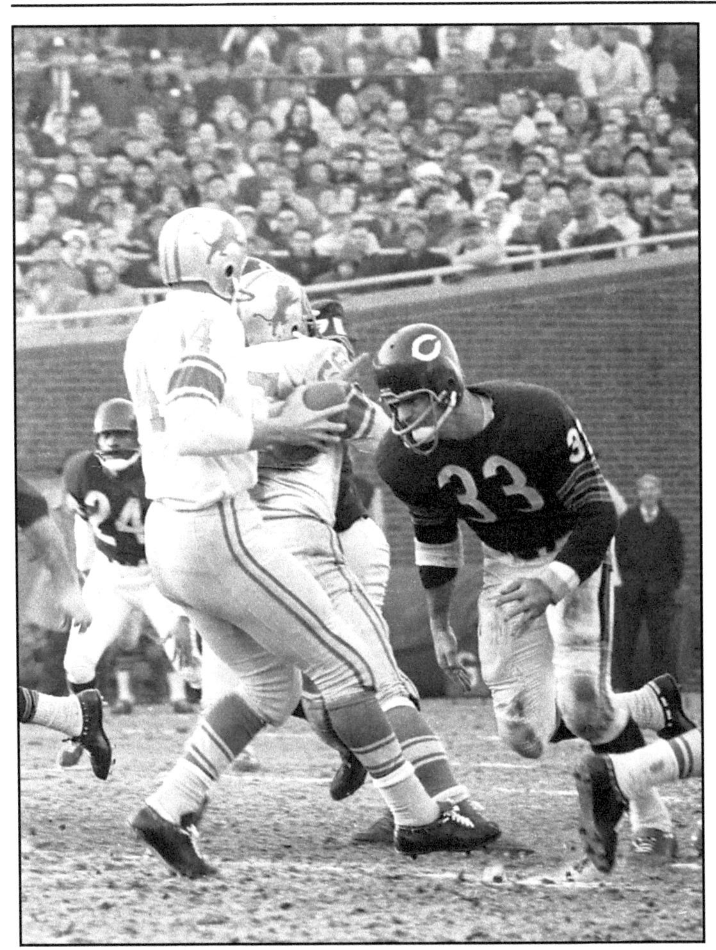
24
33

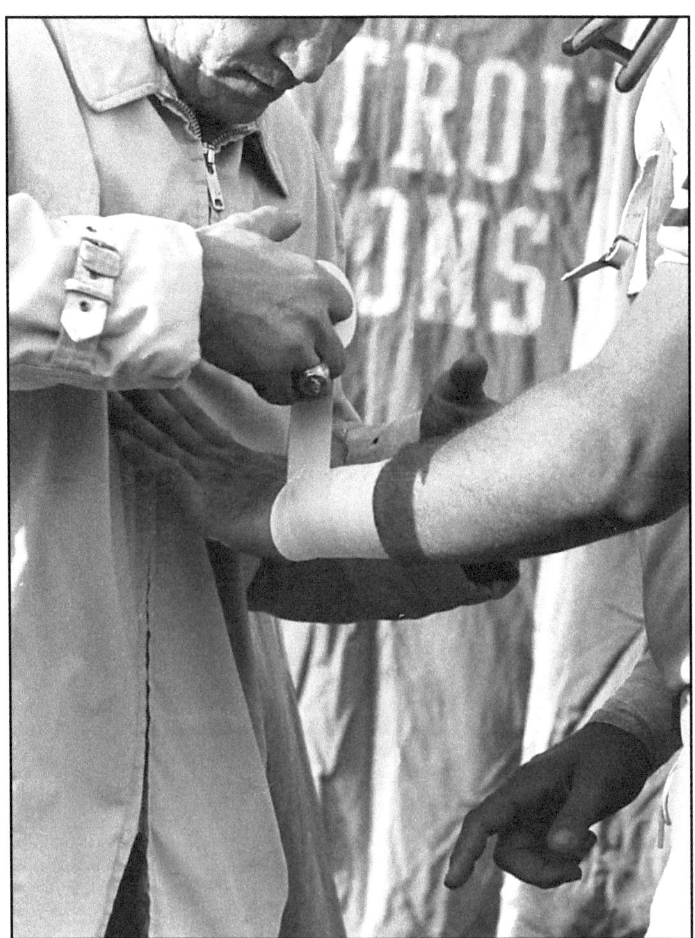

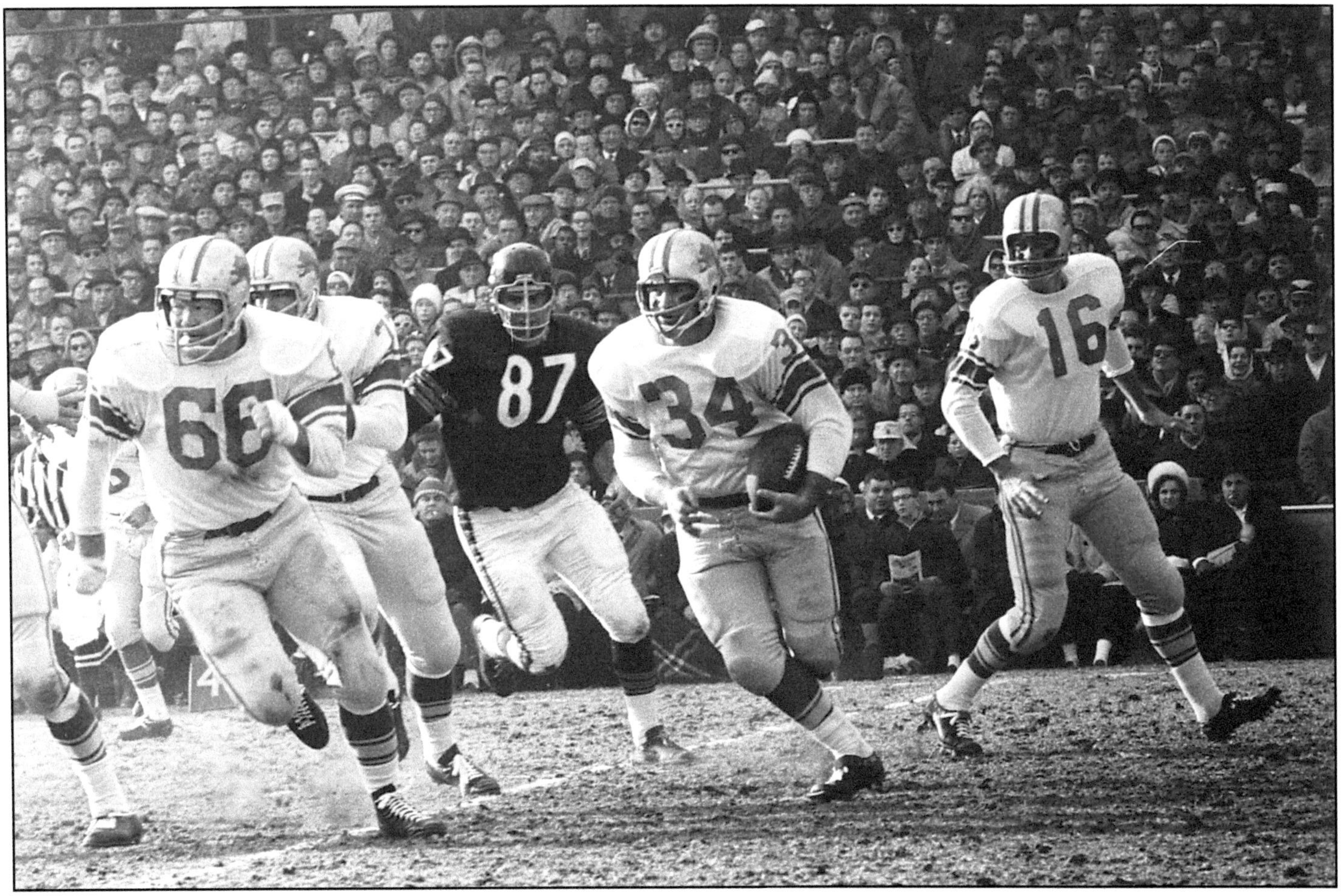

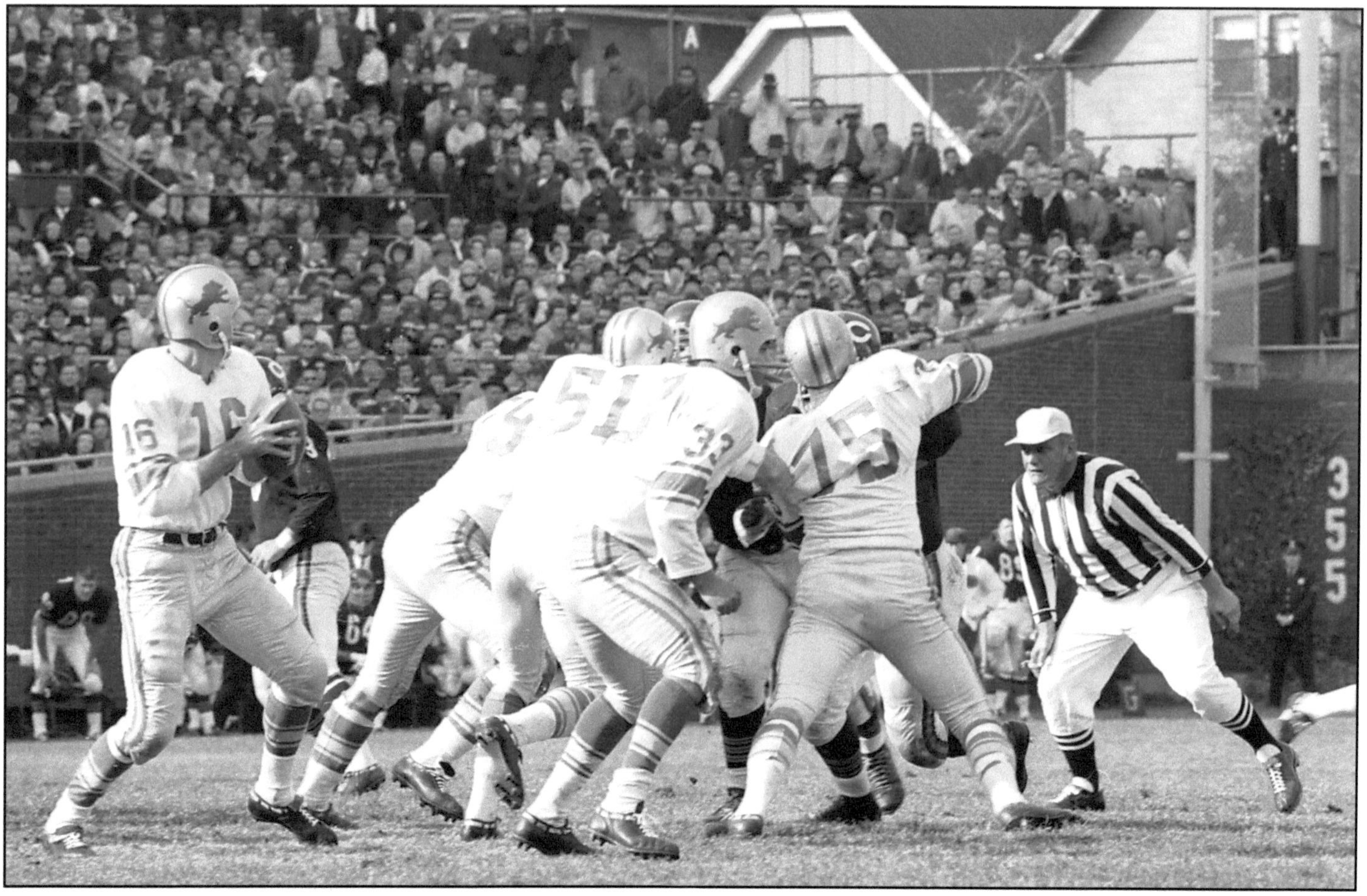

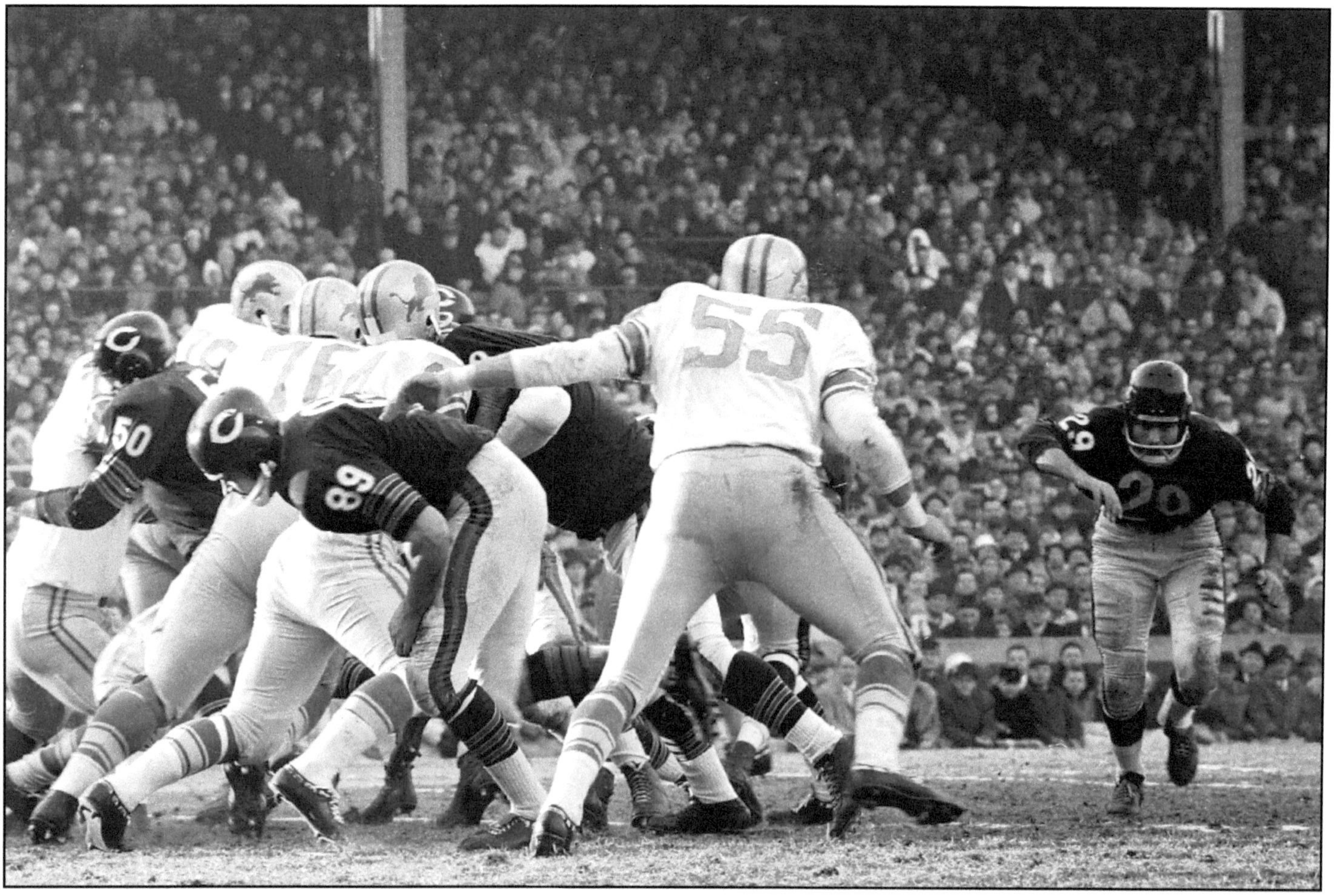

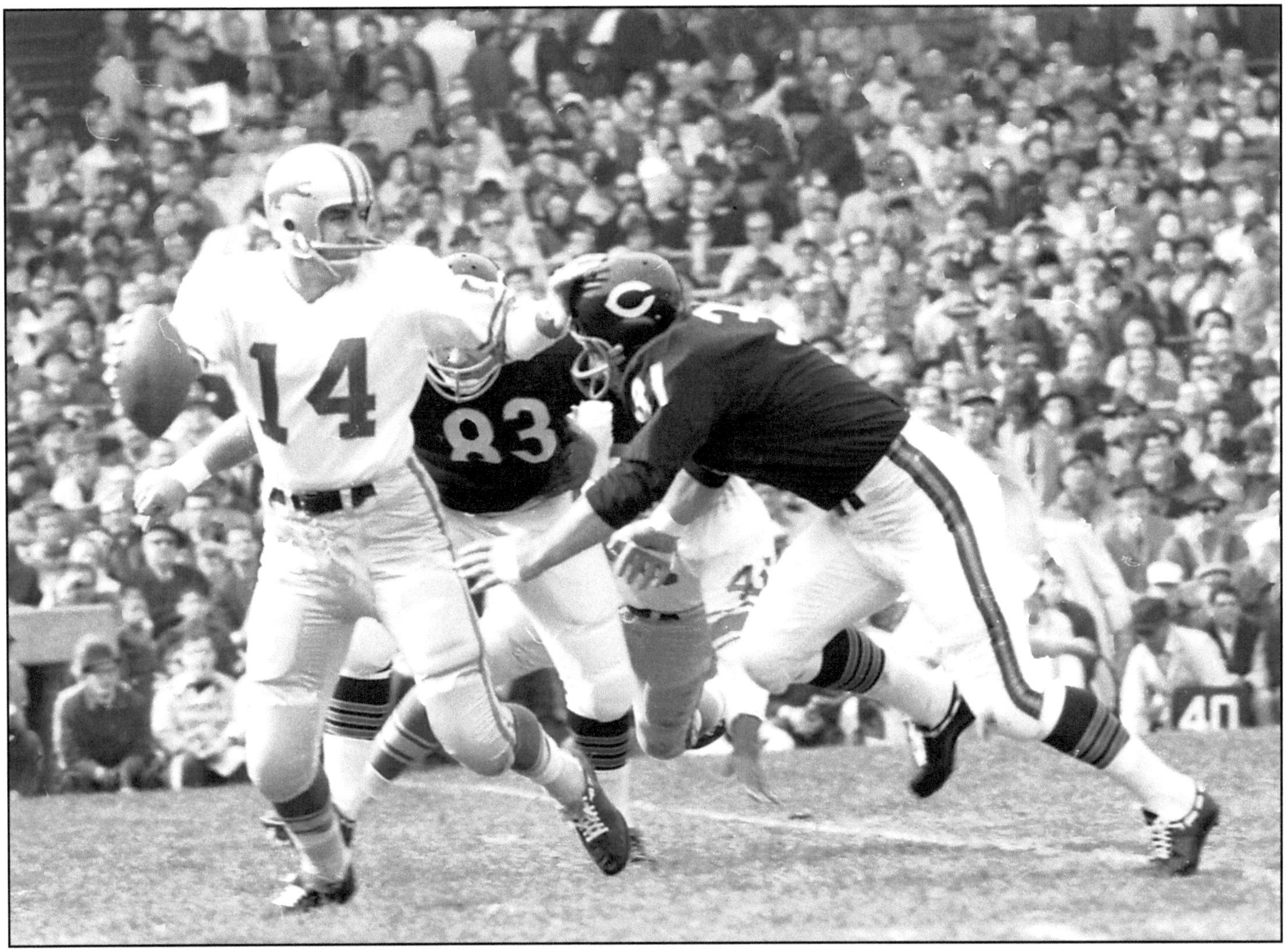

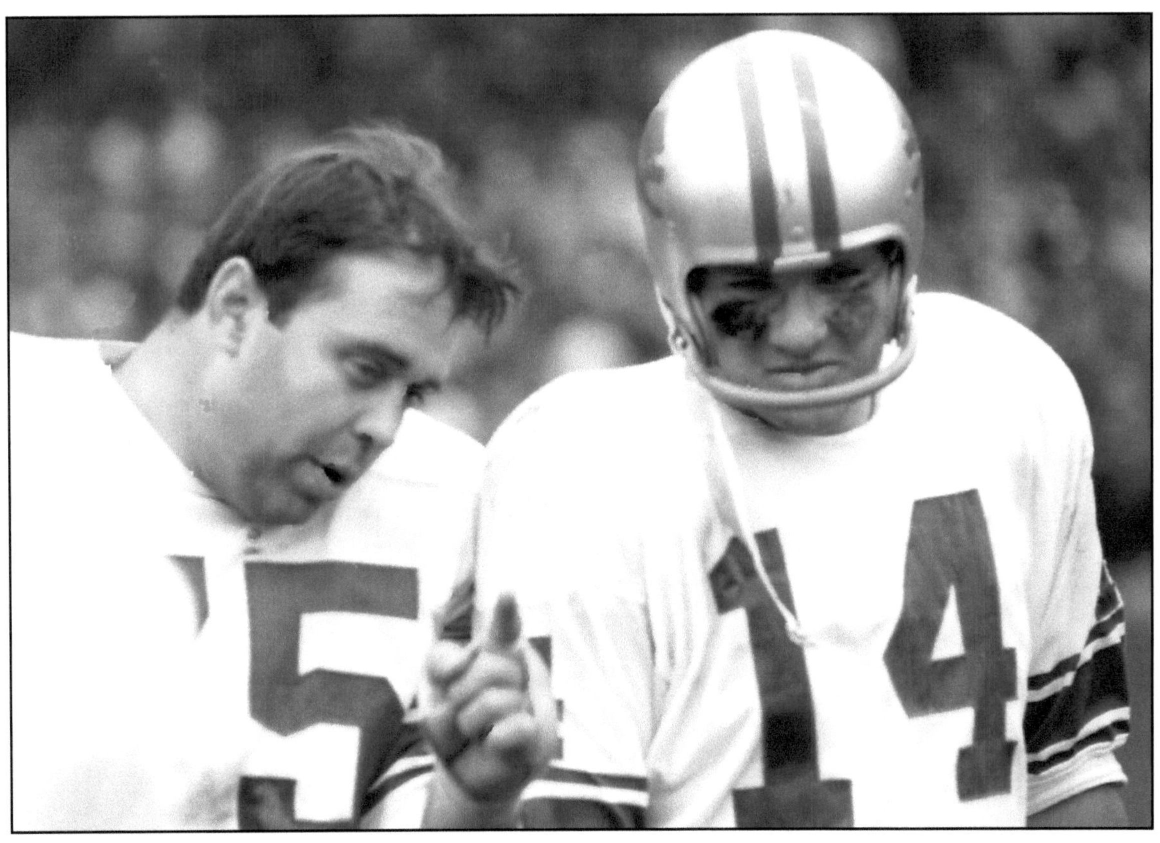

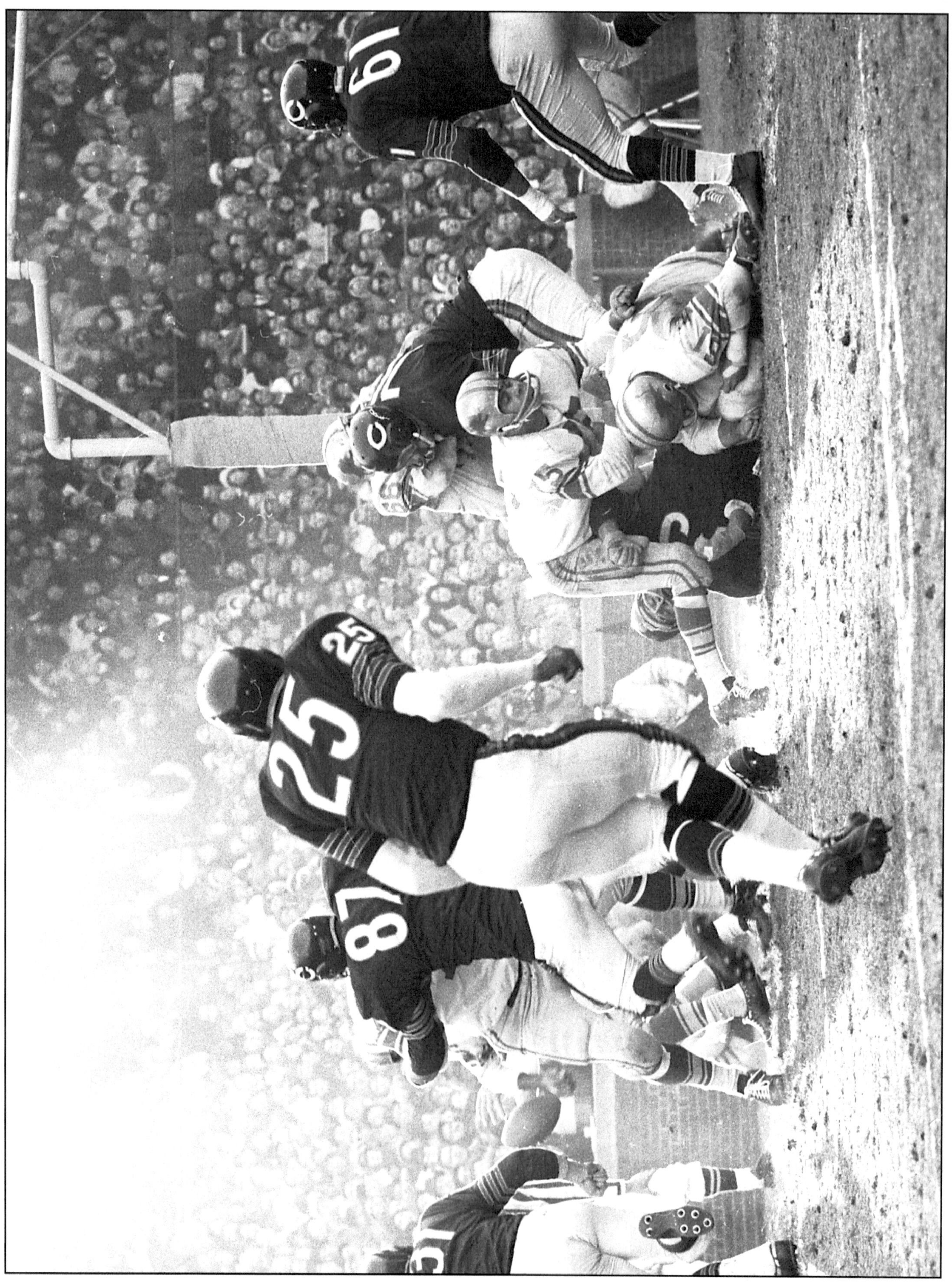

BALTIMORE COLTS

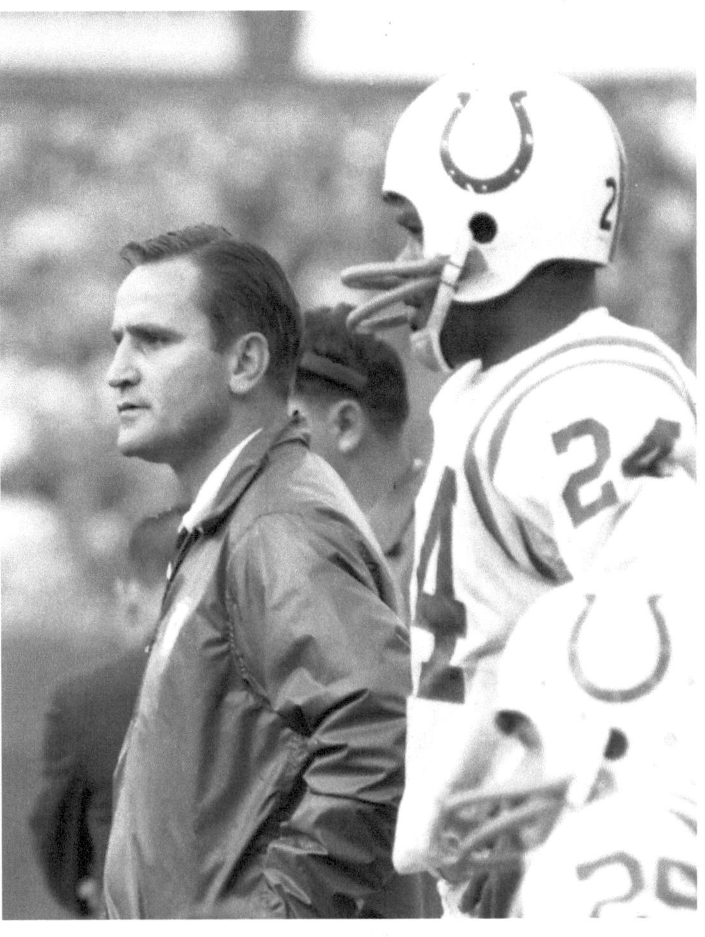

	Bears	Colts
1960	20	24
1961	24	10
1962	35	15
1963	10	3
1964	24	40
1965	21	26
1966	27	17
1967	3	24
1969	21	24

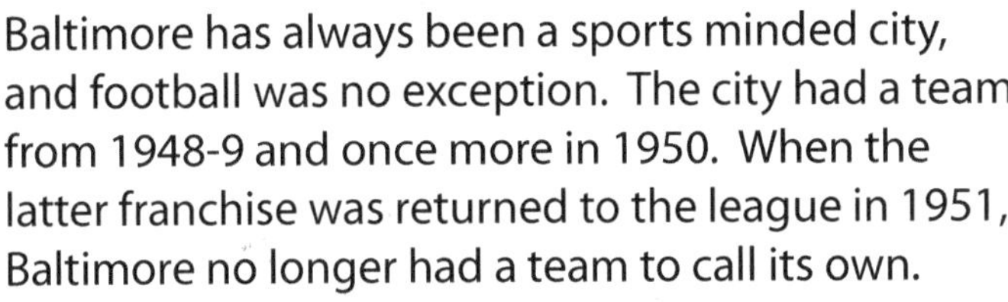

Baltimore has always been a sports minded city, and football was no exception. The city had a team from 1948-9 and once more in 1950. When the latter franchise was returned to the league in 1951, Baltimore no longer had a team to call its own.

Soon came an offer from the NFL's Commissioner Bert Bell, sell 15,000 season tickets within six weeks, and the league will give you the NFL's twelfth franchise. Local fans jumped at the opportunity to bring professional football back to Maryland and all tickets were sold well within the timeframe. Local businessman Carroll Rosenbloom and several partners backed the team financially and by early 1952, Baltimore had a football team.

By 1960, the Baltimore Colts were struggling with aging players and nagging injuries. Johnny Unitas had fractured a vertebra, a condition other teams were well aware of and often used to their advantage. Unitas' streak of 47 games with a touchdown came to an end and the team finished 6-6. 1961 was little better. The Colts finished with four wins and a tie for third place in their conference. By 1962 Unitas finally enjoyed an injury free season with 2,967 passing yards ad 23 touchdowns to finish 7-7.

In 1963 Don Shula replaced Weeb Ewbank as head coach. The team once again finished third in their division but fans were pleased that an emphasis had been placed on acquiring new young talent instead of relying solely on seasoned veterans. By 1964 the Colts won eleven games in a row and cinched the Western Division Title. The Colts lost to the Browns by a score of 27-0 in the Championship game.

Unitas suffered a season ending injury in 1965 and was replaced by backup Gary Cuozzo who soon had a separated shoulder. The team rallied under third string quarterback Tom Matte to defeat the Cowboys 35-3 in the Playoff Bowl. History repeated itself in 1966 as Unitas again suffered a devastating injury, this time to his shoulder. Baltimore won seven of its first nine games then faltered as the season drew to a close. The Colts were able to beat Philadelphia 20-14 in the Playoff Bowl to put a positive spin on the season.

In 1967 the Colts finished 11-1-2 with both its offense and defense finishing ranked second in the NFL. 1968 saw Art Donovan become the first Colt to be named to the Pro Football Hall of Fame. Earl Morrall took over quarterback duties from Unitas. The Colts made it to the Super Bowl but lost in an upset to the Jets by a score of 16-7.

Unitas remained on the roster in 1969 although his duties were limited. The team finished two and a half games behind the Rams with a record of 8-5-1.

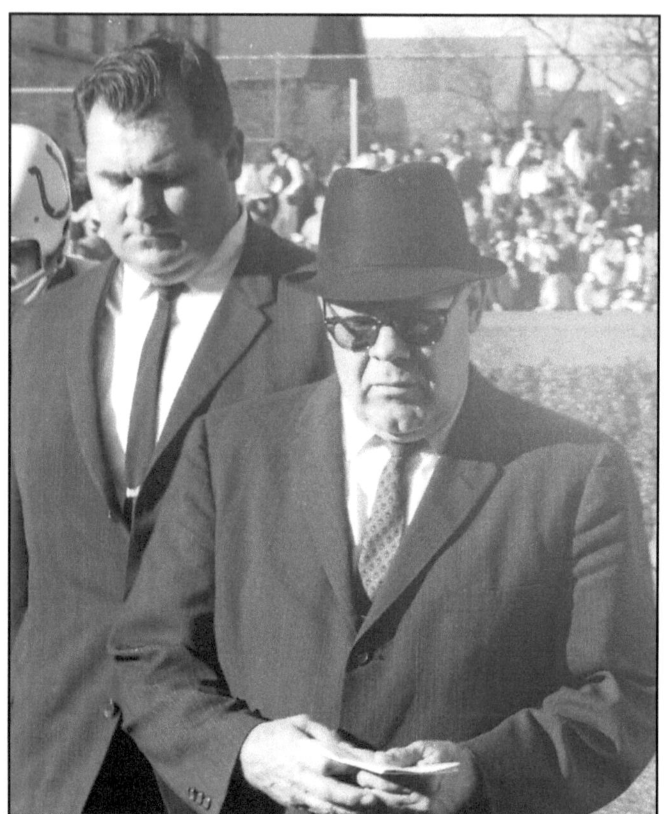

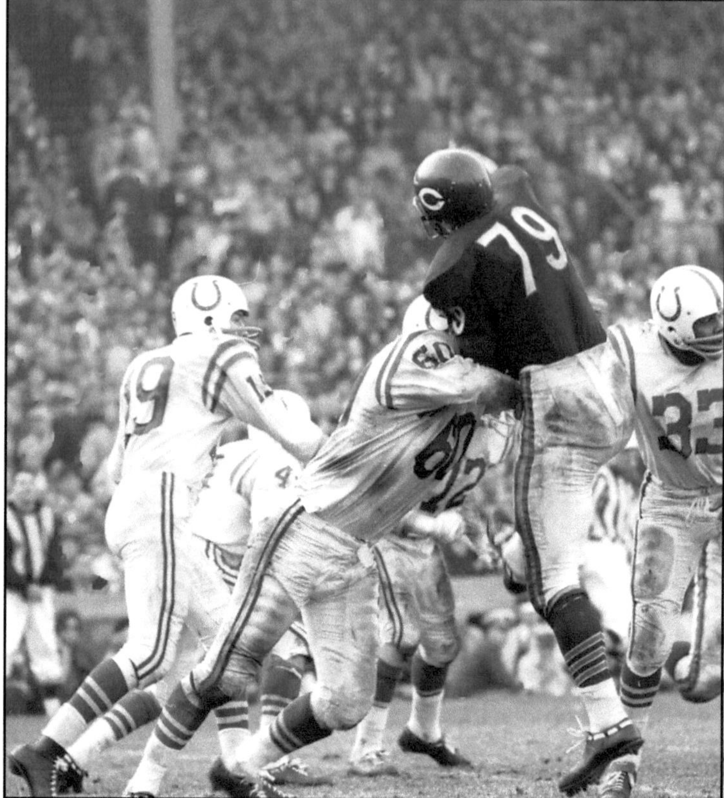

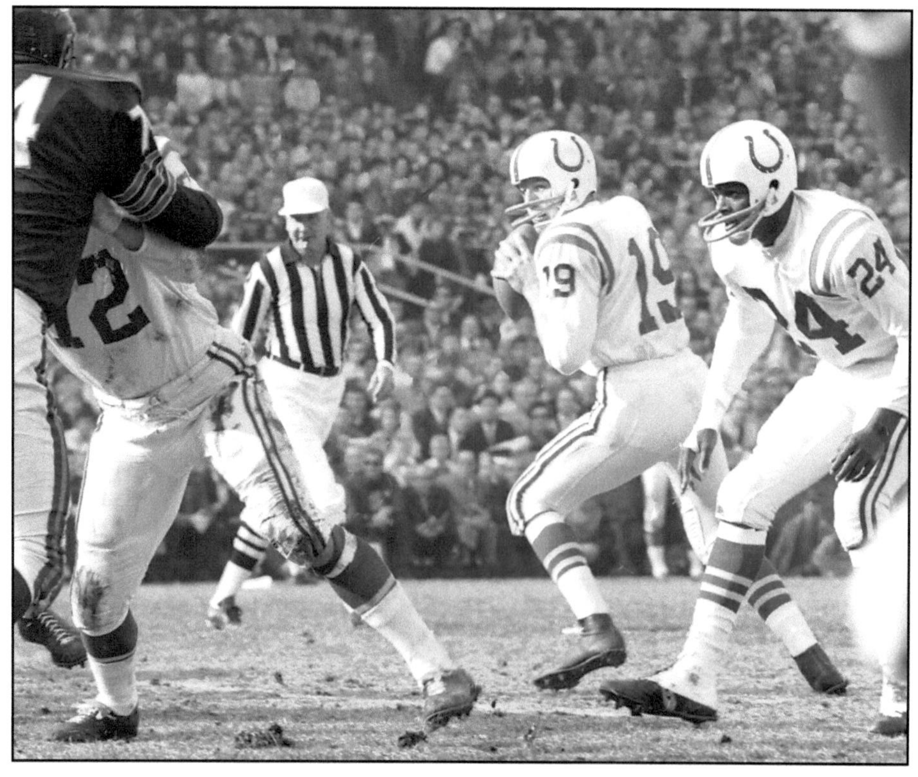

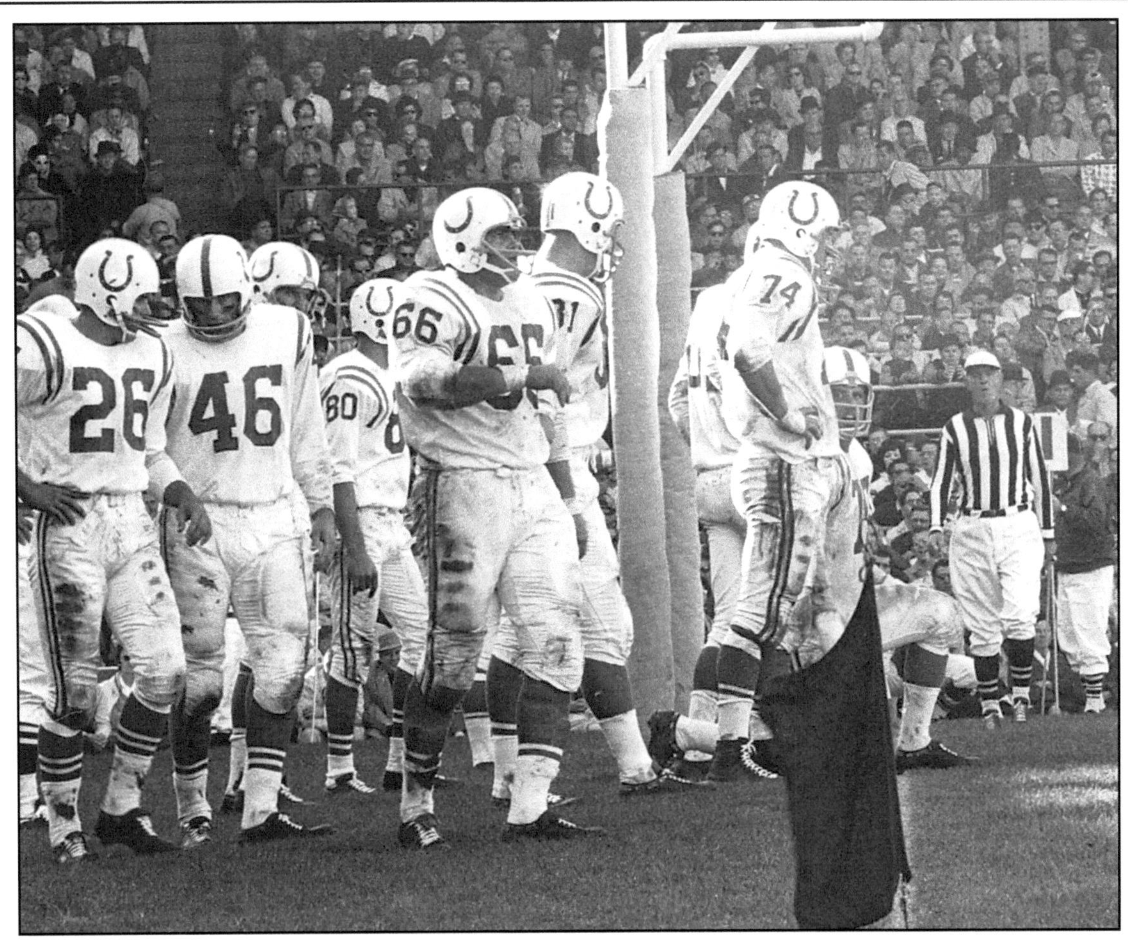
26
46
80
66
74

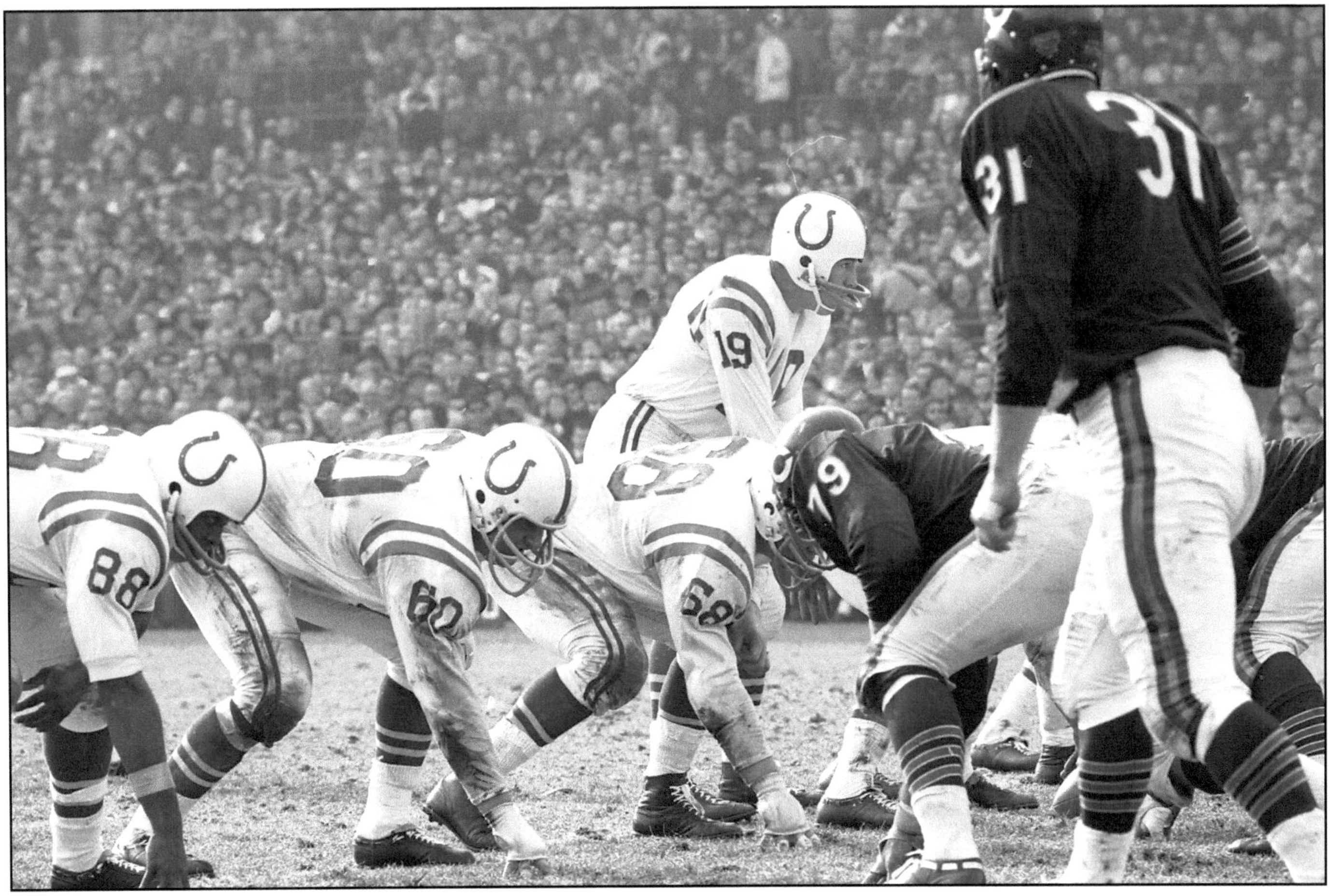

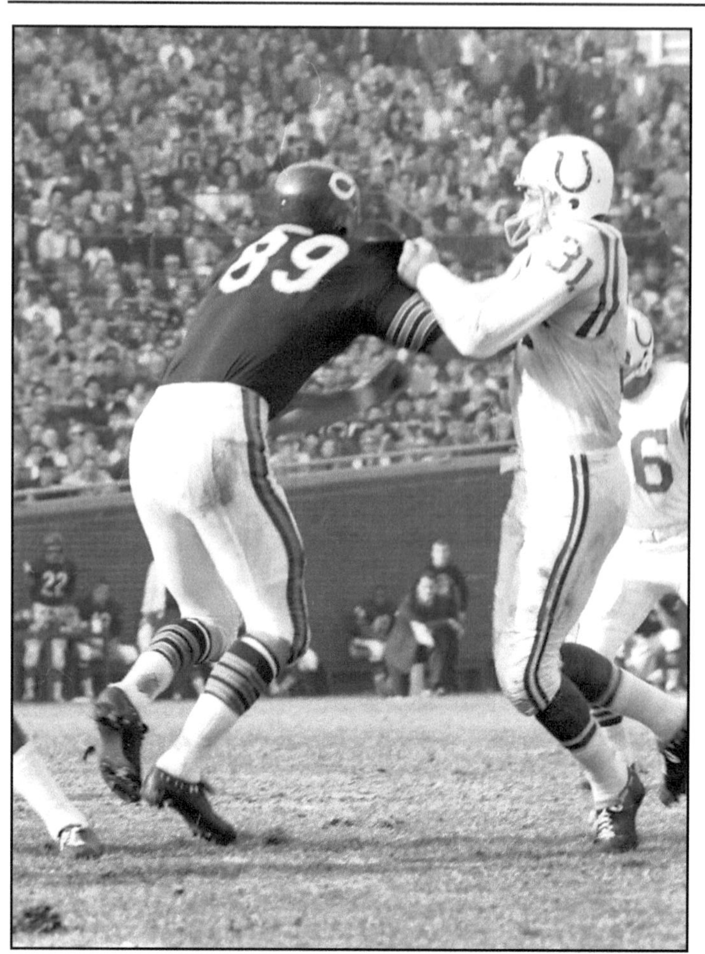

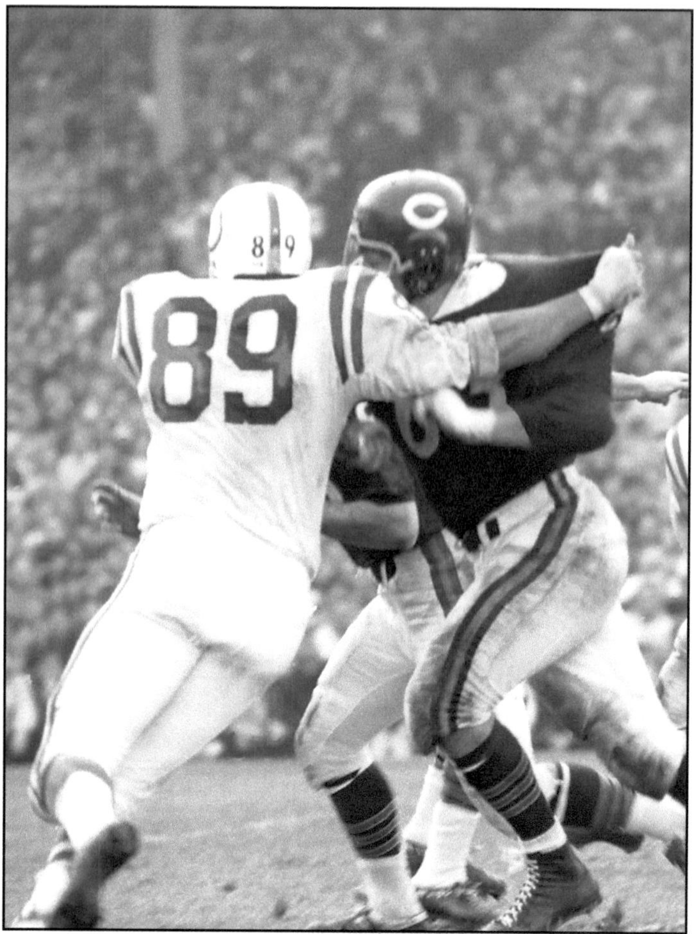

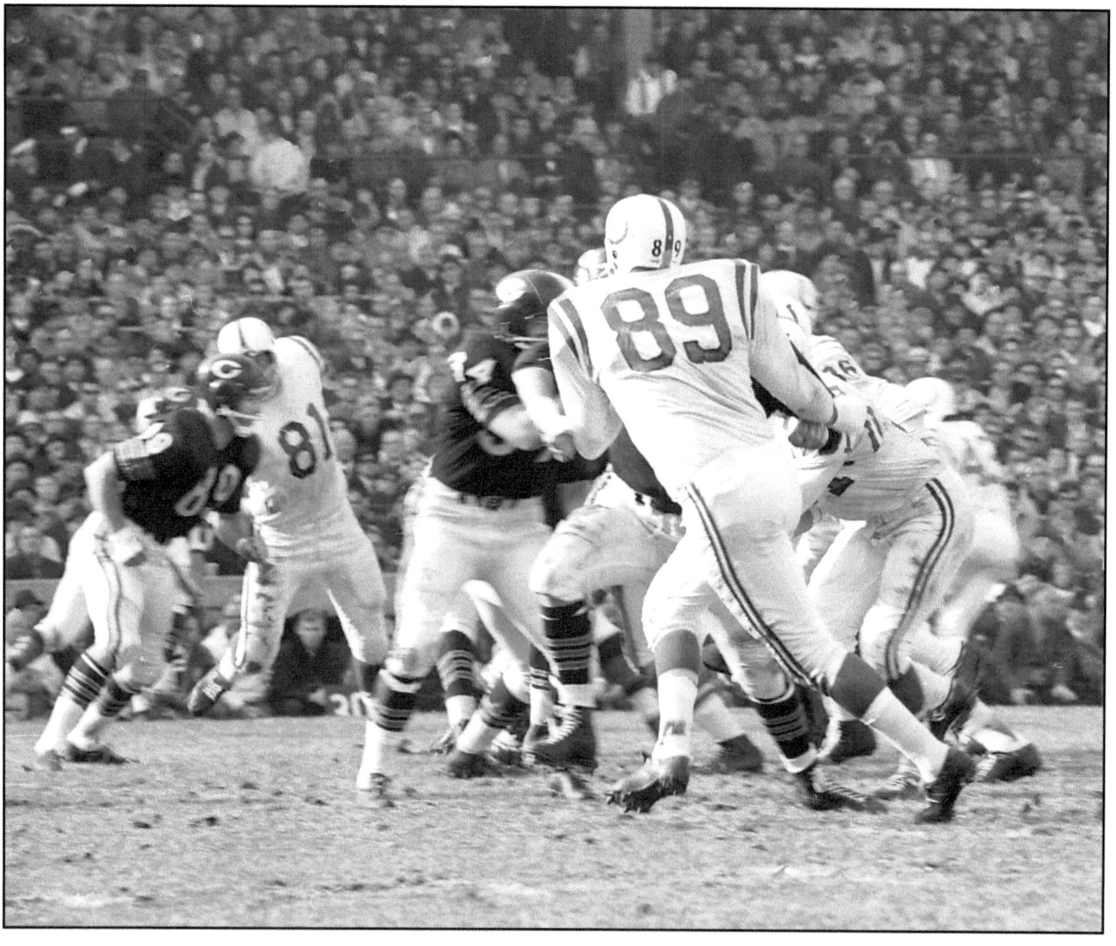

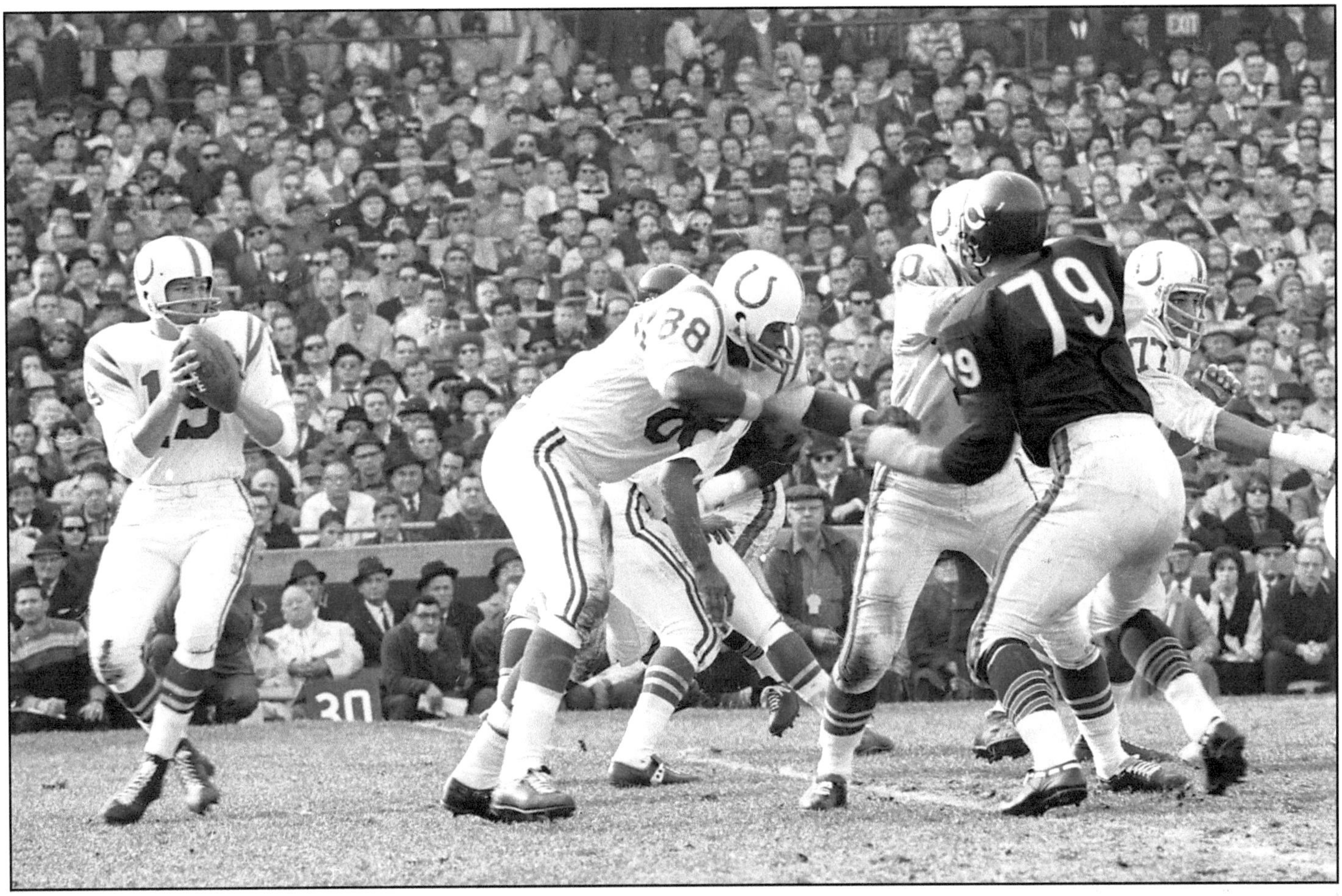

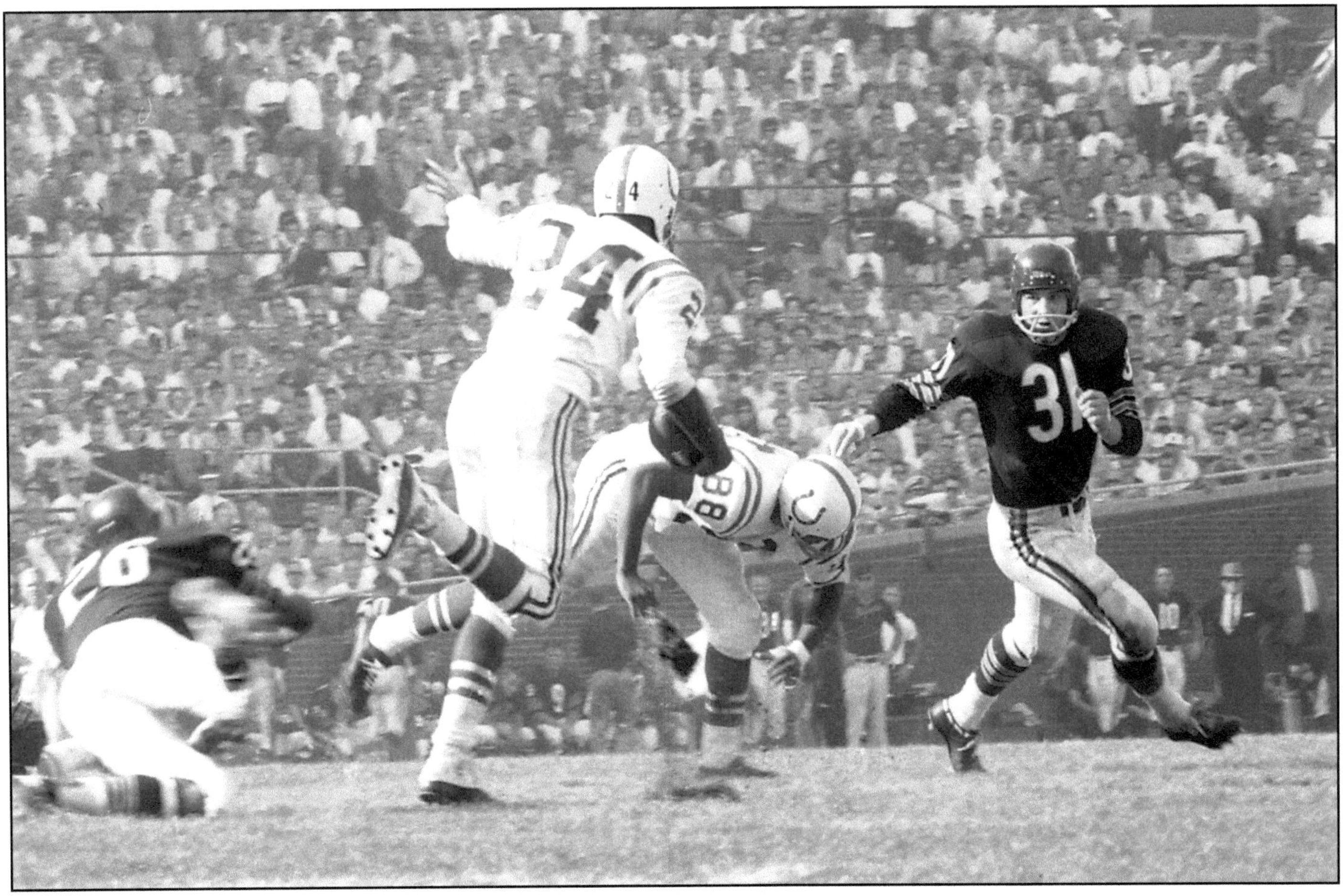

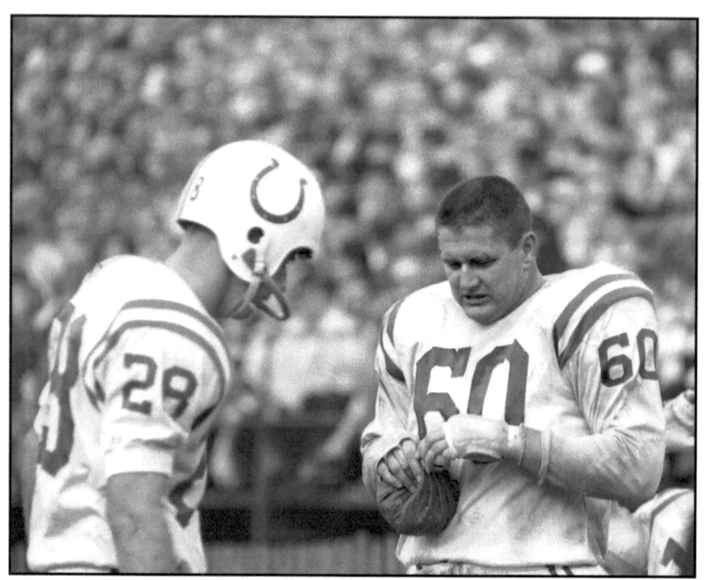

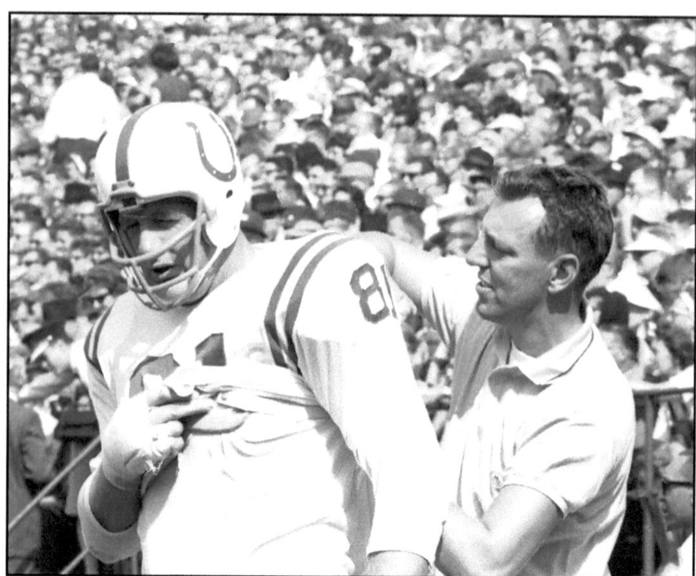

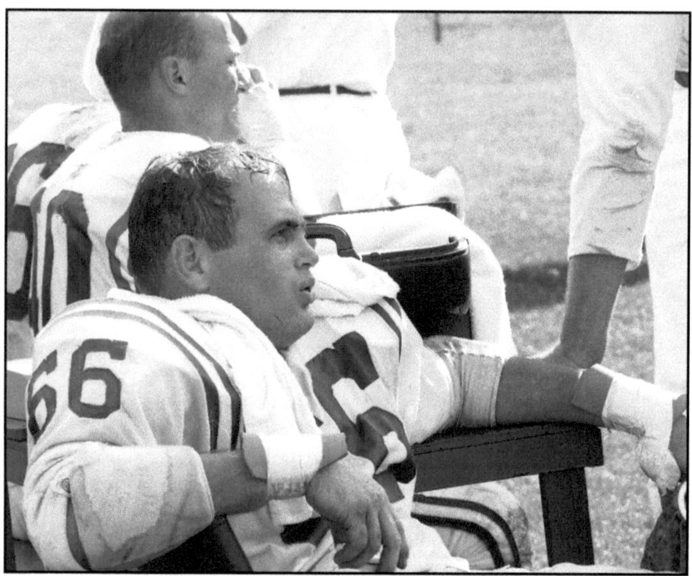

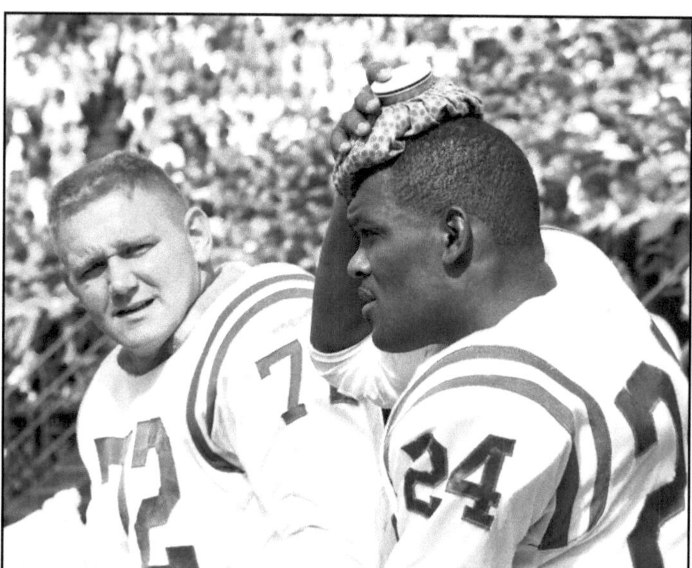

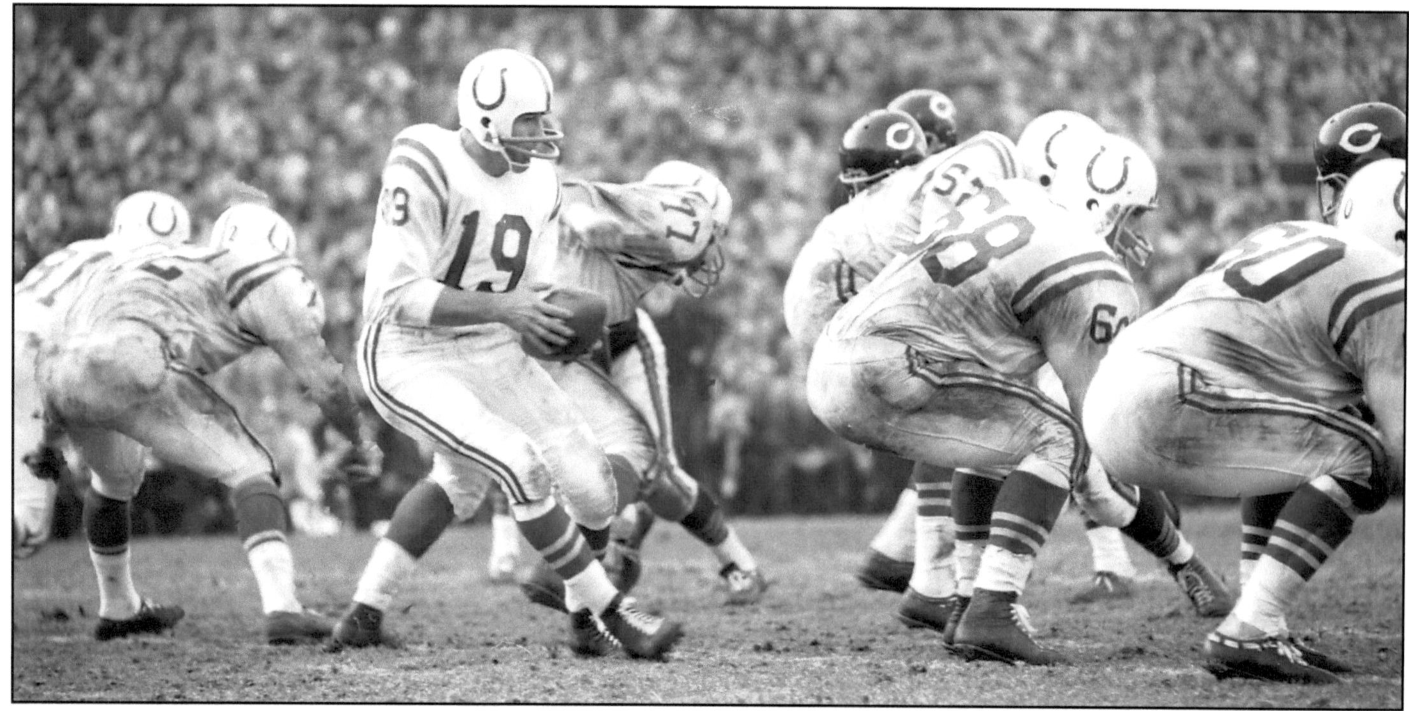

MINNESOTA VIKINGS

	Bears	Vikings
1961	52	35
1962	31	30
1963	17	17
1964	14	41
1965	17	24
1966	41	28
1967	10	10
1968	26	24
1960	0	31

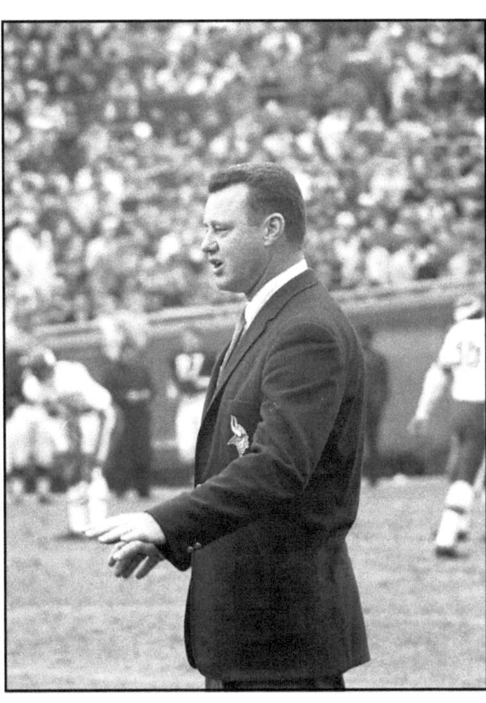

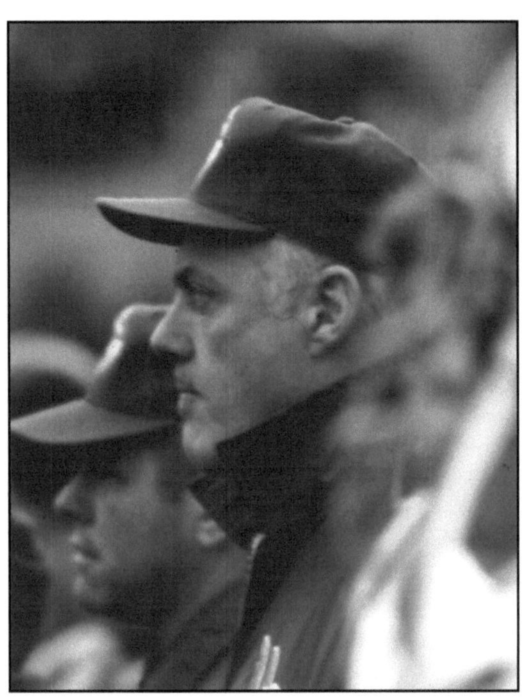

The Vikings opening game as a franchise took place on September 17,1961. Quarterback Fran Tarkenton countered a relatively slow start by the team by taking over starting duties and eventually beating the Bears that year by a score of 37-13. Head coach Norm Van Brocklin, former Eagles quarterback, brought the team to a 2-11-1 season as the team settled in.

In 1963 the Vikings came on strong beating a formidable 49ers squad twice. Minnesota faced the Bears who would go on to be champions that year and came away with a 17-17 tie. Paul Flatley a receiver form Northwestern was named NFL rookie of the year with a team leading 51 receptions.

1964 saw the Vikings winning all pre season games and also their first regular season game against Green Bay. They went on to a record of 8-5-1 after going unbeaten in the final four games. After an up and down season in 1965 with a final record of 7-7 Van Brocklin resigned as head coach. He later changed his mind and continued to coach through 1966 during which he and Tarkenton rarely spoke. The Vikings won only one of their first six games that year.

Van Brocklin resigned again in 1967 and Bud Grant took over the reins as coach. The team was able to upset Green Bay, who would later go on to win the Super Bowl, by a field goal with a score of 10-7. By 1968 the Vikings had one of the most formidable defensive lines in the league with Eller, Page,Larsen and Marshall. Minnesota made it to the playoffs but lost in the first round to Baltimore.

Although the Vikings opened the 1969 season with a loss to the Giants, the team rallied for an eleven game winning streak. They won the Western Conference Championship but lost in the Super Bowl to Kansas City 23-7.

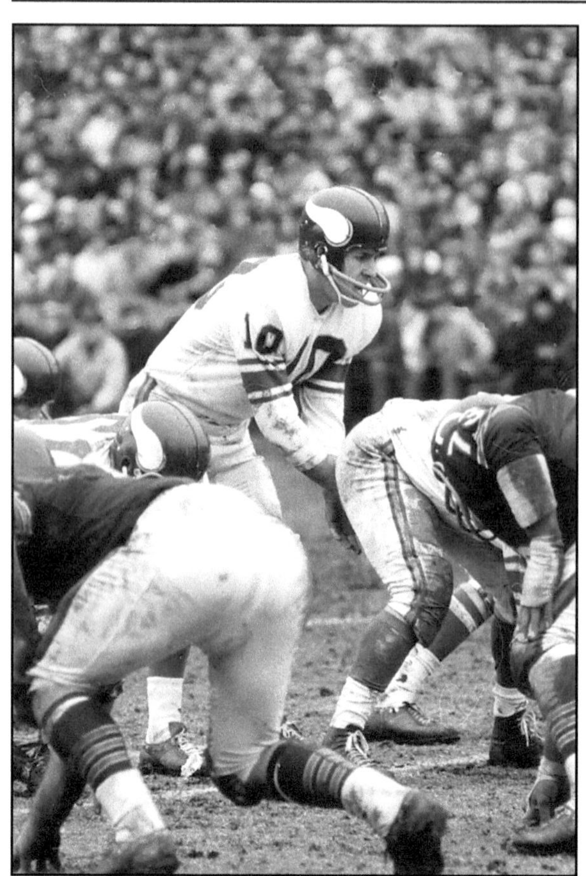

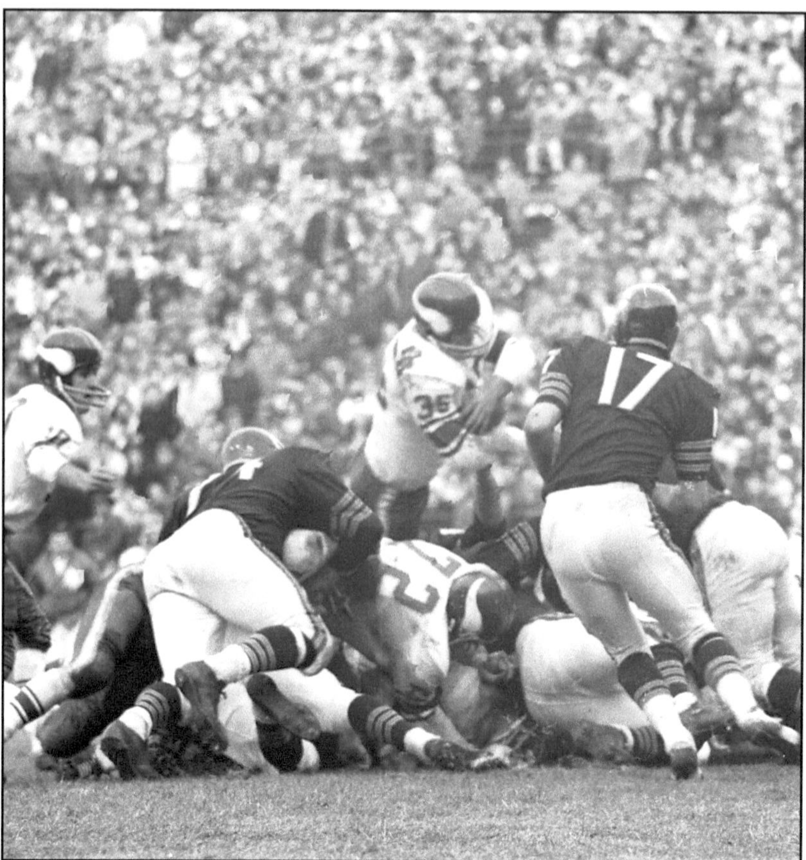

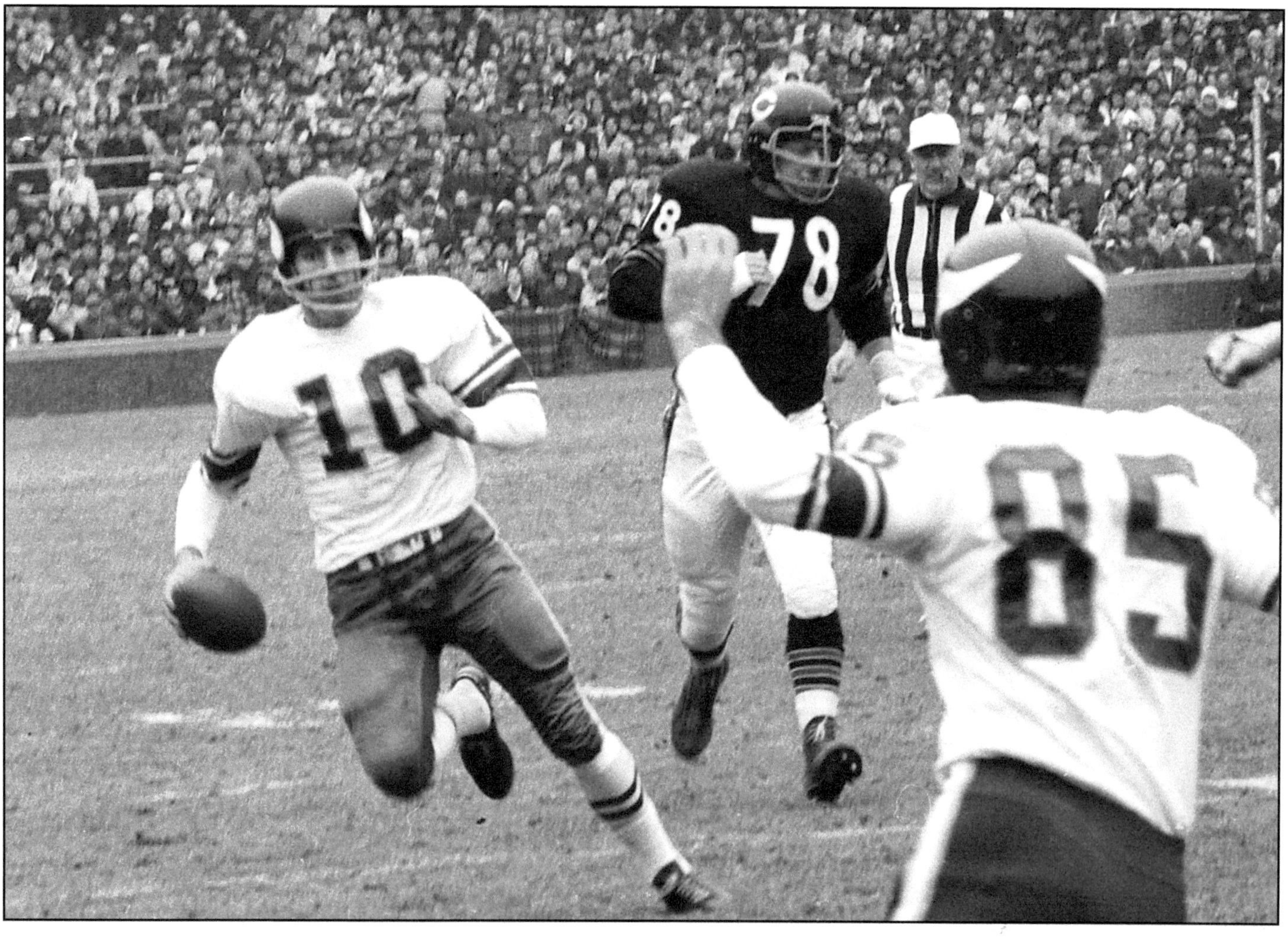

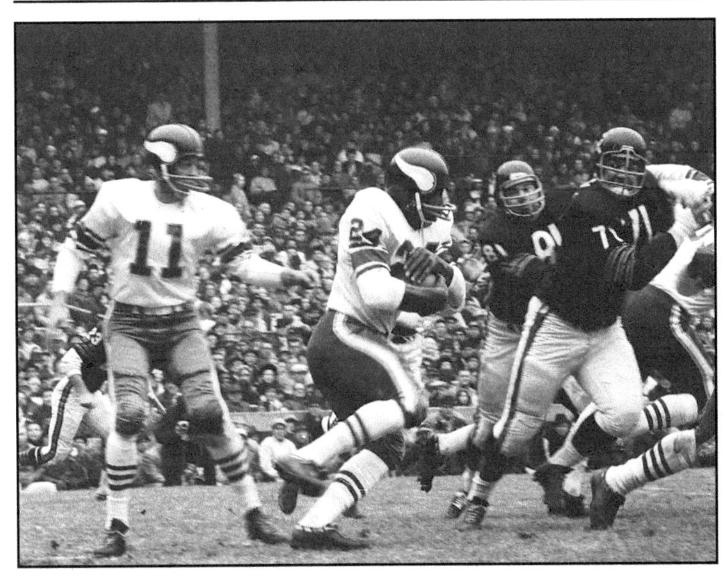

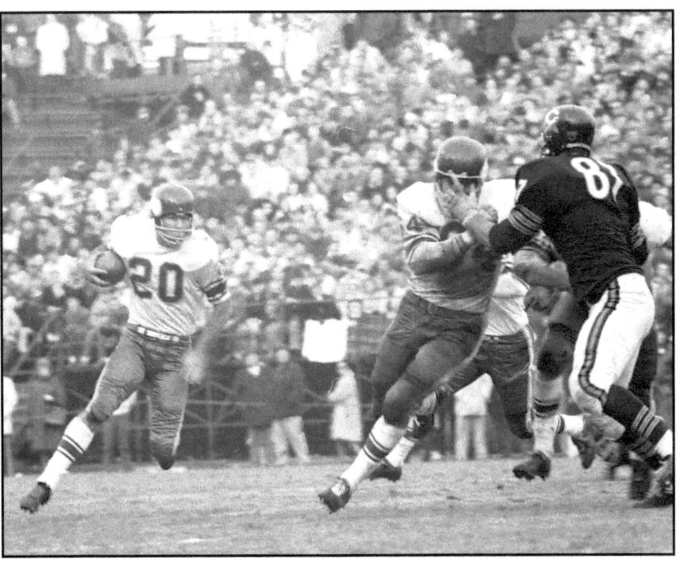

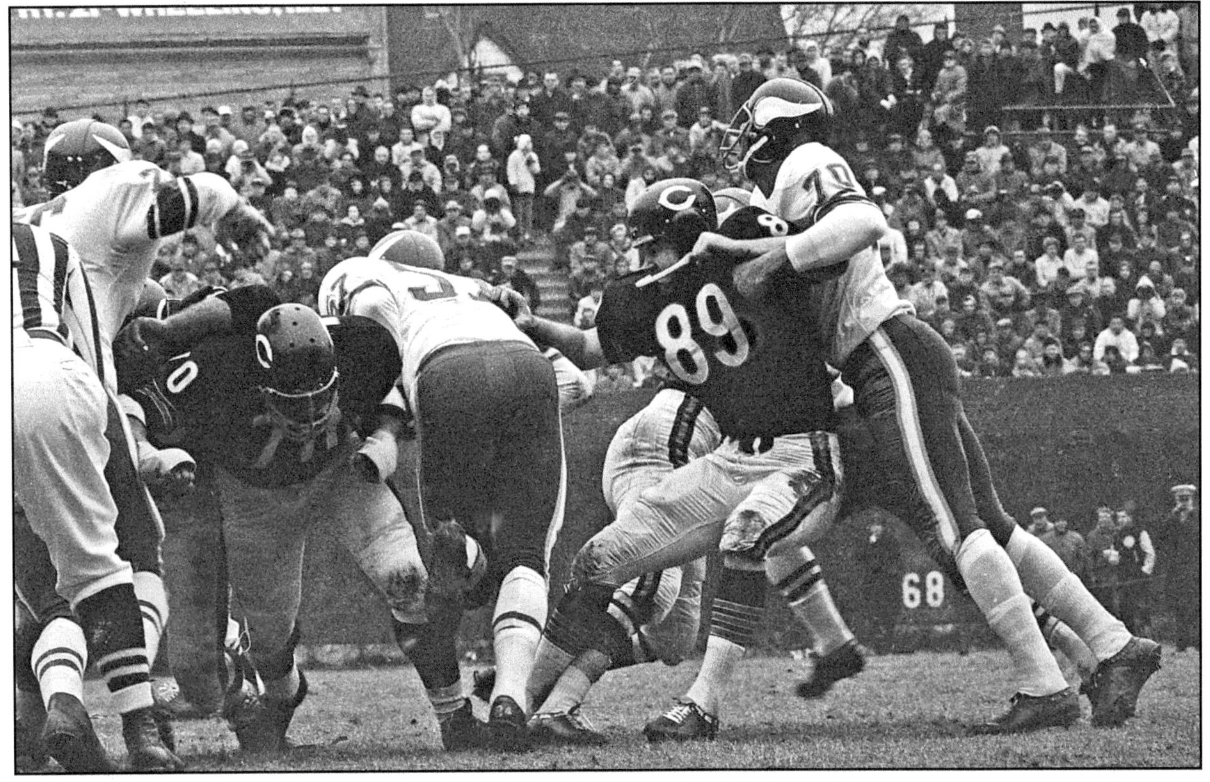

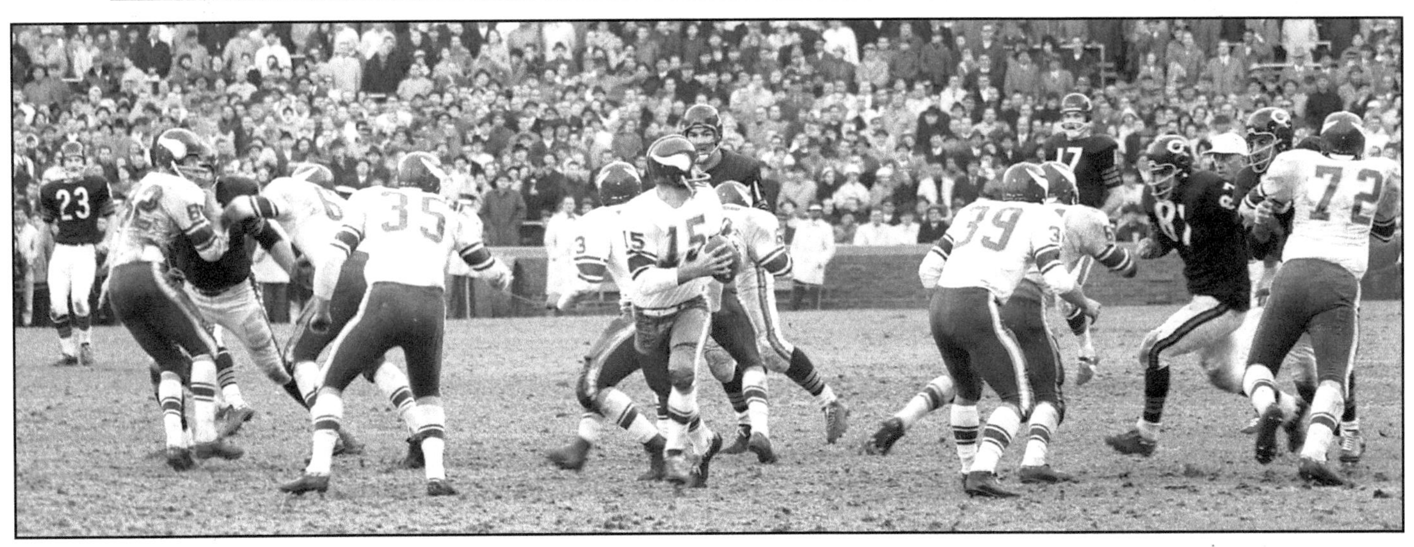

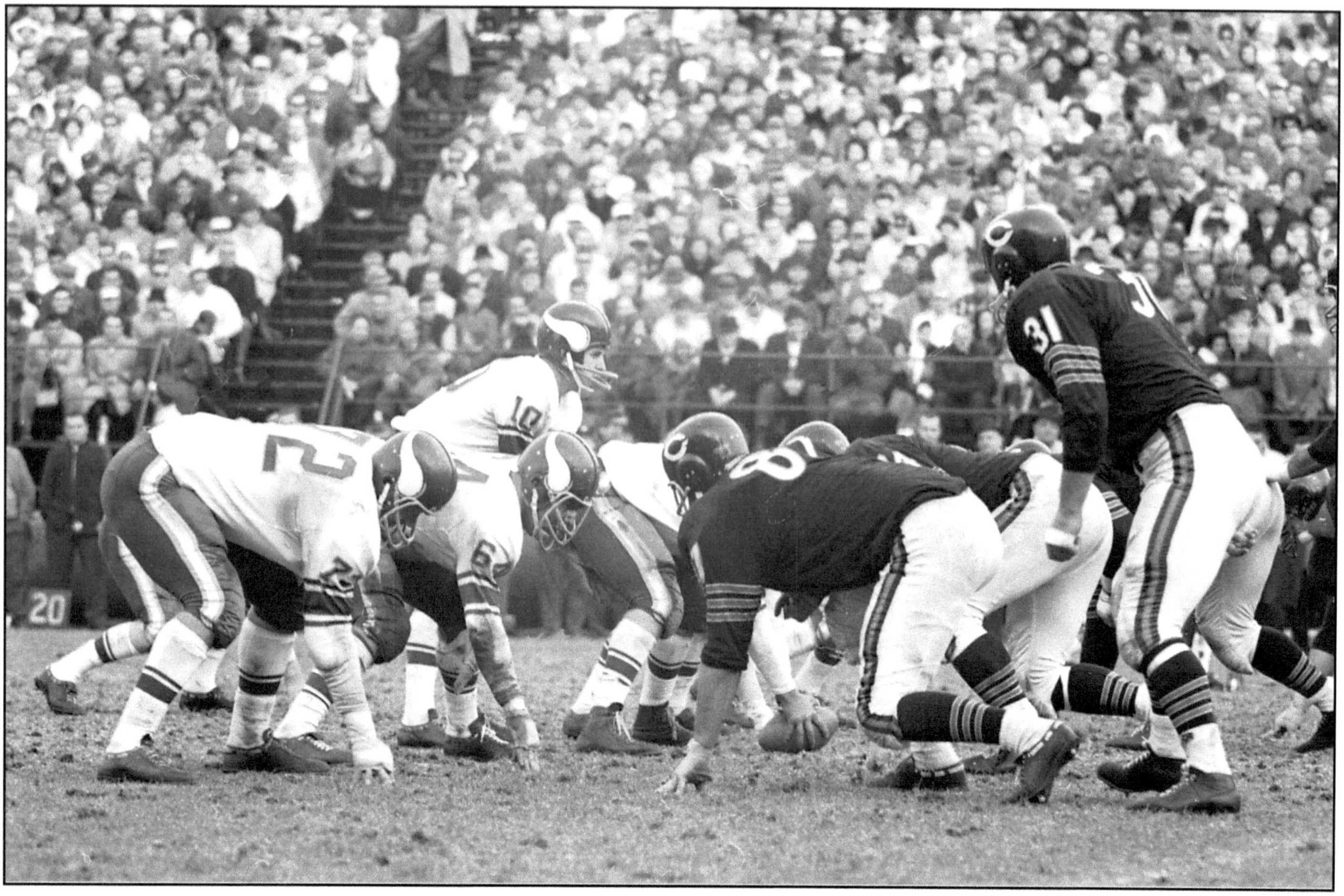

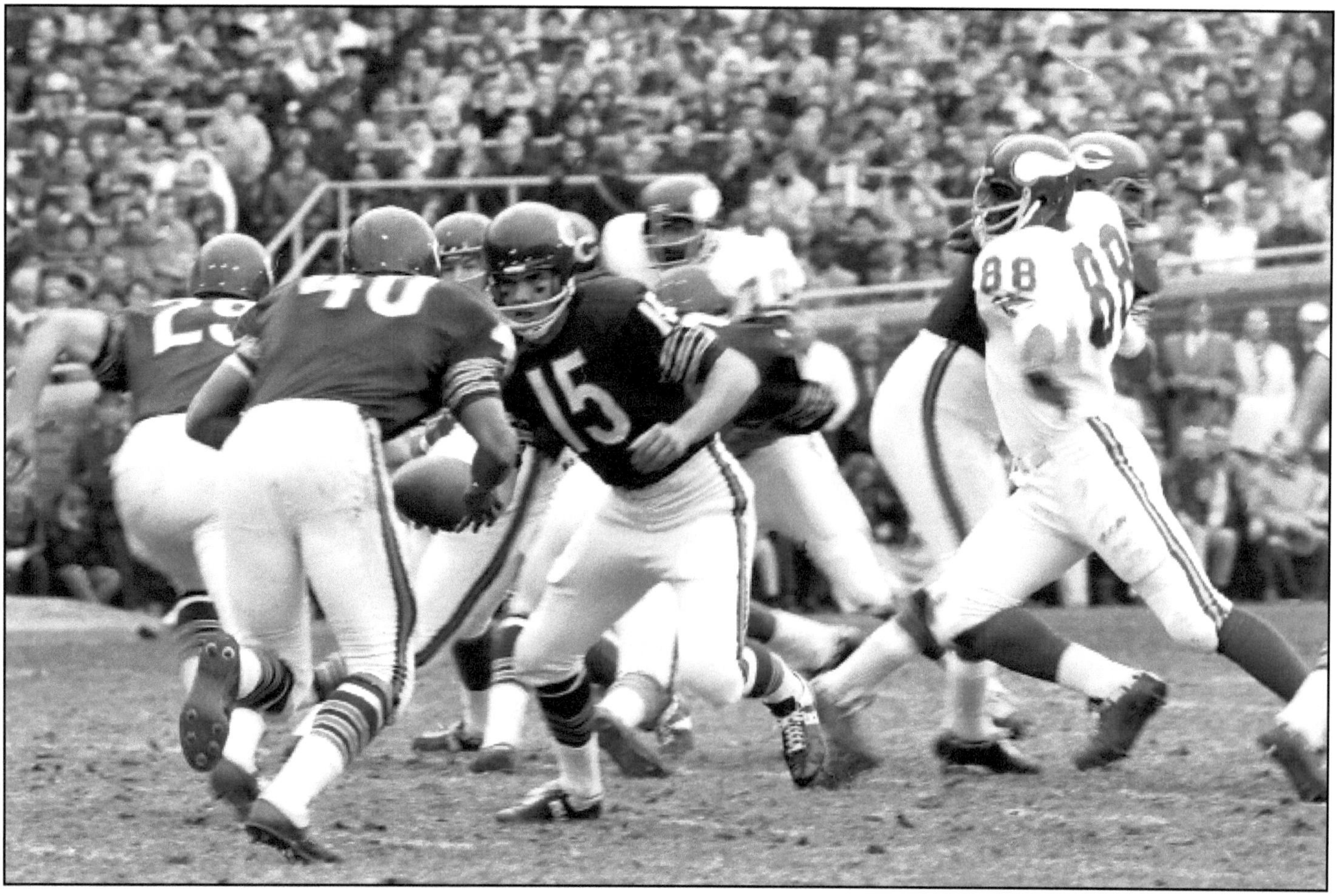

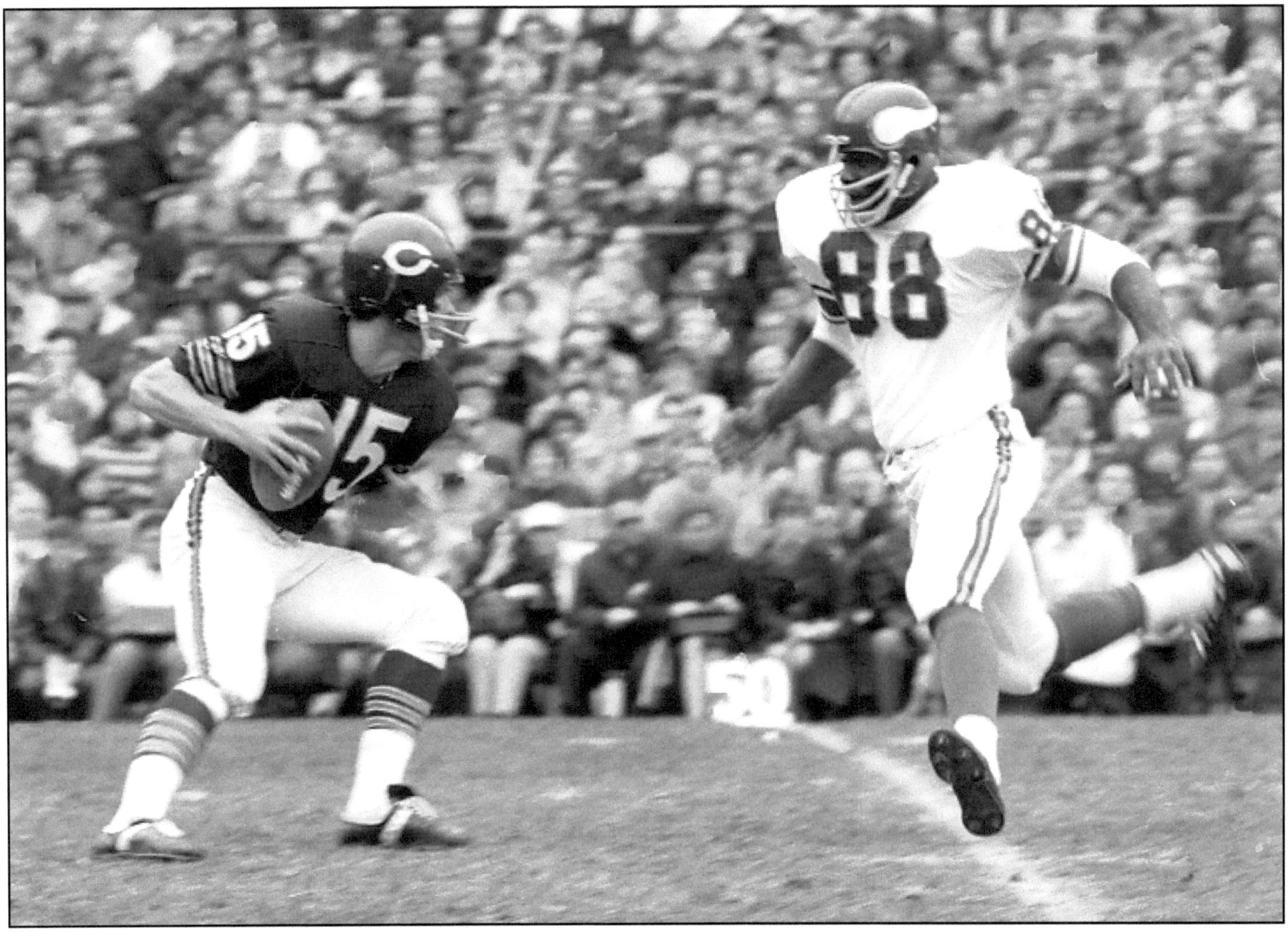

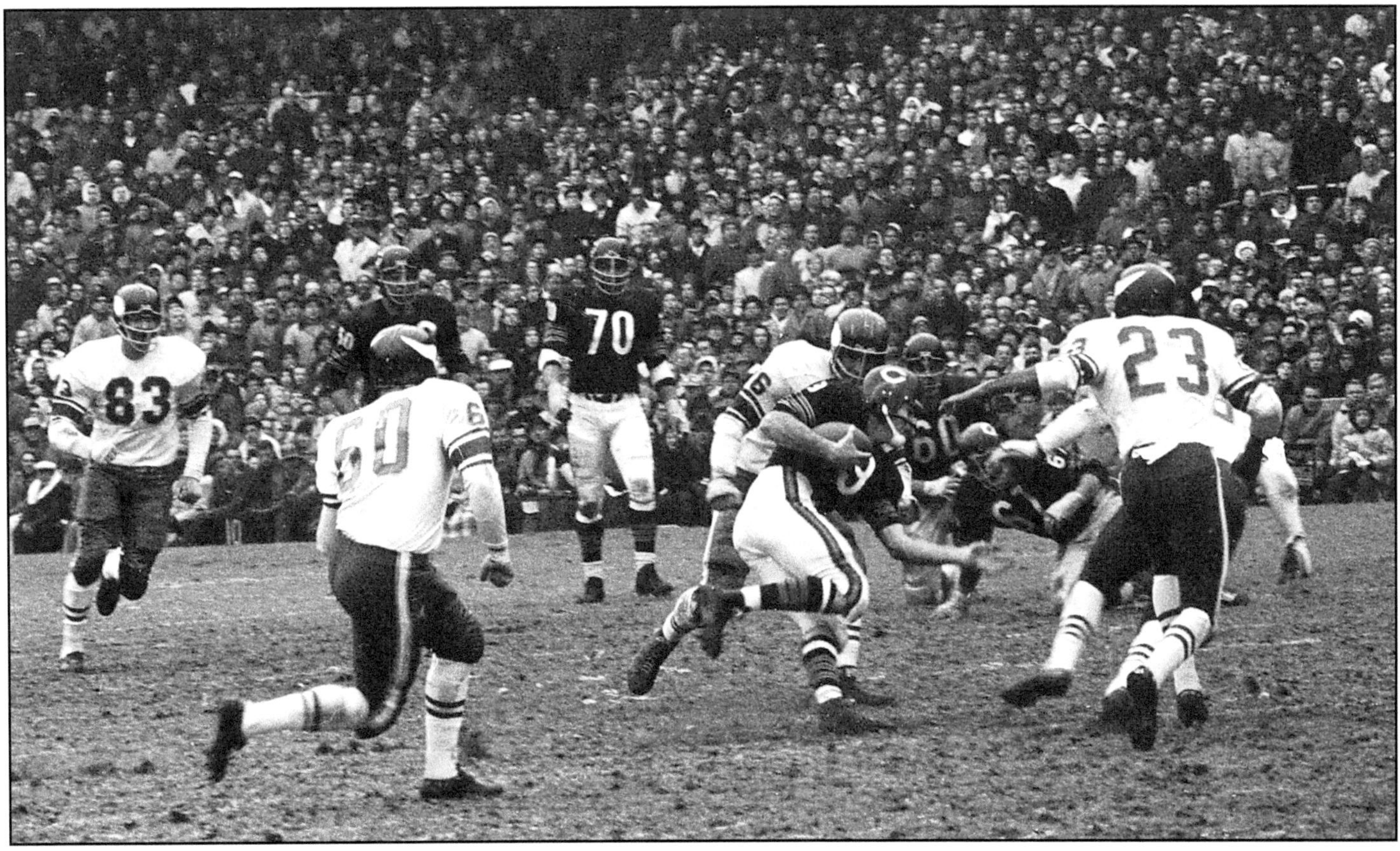

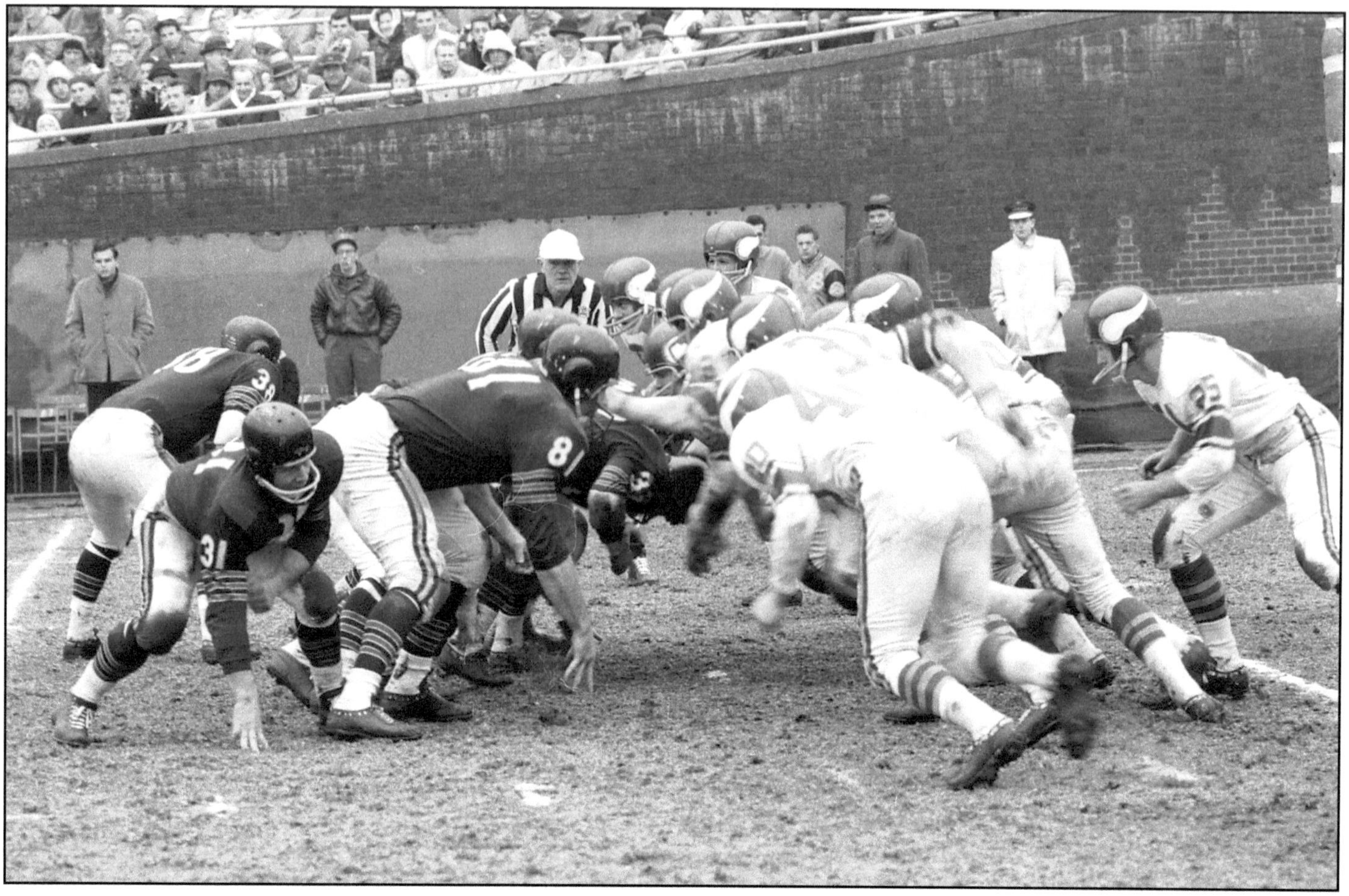

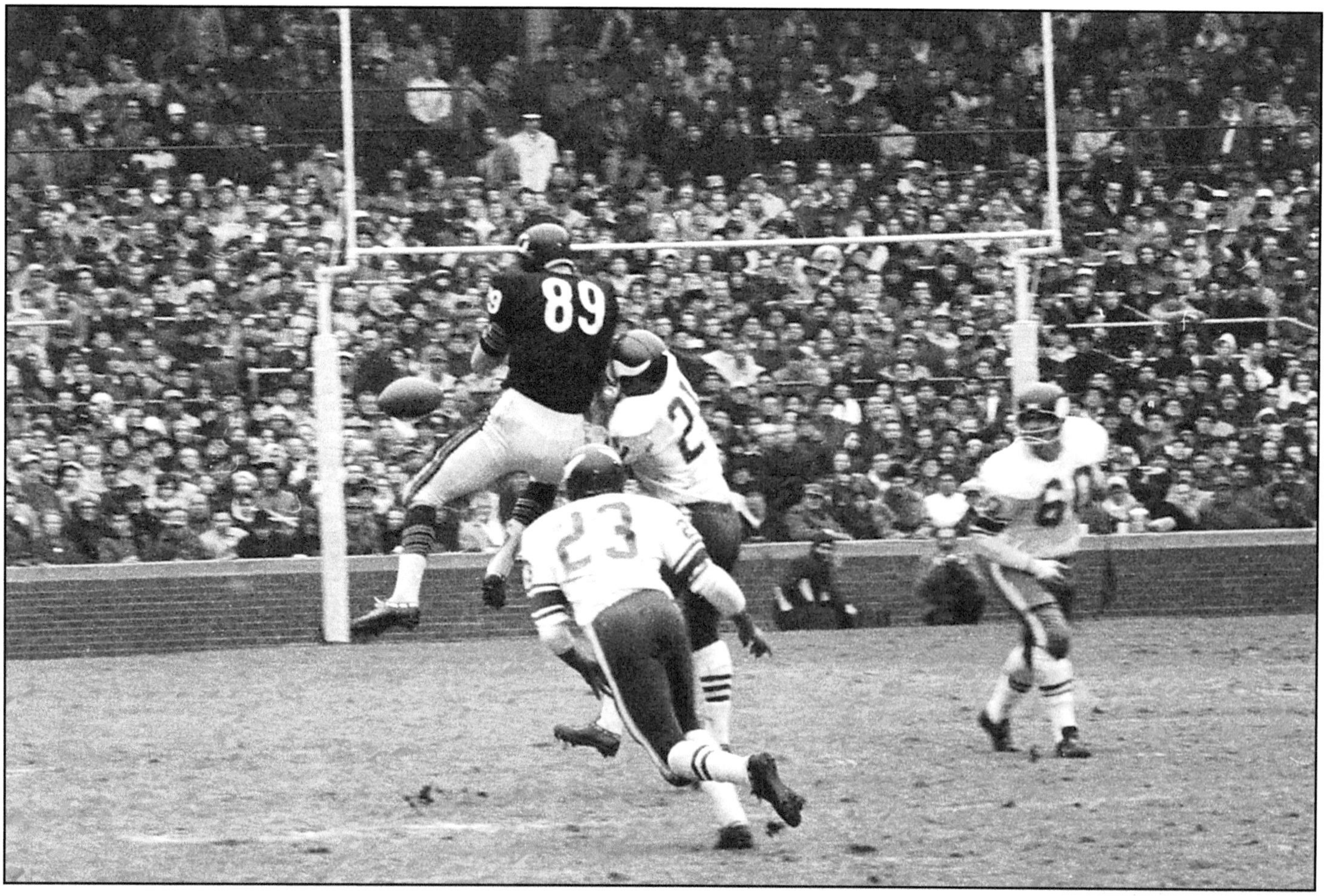

LOS ANGELES RAMS

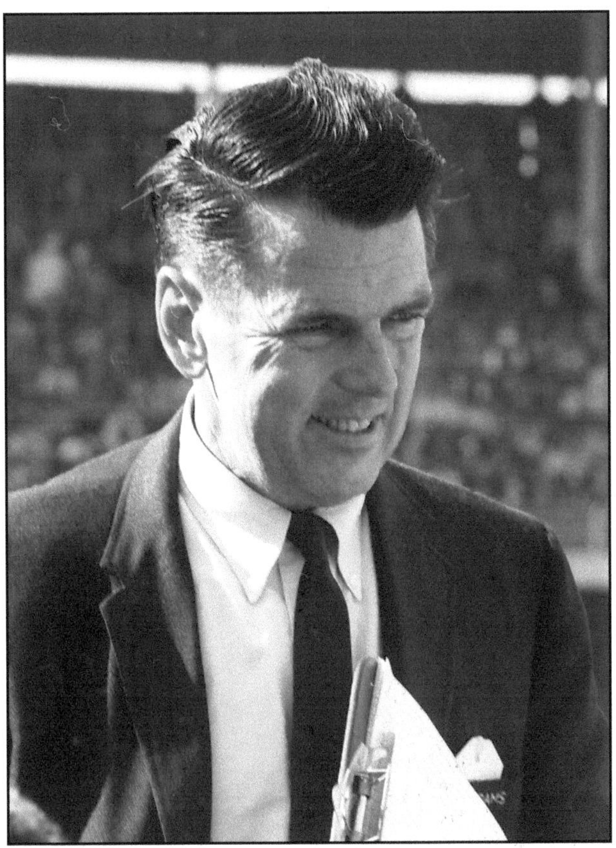

	Bears	Rams
1960	24	24
1961	20	24
1962	30	14
1963	6	0
1964	38	17
1965	31	6
1966	17	10
1967	17	28

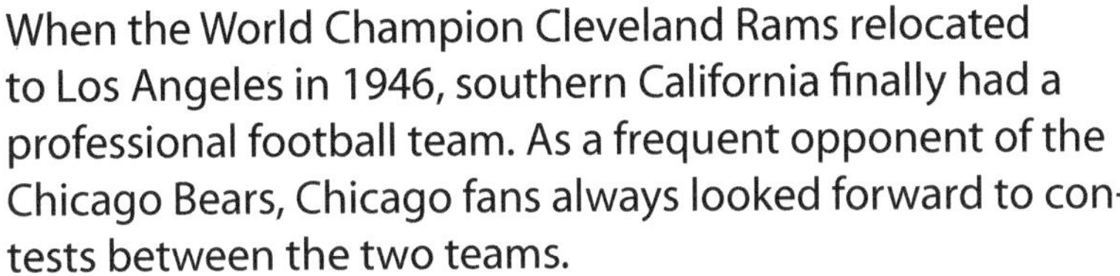

When the World Champion Cleveland Rams relocated to Los Angeles in 1946, southern California finally had a professional football team. As a frequent opponent of the Chicago Bears, Chicago fans always looked forward to contests between the two teams.

In 1960 after the death of NFL Commissioner Bert Bell, Rams GM Pete Rozelle was named to replace Bell. Former Rams WR Crazy Legs Hirsh replaced Rozelle as Rams GM. The Rams compiled a record of 4-10 in 1961, probably due in part to the trade of Bill Wade, Del Shofner and John Guzik to the Bears.

Quarterback Roman Gabriel joined the Rams along with DT Merlin Olson in 1962, both of whom would start for the team for the next decade. The Rams, however, finished this season with a lowly 4-10 record. In 1963 the Rams also acquired Rosey Grier who would join Olson, Deacon Jones, and Lamar Lundy to form the legendary Fearsome Foursome. Deacon Jones sets a record with a 22 sack season in 1964, but the Rams still finish with a mediocre 5-7-2 season.

1965 featured a slow start for the Rams with the team winning only one of their first ten games they played. The Rams manage to turn it around somewhat later in the year,winning three of their final four games. However, head coach Harland Svare is fired.

After a contentious court battle with George Halas and the Bears organization, defensive coordinator George Allen leaves Chicago to become the Rams head coach in 1966. The Rams finally notch a wining season, going 8-6.

In 1967, the Rams win their division championship. They go on to lose the Western Conference Championship to the Packers in Green Bay. By 1968,The season's record is an improved 10-3-1. The Rams finish second in their division to the Baltimore Colts.

By 1969 the Rams have won the Coastal Division title with a record of 11-3 but lose the Conference Championship to the Vikings. Roman Gabriel is named the NFL's MVP.

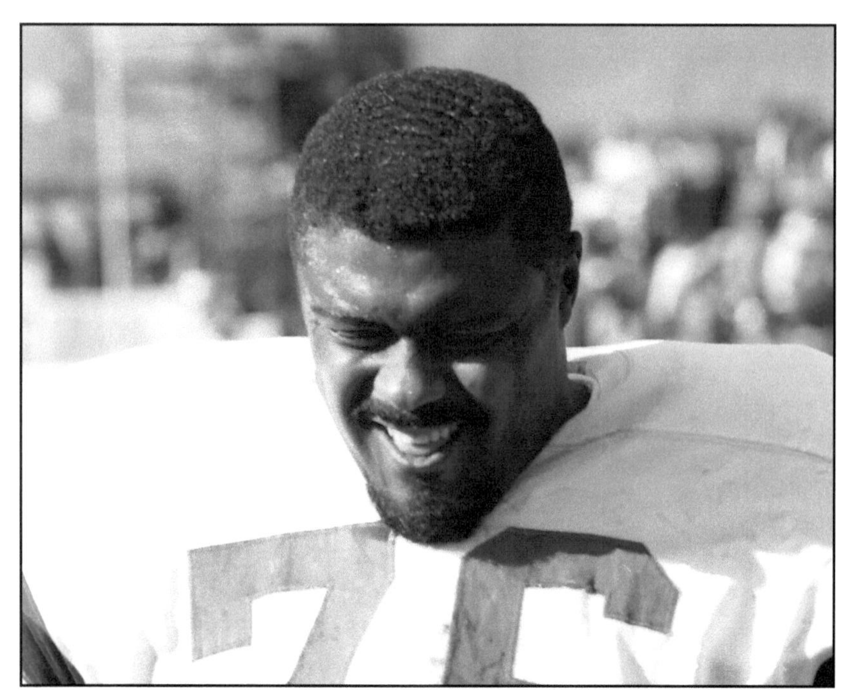

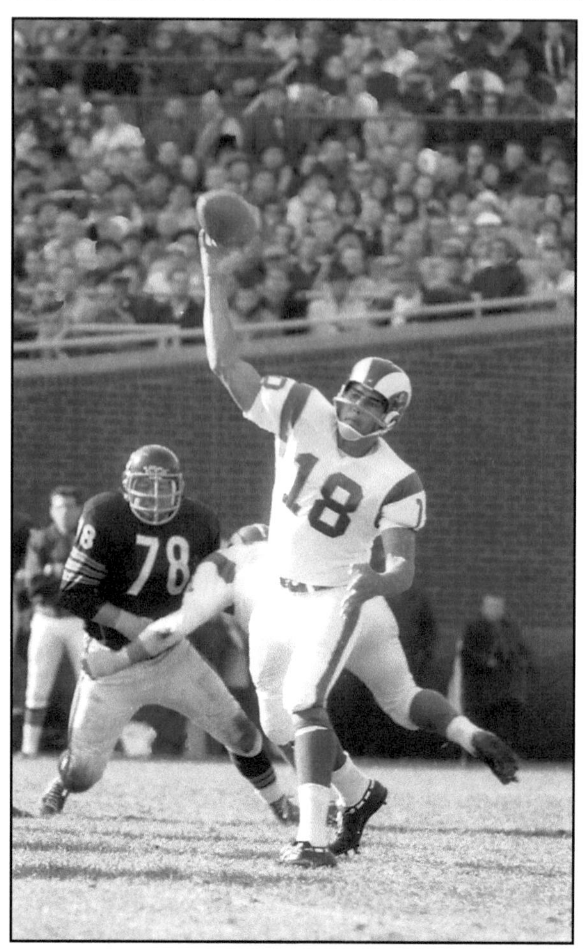

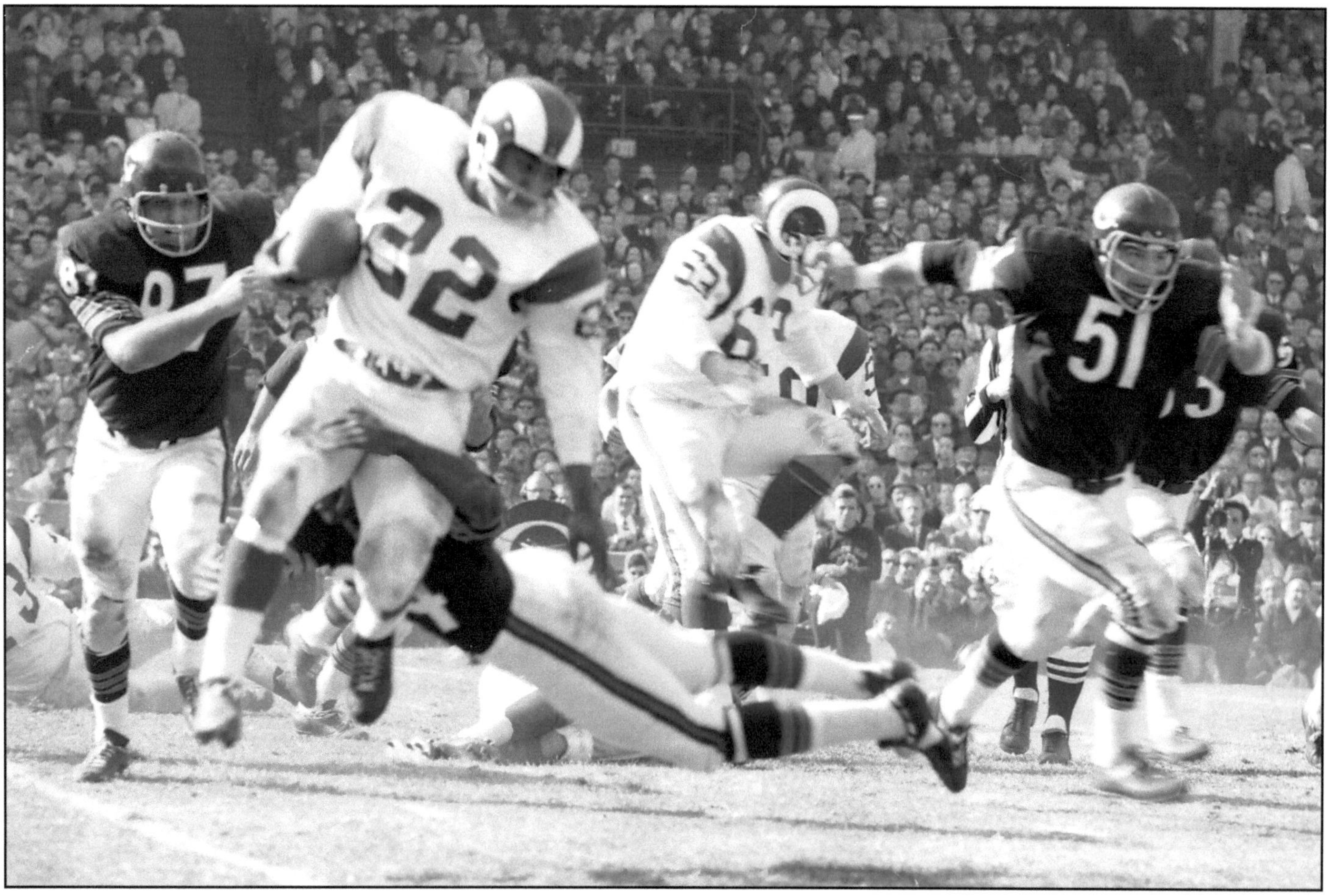

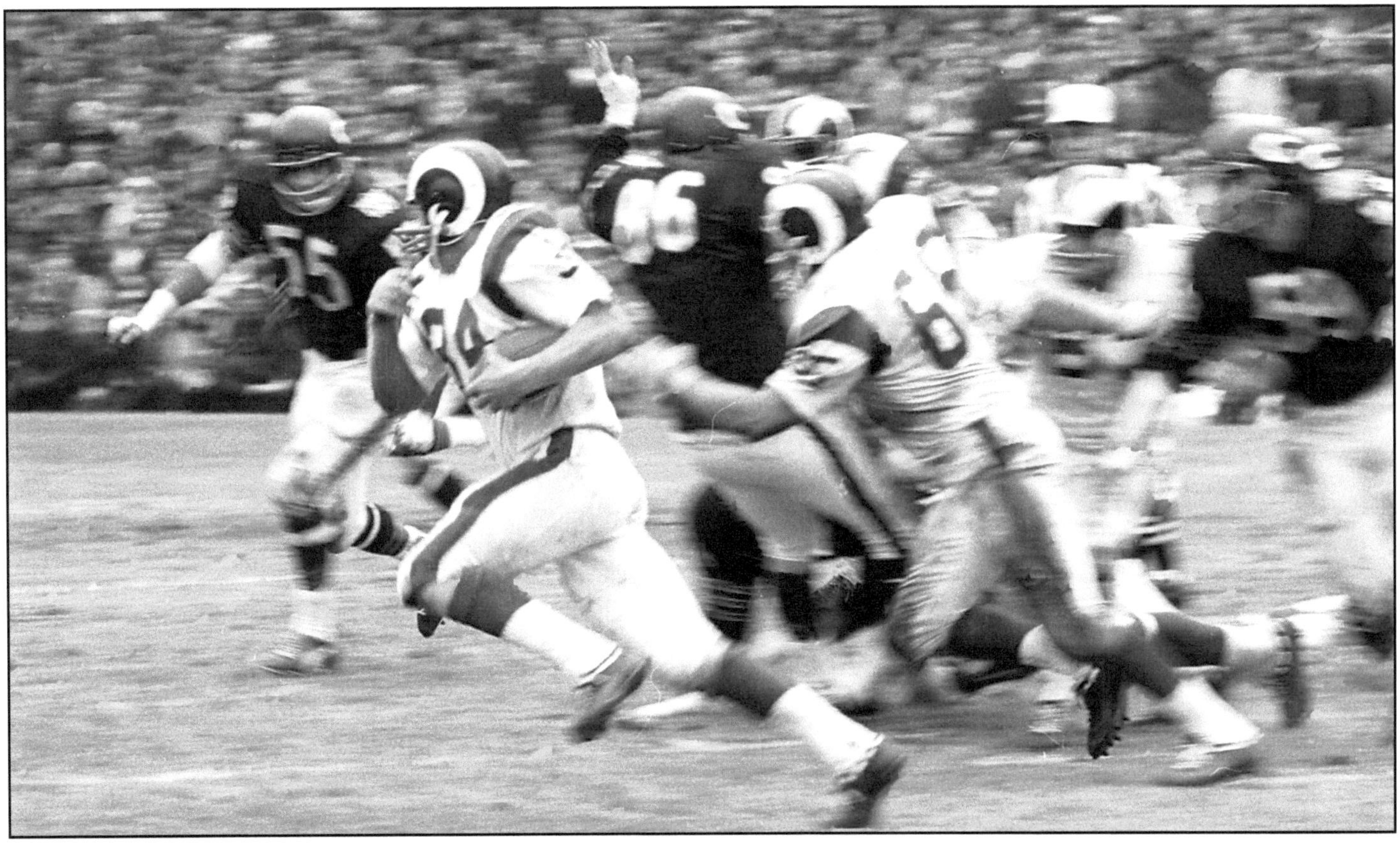

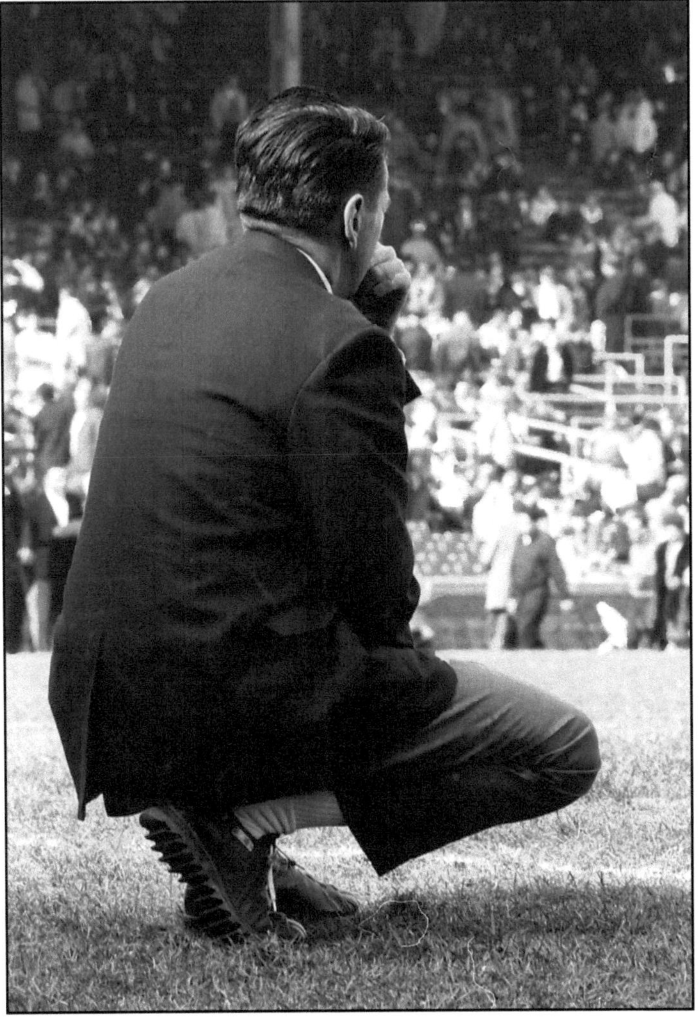

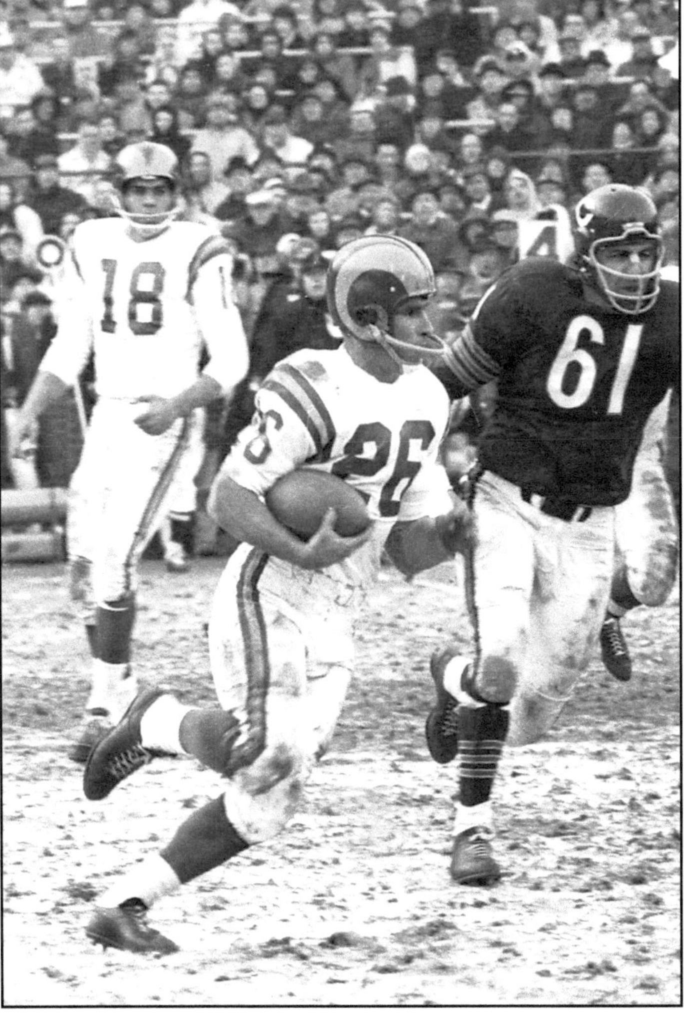
18
61

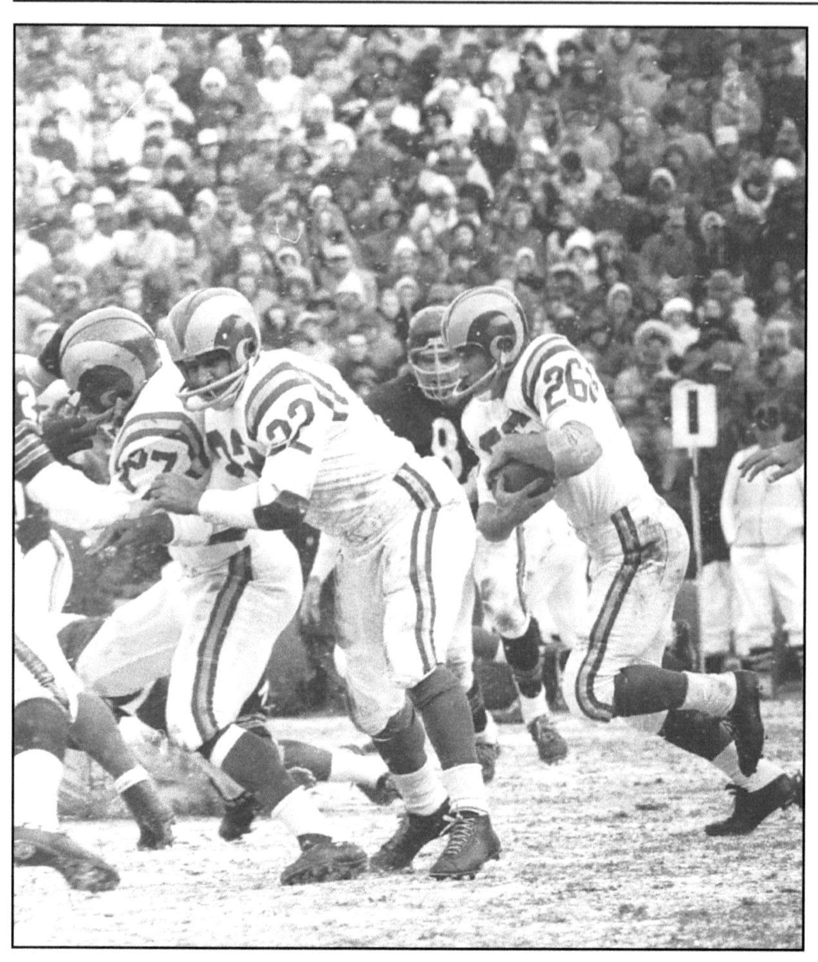

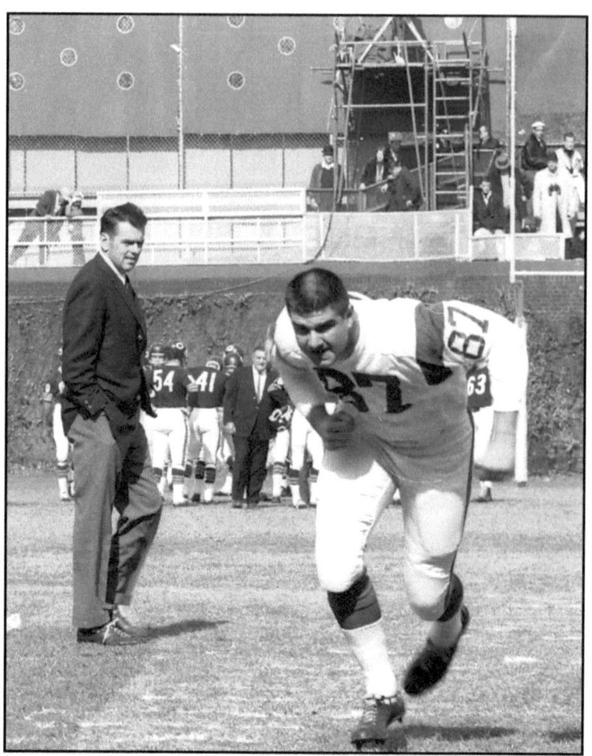

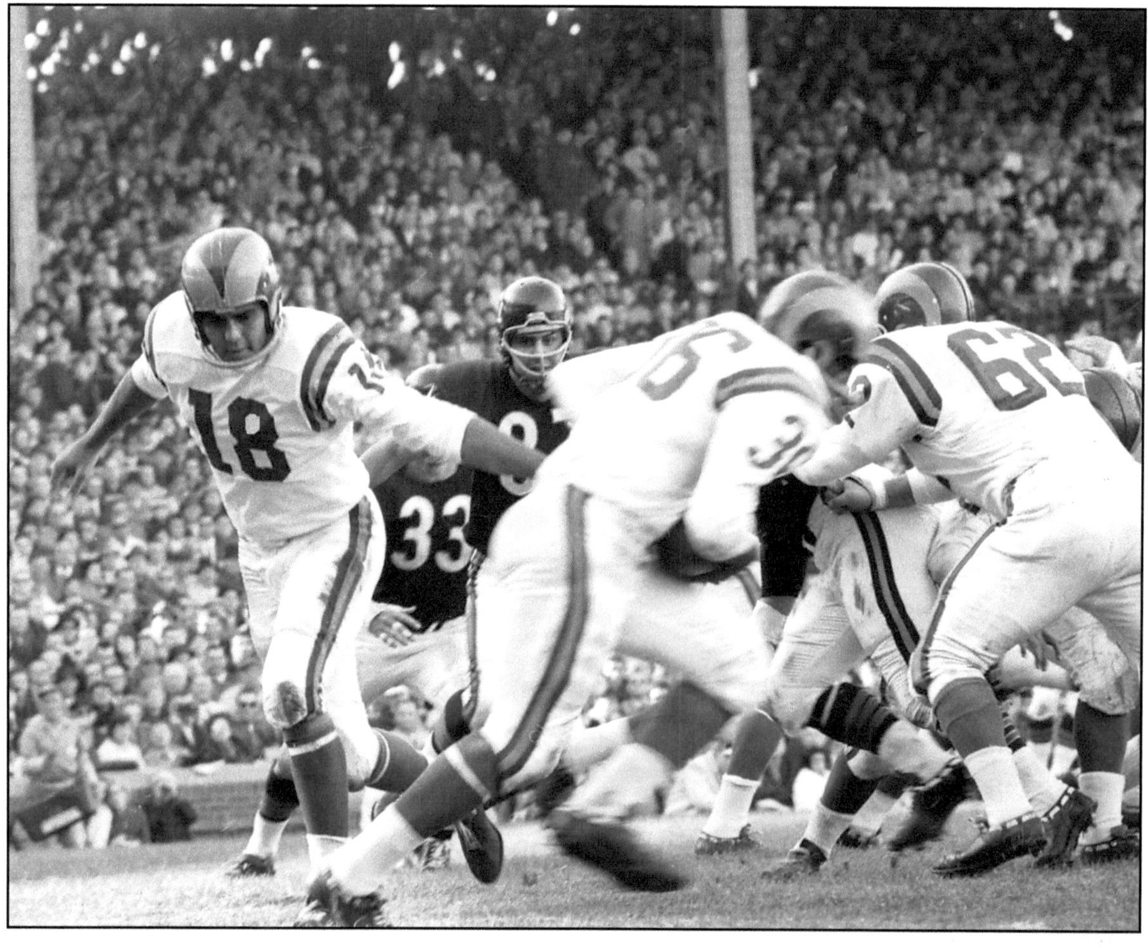

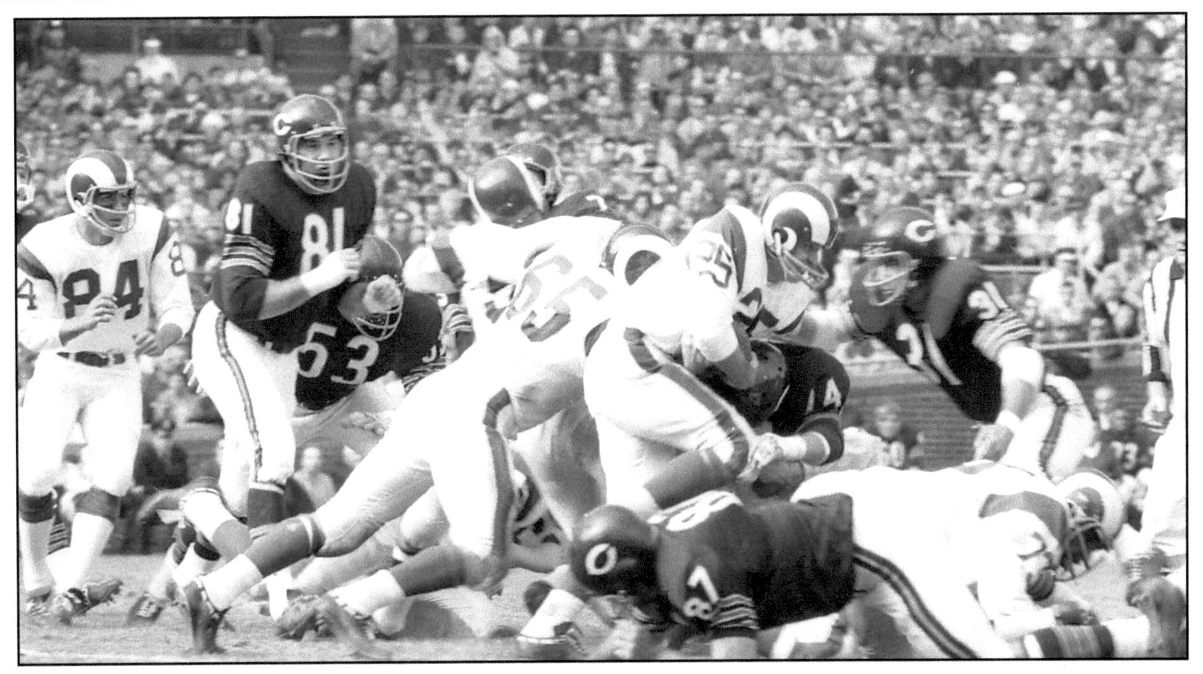

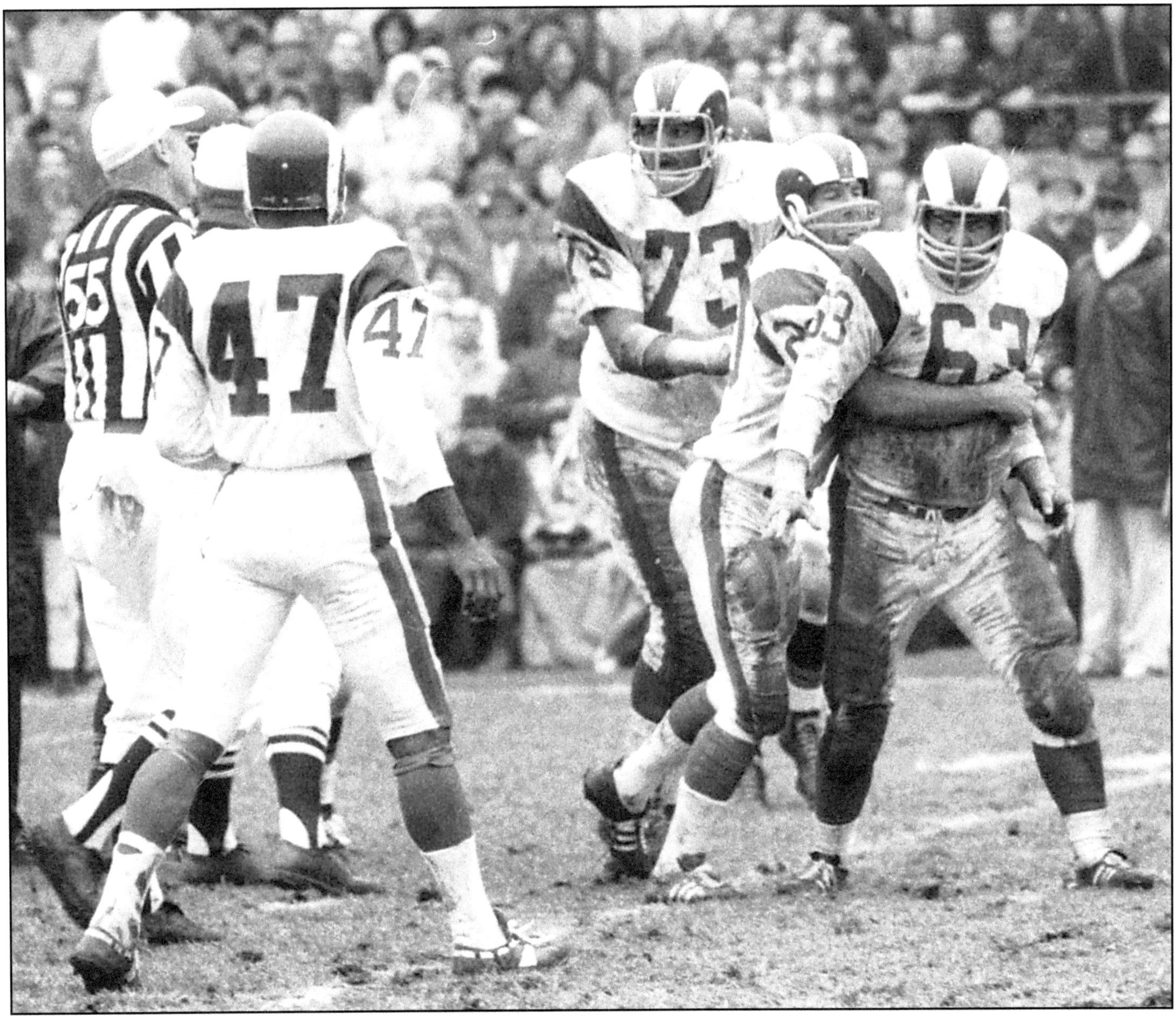

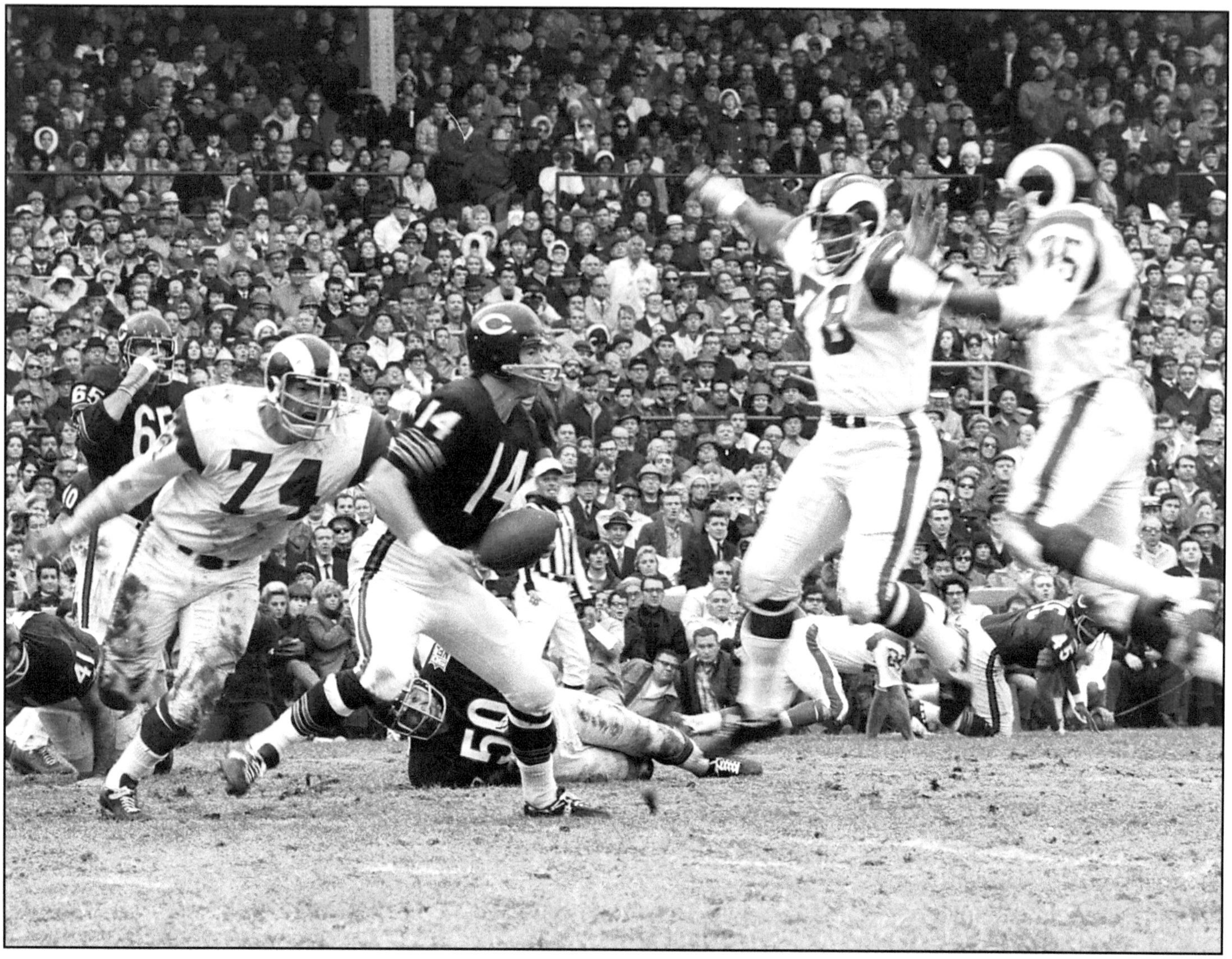

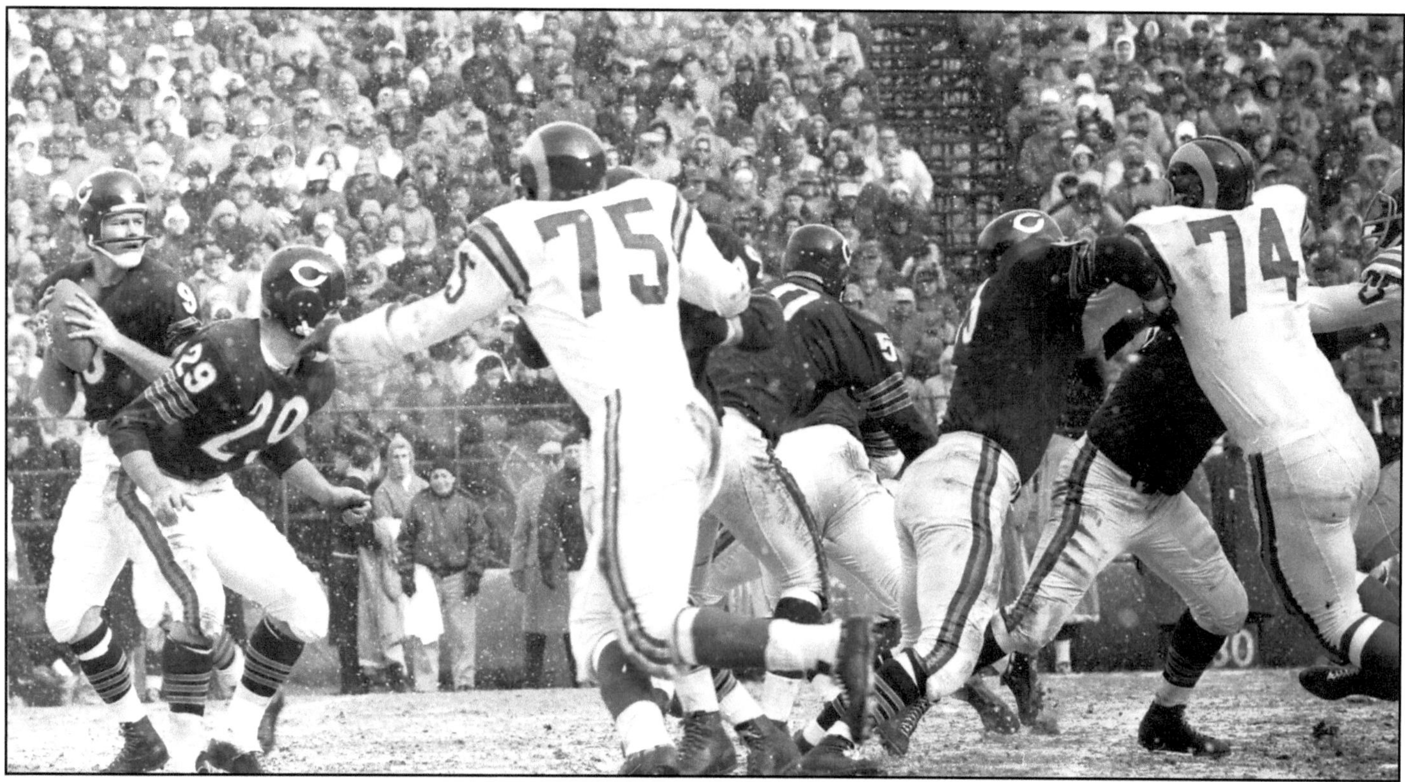

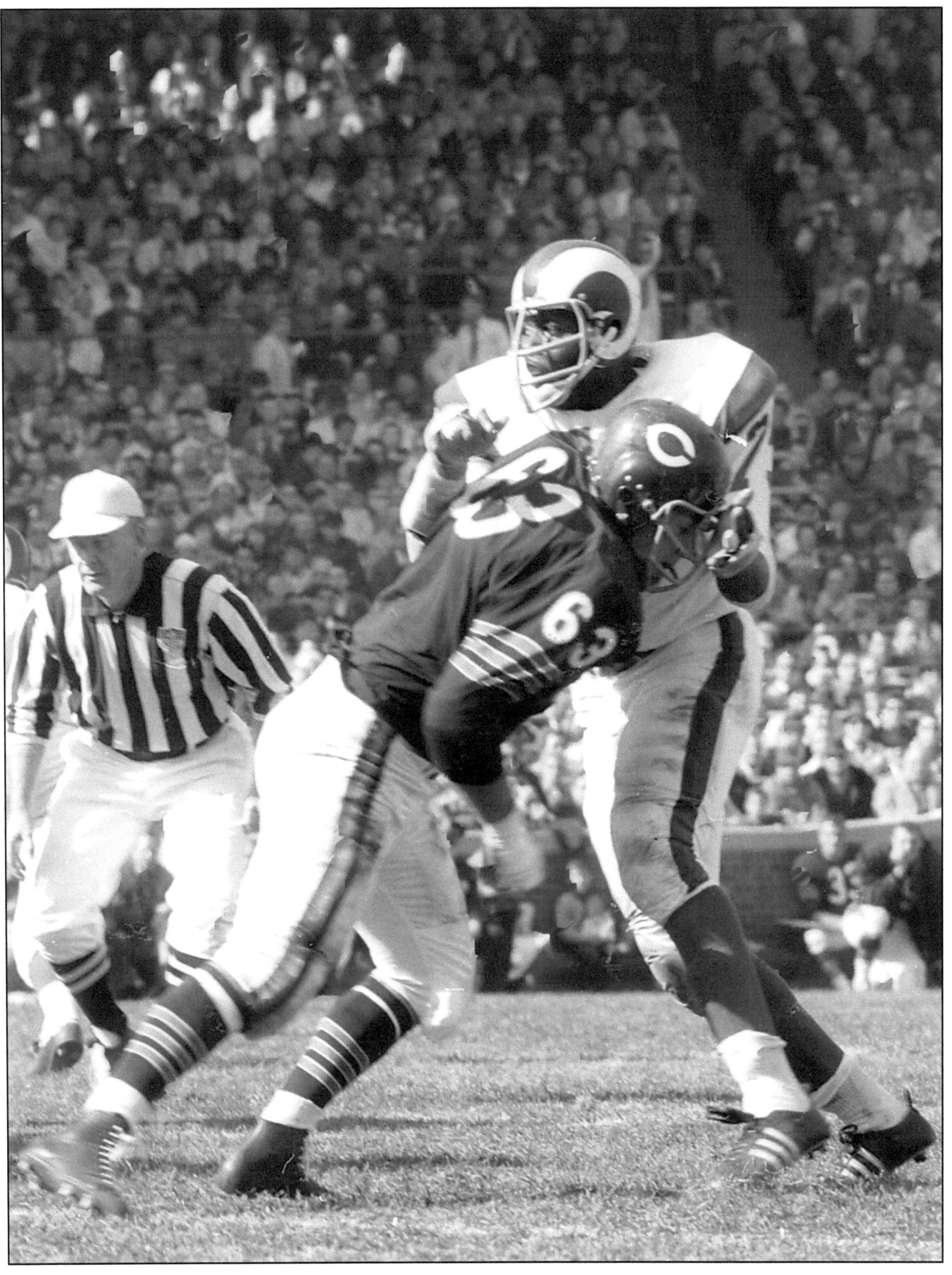
83
63

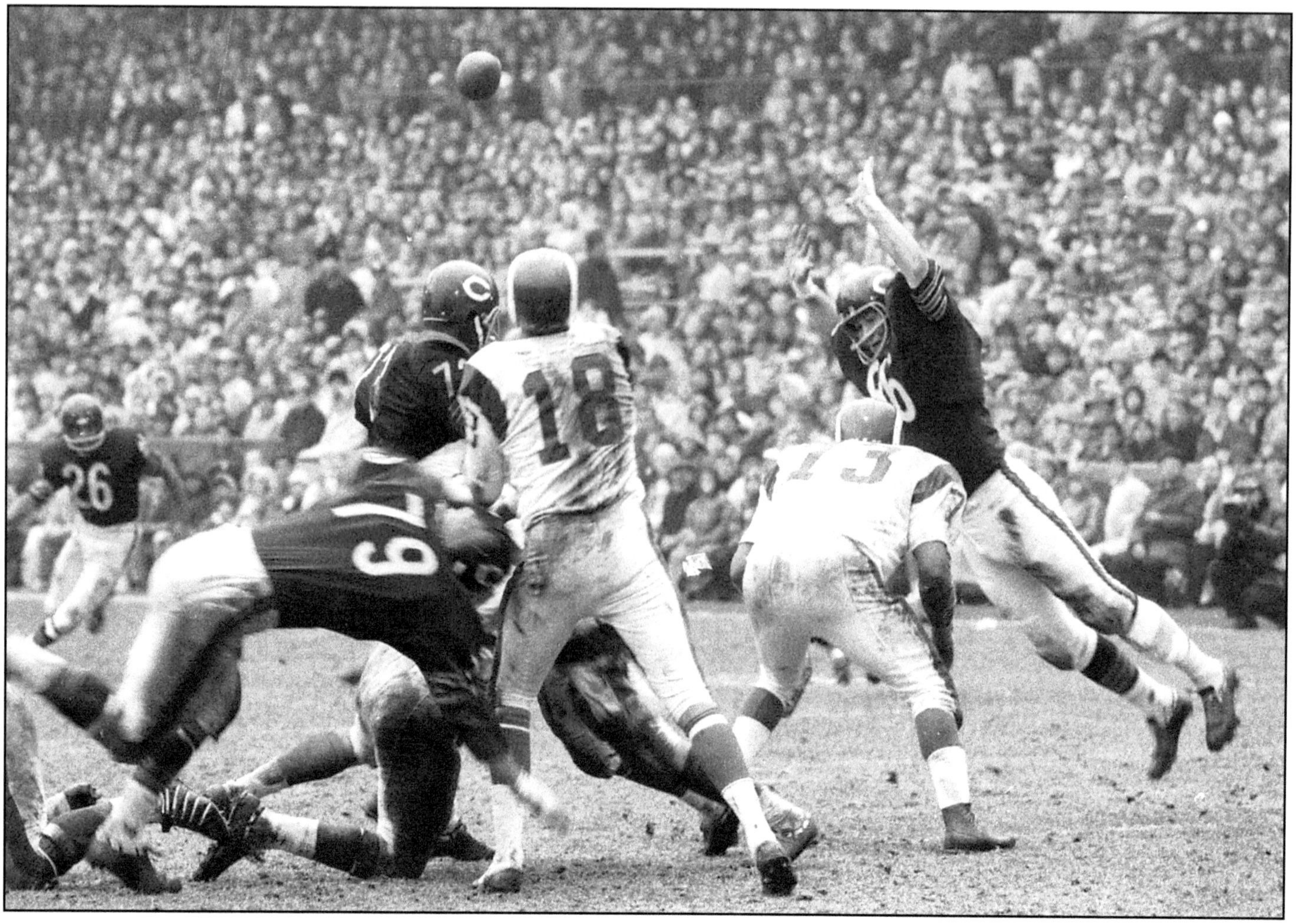

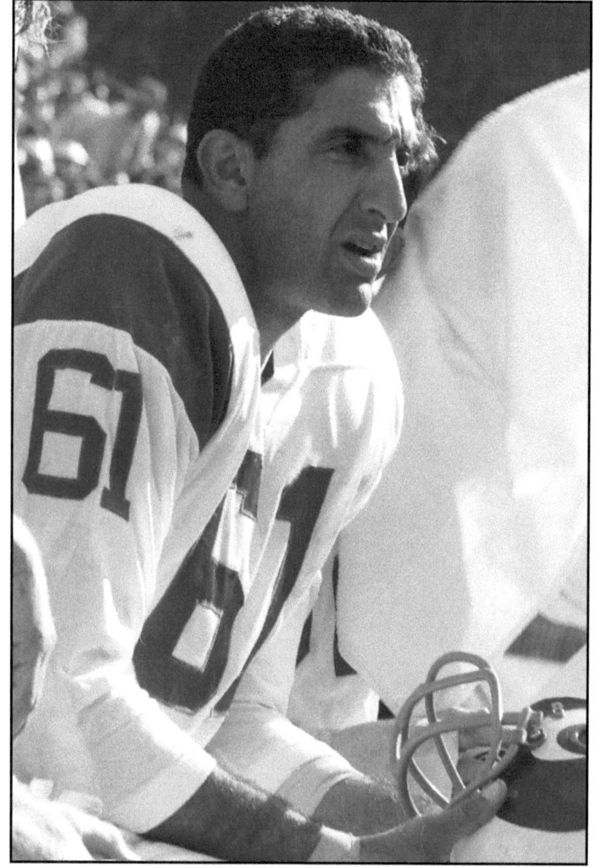
61

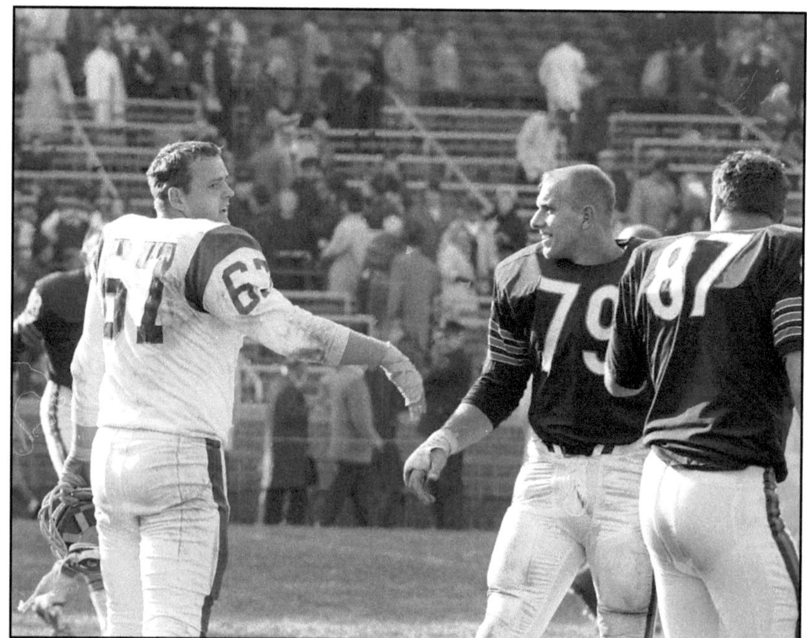
79
87

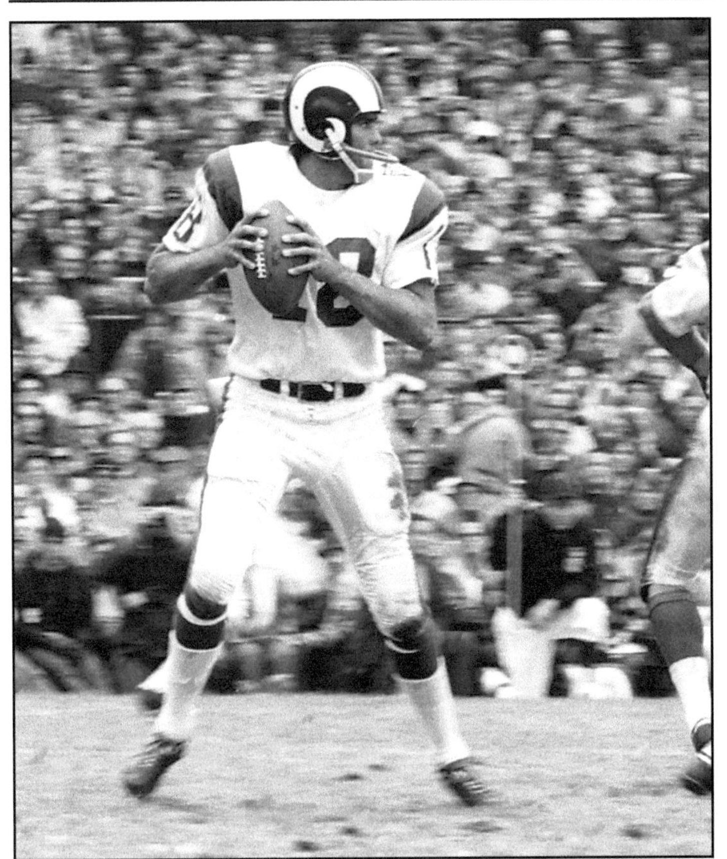

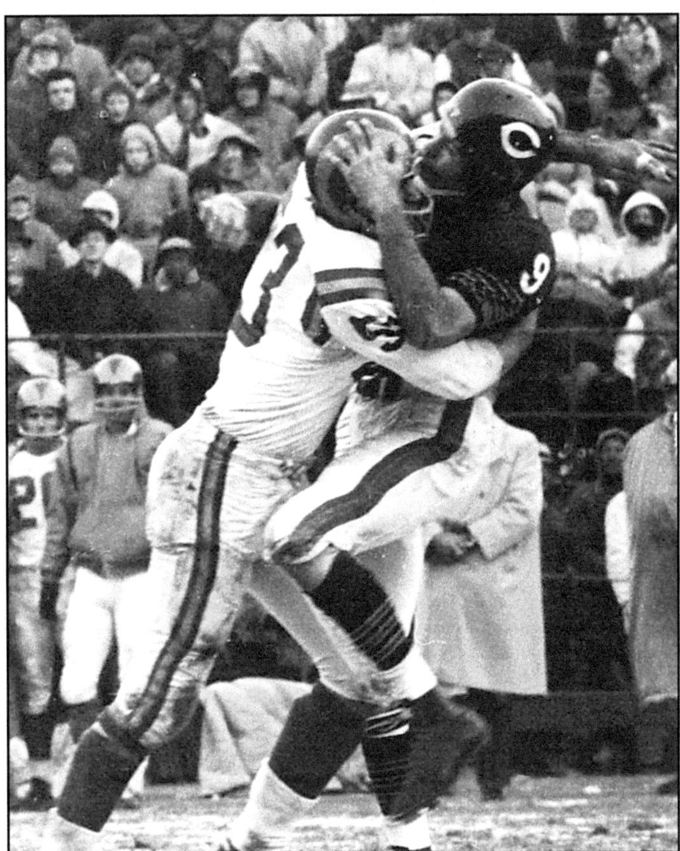

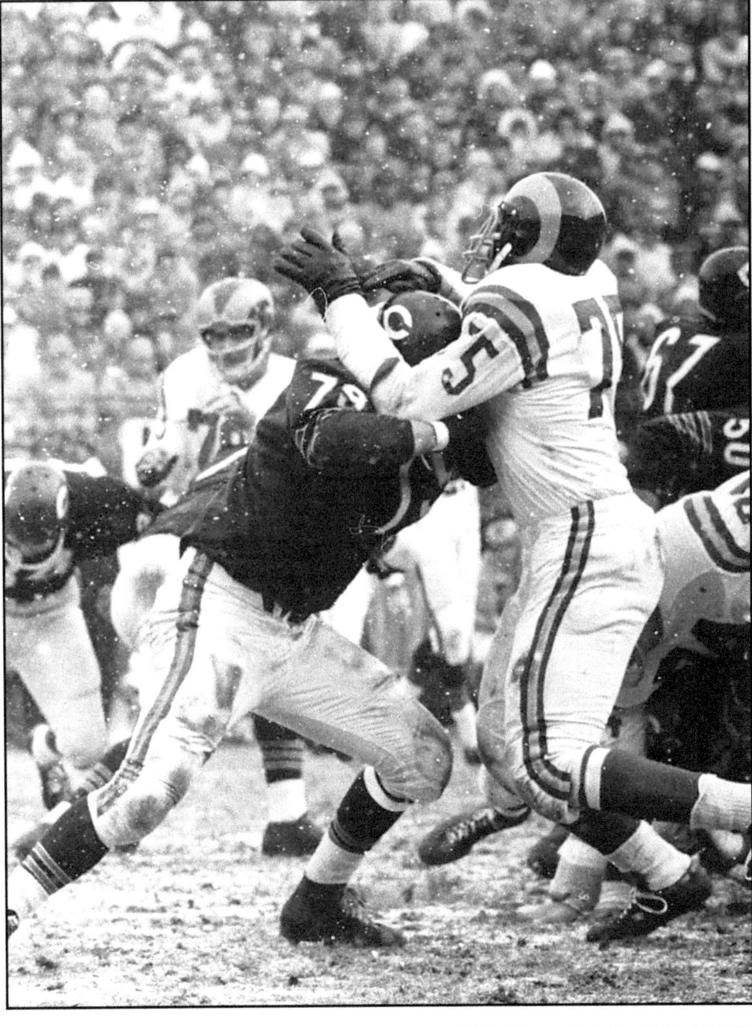

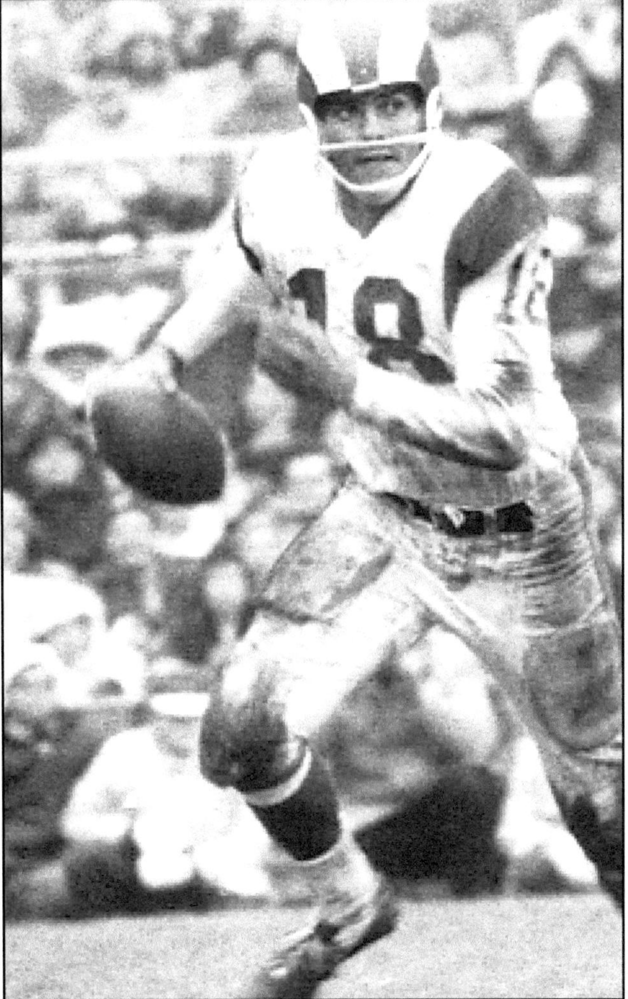

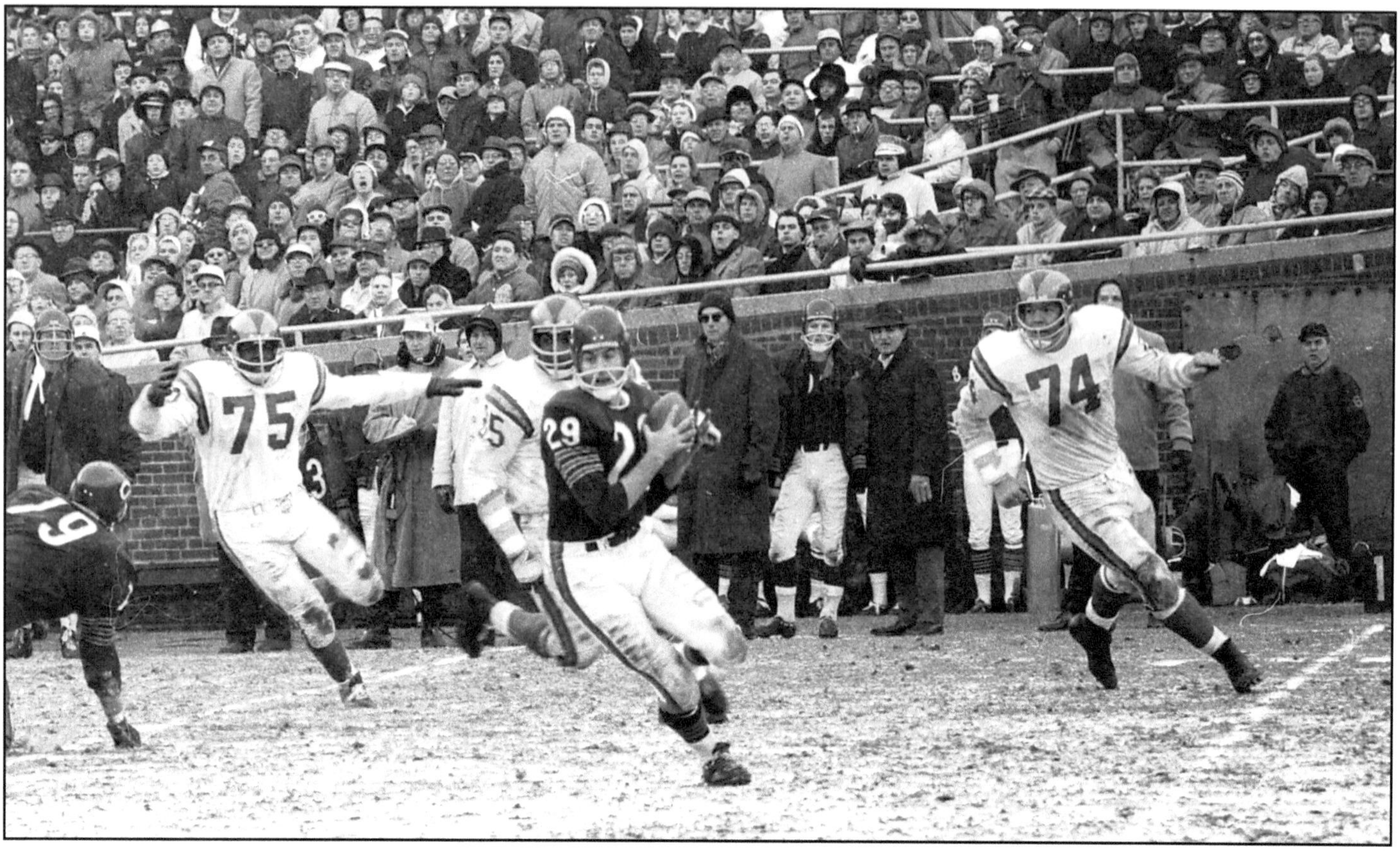

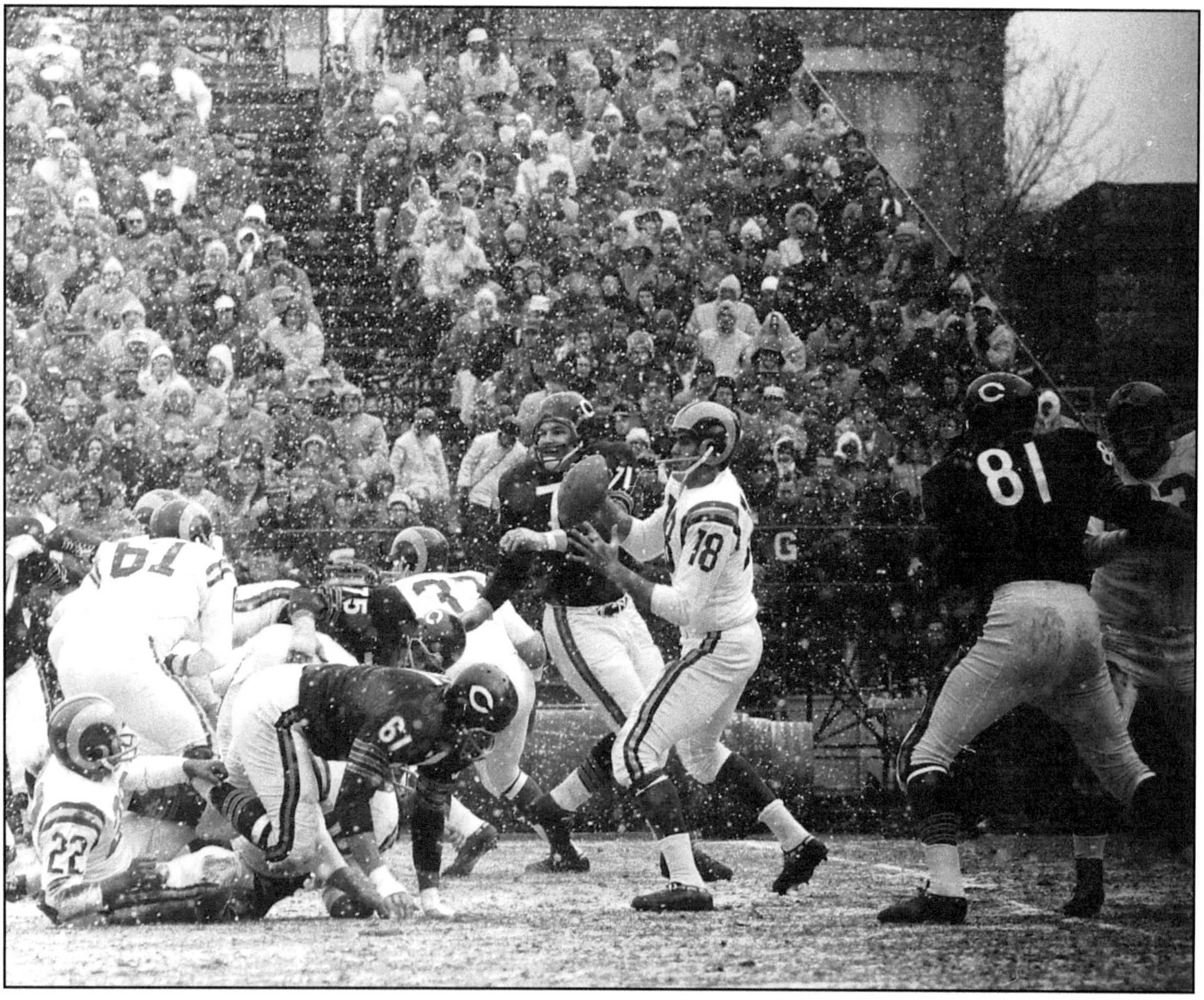

SAN FRANCISCO 49ERS

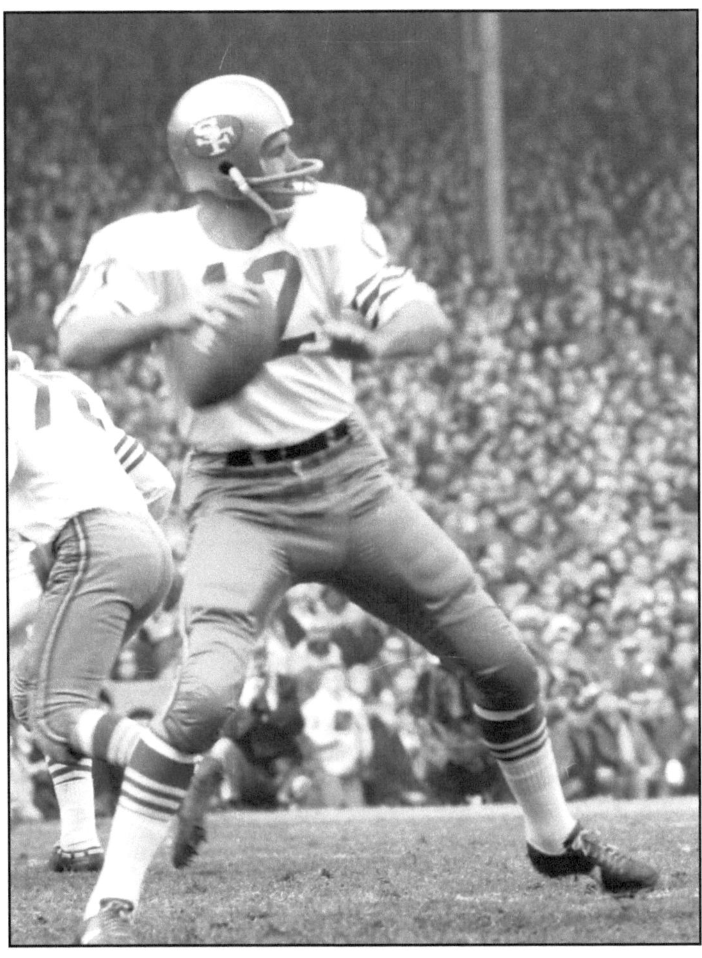

	Bears	49ers
1960	27	10
1961	31	0
1962	27	34
1963	27	7
1964	61	20
1965	23	21
1966	30	30
1968	27	19

The San Francisco 49ers were the first NFL team to use the shotgun formation in which the quarterback lines up seven yards behind center in order to get more time to throw. Invented by 49er's coach Red Hickey, the formation helped the 49ers beat the Baltimore Colts the first time it was used. The advantage it provided soon dissipated as other NFL teams also adopted the formation.

In 1961 the Bears were one of the first teams to use an effective counter attack against the shotgun. By moving players closer to the line of scrimmage, the Bears were able to shut down the quarterback ad erase the advantage he gained by dropping back. Although the shotgun did improve San Francisco's offense overall,1961 proved to be a dismal year for the 49ers with a 3-5-1 season.

In 1962 things had not improved significantly ands the 49ers won only 6 games. The team had losing seasons once more in 1963 and 1964. By 1965, they reached a 7-6-1 record. John Brodie led the league in pass attempts, completions,touchdowns and yards. The 49ers handed the Bears one of their worst losses ever, a 52-24 drubbing. In 1966 San Francisco again beat the Bears at Kezar Stadium, this time by a score of 41-14.

1967 saw the 49ers off to a fast start winning five of six games. A number of injuries to starters ended playoff dreams, however. Dick Nolan took over as Coach in 1968 and Brodie led the league with 3,020 passing yards. Despite Brodie's and Nolan's best efforts the 49ers went 4-8-2 due to continuing injury problems with starters.

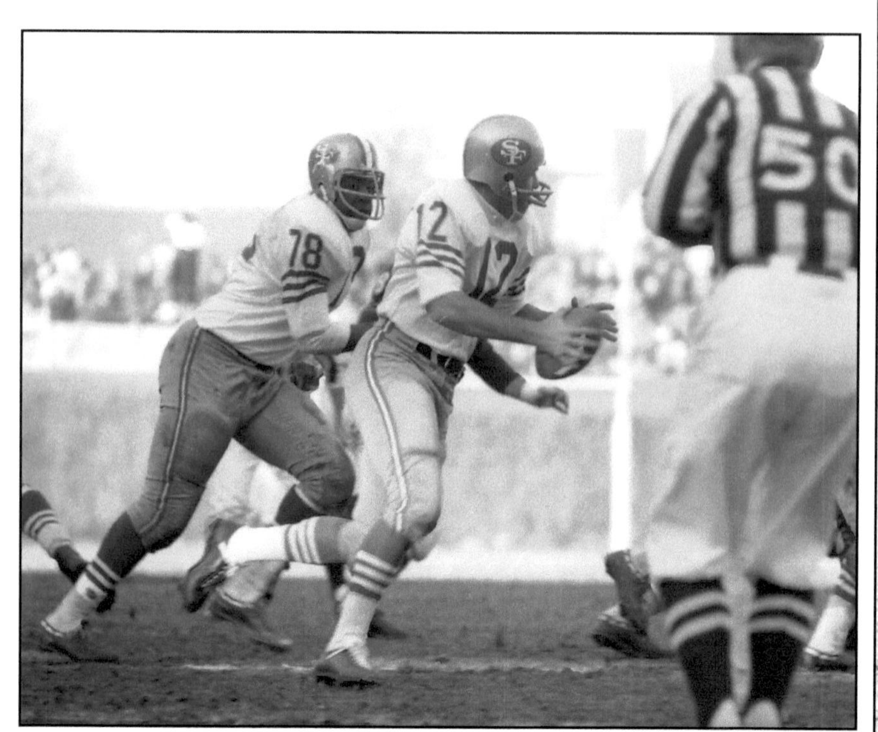
78
12
50

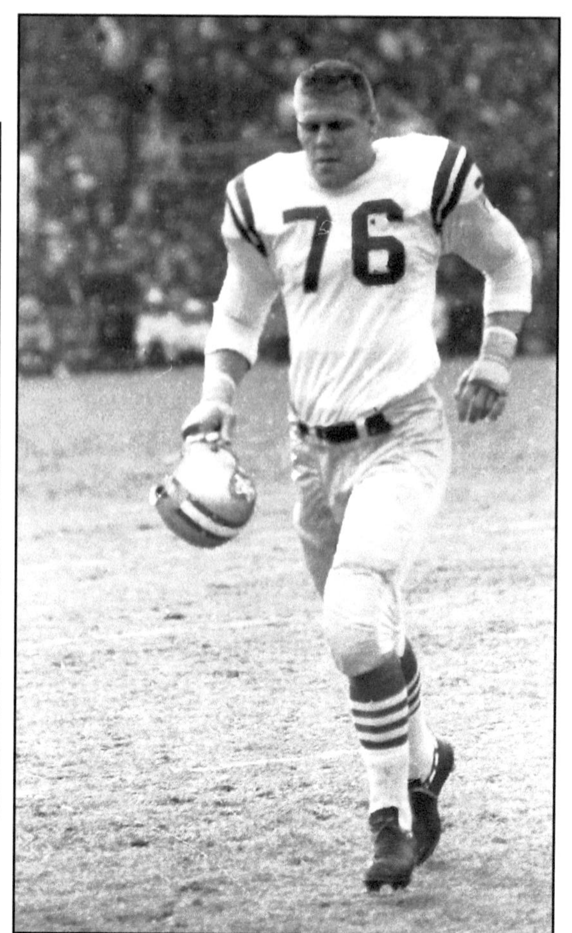
76

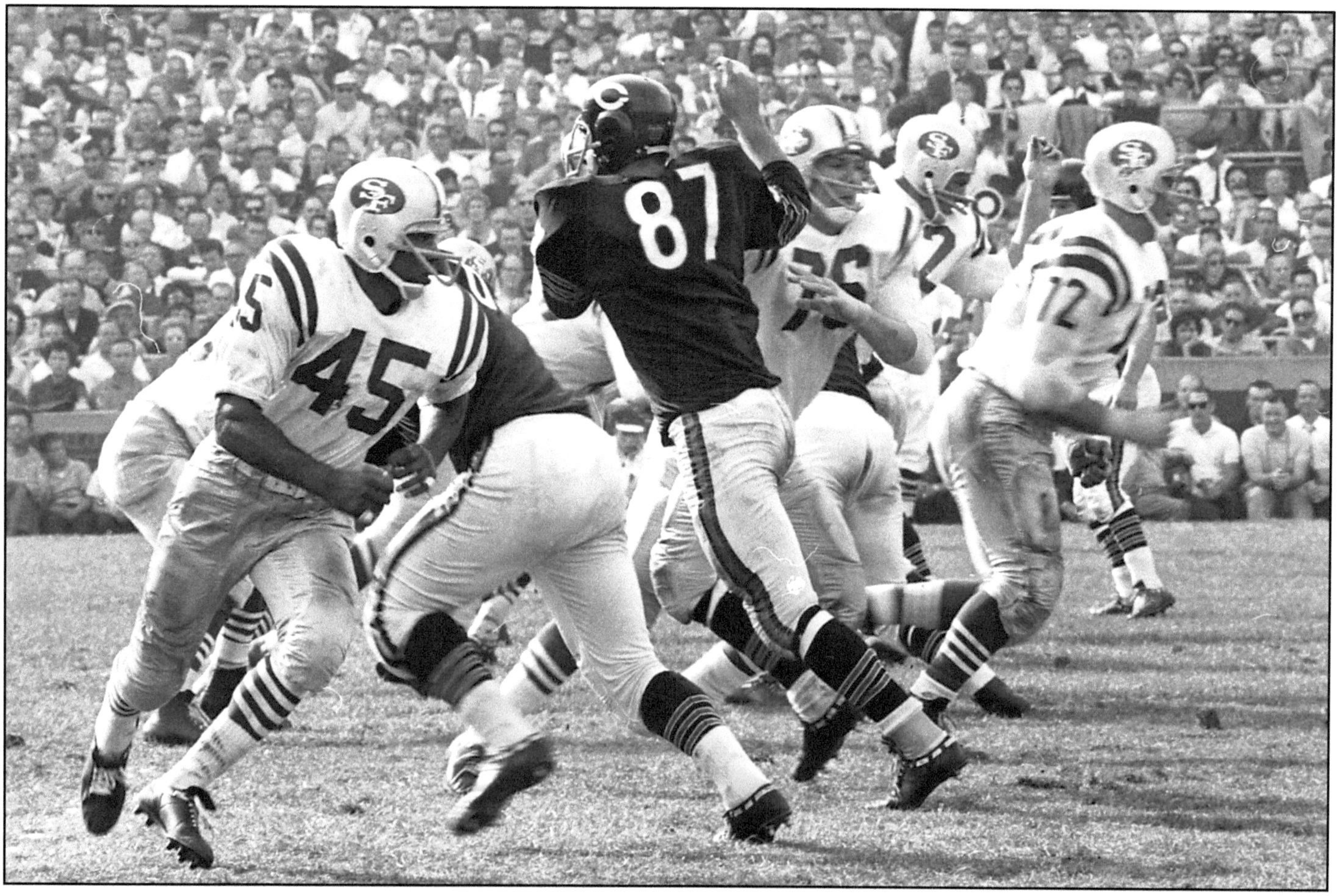

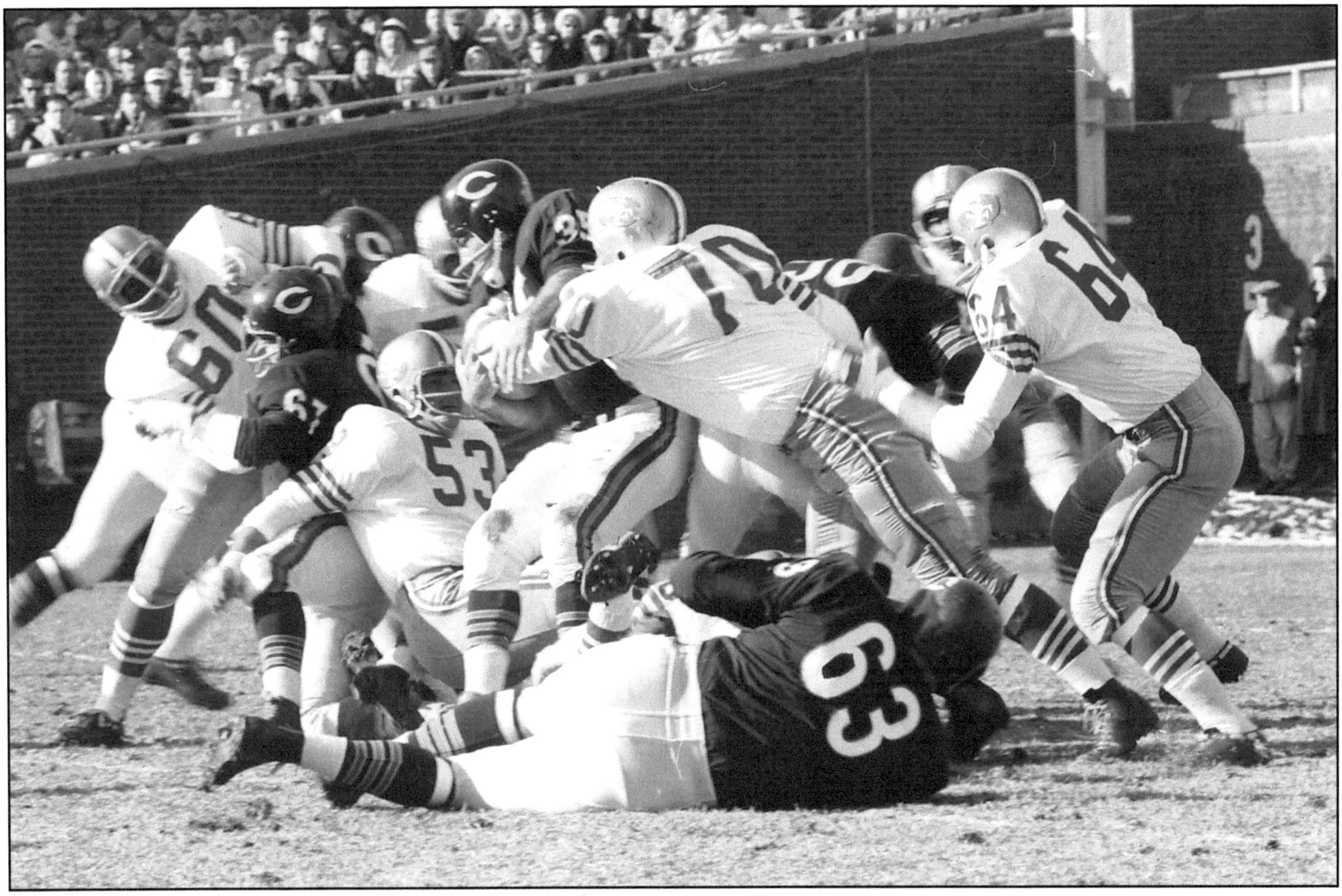

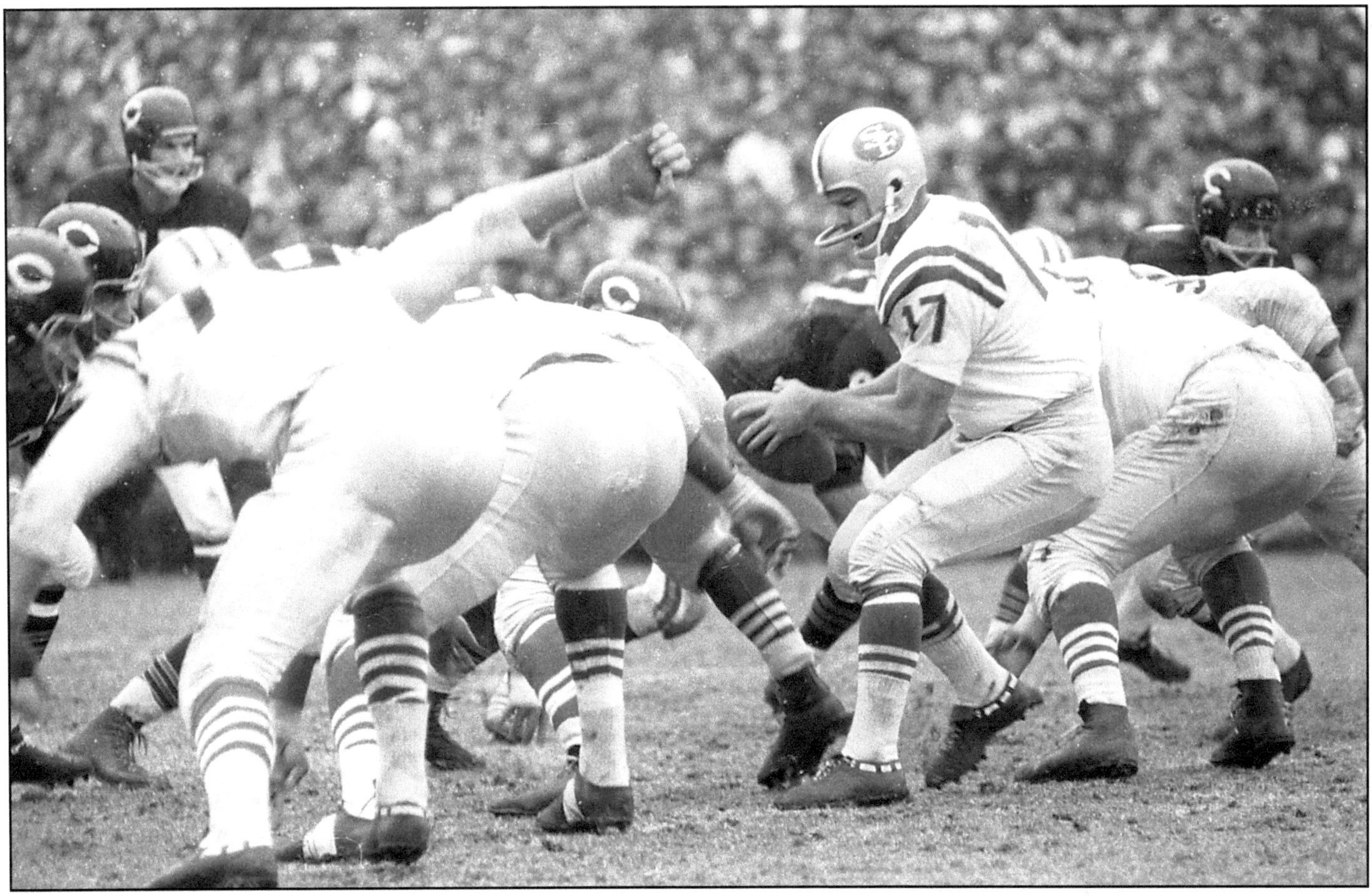

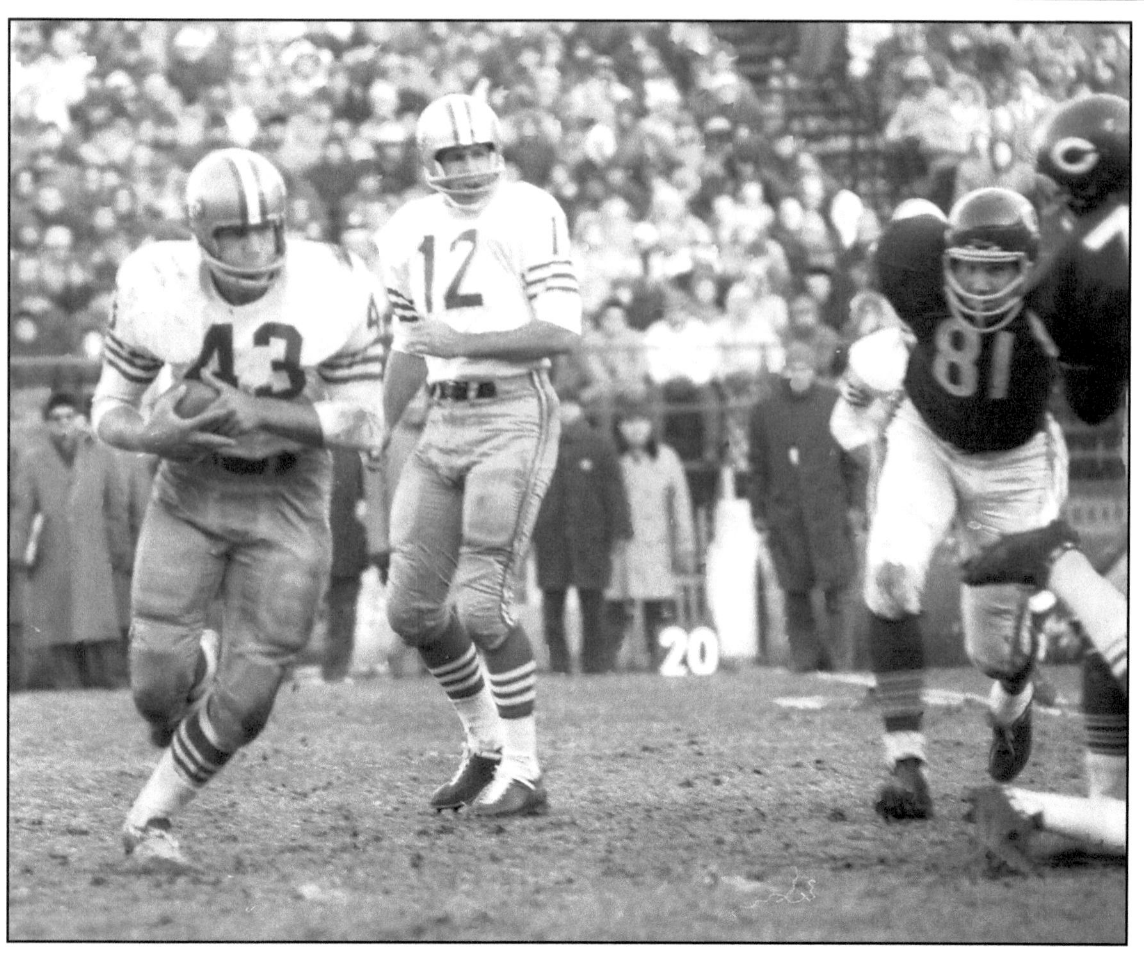
43
12
81
20

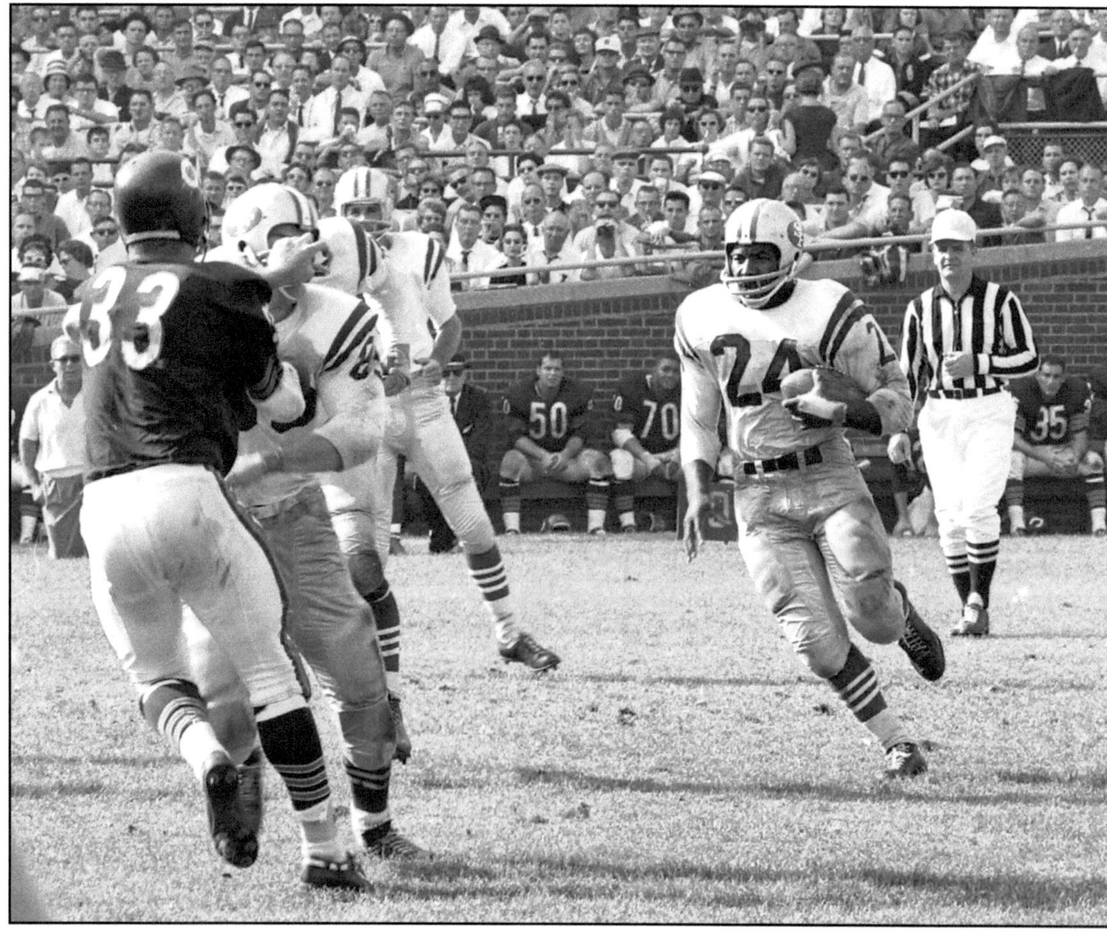
33
24
50
70
35

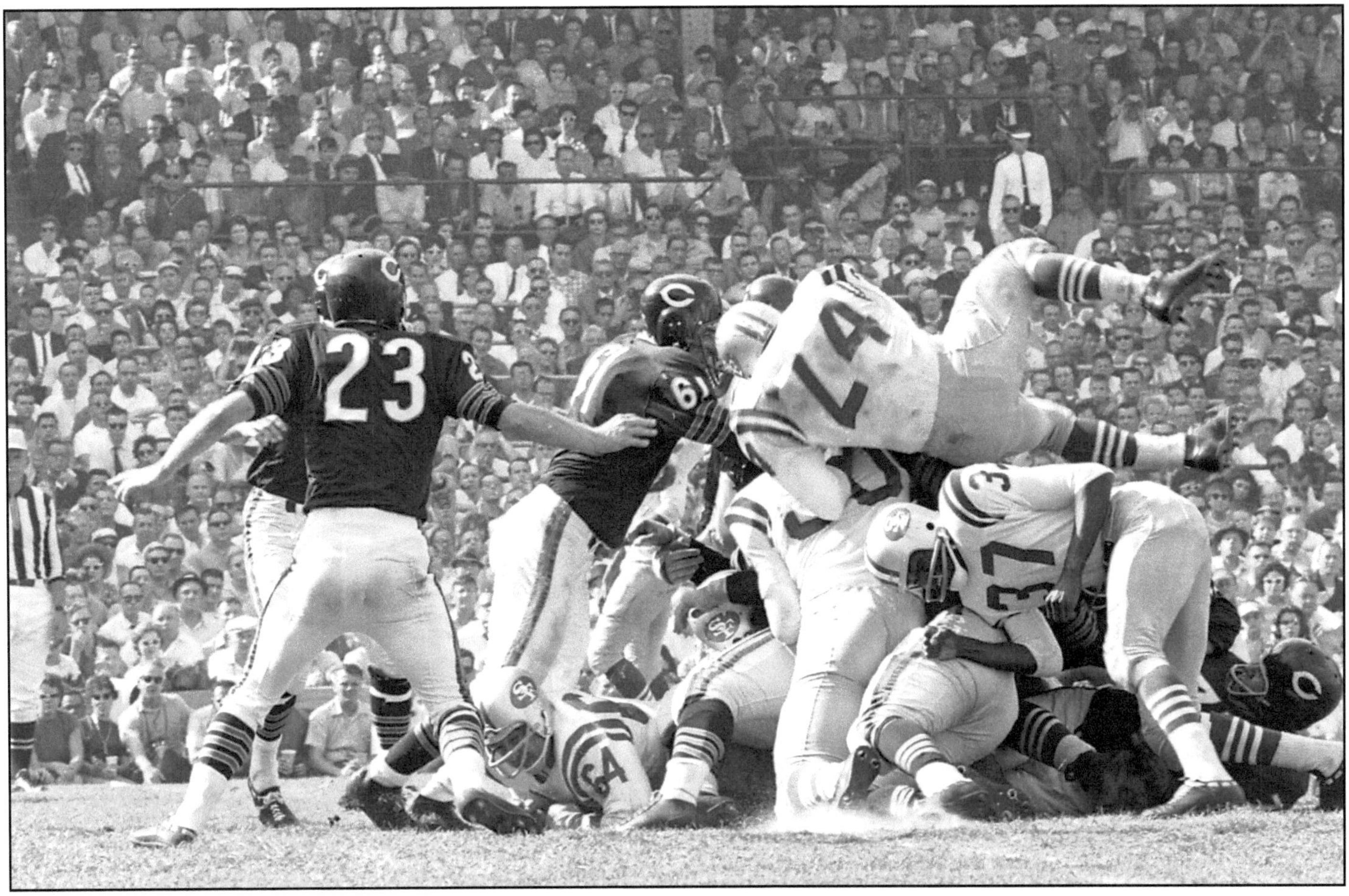

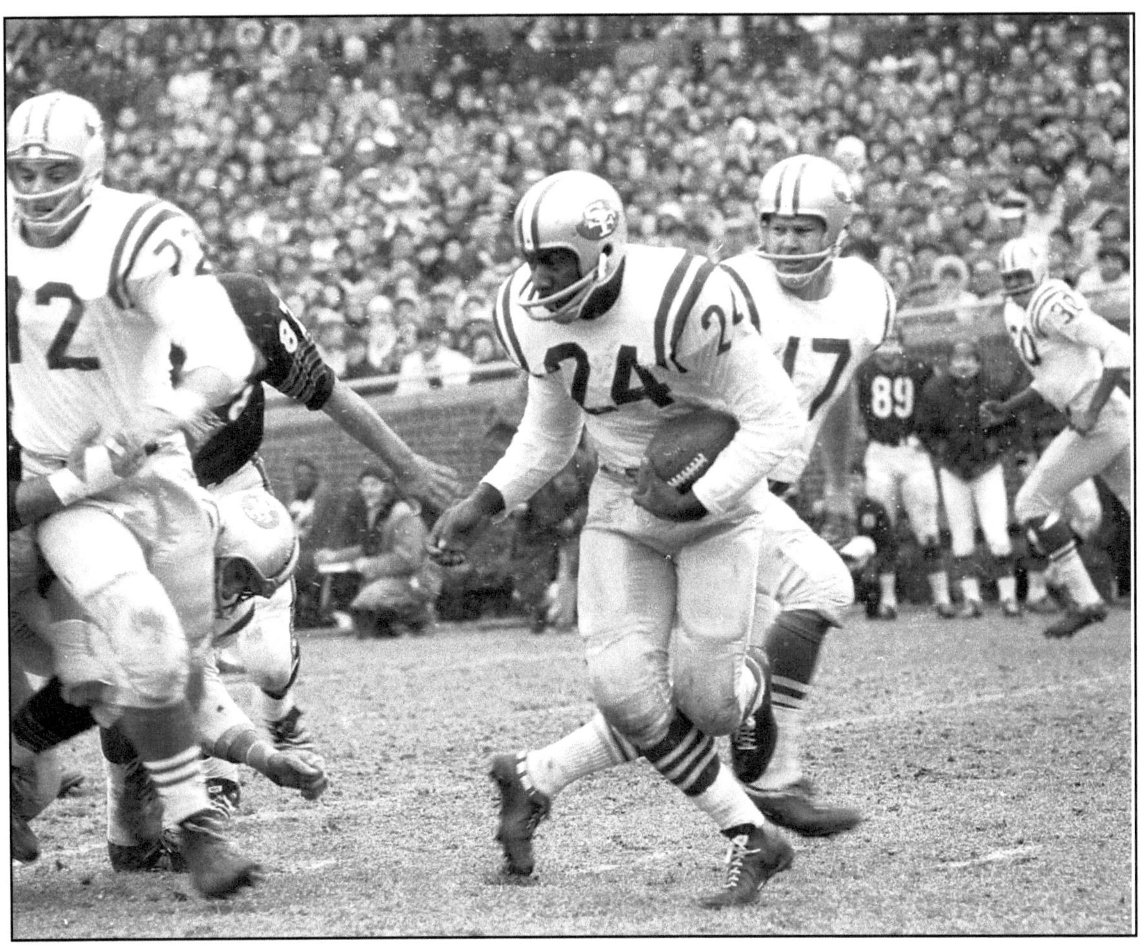
24
17
89

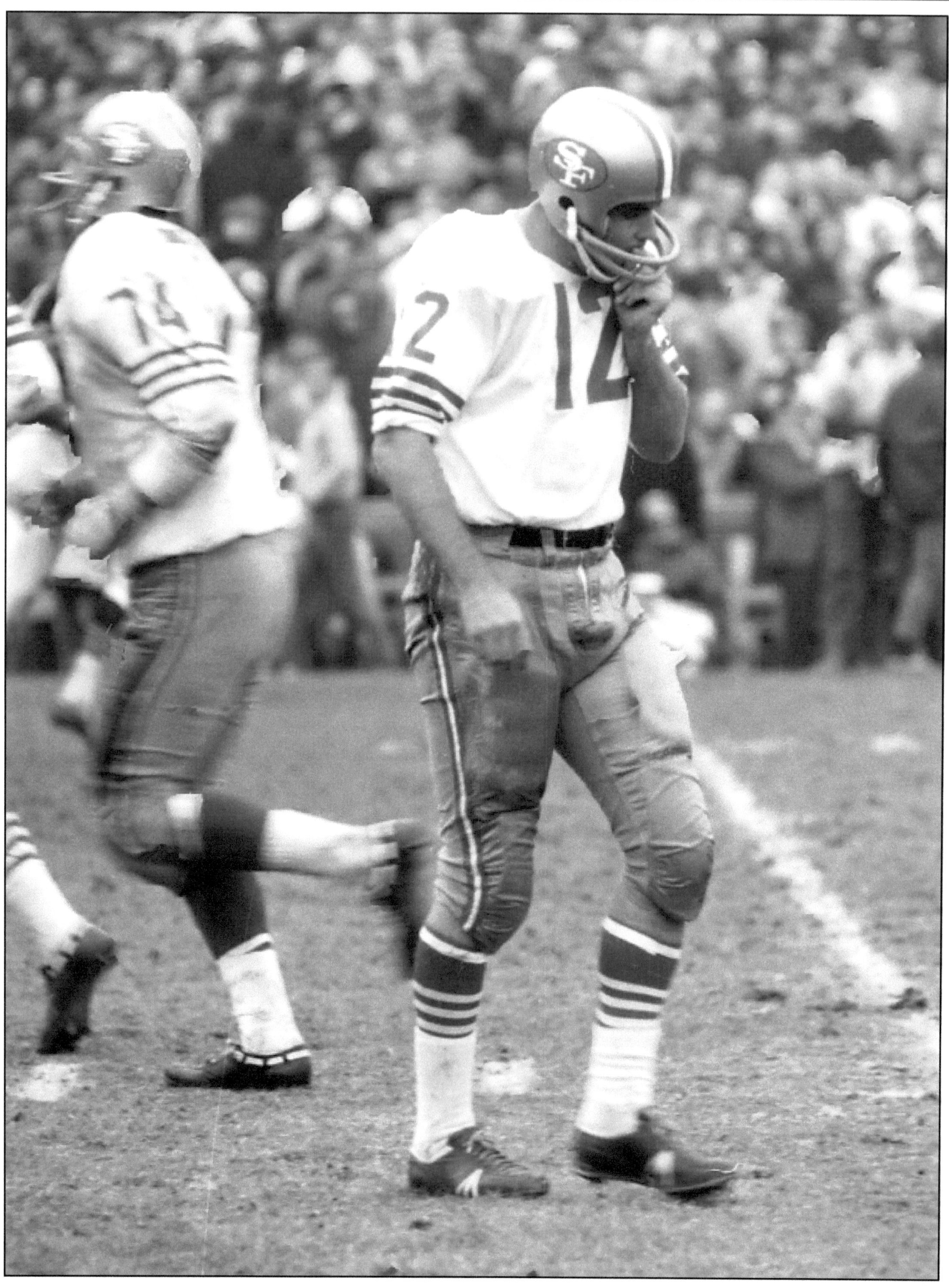
74
12

NEW YORK GIANTS

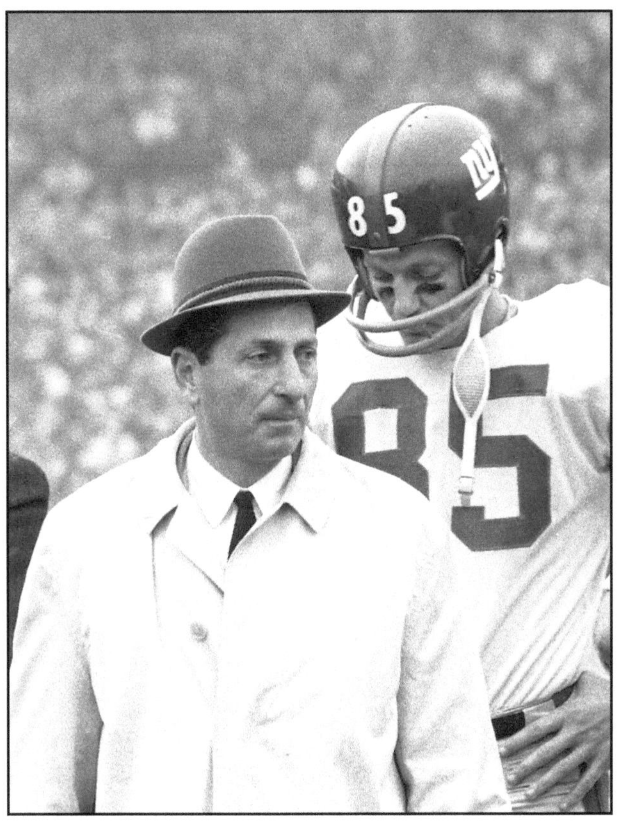

	Bears	Giants
1962	24	26
1963	14	10
1967	34	7

In 1960 the giants organization was in turmoil with the departure of head coach Jim Lee Howell. Defensive coach Tom Landry also departed to join the newly formed Dallas Cowboys. Injuries haunted key starters and the team limped to a record of 6-4-2.

Things looked up for the Giants in 1961 as Allie Sherman signed on as head coach and football legend Y.A. Tittle joined the team. Alex Webster's 928 yards rushing brought the team to the Championship game against the Packers, but the Giants lost 37-0. The Giants again lost the title to the Packers in 1962 even with the added talent of Frank Gifford who had come out of retirement, and of Andy Robustelli who was named the NFL's top player.

In 1963 the Giants lost a bitter battle for the NFL Championship,by a score of 14-10. The team that the Giants played in bone chilling temperatures at Wrigley Field was the Chicago Bears.

1964 brought a marked step back for the franchise as the Giants posted a losing season with a record of 2-10-2. Although the Giants record improved to 7-7 in 1965, the team suffered the loss of longtime president Jack Mara and also the retirement of Y.A. Tittle.

Things got even worse in 1966 with a 1-12-1 record. The Giants defense allowed an NFL record 501 points. Tackle Rosie Brown retired after 13 years. Frank Tarkenton joined the team in 1967 and brought the Giants season record to 7-7 thanks in part to the QB's 29 touchdown passes.

Again in 1968 the Giants' record was 7-7. Allie Sherman retired as head coach after four consecutive losses near the end of the season. Alex Webster replaced Sherman in 1969 and the Giants finished up with a 6-8 record.

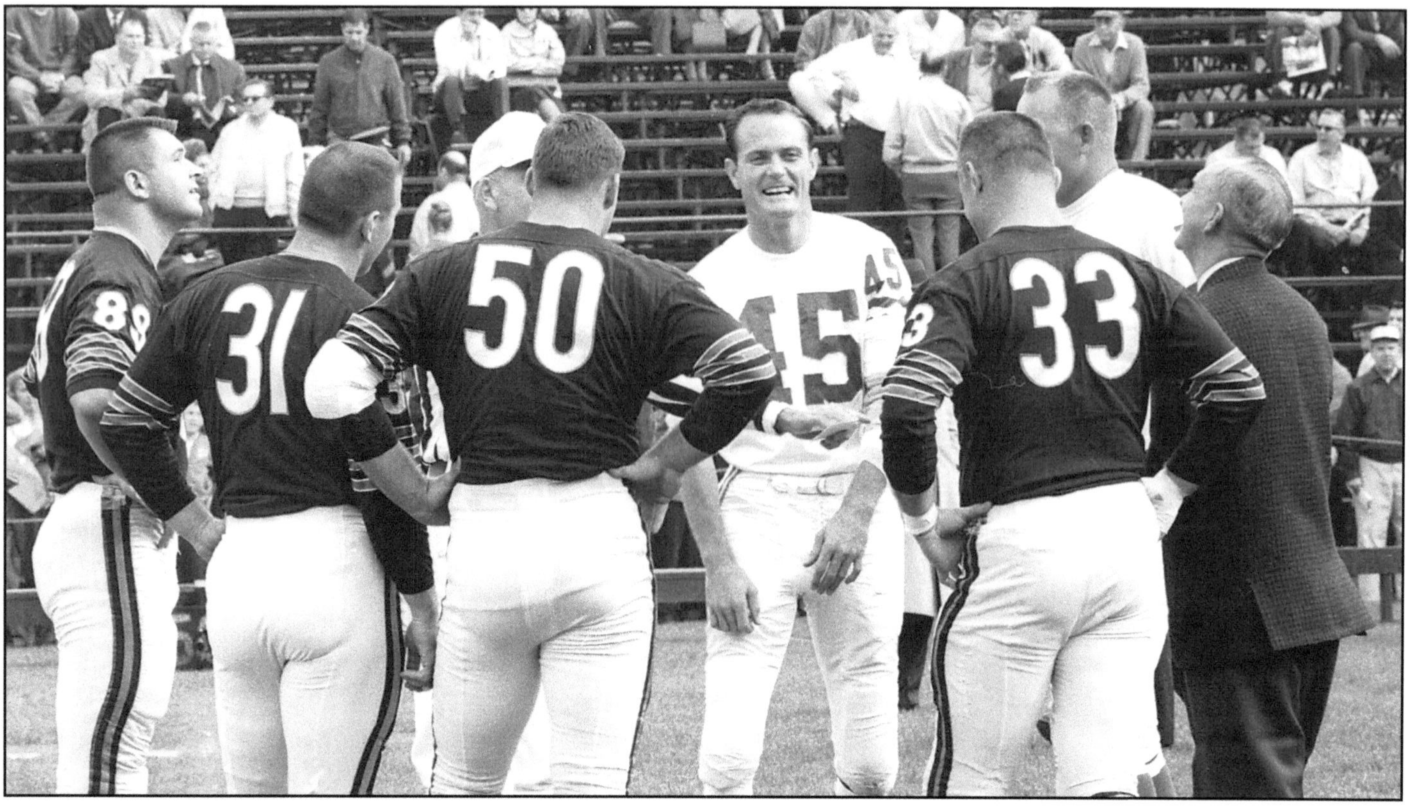

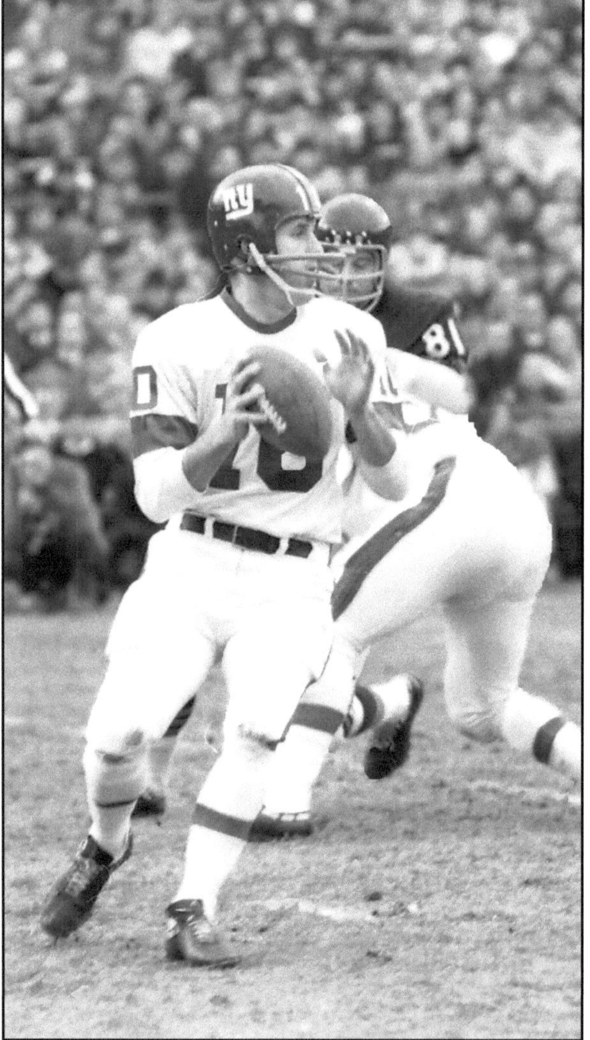

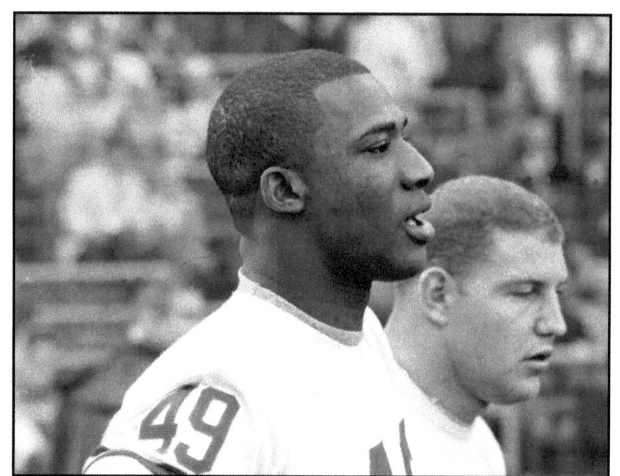

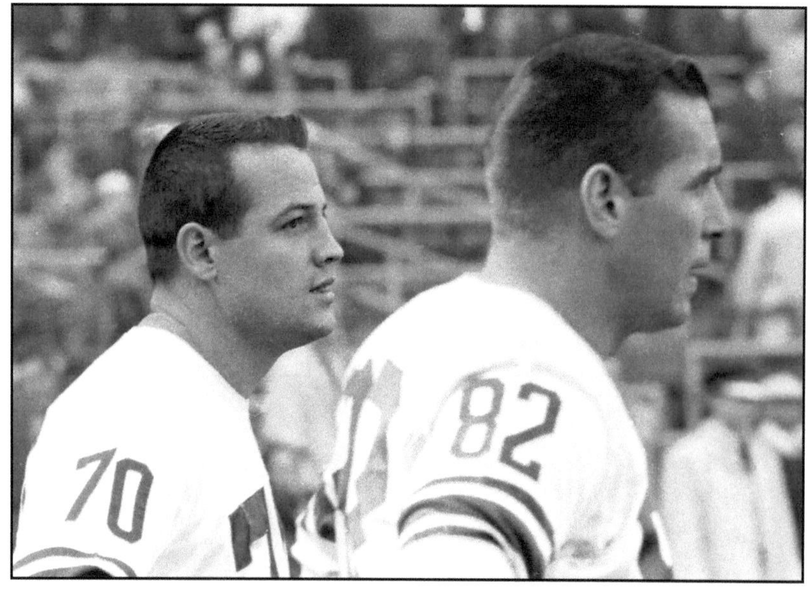

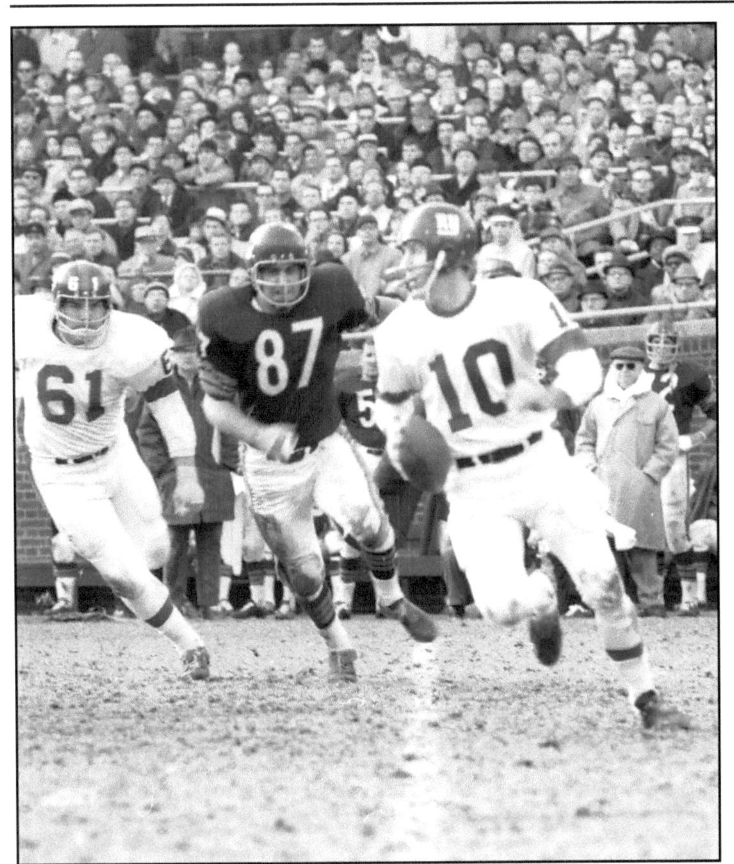

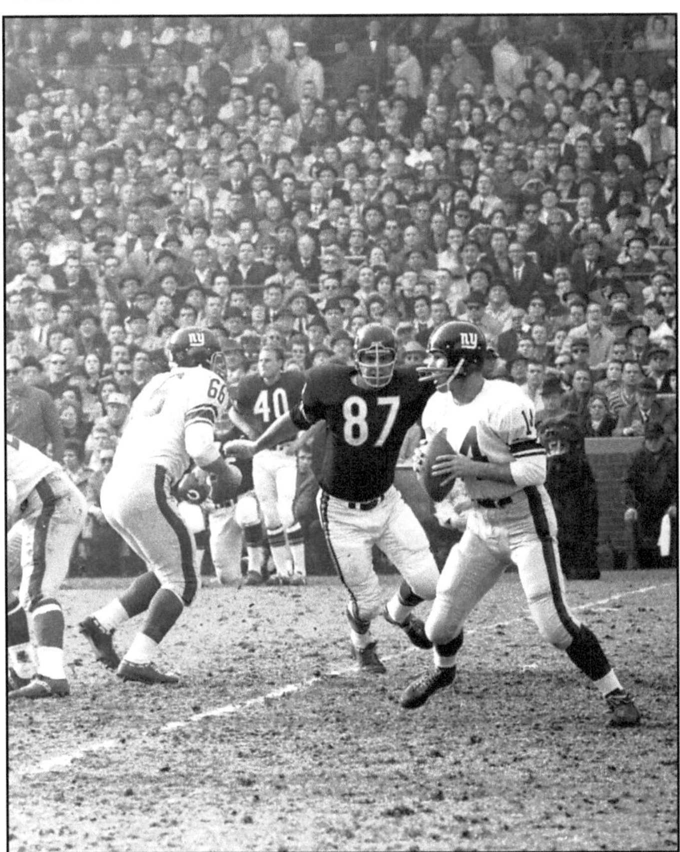

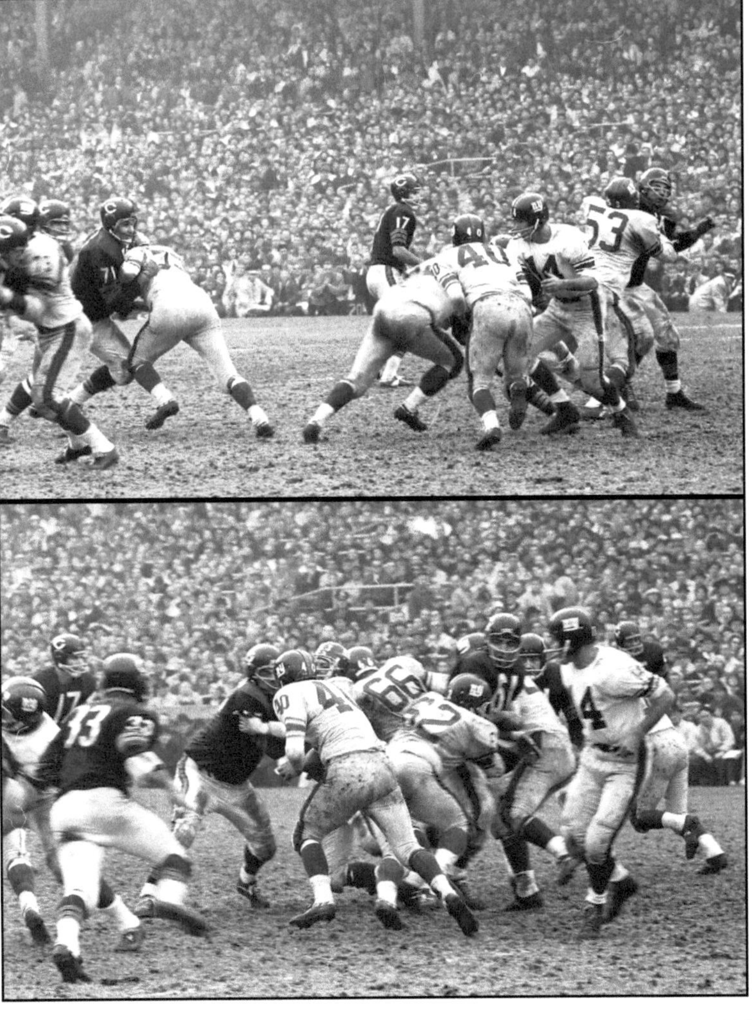

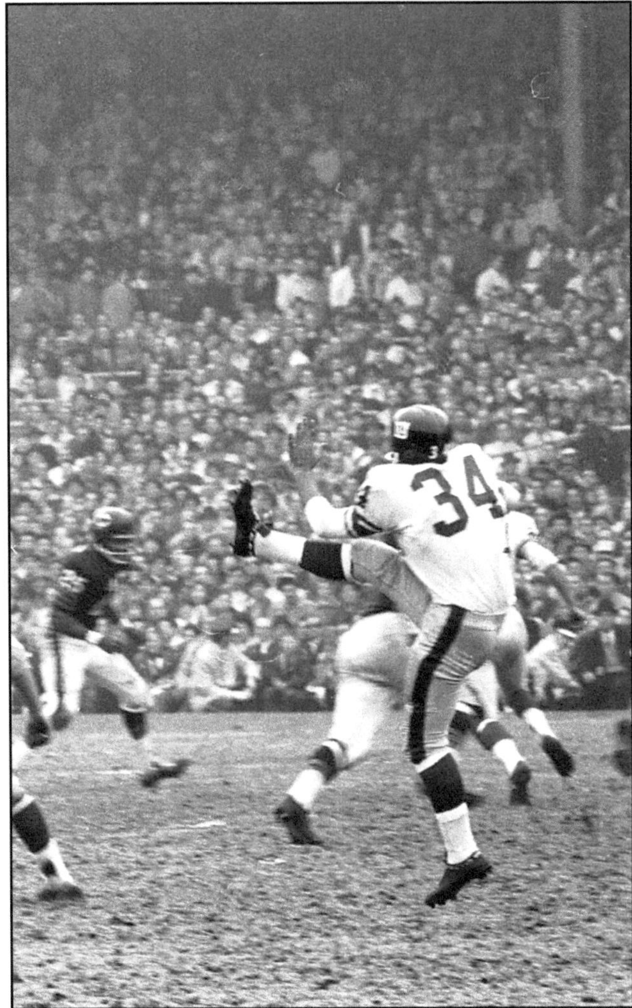

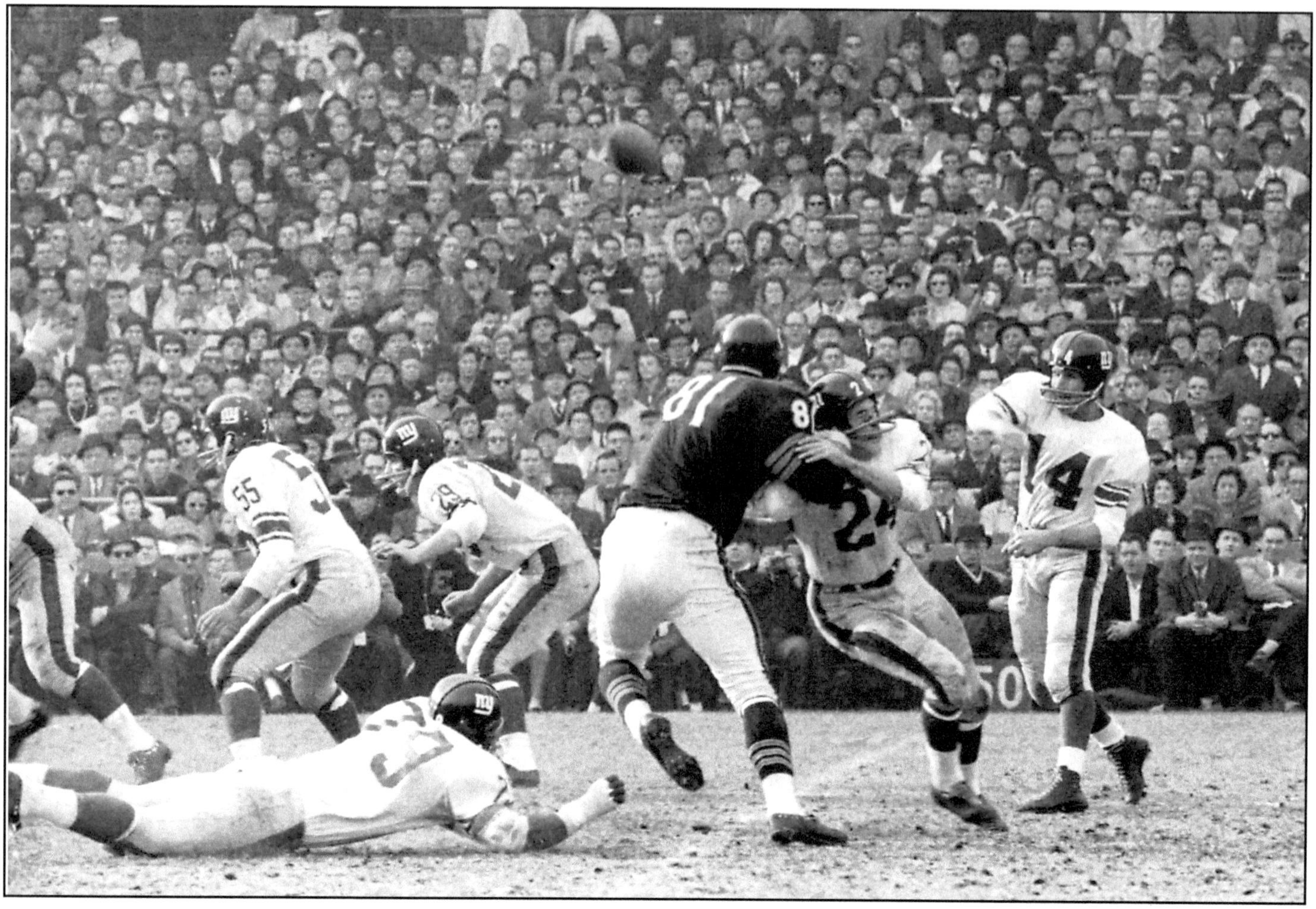

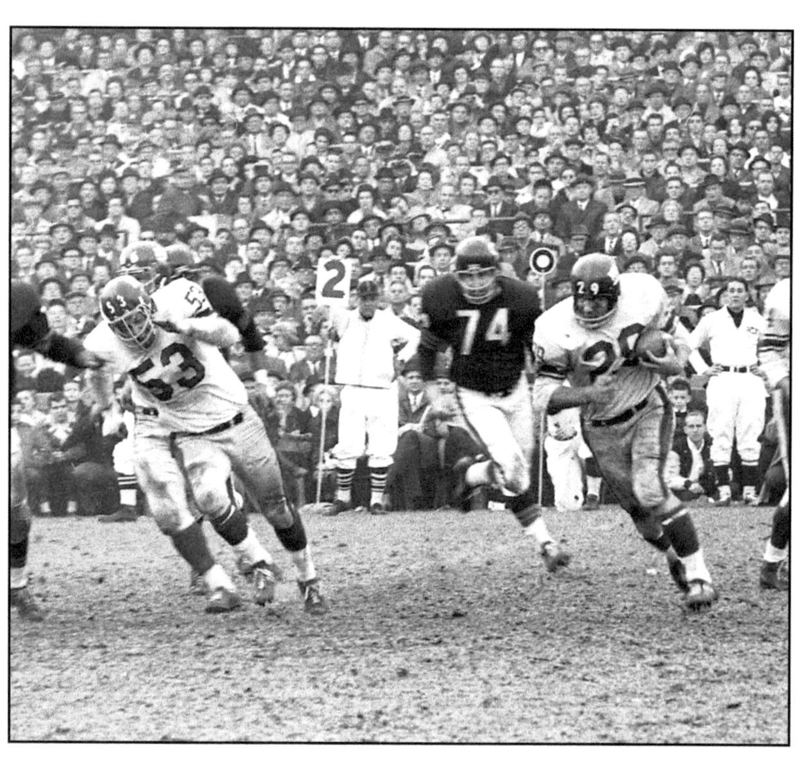
53
74
29

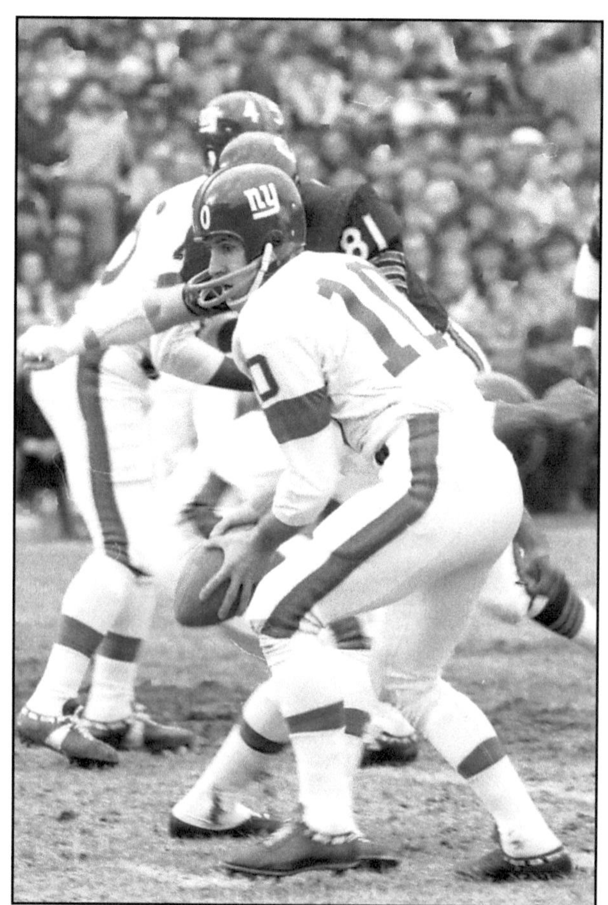
81

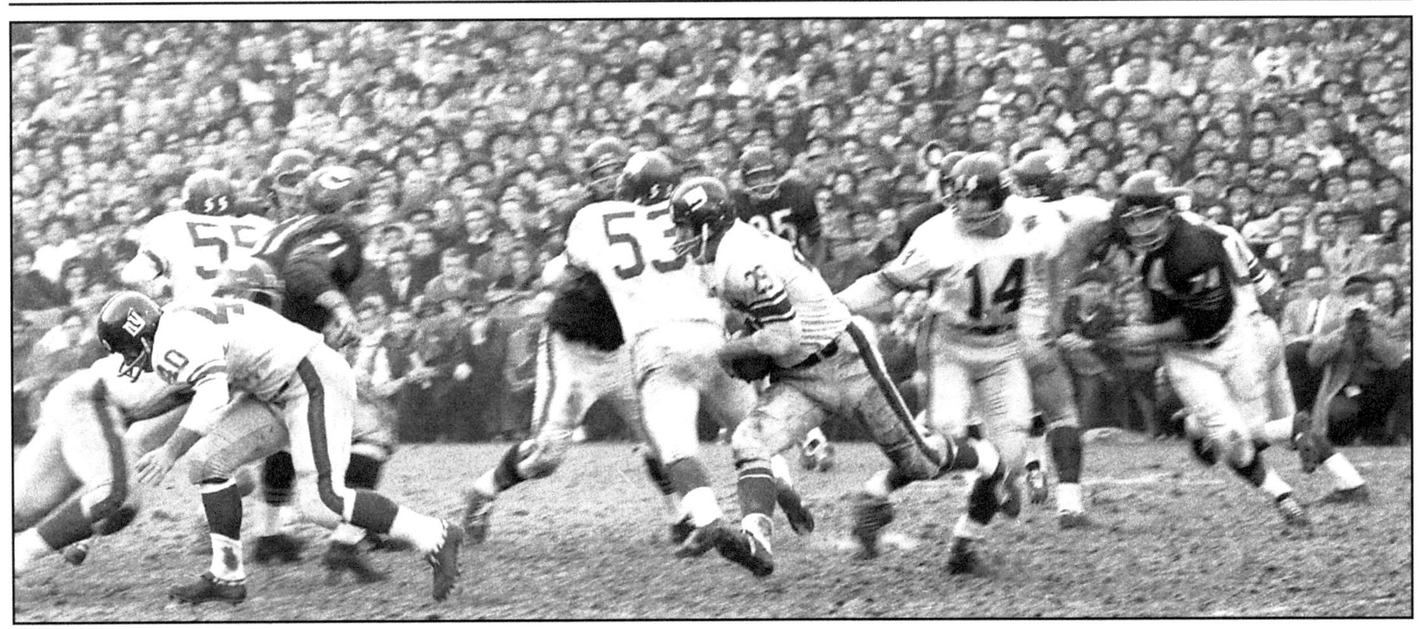

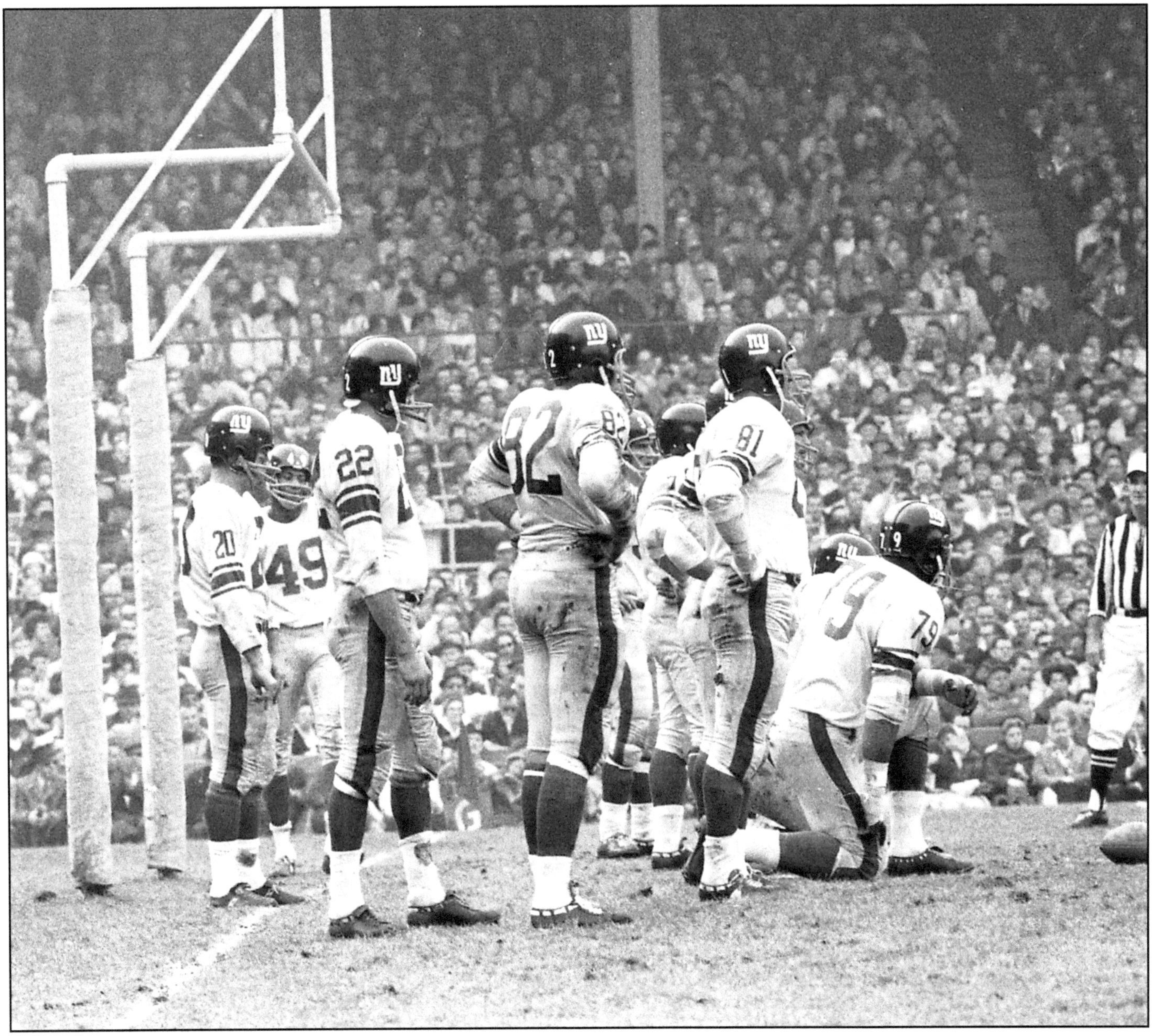

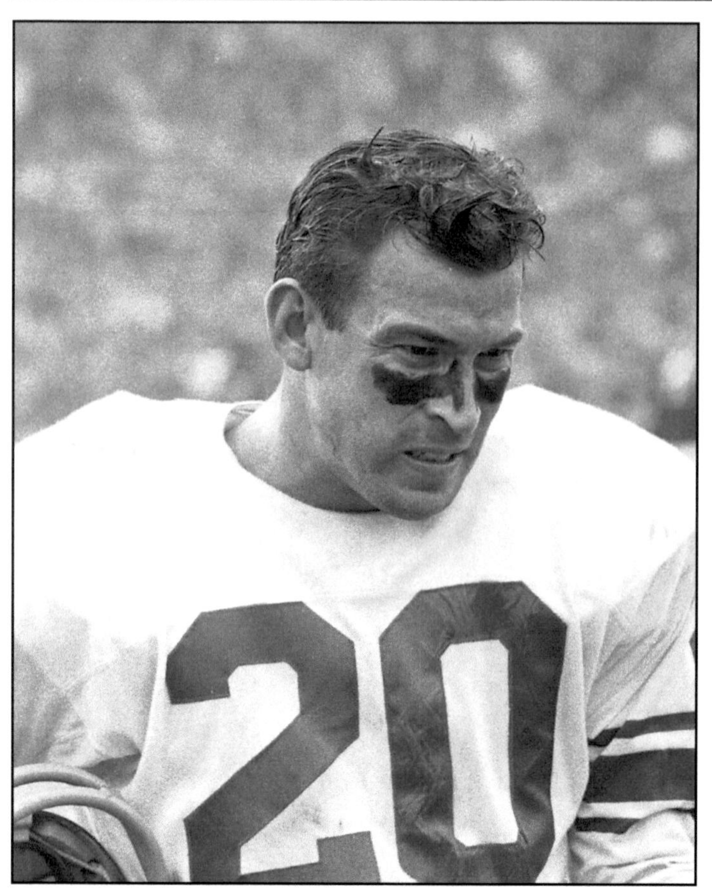
20

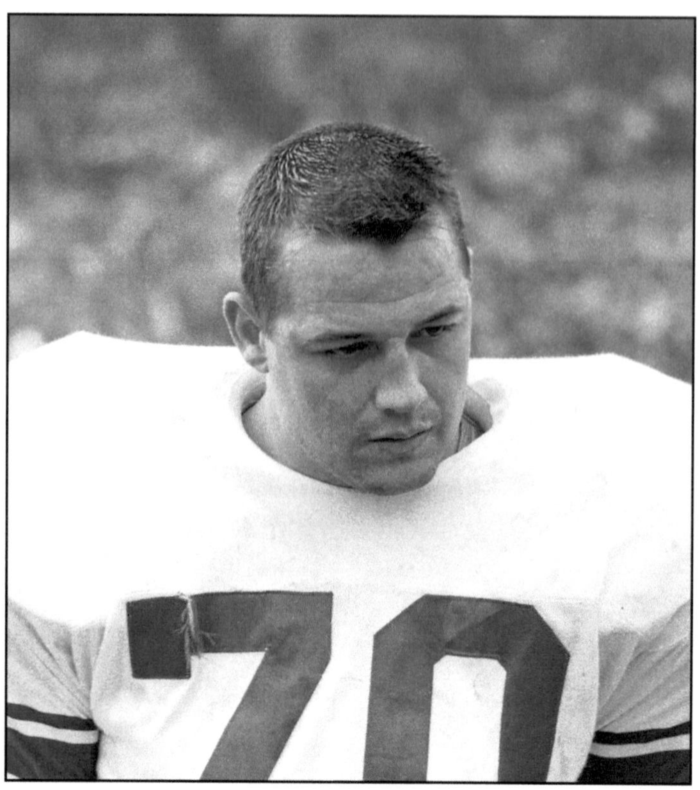
70

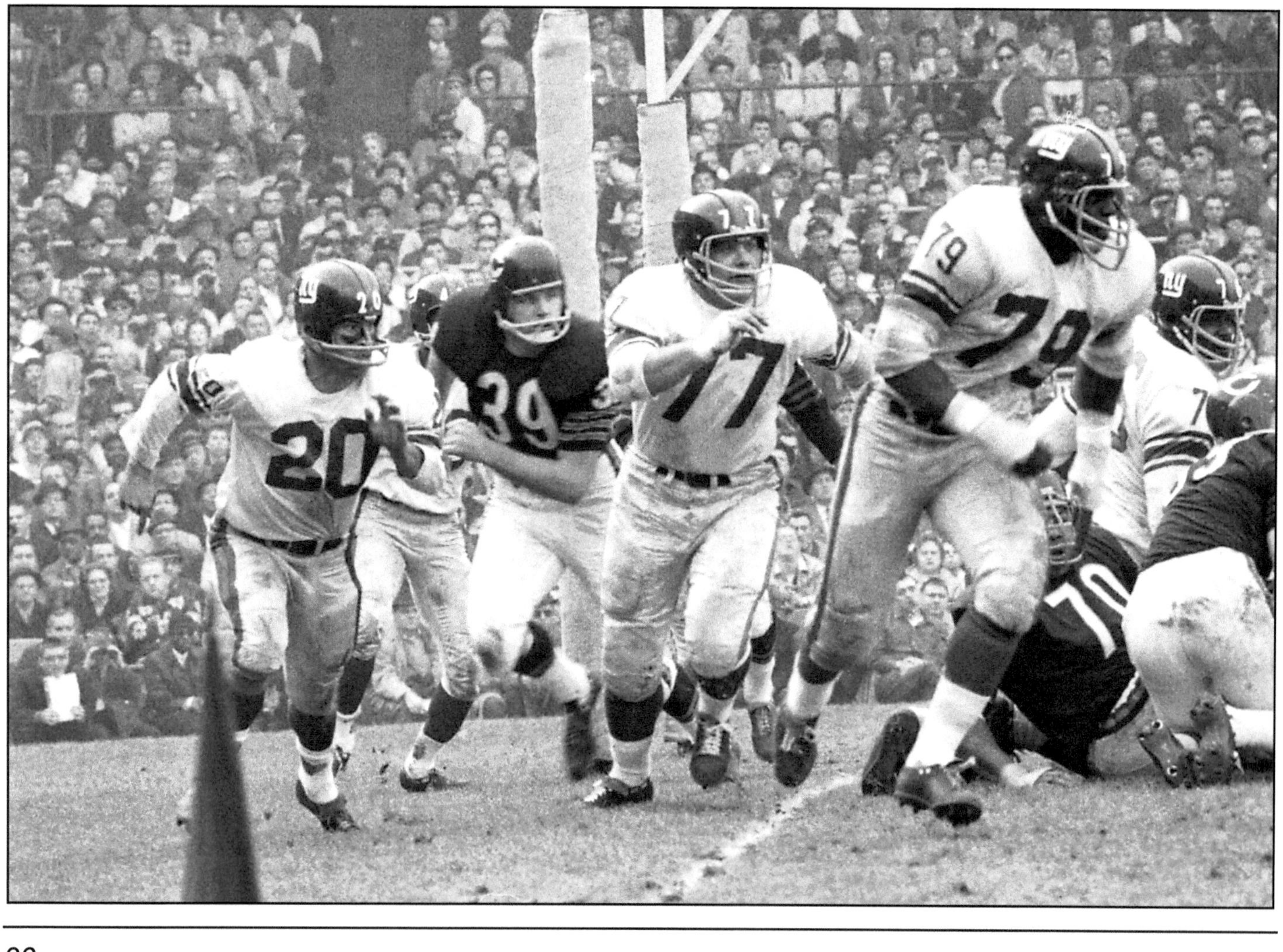

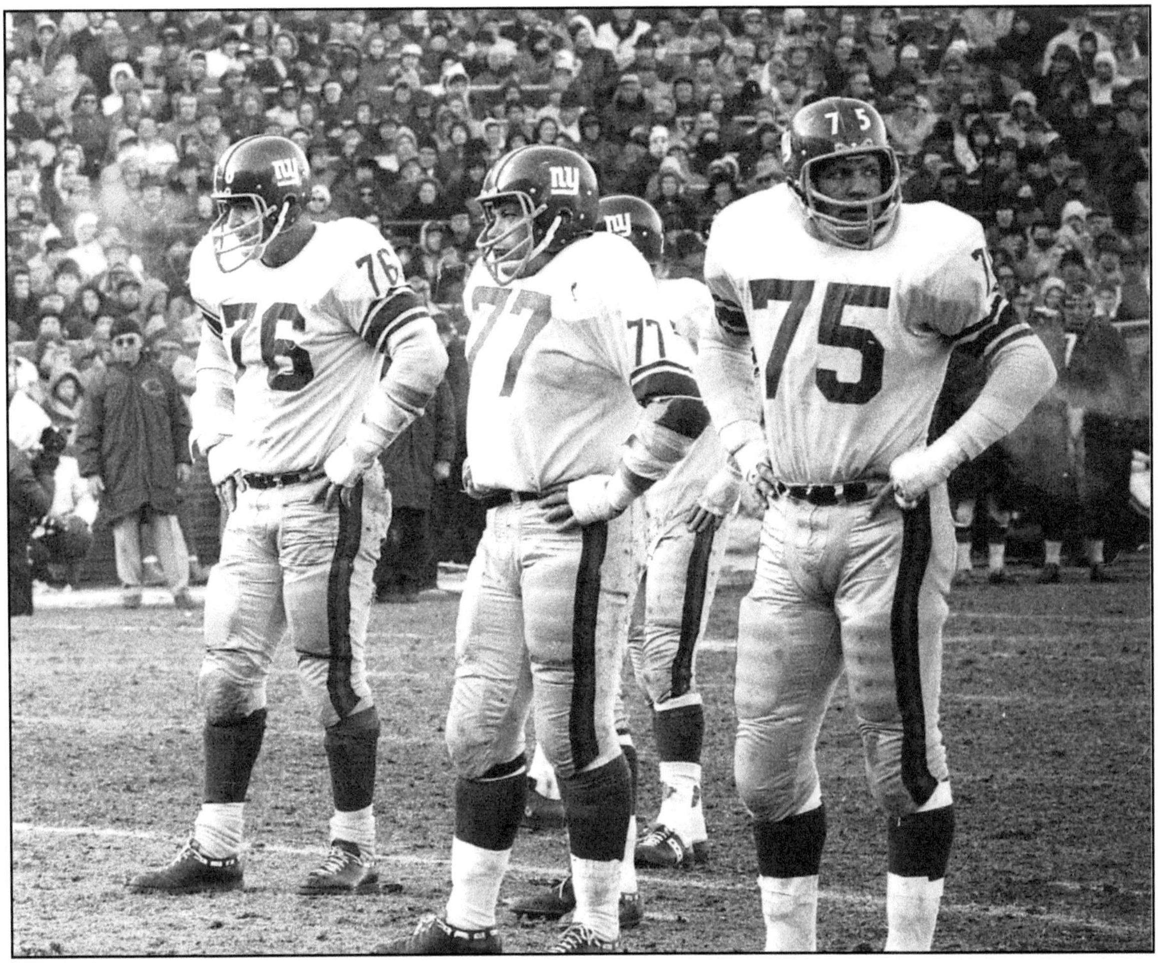

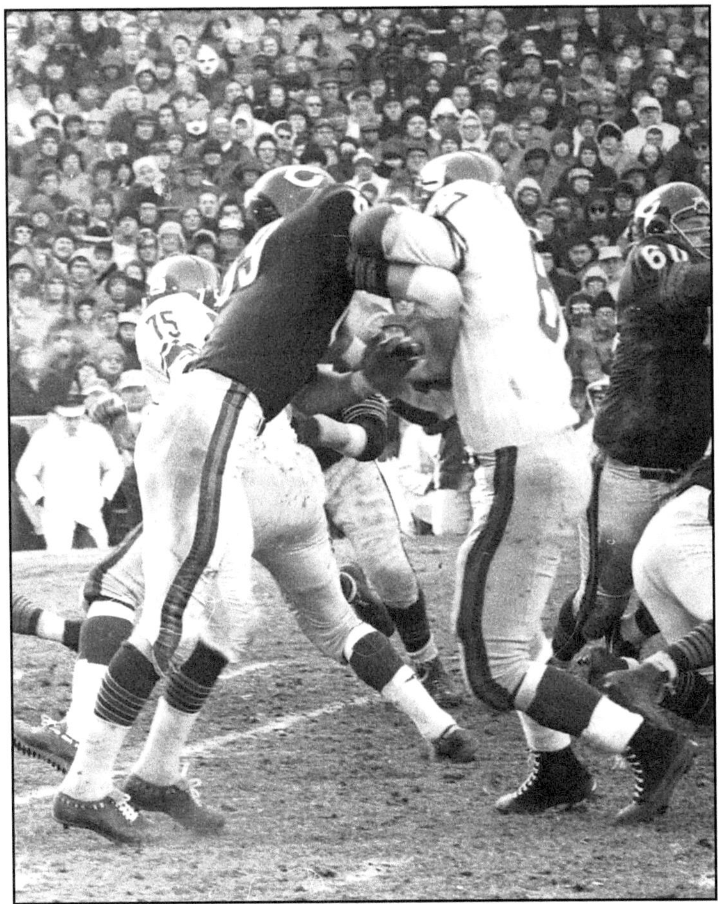

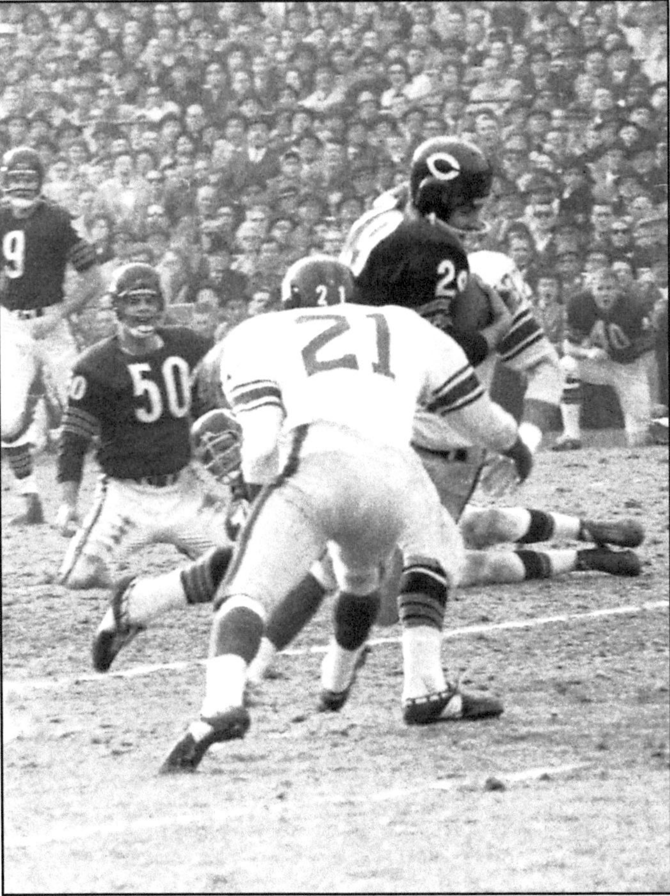

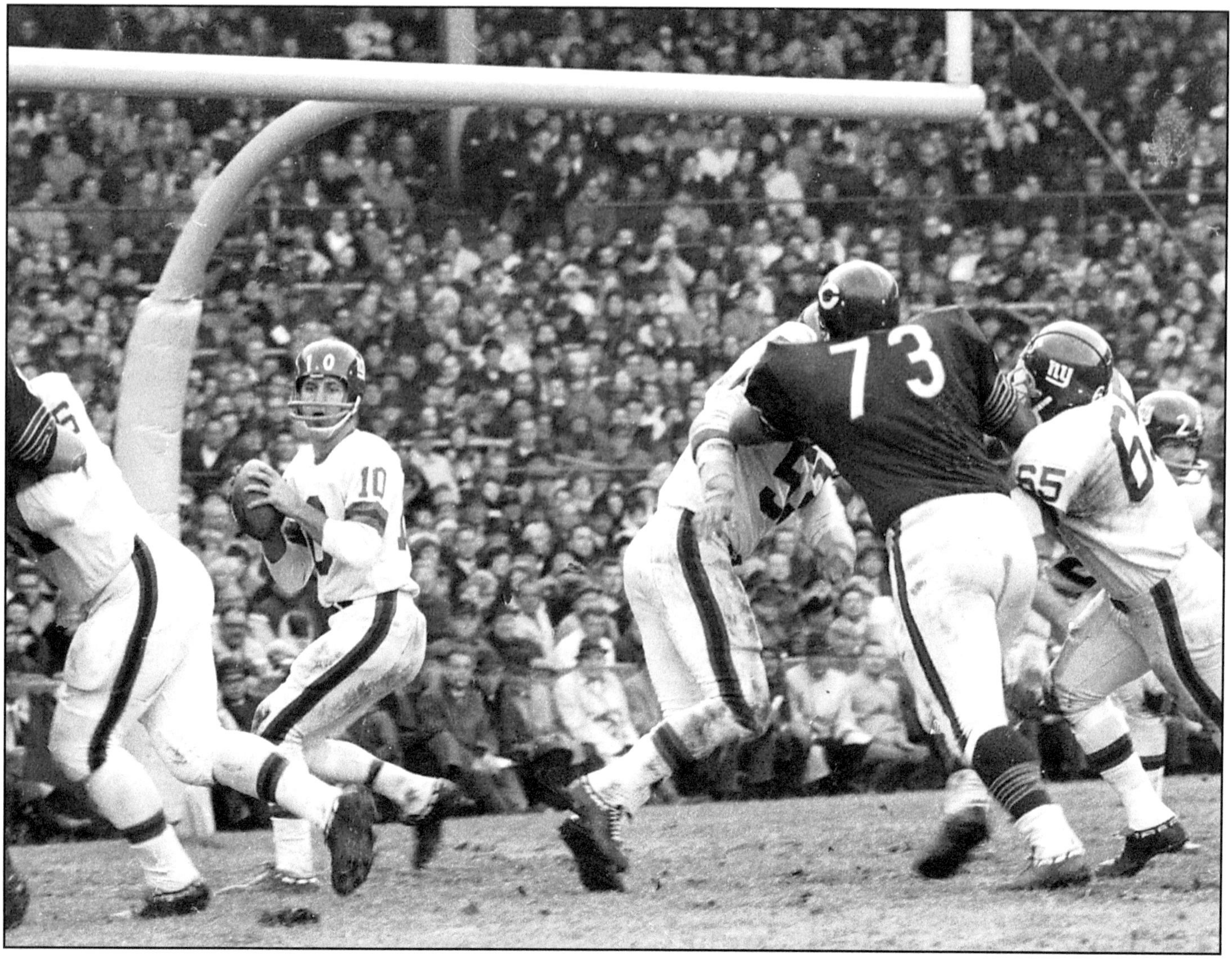

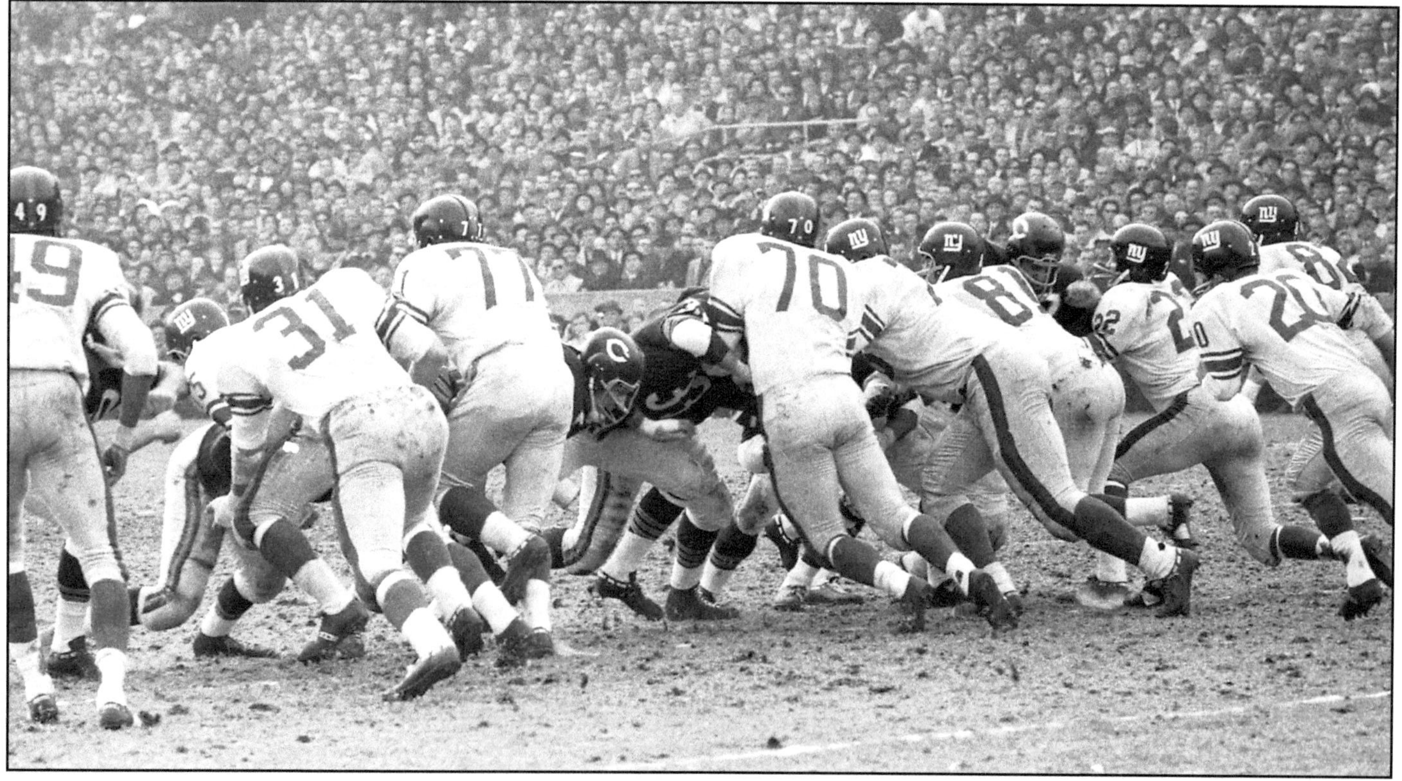

St. Louis CARDS

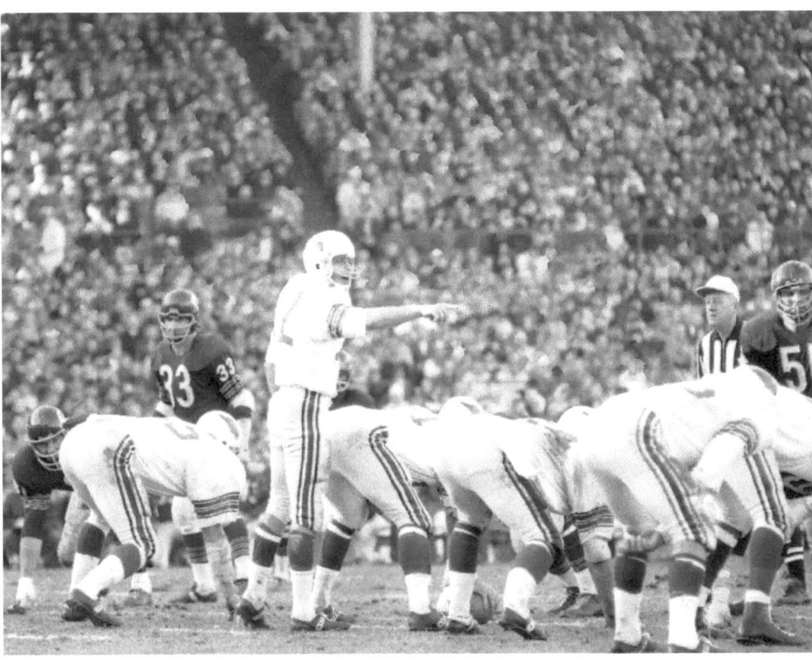

1965	Bears- 34	Cardinals- 13
1967	Bears- 30	Cardinals- 3

St. Louis Cardinals and the Chicago Bears are the only professional football franchises continuously in operation since the founding of the National Football League. Originally known as the Chicago Cardinals, the club relocated to St. Louis, Missouri in 1960. In its long and storied history the club has only won two Championships, the first in 1925 and the second in 1947 when the team played in Chicago.

Although local football fans embraced the city's new franchise, the Cardinals struggled with injuries throughout the 1961 season. The sudden resignation of coach Frank Ivy, who played for he Cardinals in the 1940s, left the team with only assistant coaches calling the plays. Ray Willsey took over coaching responsibilities near the end of the season and led the team to a record of 7-7.

Charles and Bill Bidwell became owners of the team upon their mother Violet's death in 1962. The Bidwells took an active role with the team and hired Wally Lemon as coach. Despite a strong offensive corps, the Cardinals' defense was sorely lacking, leading to a record of 4-9-1 for the season.

Through the 1963 season, the Cardinals continued to dominate the league on offense, however a weak defensive corps left the team with a record of 9-5. Ground was broken for a new all sports stadium in St. Louis with the intent of drawing more fans. The stadium was not completed as scheduled in 1964 and Atlanta tried to lure the team with its newly constructed facilities. Civic Leaders in St. Louis convinced the Bidwells to remain in the Midwest. The team's 1964 9-3-2 record was only half a game behind league leading Cleveland. The Cardinals won crucial games near the end of the season and went to the Playoff Bowl where they defeated Green Bay 24-7.

Joe Namath was drafted by the Cardinals in 1965 but the team was unable to sign him. The team lost eight of their last nine games and finished the season with a record of 5-9.

In 1966 Charlie Winner was named coach and the team moved into Busch Memorial Stadium . The team started fast going 7-1-1 in its first nine games. A series of devastating injuries to starters however, led to problems as the season progressed. The Cardinal's record that year was 8-5-1.

1967 and 1968 saw a repeat of the Cardinal's porous defense and a recurrence of injuries to starters. Things did not improve from there. At the midpoint of the 1969 season, 11 starters ahd undergone surgery. he team's offense was erratic and its defense shaky, leading to a decade ending season with a 4-9-1 record.

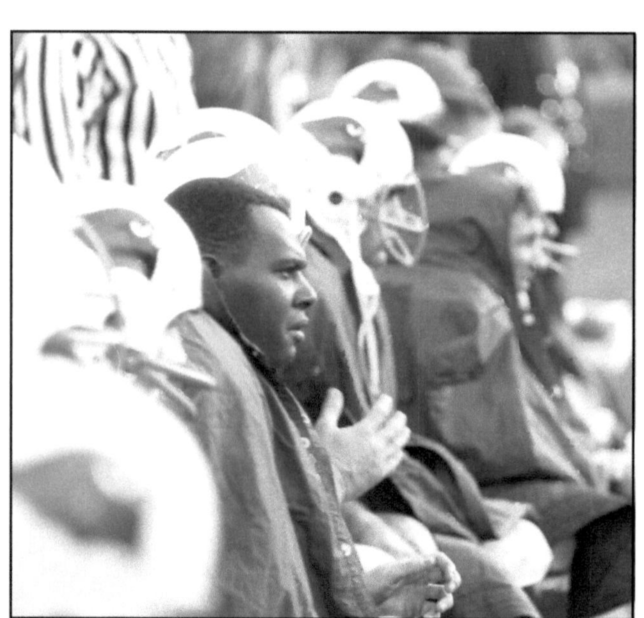

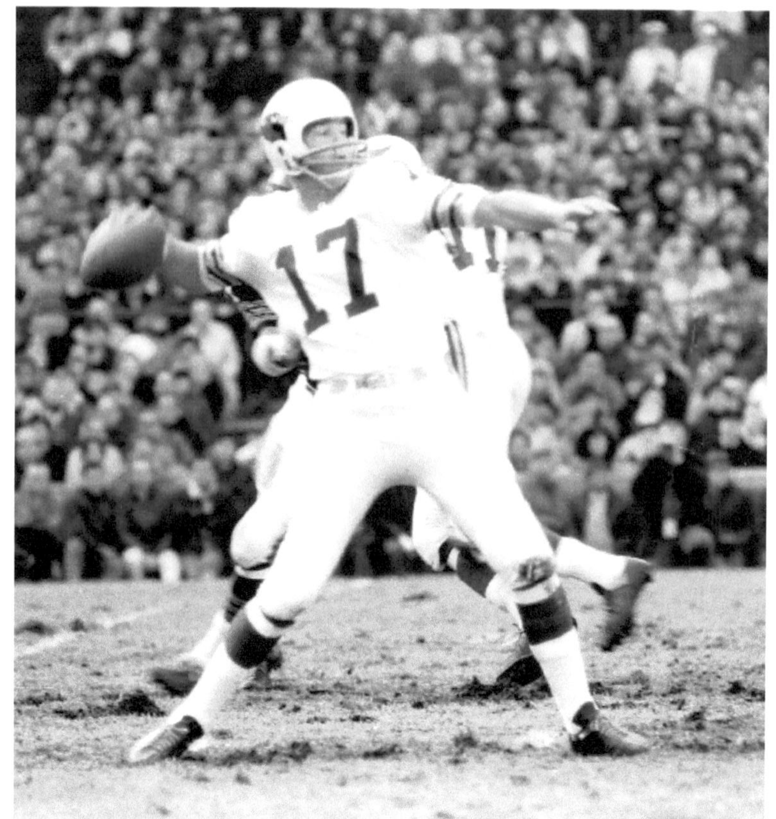
17

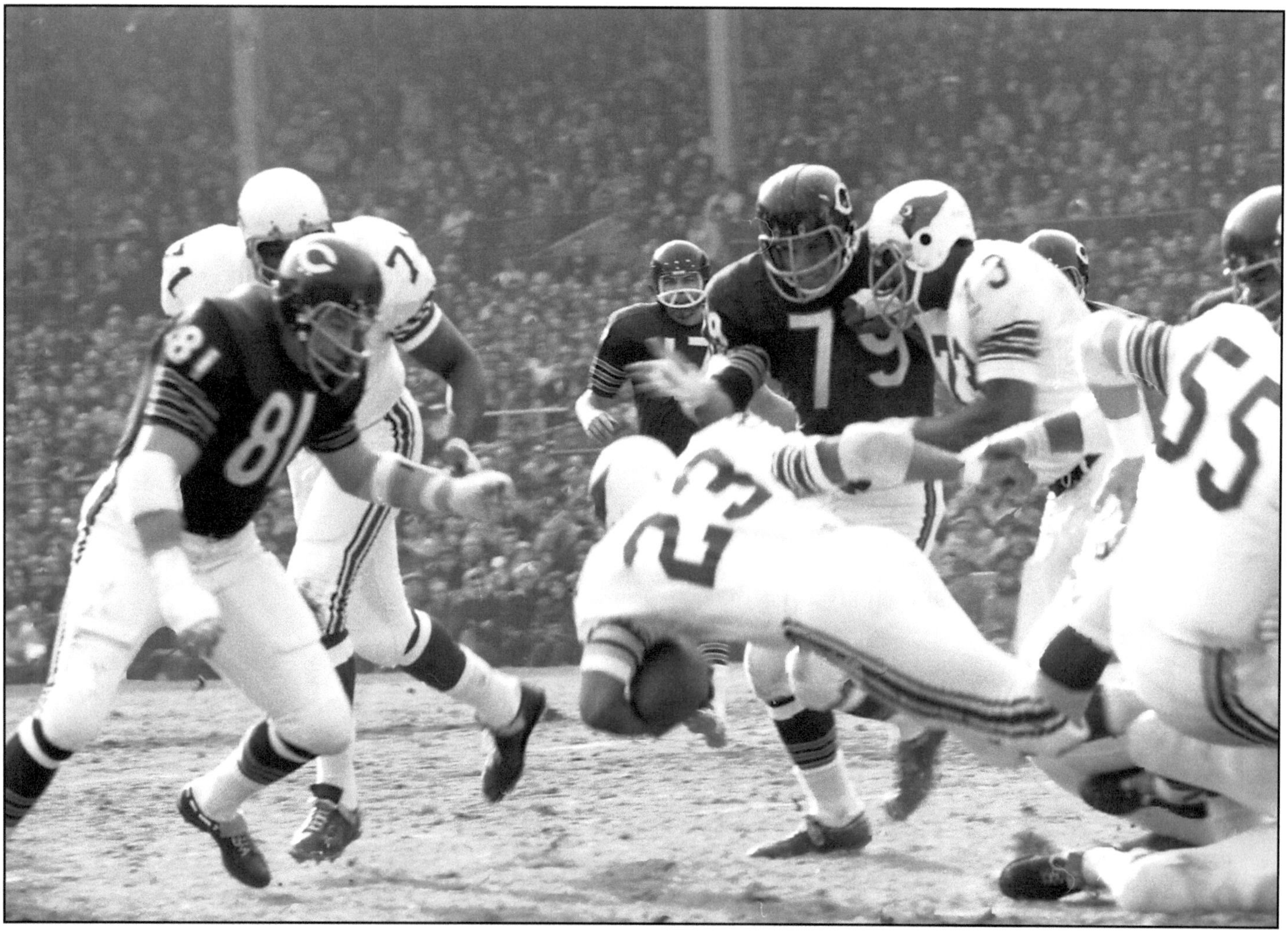

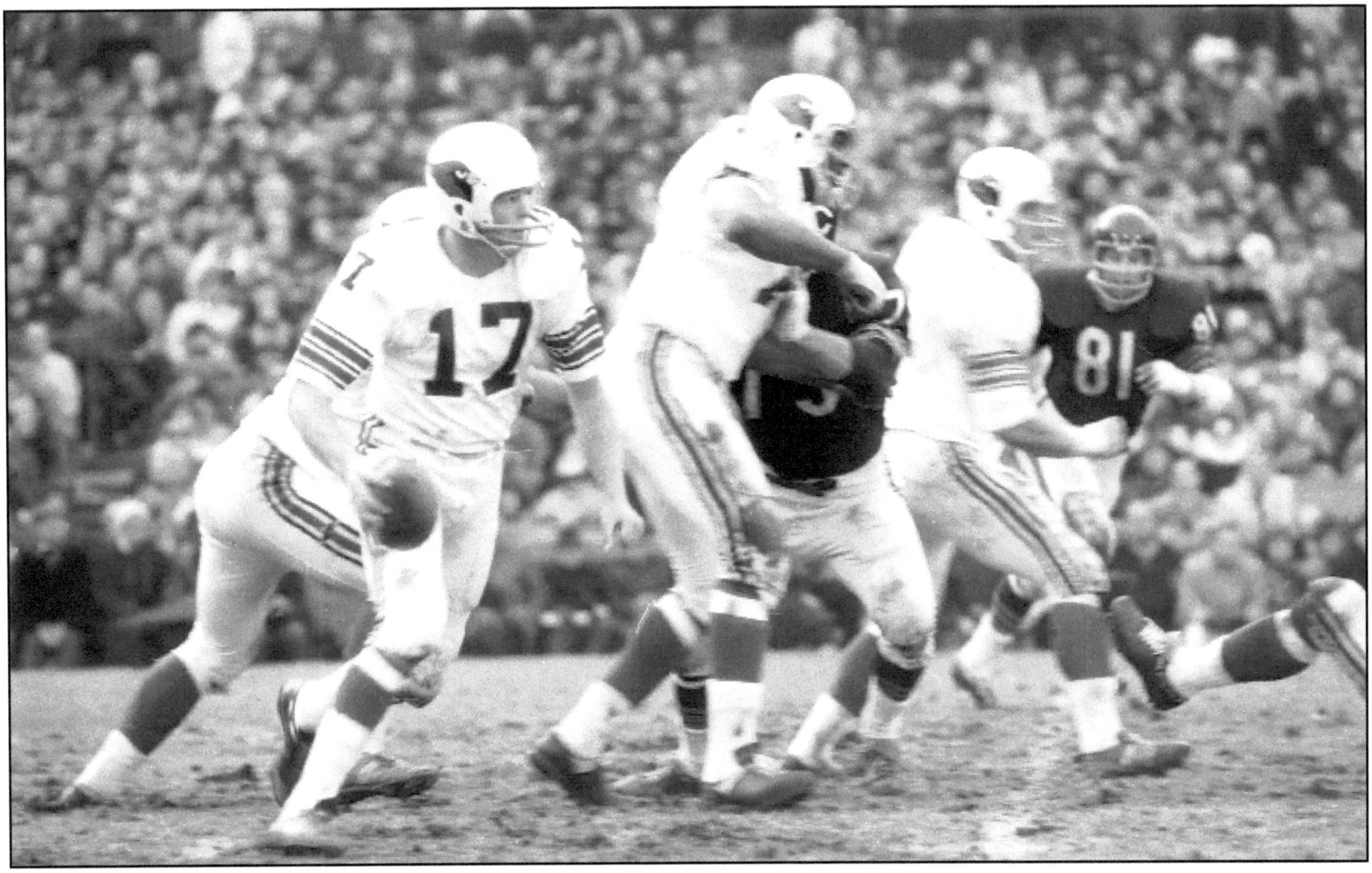

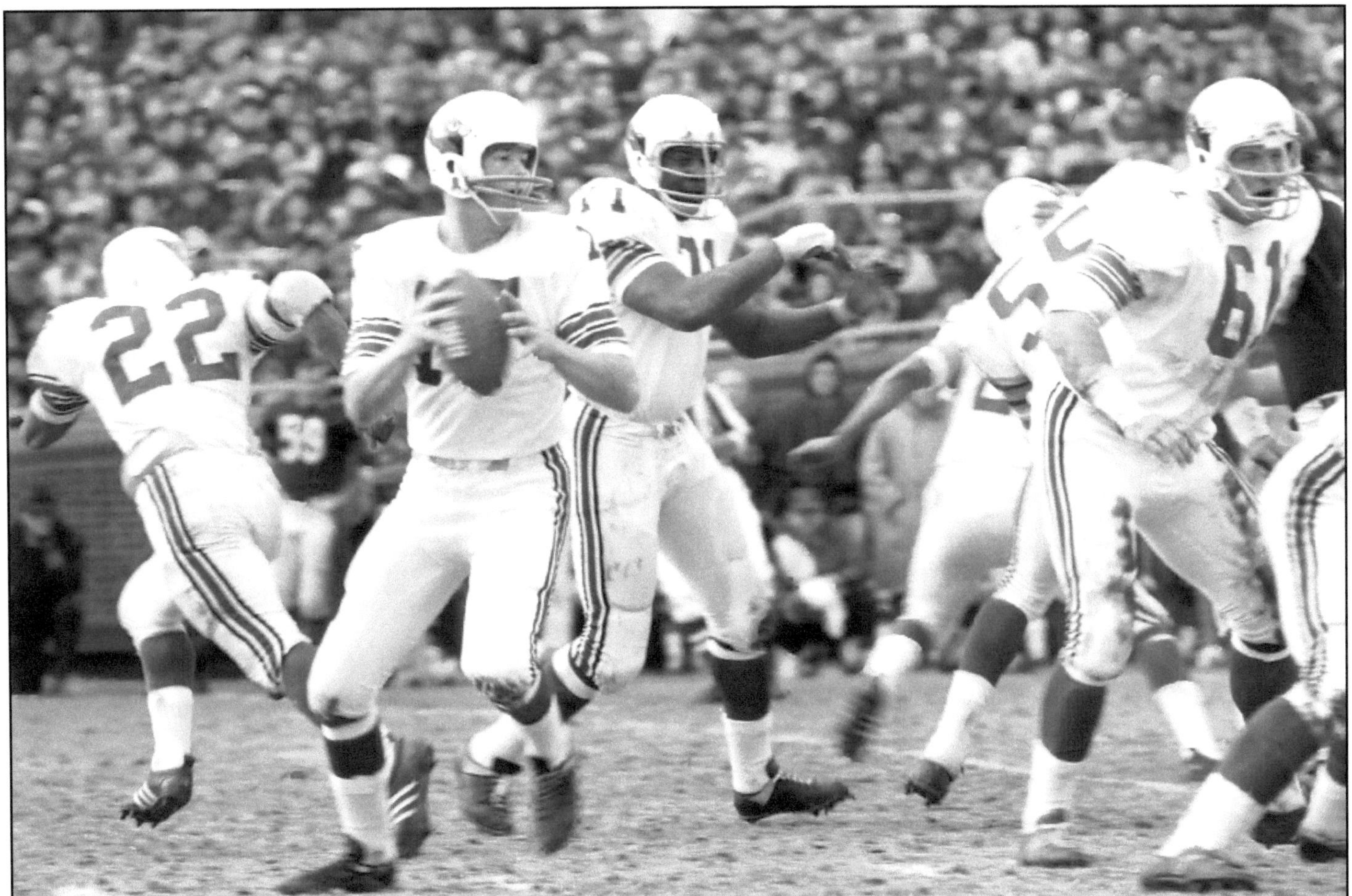

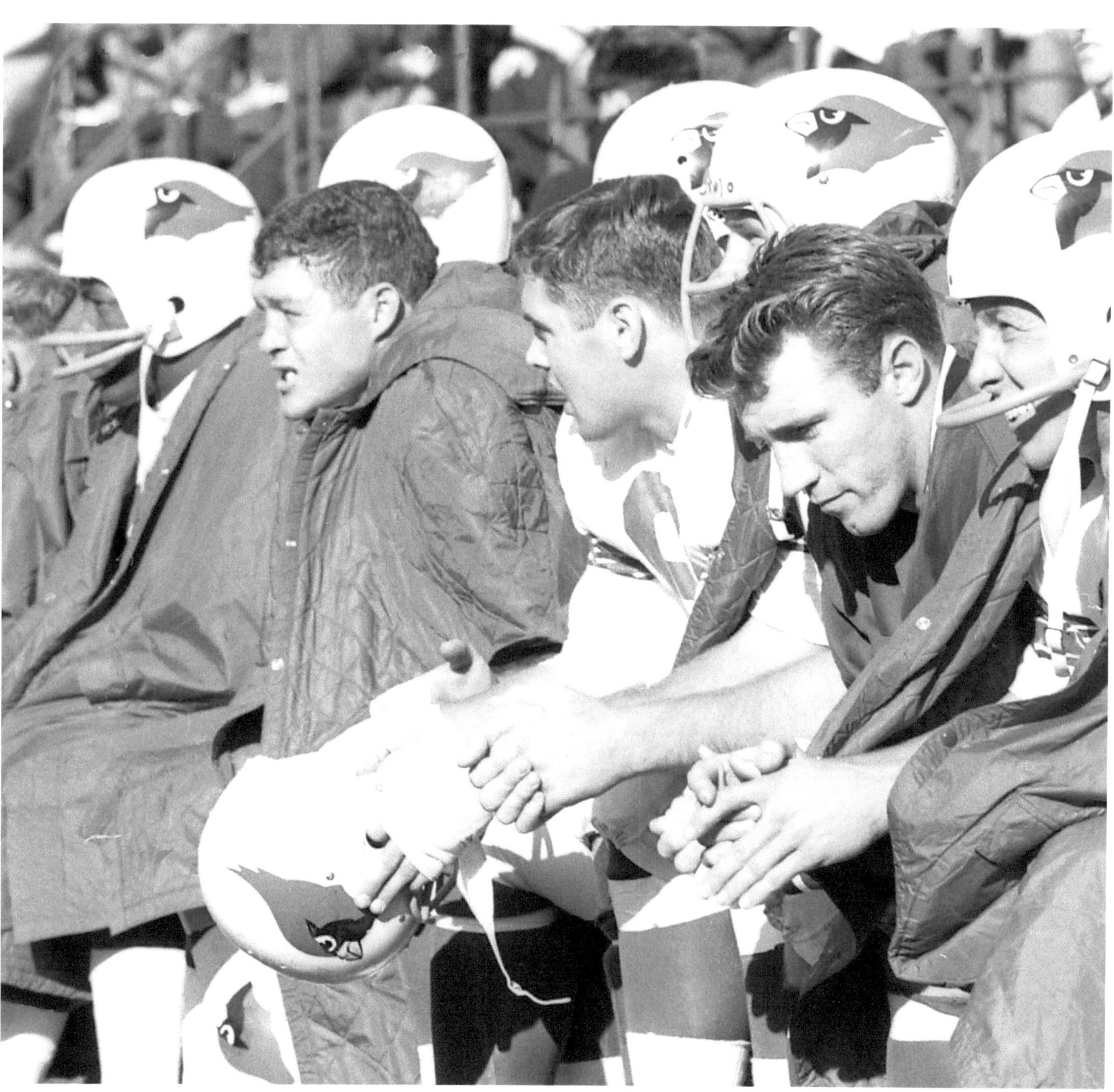

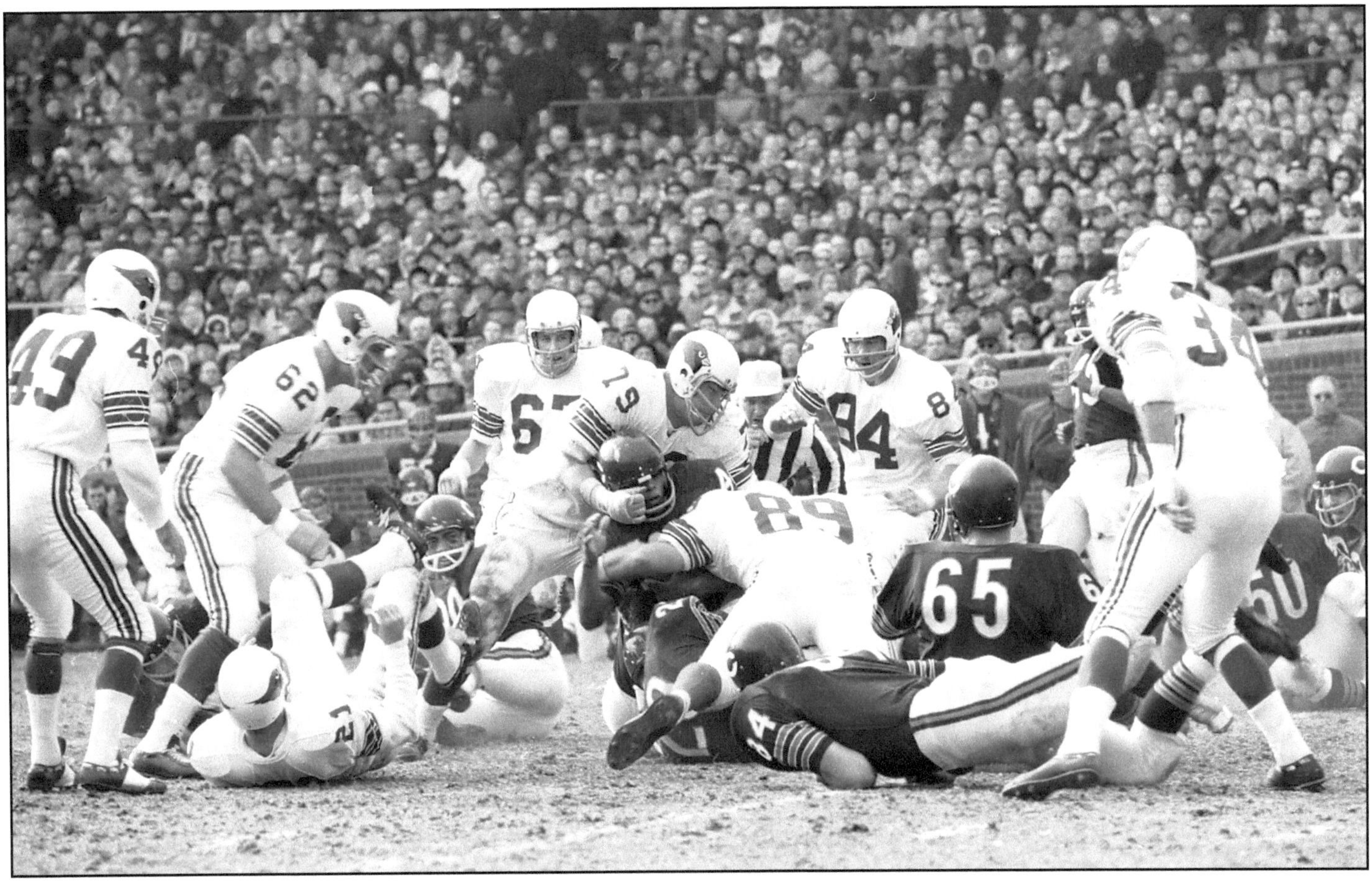

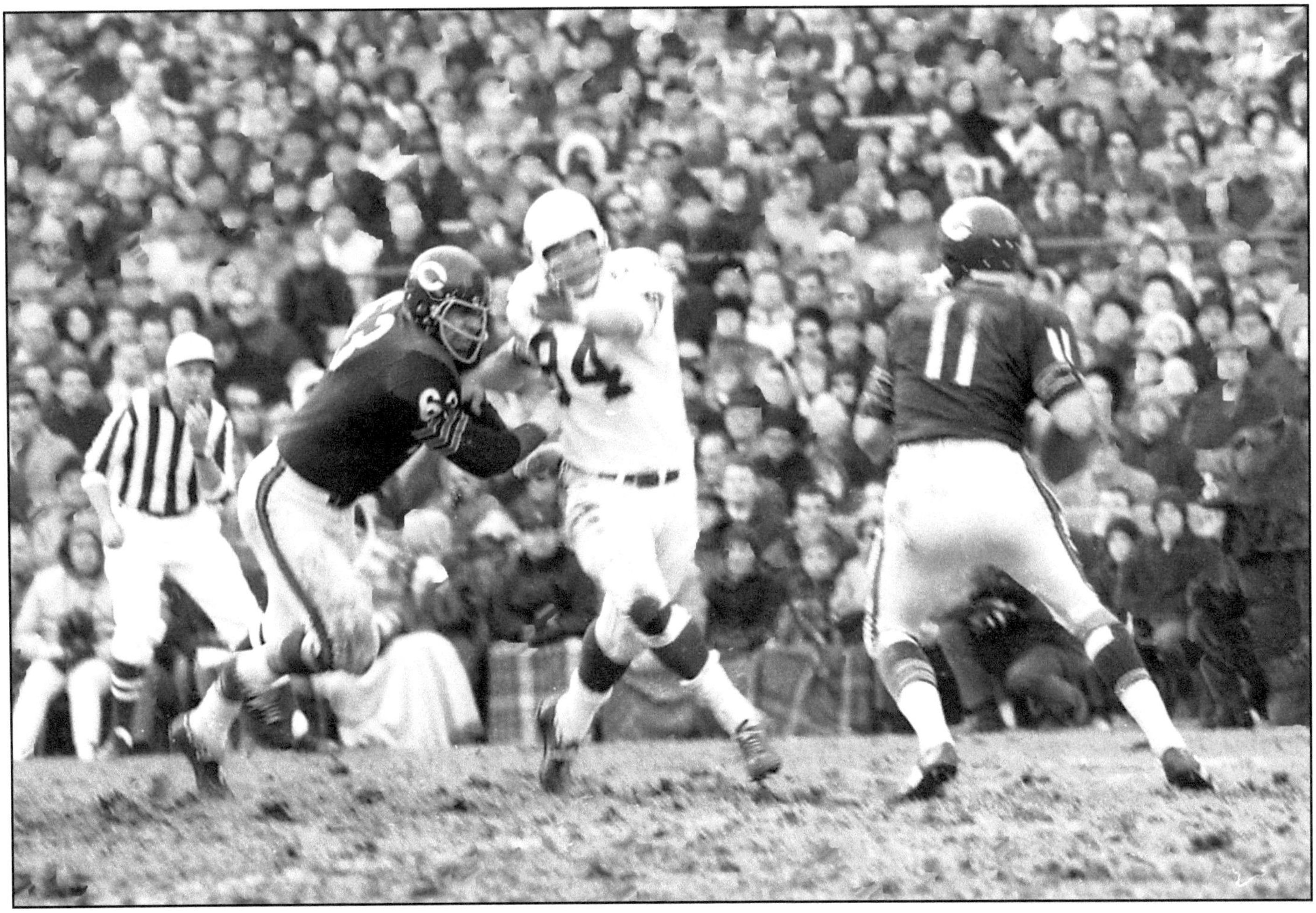

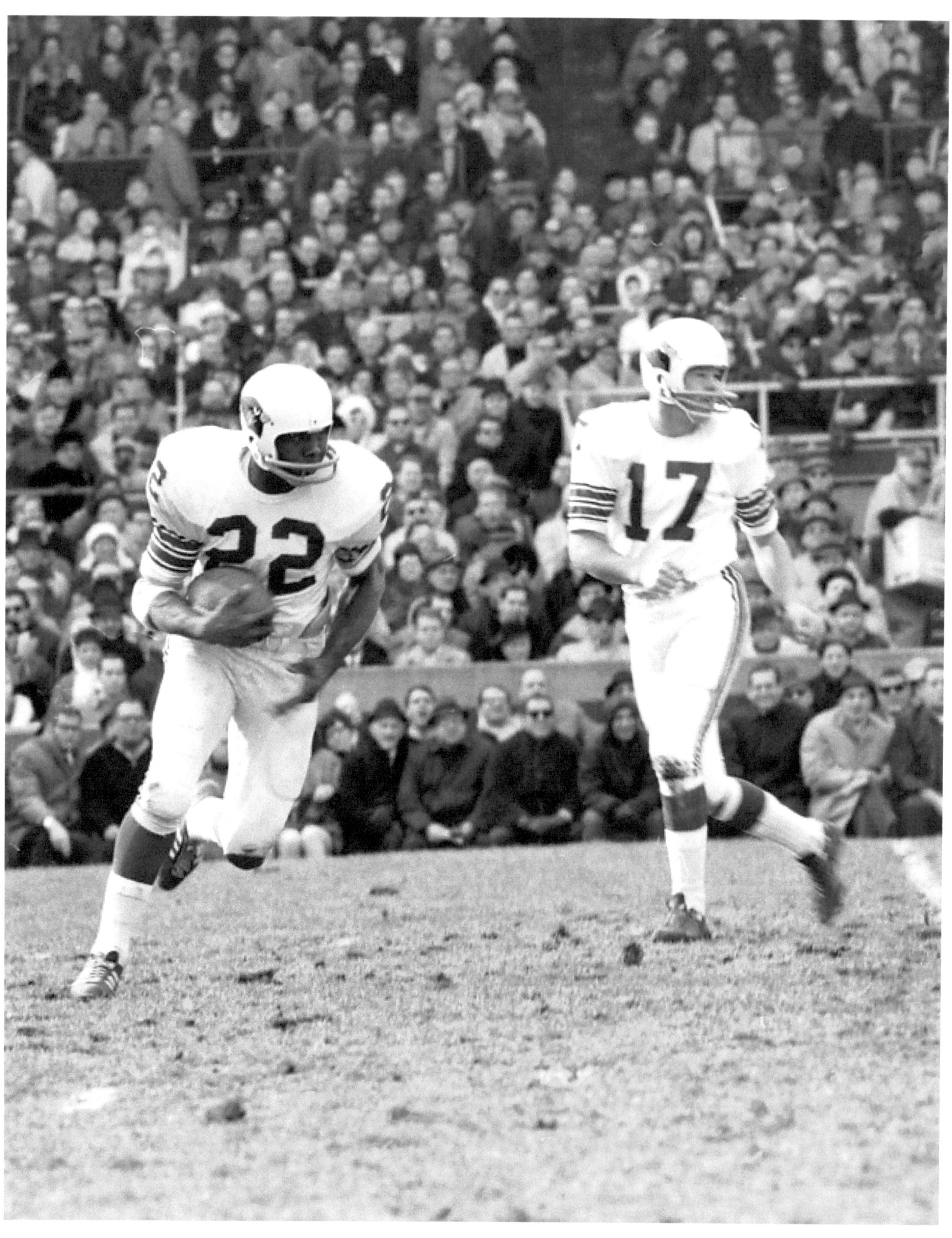
22
17

Philadelphia EAGLES

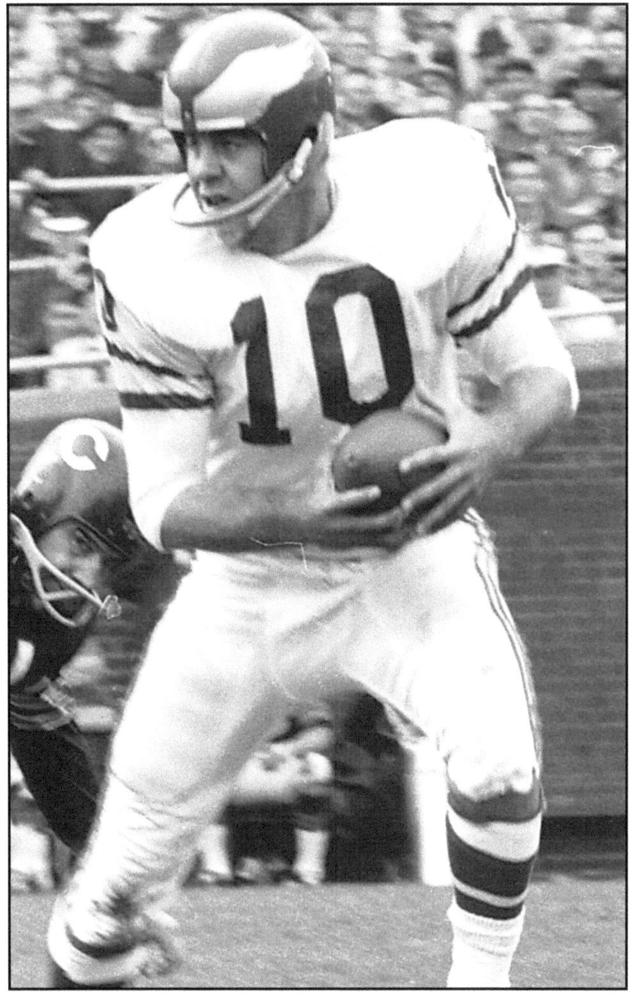

1963 Bears-16 Eagles-7

The Eagles were a formidable team in 1960, clinching their first Division Title in 11 years under the leadership of Norm Van Brocklin. Van Brocklin finished second in the NFL with 2,471 total yards and 24 touchdowns. The team won its third NFL Championship defeating Green Bay at Franklin Field before a crowd of 67,325 on December 26.

Van Brocklin unexpectedly retired in 1961 after the Eagles elevated assistant coach Nick Skorich to the head coaching position. Van Brocklin had been asked to remain as a player-coach, but he refused. Sonny Jurgensen took over at quarterback and won seven of his first eight games. Injuries plagued the season however with Jurgensen suffering a shoulder separation and tackle J.D Smith broke his leg in the playoffs.

1962 was another year marked by injuries to key players for the Eagles. Retzlaff, Watson, and Lucas all suffered broken arms. Sapp separated his shoulder. Only Tommy McDonald, the team's smallest player remained healthy.

In 1963 injuries again haunted the Eagles. Jurgensen and backup Hill boycotted games over salary disputes. Jerry Wolman, a construction tycoon purchased the struggling Eagles franchise for $5.5 million. Kucharich was brought in to coach and the team went on to wi their first seven games of 1964.

1965 saw the Eagles with a mediocre 5-9 record. Fan support slowly returned however and the team enjoyed a moderate increase in attendance. Timmy Brown rushed for 651 yards, the third best in the NFL. By 1966 the team made it to the PLayoff Brown but were unable to advance.

1967 saw the Eagles first winning season in 5 years. Mike Ditka joined the squad in a trade for Concannon. The Eagles finished in second place with a record of 6-7-1 but fans were calling for the coach to resign. The situation did not improve in 1968 when the Eagles lost their first 11 games. By winning their last two games, the Eagles lost the opportunity to draft O.J. Simpson to the even worse record Bills. With increasing fan dissatisfaction, Wolman struggled to keep the franchise from bankruptcy.

Leonard Tosse, a trucking executive, bought the Eagles for $16.1 million in 1969. Retzlaff was hired as general manager and Jerry Williams, a former Eagles halfback became coach. The team improved slightly but did not make the playoffs.

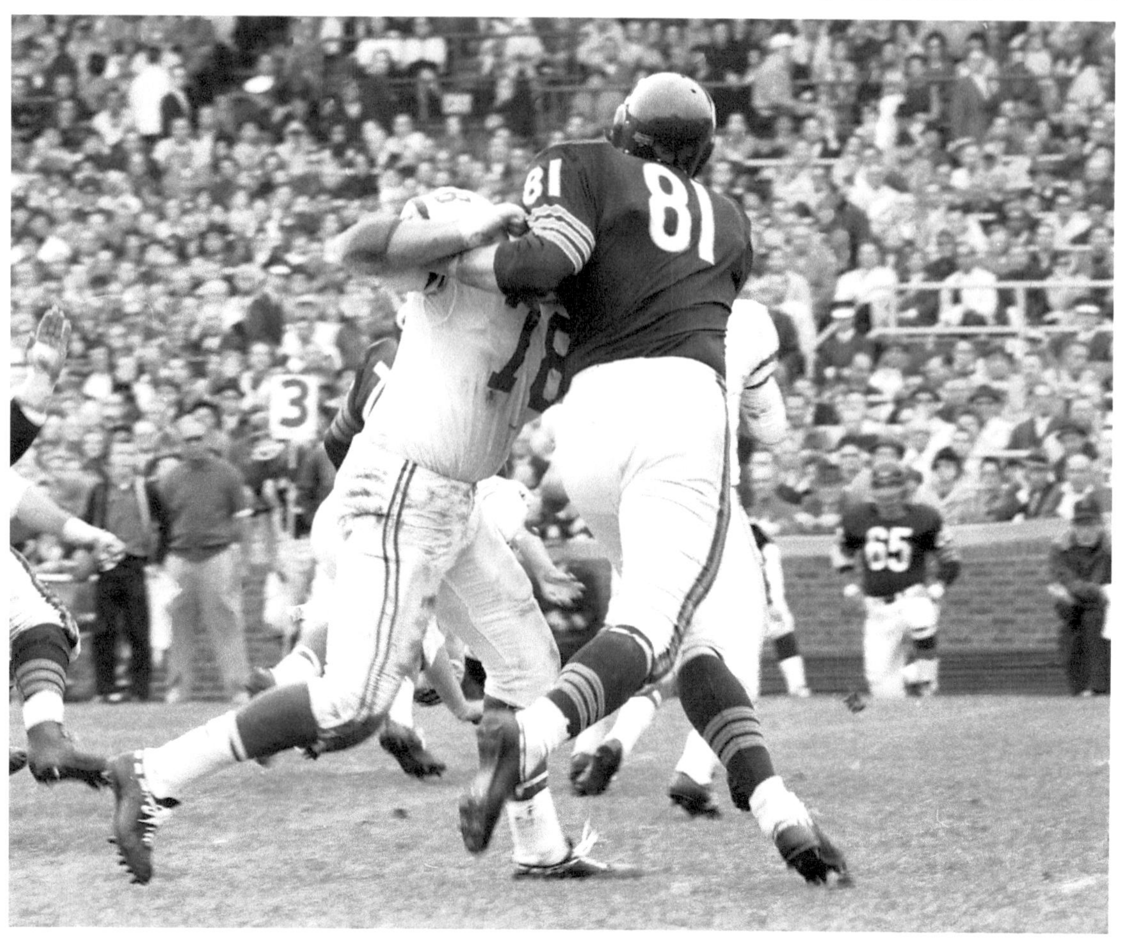
81
81
78
65

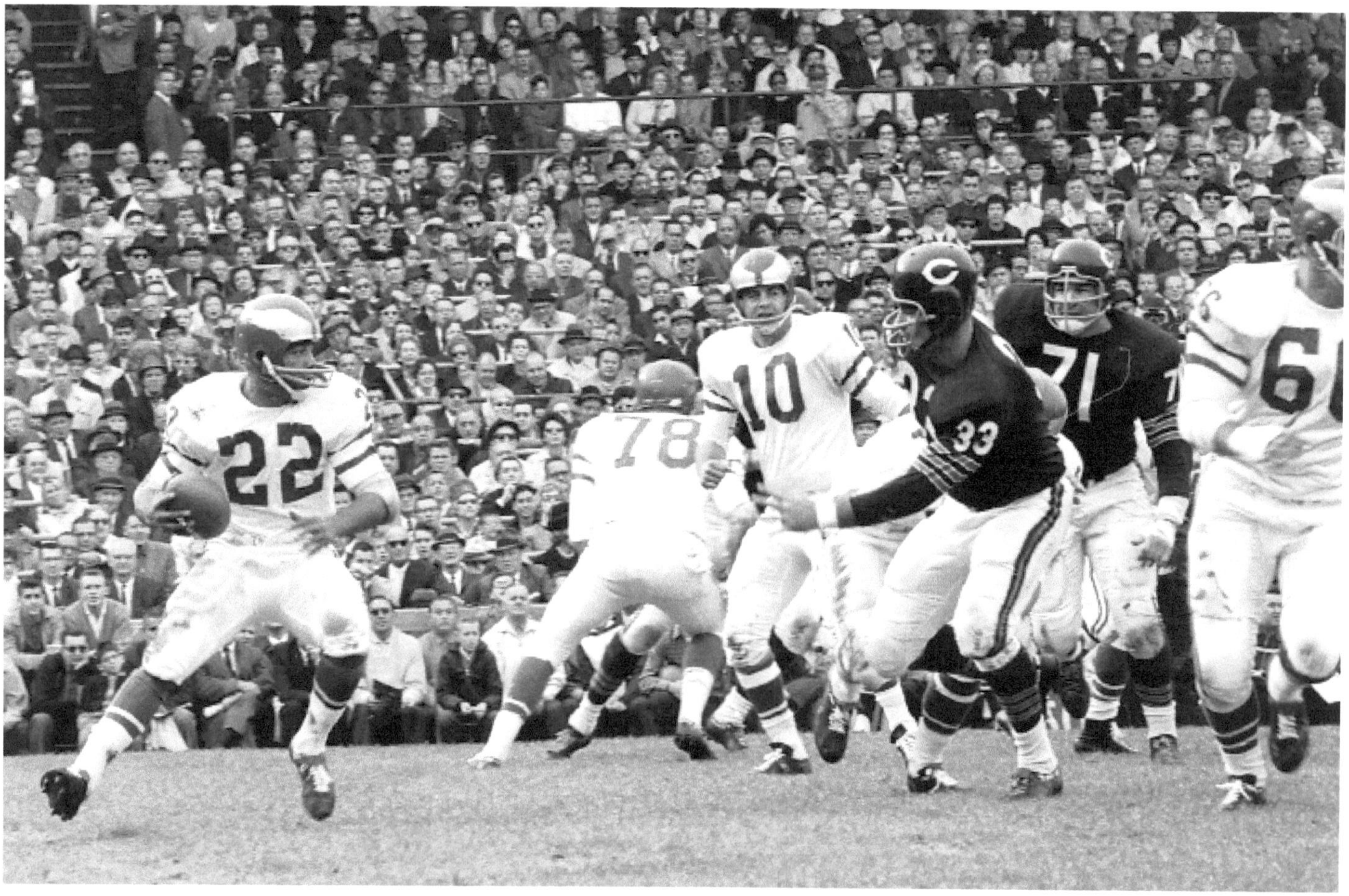

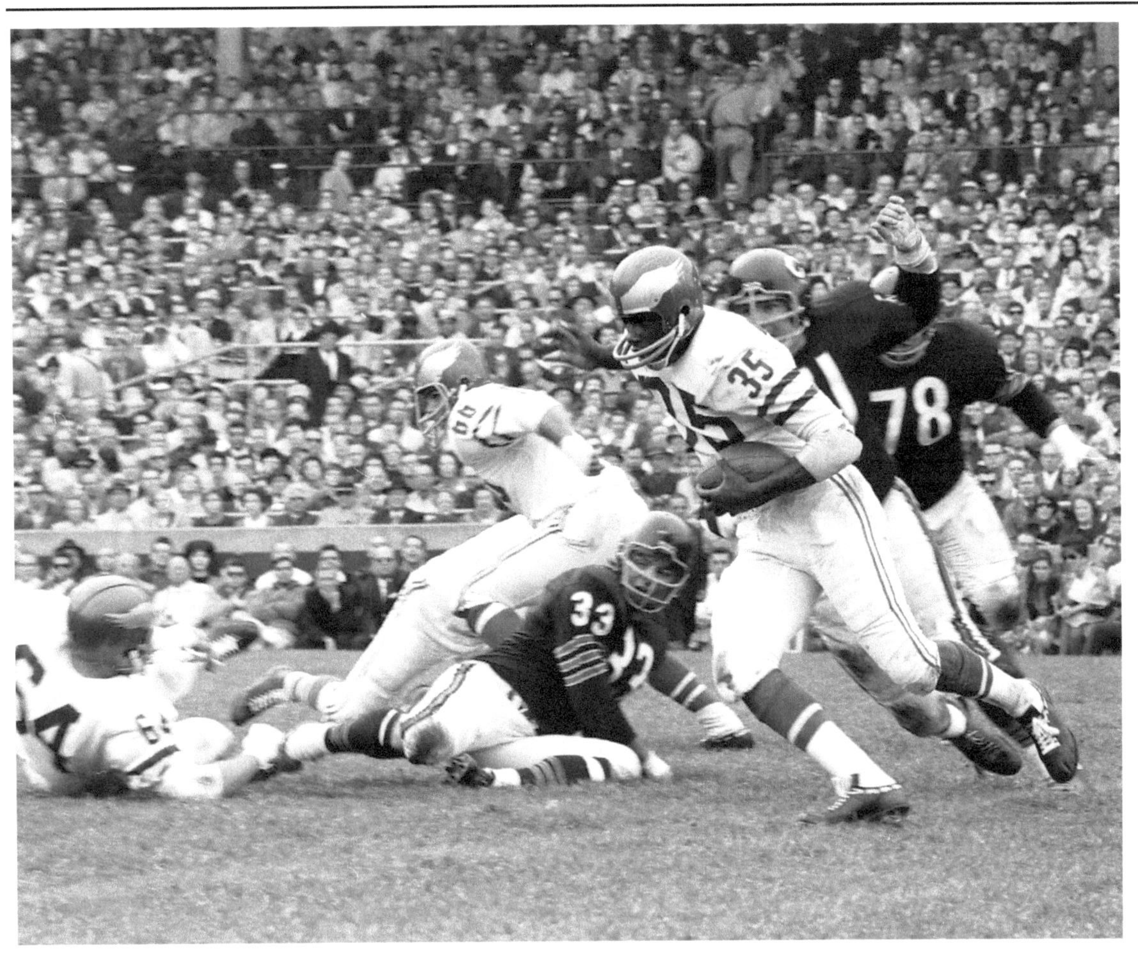
35
78
33

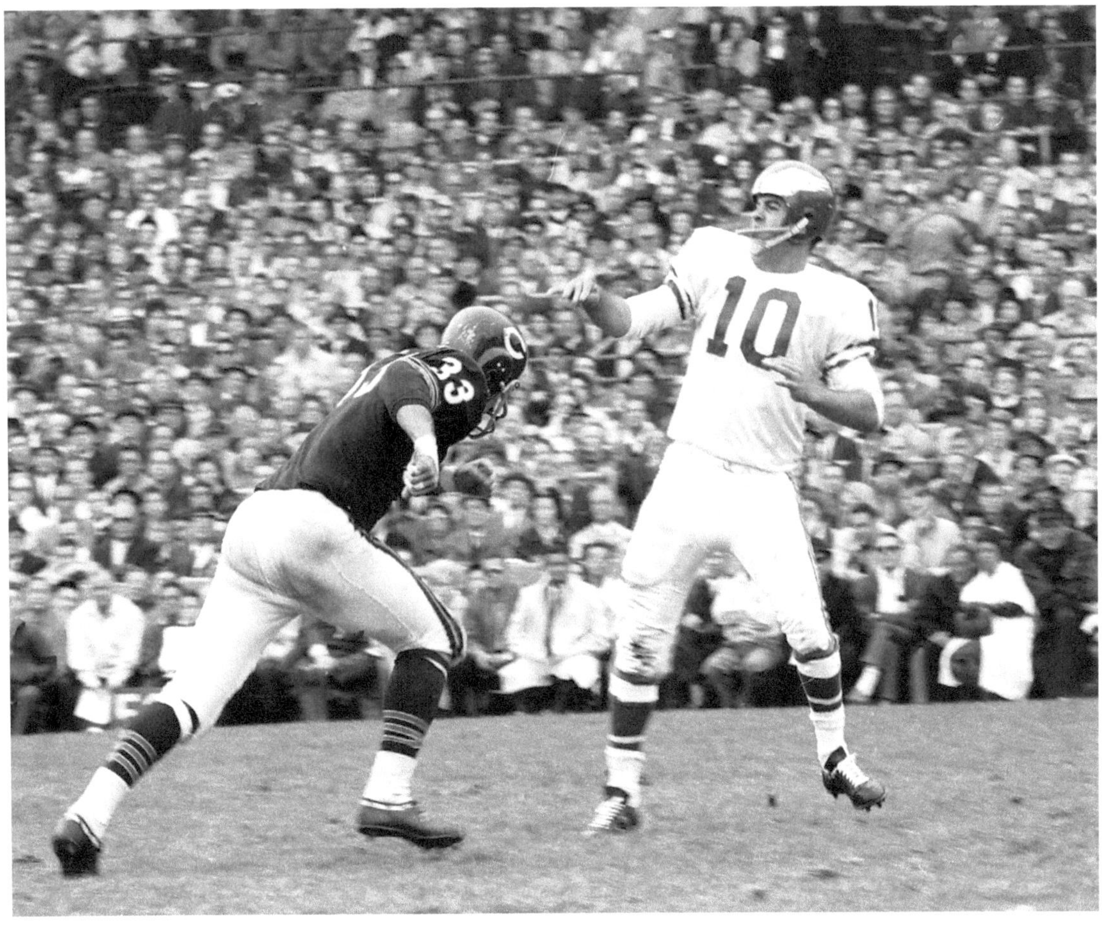
10
33

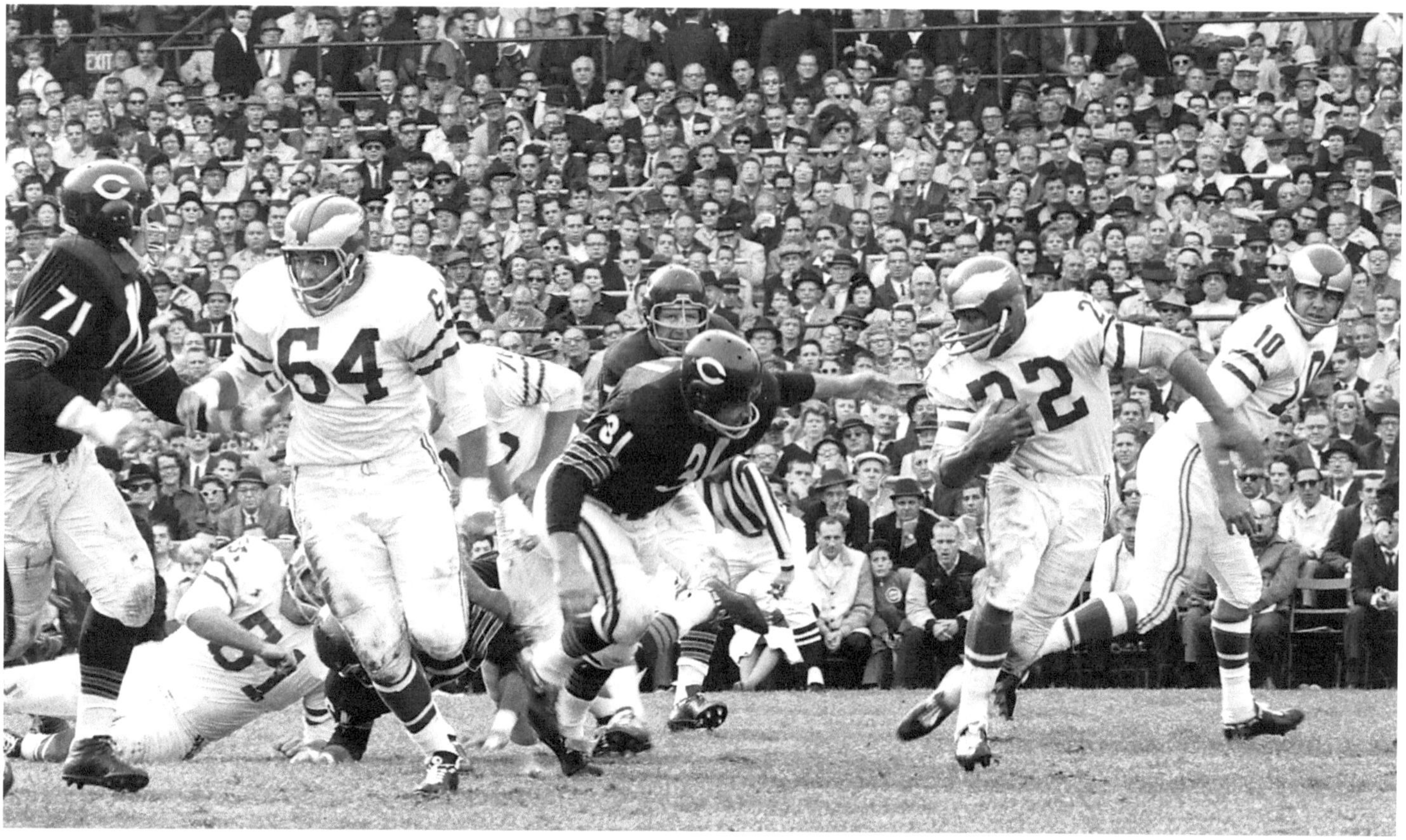

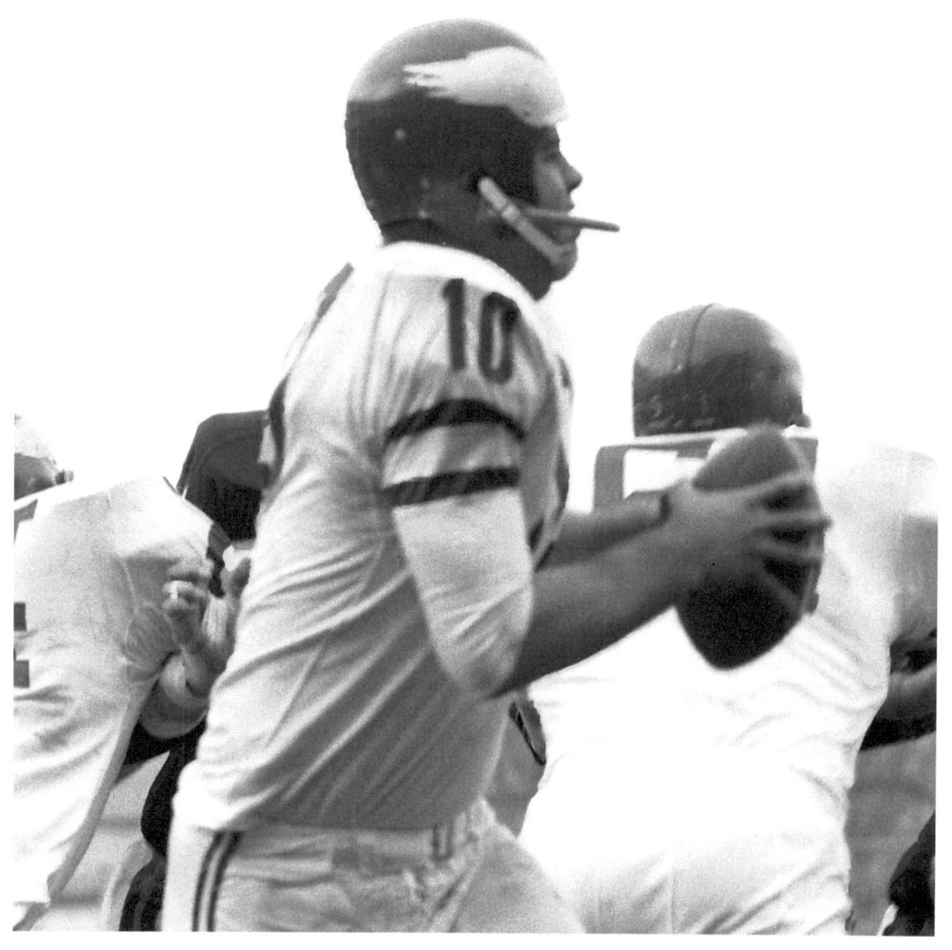

Cleveland BROWNS

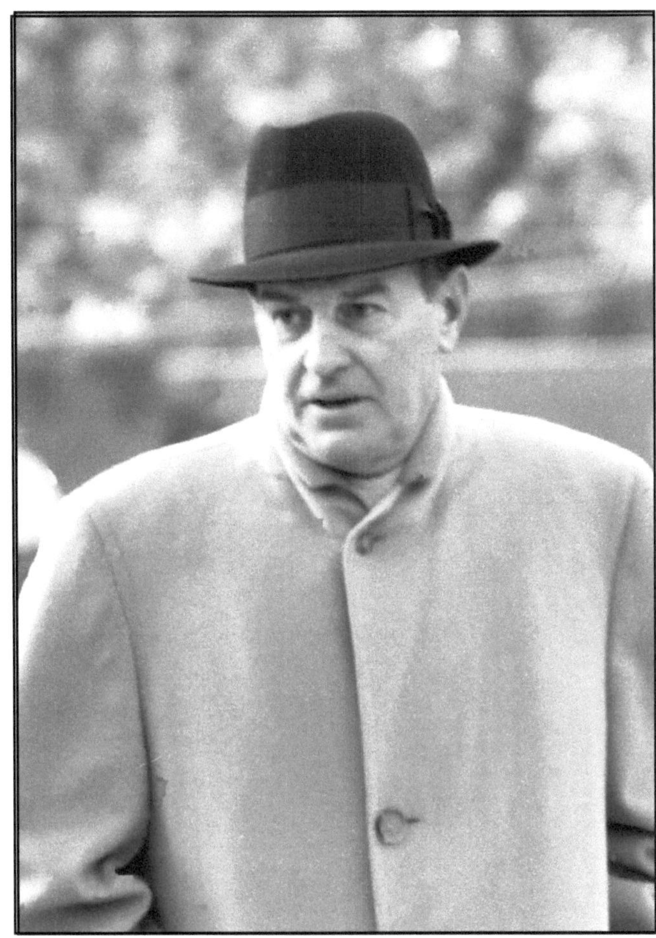

1960 Bears -7 Browns-14

In the 1960s, the Browns were one of the best, and often one of the worst, teams in the NFL. As the decade dawned, coach Paul Brown had a contentious relationship with many of his players , a situation that would become even more pronounced when Art Modell, a New York CIty television and advertising executive, bought the team in 1961.

Modell and Brown were at loggerheads from the time Modell signed the check to buy the team. Modell's emphasis was on entertainment while Brown preferred to focus on the game of football.

Heisman Trophy winning halfback Ernie Davis joined the team in 1962 to provide an additional threat combined with the talents of JIm Brown. Ernie Davis was diagnosed with leukemia and never played during the season. Jim Brown had a mediocre season and threatened to retire if Paul Brown was not replaced as the team's coach. Paul Brown was fired as coach and GM in 1963. Blanton Collier, a Brown's assistant took over the coaching duties.

In 1964 Paul Warfield of Ohio State brought a strong passing game to the team, leading the Browns to their first Conference Title since 1957. The Browns then beat the Colts 27-0 in the Championship game.

The Browns again won the Conference Title in 1965 but lost the Championship to the Packers. Warfield broke his shoulder and was out for most of the season and Jim Brown retired after that year's final game.

1966 saw the Browns with a 9-5 record and no playoff bid. In 1967, Cleveland lost the Division Championship to the Cowboys in the newly realigned league. 1968 was somewhat of an improvement with an injury devastated Browns team reaching the Championship game,but losing to the Colts by a score of 34-0.

In 1969 the Browns were back in winning form, leading the NFL in touchdowns. The Browns lost, however , to Minnesota 27-7 in the final playoff of that season.

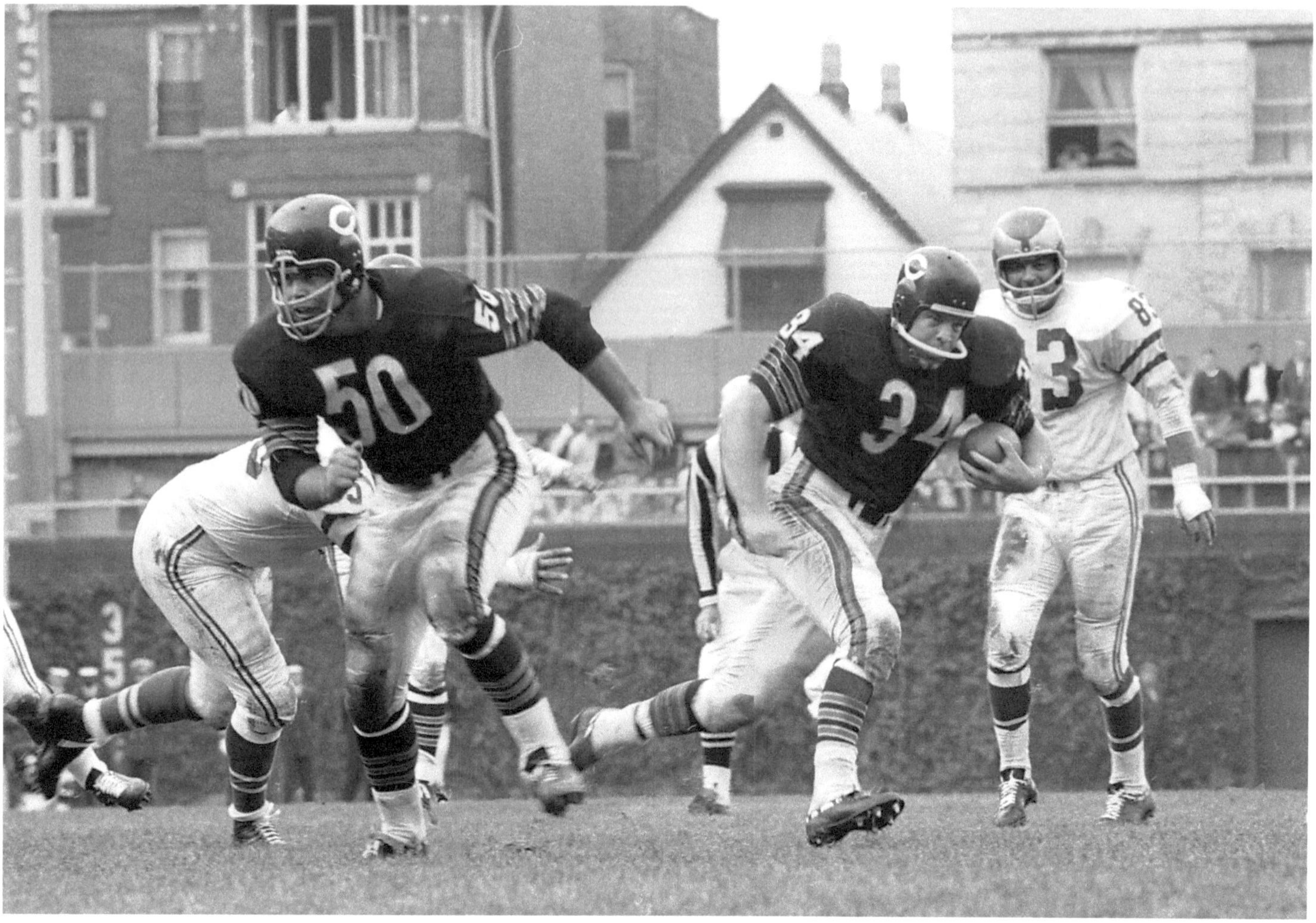

"I had watched the Bears there as a boy so I was familiar with Wrigley Field. When I was drafted by the Bears I went from the stands to the field. It was very easy for me." Mike Pyle

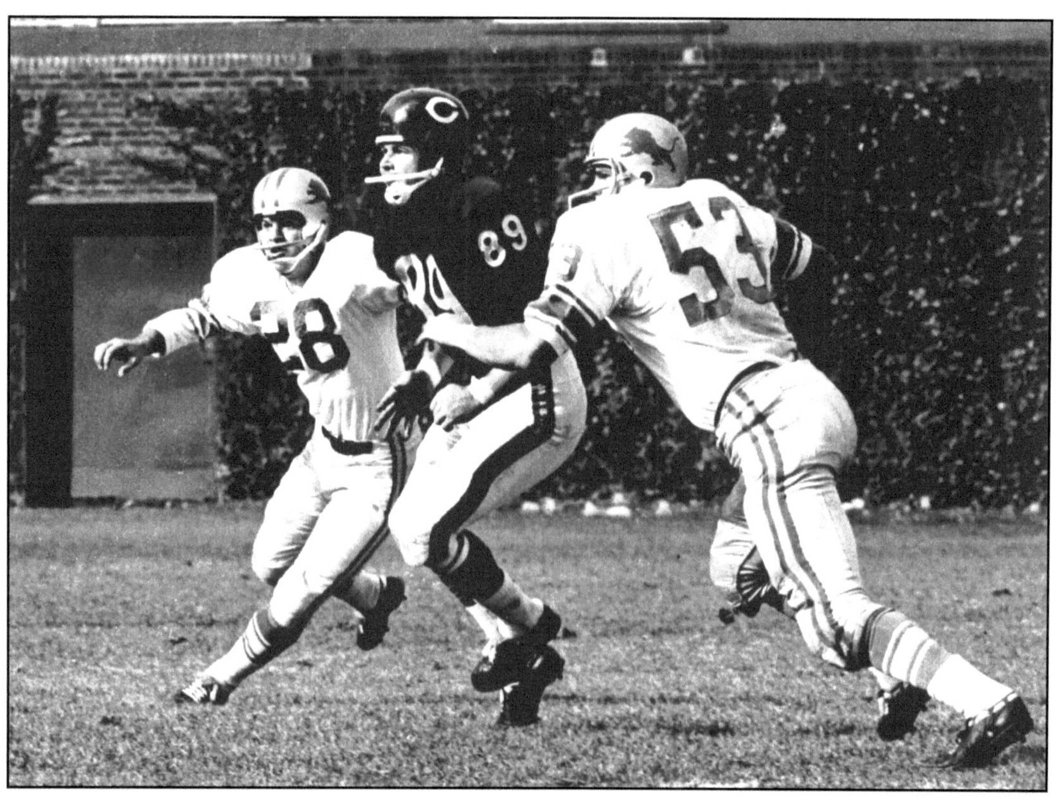

The End of an Era...

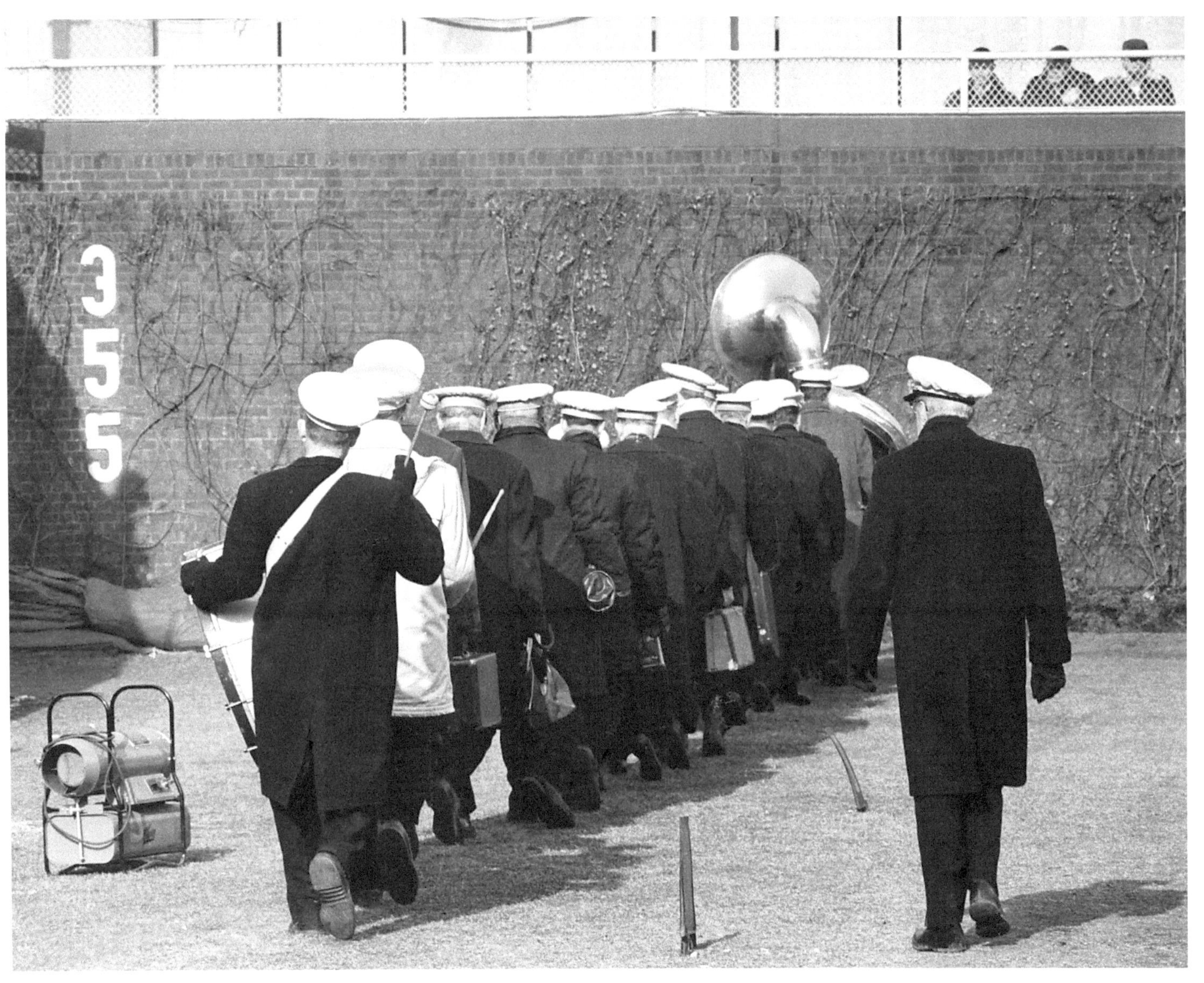

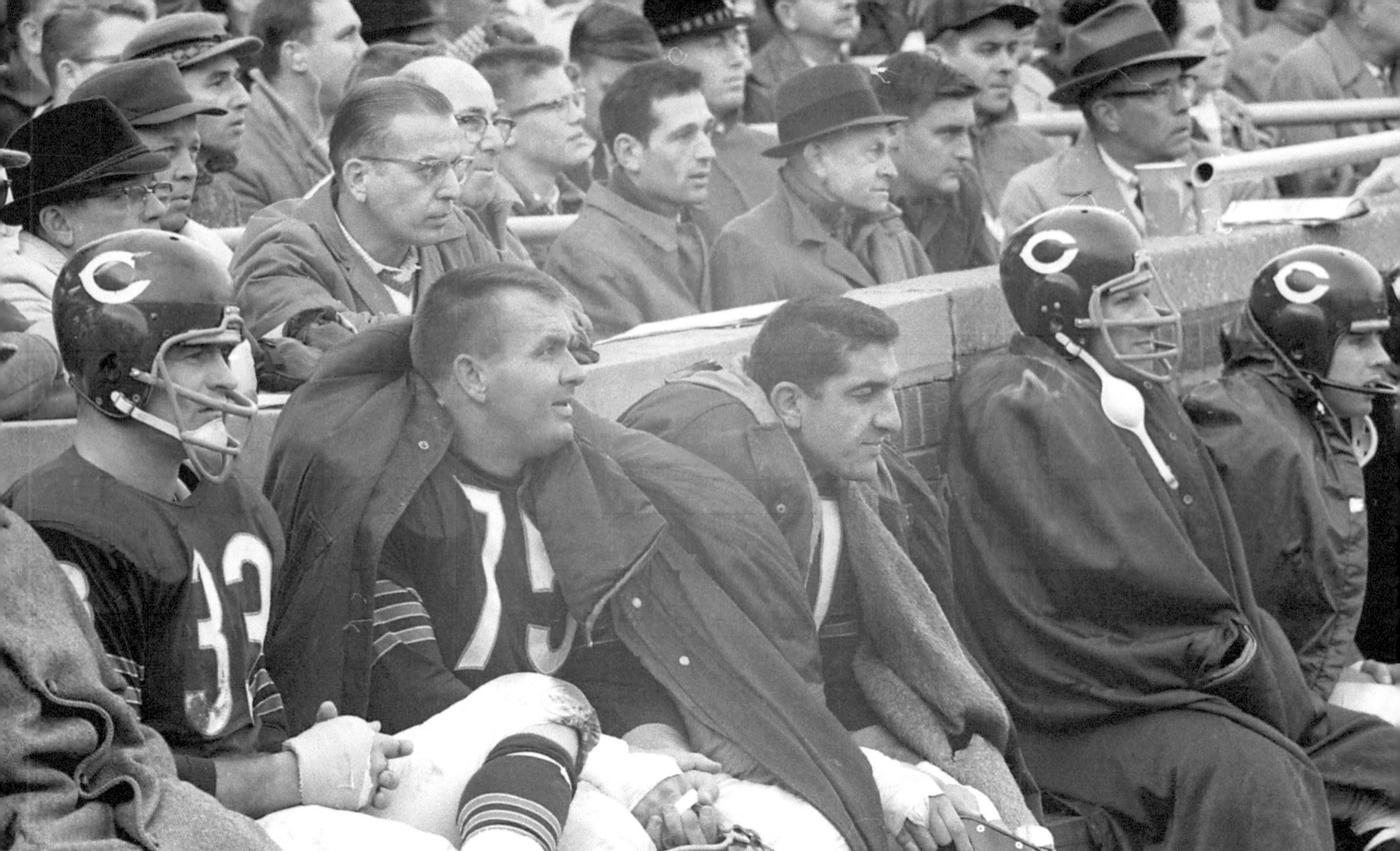

1963 NFL CHAMPIONSHIP GAME TEAM LINE-UP

NUMERICAL -GIANTS

14 Tittle, qb
15 Griffing, qb
16 Gifford, ohb
20 Patton, dhb
21 Webb, dhb
22 Lynch, dhb
23 Guy, ohb
24 King, ohb
25 Pesonen, dhb
29 Webster, fb
33 Gursky, lb
34 Chandler, k

37 Killett, ohb
39 McElhenny, ohb
40 Morrison, ohb
48 Dove, dhb
49 Barnes, dhb
53 Larson, c
60 Byers, g
62 Dess, g
63 Bolin, g
64 Walker, lb-c
65 Taylor, de
66 Stroud, ot

70 Huff, lb
71 Kirouac, ot-de
75 Katcavage, de
76 LoVetere, dt
77 Modzelewski, dt
78 Howell, o-dt
79 Brown, ot
80 Walton, oe
81 Robustelli, de
82 Scott, lb
85 Shofner, oe
87 Hillebrand, lb
88 Thomas, oe

NUMERICAL -BEARS

9 Wade, qb
10 Bukich, qb
17 Petitbon, dhb
22 Martin, ohb
23 Whitsell, dhb
24 Taylor, dhb
25 Caroline, dhb
26 McRae, dhb
28 Galimore, ohb
29 Bull, ohb
31 Fortunato, lb
33 Morris, L., lb

34 Marconi, fb
43 Glueck, dhb
46 Coia, oe
47 Morris, J., ohb
49 Bivins, ohb
50 Pyle, c
60 Davis, g
61 George, lb
63 Wetoska, ot
65 Bettis, lb
67 Karras, g
70 Lee, ot

72 Cadile, g
73 Barnett, ot
74 Kilcullen, de
75 Williams, dt
76 Johnson, dt
78 Jones, dt
80 Jencks, oe
81 Atkins, de
83 Leclerc, lb
84 Farrington, oe
87 O'Bradovich, de
88 Green, k
89 Ditka, oe

When the game started I shot a couple plays and found the film was hard to advance. It was getting brittle from the cold and breaking. The other photographers were all having the same problem. We decided the best thing to do was shoot a play, wait a minute and then just shoot the ground. It kept the film moving. The ground was covered with rolls of film that cracked and got pulled and discarded. I didn't get a lot of photographs that day. -Ron Nelson

www.ingramcontent.com/pod-product-compliance
Lightning Source LLC
LaVergne TN
LVHW070131110826
845147LV00002B/233